# Open Mind

# Open Mind

*View and Meditation in the Lineage of Lerab Lingpa*

Translated by B. Alan Wallace

Edited by Eva Natanya

Wisdom

Wisdom Publications, Inc.
199 Elm Street
Somerville MA 02144 USA
wisdompubs.org



*Library of Congress Cataloging-in-Publication Data*

Names: Las-rab-gling-pa, 1856–1926. | Wallace, B. Alan, translator. | Natanya, Eva
Title: Open mind: view and meditation in the lineage of Lerab Lingpa / Translated by B. Alan Wallace; Edited by Eva Natanya.
Description: Somerville, MA: Wisdom Publications, Inc., 2017. | Includes bibliographical references and index. | Includes translations from Tibetan. |
Identifiers: LCCN 2017018059 (print) | LCCN 2017025243 (ebook) | ISBN 9781614294047 (ebook) | ISBN 1614294046 (ebook) | ISBN 9781614293880 (pbk.: alk. paper)
Subjects: LCSH: Rdzogs-chen. | Las-rab-gling-pa, 1856–1926.
Classification: LCC BQ7662.4 (ebook) | LCC BQ7662.4 .O77 2017 (print) | DDC 294.3/420423—dc23
LC record available at https://lccn.loc.gov/2017018059

ISBN 978-1-61429-388-0 ebook ISBN 978-1-61429-404-7

22 21 20 19 18
5 4 3 2 1

Cover design by Gopa&Ted2. Cover image courtesy of The Land of Snows, www.himalayajourney.com. Interior design by Kristin Goble. Set in Diacritical Garamond Pro 11/16.

Wisdom Publications' books are printed on acid-free paper and meet the guidelines for permanence and durability of the Production Guidelines for Book Longevity of the Council on Library Resources.

This book was produced with environmental mindfulness.
For more information, please visit wisdompubs.org/wisdom-environment.

Printed in the United States of America.

MIX
Paper from responsible sources
FSC
www.fsc.org
FSC® C011935

Please visit fscus.org.

# CONTENTS

## The Vital Essence of Primordial Consciousness
### TERTÖN LERAB LINGPA

## Selected Essays on Old and New Views
## of the Secret Mantrayāna

# Foreword by His Holiness the Dalai Lama

Buddhism was established in Tibet by the great Dharma king Trisong Detsen, the abbot Śāntarakṣita, and the adept Padmasambhava more than 1,200 years ago. The ordination of monks, monastic discipline, methods for developing concentration, as well as the study of philosophy under the rubric of strict logic and epistemology make up the general structure of the teachings. Guru Padmasambhava also introduced his disciples to more specialized instructions that included the practice of tantra and the teachings on the Great Perfection.

In the Nyingma tradition a succession of nine vehicles is explained: the vehicles of śrāvakas, pratyekabuddhas and bodhisattvas; the three outer tantras of kriya, upa, and yoga tantra; and the three inner tantras of mahāyoga, anuyoga, and atiyoga. The first eight of these vehicles take the ordinary mind as the path. Atiyoga, which corresponds to the Great Perfection, takes primordial consciousness as the path.

When we speak of taking primordial consciousness as the path, we are referring to our fundamental nature, the unchanging awareness that is never tainted by the fleeting stains of discursive thought. Neither the phenomena of saṃsāra nor their causes, the karmic winds and ordinary thought patterns, have ever clouded the purity of this awareness.

The coarse level of our ordinary consciousness does not continue until buddhahood, as only the fundamental innate mind of clear light can be present in the state of omniscience. This fundamental innate mind of clear light is the primordial consciousness spoken of in the Great Perfection. It is the primordial consciousness that the Great Perfection takes as the path. The highest yoga tantras of the new translation tradition follow the same principle, using techniques reliant on the ordinary coarse mind in order to manifest the fundamental innate mind of clear light, while the Great Perfection employs nothing but the fundamental innate mind of clear light.

Taking the primordial consciousness of pristine awareness as the path is a process of revealing our subtlest level of awareness and enabling it to find its own stability by working with and experiencing the aware aspect of the fundamental innate mind of clear light. This is the extraordinary, profound, and unique feature of the Great Perfection.

Padmasambhava concealed countless spiritual treasures, or *terma*, destined to be discovered at opportune times by successive incarnations of his chief disciples. Lerab Lingpa, author of the first text in this book, was a *tertön*, a revealer of such treasures, who gave important transmissions to my predecessor, the Thirteenth Dalai Lama.

The first part of this book, a translation of *The Vital Essence of Primordial Consciousness*, consists of Lerab Lingpa's instructions—derived from treasures he had revealed—on how to practice and uncover our most subtle level of awareness.

The second part of the book consists of essays by more recent scholar-adepts on the place of specialized instructions such as the Great Perfection in the context of the general structure of Buddha's teachings. Their conclusions support the observation of the seventeenth-century master Panchen Losang Chökyi Gyaltsen, who wrote that when the numerous traditions are "scrutinized by a yogi learned in scripture, logic, and meditative experience, their definitive meanings all converge on the same intended point."

I value the care with which B. Alan Wallace has translated these works into English, making them available to a wider interested readership. I have known Alan for many years and appreciate his work as a translator, as well as his exploration of the qualities of the mind, first as a monk and later as a scientist and a contemplative.

All levels of consciousness—including the coarsest level of our ordinary minds—are permeated by an aspect of the subtlest awareness, or clear light. This can be pointed out to us by an experienced master in whom we have faith. When we recognize the nature of this subtlest awareness, we can take it—and it alone—as the basis of our practice. May this book inspire readers to develop such an understanding of the nature of the mind and to then experience it in actual practice.

Tenzin Gyatso, the Fourteenth Dalai Lama

# Preface

The Tibetan voices we hear in this volume often seem to be speaking to us directly, here and now. Though their worlds would in many ways appear to be quite foreign to us, these authors are grappling with questions of worldview and practice that are no less pressing today, even among practitioners living in modern cultures far removed from theirs. These masters frequently address crucial differences in presentation that exist across the great lineages of Tibetan Buddhism. They also offer glimpses of how to understand a deeper compatibility between those presentations in ways that are rarely explained, even among millions of pages of Tibetan literature.

The three authors whose works are translated here lived during a pivotal period of Tibetan history, from the second half of the nineteenth century through the first half of the twentieth. It was a time when the conditions were ripe for unprecedented dialogue between master scholars trained in multiple traditions, who often combined extensive knowledge of Geluk, Sakya, and Kagyü perspectives with authentic experience of the Great Perfection (Tibetan: Dzokchen) tradition associated with the Nyingma school. Determined to overcome the sectarian tensions that had run through much of Tibetan history, they wished to understand and honor the teachings from each tradition, and above all to put into practice the steps of the spiritual path in a way that would most quickly lead to complete awakening and existential transformation.

Tertön Sogyal Lerab Lingpa (1856–1926) was born in the Nyarong Valley of Kham, in southeastern Tibet, and though he spent much of his life traversing the Tibetan landscape as a visionary and teacher, especially serving the Thirteenth Dalai Lama in the capital city of Lhasa, in the last two decades of his life he remained primarily in eastern Tibet. He spent much time at Dodrupchen Monastery, on the border between Golok and Kham. There he cultivated his close Dharma relationship with the Third Dodrupchen, Jikmé Tenpé Nyima (1865–1926), who was in turn the eldest son of the great treasure revealer Düdjom Lingpa (1835–1904). Though I know of no evidence that Lerab Lingpa met Düdjom Lingpa in person, there is clearly a deep affinity between their visionary teachings and a strong familial connection through Düdjom Lingpa's sons. Lerab Lingpa served as both student and teacher to the Third Dodrupchen, even as he became the teacher of Düdjom Lingpa's youngest son, as well as several of his grandsons.

Furthermore, in his book *Fearless in Tibet* (238–39) Matteo Pistono recounts a vision that Tertön Sogyal Lerab Lingpa experienced in 1923, nearly a decade after Düdjom Lingpa had passed away and his successor Düdjom Rinpoche had been born. In that vision, Lerab Lingpa met Guru Padmasambhava surrounded by a host of ḍākinīs, one of whom spoke to him about the necessity of reaching the teacher in both peaceful and wrathful forms. This was followed by a clear vision of five famous masters, one of whom was Düdjom Lingpa. Lerab Lingpa heard an injunction from the ḍākinī: "If you can unite all of the lamas of the past, present, and future, together, as Padmasambhava, then the blessing will be swift." He then received practices associated with each of the five gurus, and when writing them down later, he heard verses echoing in the sky that included the message, "*Dudjom Lingpa can be accomplished as the Wildy Wrathful Guru.*" Again the five gurus appeared to him, and each spoke the words, "I am the great holder of all the *Complete Gathering of Teachings*. If you accomplish me, then you accomplish all the buddhas." After this they each dissolved into Guru Padmasambhava. Given such extraordinary connections between these two great treasure revealers, at both the familial and visionary levels, I believe that the text by Lerab Lingpa that comprises the first part of this volume can provide a wonderful complement to the teachings I translated in three volumes of *Düdjom Lingpa's Visions of the Great Perfection*.

Jé Tsultrim Zangpo (1884–ca. 1957), also known as Tulku Tsullo, was a learned monk from nearby Shukjung Monastery in Golok. His collected works reveal him to be a master of both the Old Translation school, or Nyingma tradition, as well as of the philosophy and tantras associated with the New Translation schools, represented primarily by the Sakya, Kagyü, and Geluk traditions. (The distinction of "Old" and "New" refers to two different historical periods during which Indian Sanskrit scriptures were translated into the Tibetan language, the former spanning from the eighth to ninth centuries CE and the latter roughly from the late tenth to twelfth centuries. Within the texts translated here, however, the terms "Old" and "New" refer more broadly to the entire body of teachings associated with each of the different lineages, even as these continued to expand during later centuries.) Jé Tsultrim Zangpo was a close student of the aforementioned Dodrupchen Jikmé Tenpé Nyima and thereby came to meet and receive extensive instruction from Lerab Lingpa as well, becoming his biographer and a primary lineage holder for all of Lerab Lingpa's treasure revelations. I believe that Jé Tsultrim Zangpo's clarifications of the subtle theory behind the practice of the Great Perfection, which reflect his sensitivity to the explanations found in both the New and Old tantras, will be of tremendous help to those who wish to understand how these traditions of practice might be harmonized without being confused.

Lozang Do-ngak Chökyi Gyatso (1903–57) was born in Golok, recognized at the age of fifteen to be a reincarnate lama, and trained by two teachers who were themselves steeped in the nonsectarian movement: Amdo Geshé Jampel Rolway Lodrö (1888–1936) and Drakkar Geshé Lozang Tenzin Nyendrak (1866–1928), from whom Lozang Do-ngak Chökyi Gyatso received full ordination as a Geluk monk. As a young man, likely while traveling with Amdo Geshé in 1919, Lozang Do-ngak Chökyi Gyatso also received transmissions from Lerab Lingpa, whom he clearly considered to be one of his root teachers. His writings reveal the depth of his love and appreciation for both the Old and New schools of thought, principally as represented by Longchenpa and Tsongkhapa, respectively. It is important to note that all but one of the essays in part 2 of this volume,

*Selected Essays on Old and New Views of the Secret Mantrayāna*, were written by this same figure. He alternatively goes by the name of Kunzang Zhepé Dorjé and by a Sanskrit version of the latter part of his monk's name: Dharmasāra. In both languages, this means "Ocean of Dharma." It is also poignant to realize that he was recognized as a reincarnation of one Japa Do-ngak Gyatso (1824–1902), who was himself a thoroughly intersectarian scholar, and was famous for having lost a debate with Ju Mipham regarding the view of the Great Perfection, after which he went into retreat for eighteen years, first meditating on *bodhicitta*, or the wish for enlightenment, and later on the stages of generation and completion. He was also a teacher of Dodrupchen Jikmé Tenpé Nyima. These details become significant when we read Dharmasāra's own views on the necessity of practicing both the stages of generation and completion—even if in previous lives—in order to become a ripe vessel for the Great Perfection. In another place, Dharmasāra praises the philosophical view of Ju Mipham as being in accord with that of Tsongkhapa on the question of simple negations, even though those two authors are often seen as being at odds with each other. Dharmasāra's works have much to reveal about the intersection between Old and New schools, both in painting the overall scope of Vajrayāna practice and in clarifying the definitive meaning of Madhyamaka, or Middle Way philosophy.

## Notes on the Texts

The first work translated here, *The Vital Essence of Primordial Consciousness*, about which I will say more in the introduction, was composed by Lerab Lingpa as a record of an oral teaching he received from the illustrious Jamyang Khyentsé Wangpo (1813–92) concerning a form of Great Perfection practice known as the *Chetsun Nyingtik*, or *Chetsun's Heart Essence*. The story of how this visionary teaching came to be appears in the opening pages of the text itself. My English translation was based primarily on Taklung Tsetrul Rinpoche Pema Wangyal's printing, circa 1985, of a manuscript edition of the entire cycle of teachings on *Chetsun's Heart*

*Essence* written by Jamyang Khyentsé Wangpo and several of his close students, including Lerab Lingpa. As an aid to Tibetan readers, the publication information for this edition (to which the bracketed page numbers correspond) appears on the first page of the bibliography. For difficult passages it was essential to consult at least two editions, so there is also reference to an alternative computer-input printing of the entire collection from Shechen Monastery. Both of these are available at the Buddhist Digital Resource Center (www.tbrc.org) as works W27867 and W27887, respectively.

The eight chapter titles were added to this English translation for ease of reading but do not appear in the original text. The traditional Tibetan outline (Tib. *sa bcad*) is also translated throughout, and appears in full at the end of *The Vital Essence of Primordial Consciousness*. Where there were disparities in the outline, for the most part I followed the choices of the Shechen Monastery Tibetan editors, who had evidently consulted several more prints and manuscripts in making such editorial decisions.

The second work translated in this volume, *Selected Essays on Old and New Views of the Secret Mantrayāna*, represents a Tibetan-language anthology that was compiled and published in 2009 by Namgyal Monastery in Dharamsala, India. Thus the six works by Lozang Do-ngak Chökyi Gyatso/Dharmasāra and the single work by Jé Tsultrim Zangpo were chosen by Tibetan editors from among the multivolume collected works of each author, specifically in order to speak to the theme of intersectarian dialogue and mutual understanding. As these ideas are pertinent for contemporary Tibetans, both lay and monastic, so I expect they will be for English readers worldwide. Again, for variant readings it was necessary to consult printed editions of the collected works of each author, for which there is publication information included in the bibliography. The bracketed page numbers herein correspond to the Namgyal Monastery publication.

All of these works contain passages that are not easy to understand upon first reading, just as they were not easy to translate. They are written in a terse and highly technical style of composition that assumes much knowledge on the part of the reader and expects that the text is being studied as part of a comprehensive training in Buddhist ideas, in the presence of qualified living teachers. Numerous footnotes supply information that the author takes as given. Nonetheless, I urge my readers to take the time to read certain passages over and over again in order to decipher the intent behind the economical expression. I believe it will be well worth the effort in trying to understand each point that is being made, especially when returning to these texts over many months and years of practice.

## Prerequisites

It is clear that the various texts included in this volume reveal the most sublime of all Dharmas—secret mantra, Vajrayāna, or the Vajra Vehicle. The Sanskrit term *vajra* signifies the nature of ultimate reality, with its seven attributes of invulnerability, indestructibility, reality, incorruptibility, stability, unobstructability, and invincibility; and *yāna* means a vehicle for spiritual practice. Such profound instructions are traditionally guarded as secrets due to their potential for being dangerously misunderstood, and also in order to protect the teachings from disparagement. It has often been said that such treatises maintain their own secrecy, for only those who are sufficiently mature in their spiritual development will even have the capacity to hear or understand what is being expressed when encountering such teachings.

Therefore, if you wish to put the meaning of these sacred texts into practice, it is essential that you seek out a qualified guru to guide you in your understanding and practice. The masters of this lineage insist that, rather than merely striving to accumulate knowledge or virtue that might benefit you in this current lifetime, or else some future lifetime, you should seize this precious opportunity—a human life in which you can practice the sublime Dharma—and generate the aspiration to achieve enlightenment in this present lifetime.

Thus the publication of these translations is indeed restricted to suitable readers, specifically those who earnestly aspire to achieve liberation and enlightenment. In setting forth specific restrictions for readers of this volume, I am adhering exactly to the stipulations made by my principal Dzokchen lama, Ven. Domang Gyatrul Rinpoche, with the original publication of my translation of *The Vajra Essence*. The teachings in this volume are no more or less esoteric or secret than those explained in *The Vajra Essence*, so I feel the prerequisites are equally applicable in this context. According to the guidance of my lama, people who are qualified to read the translations of the texts in this volume will not be fixated on material success, but because they understand the reality of suffering, they will have turned away from the allures of saṃsāra. They will honor the fundamental Buddhist teachings included in the Śrāvakayāna, or the Hearers' Vehicle, and they will revere the Mahāyāna, or Great Vehicle, as well.

This means that not only will they care about following a path toward freedom from their own experience of suffering, but they will care deeply about helping others achieve their highest and most meaningful spiritual goals, both in this life and far into the future. Thus such readers will have begun to cultivate the four immeasurables, including thoughts of limitless compassion, loving-kindness, empathetic joy, and equanimity toward all living beings. They will have begun to study and practice in the manner of a *bodhisattva*, or someone who aspires to reach the state of a buddha for the benefit of others. Such a way of life includes the six perfections: giving, ethical conduct, patience, joyful effort, meditative concentration, and wisdom. Suitable readers will also have begun to gain familiarity with the insights associated with the Yogācāra and Madhyamaka worldviews regarding the way in which all phenomena do not exist in the way that they appear. In addition, they will value all the outer, inner, and secret classes of the tantras and have a genuine desire to practice the stages of the Great Perfection known as cutting through and direct crossing over. Finally, suitable readers of this volume will treat it with reverence and care.

While those who will devote themselves to the practice of these Great Perfection teachings should receive the appropriate empowerments, oral transmissions, and explanations of the lineage masters, the texts themselves do not restrict their readership to those who have completed certain preliminary practices, such as a hundred thousand recitations of the Vajrasattva mantra and so on. Likewise, the many tantras and other secret Vajrayāna treatises originally composed in Sanskrit and eventually translated into Tibetan, which were then published in the Kangyur and Tengyur, are freely available to anyone who can read Tibetan, without restrictions placed on the readership by the translators. So I do not feel that it is appropriate for me as the translator of these texts to impose such restrictions of my own. This is a decision to be made by individual qualified lamas of this lineage, and they are bound to have different criteria by which they judge who may and may not read such secret texts.

## Acknowledgments

It was an enormous privilege for me to translate these works, and I am above all indebted to the immeasurable kindness of my root lama, His Holiness the Dalai Lama, for encouraging me to translate the anthology *Selected Essays on Old and New Views of the Secret Mantrayāna*. Both this text and Tertön Lerab Lingpa's *The Vital Essence of Primordial Consciousness* presented many challenges in the process of translating them into English, and I would not have been up to the task were it not for the great assistance of scholars and contemplatives more knowledgeable and experienced than I. I am particularly grateful for the many points of clarification about these texts pointed out to me by Tulku Orgyen Phuntsok and Geshe Dorji Damdul. Lama Chönam was also ever so helpful in clarifying especially those passages in the anthology that included phrases in the regional Golok dialect of the two authors. Happily, Lama Chönam was born and raised in that same region of southeastern Amdo, on the border with Kham, so he was a perfect consultant for this translation! I am also indebted to the conscientious editorial suggestions made by David Kittelstrom of Wisdom Publications, who has offered his unflagging support over the years for my efforts to translate and elucidate the meaning of the Buddha's teachings for modern readers. The translations in this text were also enhanced by the careful line editing of Mary Petrusewicz, to whom I offer my sincere thanks. Finally, I wish to express my heartfelt gratitude to the wonderful assistance of Eva Natanya, who brought her exceptional gifts as a scholar and translator, together with her earnest devotion to the Dharma, to editing this entire volume. In retrospect, I don't know how these translations could have been corrected, clarified, and polished in their current form without her invaluable assistance. That said, whatever errors in translation remain, they are solely my responsibility, and I hope that they will be brought to my attention so that they may be cleared up in any future editions of this work.

May the teachings in this volume be of great benefit to all those who study and practice them, resulting in their swift realization of śamatha, vipaśyanā, cutting through, and the direct crossing over. Finally, may many beings arrive at the culmination of this path by actualizing the rainbow body in this very lifetime!

B. Alan Wallace
April 11, 2017, full-moon day of the second month of the fire-bird year
Pomaia, Italy

# Translator's Introduction

This volume focuses on the teachings and legacy of one of the greatest Tibetan Buddhist contemplatives of recent history, Lerab Lingpa (1856–1926), also known as Tertön Sogyal. His life story, beautifully narrated by Matteo Pistono in *Fearless in Tibet*, was deeply intertwined with that of the Thirteenth Dalai Lama (1876–1933), for whom he served as spiritual friend and guru.[1] As the Dalai Lama devoted himself tirelessly to bringing about long-overdue, desperately needed social and religious reforms in Tibet, Lerab Lingpa similarly made it his life's mission to support the Dalai Lama's innovations and do all he could to serve the welfare of the Tibetan people and culture. Both seemed to have a profound foreboding of the crisis Tibetan civilization would face when it was fully assaulted by the ideological, military, and economic might of the modern world. The suppression of religion in Russia began in 1917 with the Communist overthrow of the czarist regime, and Mao Zedong's attempts to bring China under the heel of Communism began just ten years later. Ironically, the attempted genocide of Tibet in the twentieth century and the assault on traditional Chinese culture were perpetrated not by Europeans but by Chinese Communists, who thereby advanced a Eurocentric conquest of their own civilization. For they were seduced by European thinkers like the biologist Thomas H. Huxley (1825–95) and the economist Karl Marx (1818–83).

Thomas Huxley fused a metaphysical belief in materialism with the empirical facts of modern science. For him, human beings were simply highly

1. For a brief biography of Lerab Lingpa (*Las rab gling pa, gter ston bsod rgyal*), see http://treasuryoflives.org/biographies/view/Lerab-Lingpa/8538.

evolved animals, their behavior determined solely by physical causes. Such humans lack any form of free will and thus any basis for moral responsibility. Biological evolution is essentially a mechanical series of adaptations for the sole purpose of survival and procreation, and the universe at large a series of mindless processes. The conflation of such a barren metaphysical worldview with scientific knowledge has sparked a rejection of modernity and science by religious fundamentalists worldwide. In this way the dogma of materialistic fundamentalism reinforces the dogmas of religious fundamentalism, often leading to violence and the suppression of free thought and expression.

In his antipathy toward organized religion, particularly the Church of England, Huxley insisted that science must be practiced and taught only within the framework of materialism. In so doing, he turned a blind eye to the sophisticated writings on the constructive interface between science and theology by his eminent contemporary James Clerk Maxwell (1831–79). Widely considered the greatest physicist after Isaac Newton and prior to Albert Einstein (both of whom wrote extensively about the constructive interrelationship between science and religion), Maxwell was a devout evangelical Christian who integrated his religious beliefs with his scientific investigations. But with astonishing global success, Huxley divorced science from religion.[2]

There is no question that blind faith and uncritical allegiance to what is presented as divine authority is common among the world's religions. And science, with its ideals of objectivity, empiricism, and rationality, has brought great benefits to humanity that, when wielded well, can be an important corrective to benighted religion. But when religion is cast as a singular culprit in depicting what is wrong with the world, when religion is said to be only an obstacle and never a solution, we risk losing touch with the manifold and highly sophisticated spiritual technologies that humans have developed over millennia.

Buddhism may be uniquely poised to heal the rift between "science" and "religion," for it doesn't neatly fit into either of these Eurocentric categories.

2. For an illuminating account of Huxley's campaign for world domination of scientific materialism, see Stanley, *Huxley's Church and Maxwell's Demon*.

For example, in the *Kalama Sutta* the Buddha famously countered sectarian rivalry by encouraging his listeners to be skeptical of dogmatic claims based on nothing more than hearsay, tradition, rumor, scriptures, speculation, unquestioned beliefs, specious reasoning, personal bias, the charisma of others, and allegiance to one's own teacher. Rather, he counseled others to adopt a radically empirical and pragmatic approach to evaluating various theories, embracing them only if they are found to be true and helpful. His Holiness the Fourteenth Dalai Lama, who has taken a crucial role in advancing dialogue and collaborative research between science and religion, remains true to this spirit of constructive skepticism originally advocated by the Buddha: "A general basic stance of Buddhism is that it is inappropriate to hold a view that is logically inconsistent. This is taboo. But even more taboo than holding a view that is logically inconsistent is holding a view that goes against direct experience."[3]

The twentieth century brought many benefits to humanity as a whole, especially in the supplanting of fascist and other military dictatorships with democratic governments. This shift has supported the noble ideals of self-governance and the protection of human rights. But these same benefits have been denied in precisely the Communist regimes in which the church of scientific materialism has been united with the military and police power of the state. The violent suppression of all religions throughout Asia—including the destruction of countless churches, temples, and monasteries, and the execution of tens of thousands of priests and monks—especially under the despotic leadership of Joseph Stalin and Mao, constitutes one of the most savage ideological warfares in human history. Although waged by atheist rather than religious fanatics, this should not obscure the fact that it bears all the earmarks of religious warfare in its scientific materialist dismissal of religion as poison.

But recent history has shown that religious convictions and aspirations can survive even such intense, sustained persecution, and the revitalization of Buddhism throughout Asia bears witness to this. In this regard,

3. Varela and Hayward, *Gentle Bridges*, 37.

Lerab Lingpa's record of the observation of his teacher, Jamyang Khyentsé Wangpo, seems remarkably prescient:

> [617] . . . In this era, which is more degenerate than the dregs, even to an individual more ordinary than the ordinary, who obviously has a multitude of faults of all kinds and only feeble virtues of any sort—to an individual like myself—the time of the Jina's [i.e., the Buddha's] activity has not passed, but is extremely powerful.

This assertion is found in one of his principal meditation manuals, *The Vital Essence of Primordial Consciousness*, which lays out the entire path of the Great Perfection (Tibetan: Dzokchen), a tradition that focuses inward on the ultimate nature and ground of consciousness itself. This is the first of two translations of Tibetan texts in this volume. The work was originally conceived as an explanation of a revelatory treasure (*terma*) text of Jamyang Khyentsé Wangpo (1820–92), a cycle of Great Perfection practices called the *Chetsun Nyingtik*, or *Chetsun's Heart Essence*. In 1993 in New York City, I received the empowerment and oral teachings on Lerab Lingpa's text from an incarnation of Lerab Lingpa, Khenpo Jigmé Phuntsok (1933–2004), who was widely regarded as the most highly accomplished contemplative and teacher in Tibet during the late twentieth century. Beginning in 1980 he established Larung Gar in eastern Tibet, which has become the largest Buddhist teaching center in the world and which until recently hosted up to forty thousand Tibetan and Han Chinese monastics. In the ongoing suppression of Buddhism in Tibet by the Chinese government, roughly 80 percent of the structures in this center are currently being demolished.

The second Tibetan text translated here is *Selected Essays on Old and New Views of the Secret Mantrayāna*, composed by two of Lerab Lingpa's close disciples. The author of all but one of the essays in this anthology is Dharmasāra (1903–57), who also goes by the names Lozang Do-ngak Chökyi Gyatso Chok and Kunzang Zhepé Dorjé.[4] His six essays provide

4. For a brief biography of Dharmasāra, see http://treasuryoflives.org/biographies/view/Dongak-Chokyi-Gyatso/7945.

detailed, erudite explanations of the compatibility among the theories and practices of Great Perfection, Mahāmudrā (the "Great Seal"), and the Madhyamaka view, especially as these are interpreted by the Indian paṇḍita Candrakīrti (ca. 600–650), the Nyingma master Longchen Rabjam (1308–63),[5] and Jé Tsongkhapa (1357–1419),[6] founder of the Geluk school of Tibetan Buddhism. The second author, Jé Tsultrim Zangpo (1884–1957), also known as Tulku Tsullo, composed the only biography of Lerab Lingpa.[7] His contribution to the anthology is titled "An Ornament of the Enlightened View of Samantabhadra." Here he contextualizes the Great Perfection within the broader framework of Mahāyāna and Vajrayāna Buddhism and then elucidates all the stages of practice of the Great Perfection, unifying the profound path of cutting through and the vast path of the spontaneous actualization of the direct crossing over.[8] In 2014 I was encouraged by His Holiness the Fourteenth Dalai Lama to translate this anthology, for these essays make a major contribution to intersectarian understanding and harmony within the schools of Tibetan Buddhism.

Both the texts published here focus primarily on the teachings and practices of the Great Perfection, which are regarded especially in the Nyingma school of Tibetan Buddhism as the pinnacle of Buddhist contemplative

5. Frequently known simply as Longchenpa, one of his full names is Longchen Rabjam Drimé Özer (*Klong chen rab 'byams dri med 'od zer*).

6. Jé Tsongkhapa Lozang Drakpa (*Rje tsong kha pa blo bzang grags pa*).

7. Although there is as yet no biography for Jé Tsultrim Zangpo (*Rje tshul khrims bzang po*) at this website, his name does appear as a disciple of the Third Dodrubchen, Jigmé Tenpé Nyima: http://treasuryoflives.org/biographies/view/Dodrubchen-03-Jigme-Tenpai-Nyima/4185. There is also a brief biography of Jé Tsultrim Zangpo at http://www.rigpawiki.org/index.php?title=Tulku_Tsultrim_Zangpo.

8. Another masterful overview of the Great Perfection within the context of the Buddhadharma as a whole is found in His Holiness the Dalai Lama's *Mind in Comfort and Ease*. During the oral teaching of which that volume is a record, His Holiness praised Jé Tsultrim Zangpo in particular for his remarkable ability to make connections between the Great Perfection and "Lama Tsongkhapa's way of presenting things." See *Mind in Comfort and Ease*, xxvi. His Holiness relied heavily on Jé Tsultrim Zangpo's text (the same one translated in this present volume) for his presentation there, quoting it at length multiple times.

inquiry. Instead of focusing our attention outward in the pursuit of understanding the objective physical world, the Buddha encouraged his followers to look inward at our own minds to discover the true sources of suffering and of joy and meaning. Instead of focusing on increasing our material wealth and power, Buddhist teachings focus on exploring the inner resources of consciousness. Instead of encouraging an insatiable appetite for hedonic pleasures, Buddhism lays the foundation for genuine well being, which stems from within. And instead of perpetuating the globally self-destructive cycle of ever-increasing consumption, Buddhist tradition has always promoted the ideals of simplicity and material contentment.

Within the history of Buddhist educational institutions there has long been a widespread tradition of first becoming deeply immersed in Buddhist theory and then of devoting oneself single-pointedly to meditation with the intention to put those teachings to the test of experience. But within the Great Perfection and Mahāmudrā traditions of Indo-Tibetan Buddhism, which bear much in common, especially in terms of their primary focus on fathoming the nature and potentials of consciousness, another approach is advocated. Padmasambhava, the eighth-century Indian Buddhist master who took a seminal role in introducing Buddhism in general and the Great Perfection in particular into Tibet, wrote in this regard:

> According to the custom of some teaching traditions, you are first introduced to the view, and on that basis you seek the meditative state. This makes it difficult to identify pristine awareness. In this tradition, you first establish the meditative state, then on that basis you are introduced to the view. This profound point makes it impossible for you not to identify pristine awareness. Therefore first settle your mind in its natural state, then bring forth genuine *śamatha* in your mindstream and reveal the nature of pristine awareness.[9]

Paṇchen Lozang Chökyi Gyaltsen (1570–1662), the First Paṇchen Lama and the teacher and close ally of the Fifth Dalai Lama, composed a highly

9. Padmasambhava, *Natural Liberation*, 115, translation slightly modified.

influential text on Mahāmudrā, which he introduces with a similar comment: "Of the two approaches of seeking to meditate on the basis of the view and seeking the view on the basis of meditation, the following accords with the latter approach."[10] So rather than first moving outward to the acquisition of objective knowledge and then inward to direct, experiential knowledge, the classic approach of the Great Perfection and Mahāmudrā traditions is first to bring about a profound subjective state of meditative equipoise and to let Buddhist insights spontaneously flow from within.

Another distinctive aspect of the Great Perfection is that it presents the ground of being, the path to enlightenment, and the fruit of perfect spiritual awakening from the perspective of one who is already enlightened. His Holiness the Fourteenth Dalai Lama makes this point with great clarity regarding the writings of Longchen Rabjam, one of the most influential masters of the Great Perfection in the entire history of Tibetan Buddhism:

> As is said in an oral transmission by the great lama Jamyang Khyentse Chökyi Lodrö, when the great Nyingmapa adept Longchen Rabjam gives a presentation of the ground, path, and fruit, he does so mainly from the perspective of the enlightened state of a Buddha, whereas the Sakyapa presentation is mainly from the perspective of the spiritual experience of a yogi on the path, and the Gelukpa presentation is mainly from the perspective of how phenomena appear to ordinary sentient beings. His statement appears to be worthy of considerable reflection; through it many misunderstandings can be removed.[11]

The teachings of the Great Perfection, also known as atiyoga, constitute the highest of nine spiritual vehicles, or *yānas*, as presented in the Nyingma school. There are three classes of atiyoga teachings—the mind

10. *Collected Works of Paṇ chen blo bzang chos kyi rgyal mtshan* (New Delhi, India: Mongolian Lama Gurudeva, 1973), 4: 84. All excerpts from this Tibetan text translated by B. Alan Wallace.

11. H. H. the Dalai Lama, *The Meaning of Life*, 99.

class, the expanse class, and the pith instruction class—in successive order of subtlety and profundity. Within the culminating class of pith instructions, there is a further fourfold classification of cycles of teachings, as explained by Lerab Lingpa:

> [605] . . . The supremely distinguished avenue on which disciples with faculties that are superior, [middling,] and so on may realize and actualize this method consists of the three classes of the Great Perfection. Among those, the foremost is the secret class of pith instruction, and within this there are the outer cycle, the inner cycle, the secret cycle, and the unsurpassed, ultrasecret cycle. Among those four, this here is the unsurpassed, ultrasecret one.

Padmasambhava's teachings on the Great Perfection mystically revealed to Düdjom Lingpa (1835–1904), another of the foremost masters of the Great Perfection in nineteenth-century Tibet, are also included in this unsurpassed, ultrasecret cycle of the class of pith instructions. In the most extensive of those revealed teachings, Padmasambhava definitively sets forth the characteristics of those who are qualified to learn and practice this cycle of the view and meditation of the Great Perfection:

> The best of disciples are those in whom the following qualities are present:
>
> - Disillusion and disgust with the affairs of this life
> - Unwavering faith in the Three Jewels
> - Great compassion
> - Little avarice
> - Delight in generosity
> - No envy
> - Candor
> - Courage and fortitude
> - Dependability

- Single-mindedness
- Firm resolve

He then lists the qualities of people who are unworthy to participate in such teachings:

> If disciples with the following qualities are given practical advice, eventually they will definitely become māras for the teacher:
>
> - Obsession with saṃsāra
> - Little faith or reverence
> - Duplicity and deceitfulness
> - No compassion
> - Great avarice
> - Envy
> - Hatefulness and irritability
> - Emotional instability and fickleness
> - Crudeness, with no courage or fortitude
> - Strong distraction and spiritual sloth
> - Attraction to entertainment and obsession with those of high status
> - Great satisfaction with oneself but no interest in others
> - Shallowness
> - Penchant for divisive speech
> - Fondness for dishonesty and gossip[12]

It is quite natural to be daunted by the extremely esoteric and secret nature of this cycle of teachings, so much so that many of us may feel that they must be far beyond the reach of ordinary people like ourselves. But in those same teachings Padmasambhava encourages worthy disciples to take full advantage of the opportunity to learn and practice the teachings if they are so moved from within:

12. Düdjom Lingpa, *Vajra Essence*, 219–20.

> In this present lifetime, if you . . . have firm faith and belief in [the Great Perfection] and strong, unflagging enthusiasm—the time has come to practice. When fortunate beings come to the gateway of the profound secret mantra, apart from simply having strong faith and belief, there is never anything else—such as clairvoyance, omens, or auspicious circumstances—to make them think that the time has come to practice secret mantra. Once you have obtained a human life and encountered a guru and the secret mantra Dharma, if this is not the time to practice the Great Perfection, then there will never be a better time than this in another life—this is certain.[13]

In the unsurpassed, ultrasecret cycle of teachings in the *Vital Essence of Primordial Consciousness*, Lerab Lingpa cites the vajra words of the primordial consciousness ḍākinī, Pelgyi Lodröma:

> [753] You can also see that this has been entrusted to, or placed in the keeping of, the powerful, divine protectors, and, considering that, you may think it is better not to write about it. As for me, I have dared to propagate it, so each person may practice for themselves. If you disseminate this to others who are drawn to it and do all you can to help them connect with it, since this Dharma is appropriate for the present era, even if they have a negative connection with this, how could it not be meaningful? It is certain that even if this is not beneficial, it will bring no harm, so I ask you to do your best to hold this in mind.

With such encouragement from Padmasambhava, Düdjom Lingpa, and the primordial consciousness ḍākinī Pelgyi Lodröma, I have felt emboldened to translate and publish these two texts on the Great Perfection. Anyone wishing to put these teachings into practice, however, should first

13. Düdjom Lingpa, *Vajra Essence*, 13.

seek out a qualified guru who holds this lineage and then receive empowerment, oral transmission, and guidance in these practices, beginning with the indispensible preliminary practices.

## Preliminaries to the Practice of the Great Perfection

Just as astronomers need observatories to engage in research, so do professional contemplatives need suitable facilities to support them in their explorations of the nature of consciousness and its role in the universe. In his explanation of the preparations for the meditation session to make the mindstream a suitable vessel, Lerab Lingpa begins by highlighting the importance of retreating to a quiet place, free of mundane distractions, either in solitude or in the company of like-minded companions. An astronomical observatory must be equipped with a high-quality, well-maintained telescope, and in all other scientific research laboratories sophisticated instruments of measurement and experimentation play a central role. But for the first-person exploration of the mind, one's own body, speech, and mind are the basis of all observations, so considerable effort must be given to see that they are all balanced in a state of equilibrium. As the Buddha declared, "The mind that is established in equipoise discovers reality."[14] On this basis one offers prayers of supplication to one's guru, asking for blessings to inspire one's practice.

Lerab Lingpa then proceeds to set forth seven preliminary practices that are shared between Sūtrayāna and Vajrayāna practice: namely, (1) meditation on impermanence, (2) meditation on the way in which even the pleasures of saṃsāra are causes leading to unhappiness, (3) meditation on the way there is no closure, no matter how much we strive for favorable circumstances in saṃsāra, (4) meditation on the futility of all superficial human pursuits, whether good or bad, (5) meditation on the benefits of liberation, (6) meditation on the importance of the guru's practical instructions, and (7) how to settle the mind in its natural state, since this method is so crucially important.

14. Cited in Kamalaśīla's first *Bhāvanākrama*, in Tucci, *Minor Buddhist Texts*, 205.

In the classic literature on the stages of the path to enlightenment (*lamrim*), including Atiśa's *Lamp for the Path to Enlightenment*, Gampopa's *Ornament of Precious Liberation*, and Tsongkhapa's *Great Treatise on the Stages of the Path to Enlightenment*, *śamatha*, or meditative quiescence, is taught within the context of the six perfections that provide the framework for the bodhisattva way of life. But Lerab Lingpa's approach in this text is distinctive in that he introduces śamatha prior to his explanation of the unique preliminary practices. These preliminaries include an exceptional approach to taking refuge, cultivating bodhicitta, the combined practice of purifying obscurations and accumulating merit and knowledge, and guru yoga. Nowhere in his discussion of the shared and unique preliminary practices does he make any reference to "accumulating" a hundred thousand recitations or prostrations. Nor does Düdjom Lingpa make any such reference in any of his five principal treatises on the Great Perfection. Both these nineteenth-century masters were far more concerned with engaging in these practices until they yield the inner transformations for which they were intended, regardless of how long this may take. During a public teaching at the San Francisco Zen Center in 1980, the late Kalu Rinpoché, one of the greatest Mahāmudrā masters of the late twentieth century, was asked about the proper sequence of śamatha and the preliminary practices to Vajrayāna. He replied that if one completes the preliminary practices prior to practicing śamatha, this helps to dispel obstacles to śamatha and provides merit to help bring this practice to its culmination. On the other hand, he added, if one first achieves śamatha, this will greatly enhance the efficacy of the preliminary practices. So there is no one definitive order to these practices, but they are all indispensable.

The culmination of Lerab Lingpa's presentation of the shared preliminaries is "settling the mind in its natural state," which he emphasizes as "a sound basis for the arising of all samādhis of the stages of generation and completion," let alone the subsequent meditations that are unique to the Great Perfection. This refers to a particular approach to the achievement of śamatha—one also emphasized in the Great Perfection teachings of Düdjom Lingpa—that he calls "taking the impure mind as the path" and "taking awareness and appearances as the path." Although this phase of meditative practice is widely overlooked, misunderstood, or marginalized in Buddhism today, its function of subduing the five obscurations of the mind is crucial for all schools of Buddhism. As the Buddha himself declared, "So long as these five obscurations [attachment to hedonic pleasure, malice, laxity and dullness, excitation and anxiety, and afflictive uncertainty] are not abandoned one considers oneself as indebted, sick, in bonds, enslaved, and lost in a desert track."[15] More specifically, shortly before his achievement of enlightenment, the Buddha came to the insight that the achievement of the first *dhyāna*, or meditative stabilization, was an indispensible step on the path of awakening:

> I thought of a time when my Śākyan father was working and I was sitting in the cool shade of a rose apple tree. Quite secluded from sensual desires and disengaged from unwholesome things, I entered into and dwelt in the first dhyāna, which is accompanied by coarse and precise investigation, with well being and bliss born of seclusion. I thought, "Might this be the way to enlightenment?" Then, following that memory, there came the recognition that this was the way to enlightenment.[16]

While there are many śamatha methods, all of them having the function of overcoming the five obscurations, the particular method taught by Lerab Lingpa is especially characteristic of the Great Perfection and Mahāmudrā. He succinctly explains this method as follows:

> [640] . . . Whatever kinds of experiences and visions arise—be they gentle or violent, subtle or gross, of long or short duration,

15. *Sāmaññaphala Sutta* in *Dīgha Nikāya* I 73.

16. *Mahāsaccaka Sutta* [MN I 246], in Bhikkhu Ñāṇamoli and Bhikkhu Bodhi, *The Middle Length Discourses of the Buddha*, 340, with modification of the original translation.

> strong or weak, good or bad—observe their nature and avoid any obsessive evaluation of them as being one thing and not another. Let the heart of your practice be consciousness, naturally at rest, lucid and clear. Acting as your own mentor, if you can bring the crucial points to perfection, as if you were threading a needle, the afflictions of your own mindstream will be subdued, you will gain the autonomy of not succumbing to them, and your mind will constantly be calm and composed.

Düdjom Lingpa, as explained by his commentator, Pema Tashi, further clarifies four stages of mindfulness that are achieved along this path:

> According to the teachings, there are four types of mindfulness of the essential nature of the path. The first entails distinguishing between stillness and movement, and by the power of familiarizing yourself with their different appearances, there is *single-pointed mindfulness* of the unification of the two. Then, even while resting without strenuously observing them as you did before, as its natural power manifests, there is *manifest mindfulness*. Abiding loosely without mindfulness in a vacuous, wide-open clarity, a spacious vacuity, constitutes lying down on a bed that is *devoid of mindfulness*, which is the *substrate*. Once coarse mindfulness has subsided, resting in a luminous vacuity is called *self-illuminating mindfulness*, or the *substrate consciousness*. The former two kinds of mindfulness [single-pointed mindfulness and manifest mindfulness] directly perceive whatever creative displays arise, while during the latter two [the absence of mindfulness and self-illuminating mindfulness], apart from abiding solely in dependence upon a subtle mode of apprehension, all radiant appearances and creative displays of thoughts cease, so there is only nonconceptuality. These kinds of mindfulness are aroused by the path, and since

> they descend to the two types of substrate,[17] they are called the *substrates of descent*. Some teachers regard the first as the "one taste" and the second as "freedom from conceptual elaboration." Others claim it is ethically neutral, but whatever they call it, you have arrived at the essential nature of the mind.[18]

In this passage Pema Tashi, following Düdjom Lingpa, refers to the *substrate* (Skt. *ālaya*) and *substrate consciousness* (Skt. *ālayavijñāna*), commonly associated with the Cittamātra, or Mind Only, school of Indian Buddhism, which presents them as being inherently existent. In contrast, in the pith instructions of the Great Perfection, these terms refer to aspects of the mind that are directly experienced when one comes to the culmination of the path of śamatha, and their inherent existence is explicitly refuted. So there is nothing in these references that is incompatible with the Prāsaṅgika Madhyamaka view, which is discussed in detail in the *Selected Essays on Old and New Views of the Secret Mantrayāna*. While many practitioners in Tibet have mistaken the experience of the substrate consciousness for exalted states of Mahāmudrā realization within the context of the four yogas, such as "one taste" and "freedom from conceptual elaboration," Düdjom Lingpa brushes such claims aside and instead claims simply that one has realized the "essential nature of the mind." Here he is not referring to its ultimate nature, but rather the phenomenal, defining characteristics of ordinary consciousness, namely, luminosity and cognizance. Paṇchen Lozang Chökyi Gyaltsen explains the same śamatha practice and its significance in the following passage:

17. The two types of substrate are the actual substrate (corresponding to the absence of mindfulness) and the temporarily luminous substrate (corresponding to self-illuminating mindfulness). The former is a mindless vacuity, like the sky at dusk, covered over by darkness, while the latter makes it possible for thoughts to appear, just as a polished mirror reflects a face. By letting the temporarily luminous substrate consciousness rest in the pristine nature of emptiness, the assemblies of roving thoughts cease, causing a radiant vacuity to appear. This corresponds to the second type of substrate.

18. Düdjom Lingpa, *The Heart of the Great Perfection*, 52–53.

> The nature of meditative equipoise is not obscured by anything, but is lucid and clear. Not established as anything physical, it is a clear vacuity like space. Allowing anything to arise, it is vividly awake. Such is the nature of the mind. This is superbly witnessed with direct perception, yet it cannot be grasped as "this" or demonstrated with words. "Whatever arises, rest loosely, without grasping": nowadays, for the most part, contemplatives of Tibet uniformly proclaim this as practical advice for achieving enlightenment. However, I, Chökyi Gyaltsen, declare this to be an exceptionally skillful method for novices to achieve mental stillness and to identify the phenomenological nature of the mind.[19]

As indispensable as this meditation is, especially as a preparation for the main practices of the Great Perfection, the achievement of such meditative equipoise by itself does not bring about any irreversible transformation or liberation of the mind. As Düdjom Lingpa clarifies:

> I think people who spend their whole life at this and regard it as the best of practices may be fooling themselves by compounding one delusion with another . . . If I examine those whose lives pass in this way, I see that in the past they have created the causes for spinning around and around in saṃsāra under the influence of dualistic grasping. It seems to me that if they persist in overdoing such meditation, what need is there to say that this will act as a great anchor, further grounding them in saṃsāra?[20]

Settling the mind in its "natural state" entails the ordinary, coarse, dualistic mind (which arises from moment to moment in dependence upon physical processes within the body) dissolving into an underlying, subtle continuum of individual mental consciousness that precedes the formation of the body and continues on after its death. This continuum, which is strongly

19. *Collected Works of Paṇ chen blo bzang chos kyi rgyal mtshan*, 4: 86.

20. Düdjom Lingpa, *Heart of the Great Perfection*, 145.

configured by the body and physical environment, is reduced to its essential nature of luminosity and cognizance, which bear no human characteristics. This is the ground of each sentient being's succession of lifetimes in saṃsāra, and it has been experientially verified countless times by contemplatives of diverse schools of Indian and Tibetan Buddhism. In his classic treatise *The Path of Purification*, the fifth-century Theravāda commentator Buddhaghosa refers to it as the *bhavaṅga*, or "ground of becoming." The fourth-century Mahāyāna contemplative Asaṅga explains that with the achievement of śamatha, "due to the absence of mindfulness and of mentation, when the meditative object is dissolved and released, the mind rests in the absence of appearances."[21] His brother Vasubandhu, equally renowned as a master of Buddhist theory and practice, likewise declared that with the achievement of śamatha, technically known as the "threshold to the first dhyāna, or meditative stabilization in the form realm, the five sense consciousnesses are dormant."[22] In accordance with the Mahāyāna sūtras and authoritative Indian commentaries, Tsongkhapa states in his *Medium Exposition of the Stages of the Path to Enlightenment* that with the achievement of śamatha, specifically referring to the threshold of the first dhyāna, only the aspects of the sheer awareness, clarity, and vivid joy of the mind appear, without any sensory appearances arising to one's awareness. This, he says, is needed as the basis for eliminating the mental afflictions of both non-Buddhist and Buddhist contemplatives, and by cultivating insight on that basis, it is possible to achieve liberation from all the fetters of saṃsāra.[23]

The achievement of śamatha is foundational for the realization of all the four yogas that constitute the path of Mahāmudrā, namely, the yogas of single-pointedness, freedom from conceptual elaboration, one taste, and nonmeditation. Domang Gyatrul Rinpoché (1924–), a lineage holder of both the Mahāmudrā and Great Perfection traditions, explains that "the first stage of single-pointedness occurs with the accomplishment of

21. *Śrāvakabhūmi*, *Yogasthāna III*, Bihar MS., 12a6–5, translation by B. Alan Wallace.

22. Vasubandhu, *Abhidharmakośabhāṣyam*, 4: 1231.

23. See the section "A General Presentation of the Way to Proceed along the Path on the Basis of Quiescence," in Wallace, *Balancing the Mind*, 213–17.

śamatha, wherein one single-pointedly attends to one's own awareness, which is primordially unceasing and luminous."[24] The Third Karmapa, Rangjung Dorjé (1284–1339), associates the small stage of the yoga of single-pointedness with the Mahāyāna path of accumulation, the first of the five paths culminating in perfect enlightenment, but this requires that one's experience of śamatha be augmented by the practice of vipaśyanā, which yields insight into the mind's empty nature. In his classic treatise *The Extensive Mahāmudrā: The Ocean of Definitive Meaning*, the Ninth Karmapa, Wangchuk Dorjé (1556–1603), concurs that full achievement of śamatha, in which one does not sense either the movements or presence of one's breath or body, is the optimal preparation for effectively engaging in the practice of vipaśyanā.[25] This describes a distinctive characteristic of resting in the ground of becoming upon having reached the threshold to the first dhyāna.

After his presentation of the unique preliminary practices, which prepare one for Vajrayāna practice, Lerab Lingpa gives concise explanations of key elements of the two stages of tantra: the stage of generation and the stage of completion. According to all the New Translation schools of Tibetan Buddhism—including the Kagyü, Sakya, and Geluk traditions—in order to achieve the enlightenment of a buddha, each of these two stages of anuttarayogatantra practice must be perfected. First one must perfect the stage of generation with the full achievement of śamatha, insight into emptiness by way of vipaśyanā, and realization of pure vision and divine pride. On that basis one must perfect the five stages of the stage of completion,[26] culminating in buddhahood. Within the context of the Great Perfection, Lerab Lingpa indicates that an abbreviated practice of these two stages is sufficient as long as they are supplemented by the two main types of meditation according to the Great Perfection, namely, *cutting through* and the *direct crossing over*. Among the five principal treatises on the Great Perfection by

24. Karma Chagmé, *Naked Awareness*, 223.

25. Karma pa dbang phyug rdo rje, *Phyag rgya rgyas pa nges don rgya mtsho* (Sarnath, India: Vajra Vidyā Institute Library, 2006), 102.

26. See Tsongkhapa, *A Lamp to Illuminate the Five Stages*.

Düdjom Lingpa, only *The Vajra Essence* gives detailed explanations of the stages of generation and completion, but it states that these phases are not indispensible for everyone following the path of the Great Perfection. Two of the other four of those treatises focus only on four indispensible elements of the Great Perfection: śamatha, vipaśyanā, cutting through, and the direct crossing over. One explains only the first three of those practices, and one discusses in detail only vipaśyanā and cutting through.

In a similar vein Lerab Lingpa highlights the distinctive features of the Great Perfection relative to the stages of generation and completion:

> In dependence upon such splendid pith instructions on any of the elaborate or concise methods of the authentic generation stage practices of the unsurpassed Mantrayāna, [670] there are numerous, extraordinary methods for experiencing the clear light as the culmination of vital energies entering, remaining, and dissolving into the central channel by way of the stage of completion. But here, without needing to resort to them, there are pith instructions for directly severing delusive thoughts, which are potent and easy to practice. If you follow them correctly, delusive thoughts, along with their karmic energies, naturally cease. When that happens, whether you recognize it or not, it is inevitable that the undeluded, actual nature of the mind will nakedly emerge.

## Vipaśyanā Meditation

Nowadays the practice of Buddhist insight meditation, commonly known by the Pāli term *vipassanā*, has often been simplified and denuded of all its uniquely Buddhist aspects under the rubric of "mindfulness meditation." Casting aside the extraordinary theoretical and epistemological richness of the Buddha's own explanation of the four applications of mindfulness,[27] the popularized version of vipassanā is reduced to moment-by-moment

27. See Anālayo Bhikkhu, *Satipaṭṭhāna*, and Wallace, *Minding Closely*.

awareness of whatever arises in the field of one's awareness. Many of its proponents proclaim that this is the "essence of Buddhist meditation without the Buddhism" and even go so far as to claim this as the universal essence of all meditation, equating it with the Theravāda practice of "bare attention," Krishnamurti's "choiceless awareness," the Zen practice of "just sitting," and "open monitoring" as taught in Mahāmudrā and the Great Perfection. For all the success of this propaganda campaign, such claims are false. In his commentary to his own treatise, the *Treasure of Wish-Fulfilling Jewels*, Longchen Rabjam states: "Nowadays many people say it is enough to recognize the awareness of the present moment, and there's no point to there being many teachings. If that were enough, there would be no need for the Buddha's other teachings. But in fact this single-pointed awareness of the present moment must depend precisely upon listening [to teachings] and upon guru yoga, so they refute themselves with their own words."[28]

Lerab Lingpa explains the practice of vipaśyanā after his explanation of the stages of generation and completion in his discussion of "The Preliminary Practice of Cutting the Basis of Delusion from the Root." While it is necessary to fathom the empty nature of all phenomena, the classic approach of vipaśyanā meditation in both the Great Perfection and Mahāmudrā traditions is to investigate analytically the origins, location, and destination of the mind that is now under direct, unmediated scrutiny. Lerab Lingpa comments:

> . . . Therefore, however much mere appearances that are empty of causes, consequences, and an essential nature may arise in the aspects of the birth, cessation, and abiding of a deceptive mind—or else in the aspects of its origin, location, and destination—[679] from the very moment they arise, ultimately such movements and transformations have never existed. Recognition of that is known as *realization of the actual nature of the mind*.

28. Cited in Dharmasāra's essay "A Jeweled Mirror of Pure Appearances" in the present volume, at Tibetan page [208].

In "Oral Instructions of the Wise" in the present volume, Lerab Lingpa's disciple Dharmasāra clarifies the relationship between śamatha focused on the mind and the vipaśyanā practice of engaging in ultimate analysis of the origin, location, and destination of the mind:

> [132] . . . When engaging in this kind of Mahāmudrā meditation, śamatha is achieved by focusing on the mind, such that one seeks the view on the basis of meditation. In dependence upon this śamatha, the mind is settled with the aspect of things as they are, once one has correctly determined the birth, cessation, and abiding of the mind as being without identity.

Having experientially isolated the essential nature of the mind, free of the five obscurations, the contemplative is now optimally prepared to explore that actual nature of the mind, examining whether or not it bears its own inherent identity, independent of conceptual designation. When it comes to fathoming the origins, location, and destination of consciousness and its role in nature, beyond the distorting influences of laxity, excitation, and the vagaries of the human mind, the achievement of śamatha may be likened to launching a telescope into space, beyond the distorting influences of the Earth's atmosphere. To fathom the origins, constitution, and eventual fate of celestial phenomena, it is not enough to examine the terrestrial correlates of the relative movements of the sun, moon, planets, and stars, as was done by generations of astrologers before Kepler and Galileo. Likewise, to determine the phenomenological nature of one's own mind, let alone to gain the ontological insight that its origin, location, and destination are empty of inherent nature, it is not enough to examine the neuronal and behavioral correlates of mental processes and states of consciousness. Scientifically and contemplatively, there is no substitute for directly observing, with the highest possible degree of sophistication and precision, the phenomena one is seeking to understand.

Scientific inquiry into the nature of the mind did not even begin until roughly three hundred years after the rise of the scientific revolution in the sixteenth and seventeenth centuries, and especially over the past century, cognitive scientists continue to limit their observations mostly to the neuronal correlates and behavioral expressions of the mind. Given the limitations of this methodology, it is inevitable that virtually all scientific theories of the mind reduce it to a function or emergent property of physical processes that are amenable to such objective research. The actual nature of mental events, their relation to the body, and the role of consciousness in the natural world therefore remain as much a mystery now as they were when the scientific study of the mind began roughly 135 years ago.

The Buddhist approach in general, and the approach of the Great Perfection and Mahāmudrā in particular, are diametrically opposed to the reductionist beliefs of scientific materialism. This approach begins with an observation made by the Buddha himself: "All phenomena are preceded by the mind, issue forth from the mind, and consist of the mind."[29] The Great Perfection and Mahāmudrā explore this hypothesis in great depth and conclude that insight into the mind's empty nature readily leads to universal insight into the emptiness of all phenomena that arise as objects of consciousness. In "An Ornament of the Enlightened View of Samantabhadra" in this volume, Lerab Lingpa's disciple Jé Tsultrim Zangpo writes, "If you ascertain this mind of yours as being empty of true existence, simply by extending that reasoning you will ascertain all phenomena to be empty of true existence." He elaborates on this point:

> [58] . . . Moreover, a person with sharp faculties who can determine that this mind, which plays such a dominant role, cannot be established as truly existing from its own side, as something really, substantially existent, is someone who can determine the absence of true existence even with subtle reasoning, simply by having been shown partial reasons for establishing that absence. For such a person, just by force of a revelation as to whether or not the mind has any color or shape, and just by force of being

29. *Dhammapada* 1.1.

> taught the reasons why the mind is devoid of any [true] origin, location, or destination, that person will proceed to establish the fact that the mind lacks true existence by way of subtle reasoning that refutes a subtle object of negation. Thus, by the extraordinary power of relying on such reasoning, people with superior faculties are able to realize the emptiness of all phenomena.

This brings us back to a salient characteristic of the Great Perfection and Mahāmudrā: the theme of first balancing the mind in meditative equipoise through the achievement of śamatha focused on the mind, and then letting the view of emptiness and the ultimate ground of consciousness experientially emerge from within. Karma Chagmé (1613–78), one of the greatest Tibetan scholars and contemplatives who was a lineage holder of both the Great Perfection and Mahāmudrā, explains this point by way of the analogy of cutting down a tree in order to procure firewood:

> In some scholarly, discursive meditations in the *sūtra* tradition, one continually seeks out the mind, and there is a tradition in which investigation is needed. Here, in the tradition of Mahāmudrā and Atiyoga, it is enough to seek and investigate during this phase of Dharma practice, but afterwards it is not necessary to continue to search . . . Geshés dwell in the monastic colleges for many years and study both Madhyamaka and the Prajñāpāramitā. They memorize many volumes, and, devoting their lives to explanations and discussions, they cut through conceptual elaboration from the outside. That way is difficult to learn, difficult to understand, difficult to know, and difficult to realize; and among those who study and acquire knowledge in that way, there are many who fail to realize the meaning. The entire meaning of all that education is included in this examination of the mind. This cuts through conceptual elaborations from within, so it is easy to learn, easy to understand, easy to know, and easy to realize. Cutting through conceptual elaboration from the

> outside is like wanting dried pine wood, and drying it by cutting off the pine needles and branches one by one. So it is difficult. In contrast, cutting through conceptual elaboration from within is easy, for it is like cutting the root of the pine tree so that the branches dry up naturally.[30]

At first glance the Mahāmudrā and the Great Perfection approach of determining the mere absence of any color or shape of the mind and then recognizing the mind to be empty of any true origin, location, and destination may seem much easier than laboriously studying the great Madhyamaka treatises by Nāgārjuna, Candrakīrti, Longchen Rabjam, and Tsongkhapa and then painstakingly identifying the object of refutation, namely, inherent existence. For contemplatives with very sharp faculties who have realized the phenomenological nature of the mind by achieving śamatha focused on the mind and who are under the close guidance of an accomplished master of Mahāmudrā or the Great Perfection, the ontological analysis of the mind's origin, location, and destination may indeed be the most effective manner of realizing emptiness. But without that meditative preparation and without such close guidance, one may simply realize that the mind has no physical qualities and that one cannot identify the origin, location, or destination of the mind. Such insights are relatively trivial and do not bring one onto the Buddhist path.

## The View, Meditation, and Conduct of the Great Perfection

Eurocentric, secular modernity, which has now achieved global domination, is characterized by and is rooted in the triad of materialism, hedonism, and consumerism, each element of which is inextricably bound up with the other two. The worldview of materialism proposes that everything in the universe consists solely of matter and its emergent properties, or more broadly, of configurations of space-time and matter-energy. Such a way of

30. Karma Chagmé, *A Spacious Path to Freedom*, 100–101.

viewing reality necessarily implies that one will value only this aspect of reality, resulting in the relentless, insatiable pursuit of physically aroused, hedonic pleasures and the avoidance of physically caused bodily and mental suffering. Such a system of values, in turn, supports a consumer-driven way of life, which—with the ever-growing human population—is resulting in the catastrophic degradation of the natural environment.

Similarly, scientific research operates within a triad of views, values, and conduct. All such research requires a theoretical framework, which includes hidden, often unquestioned assumptions and working hypotheses, and that framework is materialist to the core. With that foundation, the only kind of evidence that is considered scientifically compelling is physical evidence acquired with the use of instruments of technology. Scientific inquiry also requires certain ethical standards on the part of researchers, including rigor and honesty in the collection, analysis, and reporting of their data; and for research involving human and animal subjects there are further ethical standards that must be met.

The triad of view, meditation, and conduct is equally relevant to all schools of Buddhist and non-Buddhist contemplative inquiry. Specifically, with respect to this triad as it relates to the Great Perfection, Lerab Lingpa writes:

> Furthermore, the *view* is seeing with the primordial consciousness of each one's own awareness, which nakedly perceives the nonduality of subject and object, free of conceptual elaboration, and without support. A yogin who realizes that practices the great freedom from extremes, which is the naturally luminous, nonconceptual inner space of the actual nature of the mind. The *meditation* is the achievement of the yoga—or of the stability in clarity—that comes from familiarization with such practice. The *conduct* is not to follow after good and bad objects and mental states, [660] but to gain mastery over the experience of everything arising naturally as ornaments of pristine awareness. If you can continuously apply yourself

> day and night to such conduct, meditation, and view for seven days, you will simultaneously achieve the yogas of śamatha and vipaśyanā.

A central feature of the view of the Great Perfection is drawing a clear distinction between the ordinary, dualistic mind, which reifies the distinction between subject and object, and pristine awareness, which is the ultimate ground of all of existence, transcending all conceptual frameworks and articulation. In his opening essay, "Oral Instructions of the Vidyādhara Gurus," Dharmasāra emphasizes the centrality of experientially seeing this distinction:

> [33] . . . Now even though one understands that the Great Perfection is a swift path that is devoid of conceptual elaborations, without precise knowledge of what that means, one will mix this up with the three kinds of laziness, such as lethargy. So even if one spends a lot of time diligently sustaining the sense of luminosity and cognizance but without distinguishing between the mind and pristine awareness, there is the great danger that one will go astray without attenuating attachment and hostility in the least.

The main practices of meditation in the Great Perfection are two: cutting through to the original purity of pristine awareness and directly crossing over to the spontaneous actualization of the creative expressions of pristine awareness. Jé Tsultrim Zangpo's essay "An Ornament of the Enlightened View of Samantabhadra" discusses both of these core meditations, with the first, cutting through, comprising four kinds of open presence. All of these are rooted in the prior, experiential ascertainment of pristine awareness, experienced as a dimension of reality quite distinct from one's ordinary, causally conditioned mental states. Gaining such experiential recognition is therefore key to the entire point of the practice of the Great Perfection. Jé Tsultrim Zangpo then provides an exceptionally clear presentation of how to take the first steps in such practice, based on the prior achievement of śamatha and insight into the empty nature of the mind and all other phenomena by way of vipaśyanā:

> Well, if you wonder how you can sustain the essential nature of pristine awareness by embracing from the very beginning the raw, indwelling, actual primordial consciousness, clear light, in reliance on the guru's pith instructions, [81] it is like this. Beginners are not able from the outset to take as the path the clear light primordial consciousness, pristine awareness that has never come in contact with any of the karmic energies. However, as stated previously, the cognizance that is the radiance, or rays, of the ground pristine awareness pervades all the good and bad thoughts that arise in the present, and it is present in the nature of this mind. While the distinct thoughts that arise in the present moment are not themselves pristine awareness, their nature, or basic disposition, is pristine awareness. So you must be able to recognize that basic disposition and remain there. Therefore the consciousness that is present in this very moment is not pristine awareness, but, as stated previously, in this present consciousness there is one aspect of the *mind*, the conceptual fabrications that have come under the influence of fluctuating karmic energies, and then there is the aspect of *cognizance* that has achieved autonomy so that it cannot be moved by fluctuating karmic energies. So if you can distinguish between those two, you can cast off the aspect of the mind, hold to that cognizance, and find that you can remain there.

In the practice of cutting through, it is imperative to realize not only the primordial luminosity of pristine awareness but also the indivisibility of this awareness and the emptiness of all phenomena. This is the referent of the phrase "the union of luminosity and emptiness," which appears frequently in the meditative literature of the Great Perfection and Mahāmudrā. Jé Tsultrim Zangpo adds: "If you remain in cognizance simply without abandoning the sphere of empty space that is the nature of existence of such pristine awareness, and sustain that, you are both sustaining cognizance and remaining in the space of emptiness. So that is also the meditation where you meditate on both pristine awareness and emptiness simultaneously." Finally, he clarifies how such nonconceptual meditation on awareness and emptiness relates to the teachings on emptiness as presented in the Madhyamaka Prāsaṅgika tradition, in accordance with the writings of both Tsongkhapa and Longchen Rabjam:

> [110] . . . Therefore you should loosely rest pristine awareness in the nature of the empty space of cognizance and remain there without modification. That must be a stabilizing meditation alone, without analyzing the object of negation. This must lead to the ascertainment of emptiness by way of stabilizing meditation, without reliance upon rational analysis regarding the absence of an object of negation that is either one or many, and so on. For that to happen you must first ascertain how connate self-grasping holds to the very subtle object of negation, as taught in the Madhyamaka Prāsaṅgika tradition.

The final culmination of the stages of cutting through and the direct crossing over is the achievement of the rainbow body, which manifests in different ways in accordance with the depth of one's practice. Nowadays many Tibetan contemplatives both inside and outside Tibet have demonstrated their ability to rest in pristine awareness during the dying process, which manifests outwardly as the cessation of the heartbeat, respiration, and brain activity but with no decomposition of the body over a period of days or even weeks. Other less-accomplished contemplatives reach the culmination of the dying process in which their mind dissolves into the substrate, but without realizing pristine awareness. Depending on the stability of their concentration, they may unconsciously remain in the substrate for as long as three days. After dissolving the mind into the substrate, for accomplished contemplatives the "clear light of death," which is none other than pristine awareness, arises spontaneously, and with sufficient preparation one may linger in this realization of pristine awareness and emptiness. This ability manifests physically in ways that can be studied scientifically, but the inner experience of the yogi remains hidden to all those who have not ascertained pristine awareness for themselves. Regarding the relationship between one's stage of meditation while still alive and the duration of one's experience of pristine awareness at death, Padmasambhava explains:

> The number of days you remain in meditation in the clear light of the dying process corresponds to the stability and duration of your present practice. Those who have achieved stability of practice lasting throughout the day and night may achieve stability lasting seven human days at death. But for those who have not entered the path, the clear light will not appear for longer than the time it takes to eat a bowl of food.[31]

Here again, in his teachings mystically revealed to Düdjom Lingpa, Padmasambhava gives a clear and definitive account of the different levels of achievement of the rainbow body:

> Those of the most superior faculties are liberated as a great transference body, extending infinitely into the all-pervasive dharmakāya, like water merging with water or space merging with space. Those of middling faculties attain enlightenment as a great rainbow body, like a rainbow vanishing into the sky. For those of inferior faculties, when the clear light of the ground arises, the colors of the rainbow spread forth from absolute space, and their material bodies decrease in size until finally they vanish as rainbow bodies, leaving not even a trace of their aggregates behind. That is called the *small rainbow body*. When the clear light of the ground arises, the material bodies of some people decrease in size for as long as

31. Düdjom Lingpa, *Vajra Essence*, 263.

> seven days. Then, finally, they leave only the residue of their hair and nails behind. The dissolution of the body into minute particles is called the *small transference*. For those of superior faculties, this dissolution of the body into minute particles may occur even during the practice of cutting through.[32]

The practices of the Great Perfection and Mahāmudrā begin by turning the attention inward on the nature of one's own mind and consciousness itself. As the meditation progresses, it results in changes in one's body and mind, some of which may be studied scientifically. Even in the recent past there have been accounts of Tibetan contemplatives in Tibet manifesting the rainbow body.[33] The teachings and practices leading to such a remarkable transformation are available to us all today, and when people in the modern world prove themselves capable of manifesting the rainbow body in full collaboration with open-minded scientists, this may trigger an unprecedented revolution that will have profound repercussions for all branches of the natural sciences, from the cognitive sciences down to the foundations of modern physics.

32. Düdjom Lingpa, *Vajra Essence*, 254.

33. For a provocative discussion of the rainbow body, including eyewitness accounts of a Tibetan who recently achieved this state of realization, see Tiso, *Rainbow Body and Resurrection*.

# The Vital Essence of Primordial Consciousness

An Essential Synthesis, Fluidly Presented as a Commentary, of Practical Guidance on the Great Chetsun's Profound Quintessence from Vimalamitra, the Three Units of Letters on the Five Expanses, the Sovereign of All Pith Instructions, a Vessel of the Vital Essence Taken from among the Classes of Pith Instructions on the Great Perfection

༄༅། །རྫོགས་པ་ཆེན་པོ་མན་ངག་སྡེའི་བཅུད་ཕུར་མན་ངག་ཐམས་ཅད་ཀྱི་རྒྱལ་པོ་ཀློང་ལྔའི་ཡི་གེ་དུམ་བུ་
གསུམ་པ་ལྕེ་བཙུན་ཆེན་པོའི་བི་མ་ལའི་ཟབ་ཏིག་གི་ཉམས་ཁྲིད་ཆུ་འབབས་སུ་བཀོད་པ་སྙིང་པོའི་བཅུད་དྲིལ་
ཡེ་ཤེས་ཐིག་ལེ་ཞེས་བྱ་བ་བཞུགས་སོ།། །།

Tertön Lerab Lingpa

# 1 The Treasure Text, Its Lineage, and Empowerment

Namo Gurave!

[600] Among the limitless modes of Dharma, both profound and vast, which belong to the mind, expanse, and pith instruction classes of the clear light Great Perfection, and which were held within the mind of the great master Vimalamitra, this sovereign of all pith instruction, the vessel of the vital essence that contains the unsurpassed, ultrasecret class of pith instruction, remained as a hidden treasure in the form of a textual tradition related to the profound accomplishments of Vimalamitra. That was bestowed on [601] Chetsun Senggé Wangchuk[1] by a glorious guardian of the Mantrayāna. When he was practicing this in secret, the primordial consciousness embodiment of Mahāpaṇḍit Vimalamitra actually came to him, not as if in a dream or a vision. The master remained together with his disciple for a long time and granted the complete [empowerments of] ripening and liberation. By meditating in accordance with [Vimalamitra's] instructions, Chetsun manifested the vajrakāya of the great transference rainbow body.

1. Tib. *Lce rigs kyi btsun pa seng ge dbang phyug*, ca. twelfth century. The name means "Lion Lord, Venerable One of the Ché Clan." For a brief biography, see http://treasuryoflives.org/biographies/view/Chetsun-Sengge-Wangchuk/TBRC_P0RK1222.

The vajra words of his final testimony, consisting of these three units of letters of pith instruction, [602] were given to the ḍākinīs. Then once a vast number of pure realms of vīras and ḍākinīs were reverently invited to places such as the land of Orgyen,[2] they rendered inconceivable service to myself and others, and continue to do so. Once again, this, which has been set forth by myself, Ösel Trulpé Dorjé,[3] by way of recollection, is resulting in a variety of benefits for the world in accordance with the fortune of disciples. Now the excellent teaching for you also consists of three topics: (I) the introductory topic of the special title, together with the homage of the assembly of ḍākinīs, (II) the meaning of the text, namely, the three units of profound pith instructions, together with a song of realizations, the consignment to the treasure custodians, and prayers, and (III) the meaning of the conclusion, namely, the final ornament of vajra words, advice from the primordial consciousness ḍākinī.

## I. The Introductory Topic of the Special Title, Together with the Homage of the Assembly of Ḍākinīs

Here there are two sections: (A) the meaning of the title, and (B) the homage.

### A. The Meaning of the Title

Among the three distinctive features of the title, the first is "perfection." Where is there perfection? There is primordial perfection, indivisible and

2. Tib. *O rgyan*, Skt. *Oḍḍiyāna*.

3. Tib. *Od gsal sprul pa'i rdo rje*: "The Vajra Emanated from the Clear Light." This name refers to Jamyang Khyentsé Wangpo (*'Jam dbyangs mkhyen brtse'i dbang po*, 1820–92), who granted this teaching in the form of an oral transmission to Lerab Lingpa and a few other close disciples, c. 1887. The first-person voice in this section seems to be his. Jé Tsultrim Zangpo's biography of Lerab Lingpa records that after each session of Jamyang Khyentsé Wangpo's explanation, Lerab Lingpa "wrote down from memory what had been taught. At the end of the many days of teachings, [he] presented his notes to Khyentse, who looked at them and commented, 'This is exactly what I said, without anything missing or added.'" Pistono, *Fearless in Tibet*, 76–78.

of one taste, in the essential nature of the great, all-pervasive expanse of the absolute space of phenomena,[4] which is free of all elaborations. What is perfected? [603] All phenomenal realities, without exception, included in saṃsāra, nirvāṇa, and the path, are perfected. In what manner are they perfected? How could it ever be the case that the "absolute space of phenomena" could be like a big empty container in which the many good and bad substances known as "phenomena"[5] are inserted? Or how could it ever be that what are known as "phenomena"—as though they were individual substances—could have their own separate signs, as though each of them could be inserted into its corresponding actual nature,[6] as if each were being put inside its own individual, empty container?

How is it, then, that they are perfected? To speak in terms of their ultimate, final mode of existence, everything that manifestly appears in the universe, including saṃsāra and nirvāṇa, the good and the bad, oneself and others, the physical world and its inhabitants, matter and consciousness, as well as every unimaginable, inexpressible, diverse variety of phenomena, is primordially and solely of the same taste and exists in the same manner as the absolute space of phenomena, free of elaborations. Apart from existing that way primordially, there has never been in the past, it is impossible for there to be now, [604] and in the future there will never be a place or a time when there will be even the tiniest particle that is different from that absolute space.

The final syllable of "perfection"[7] signifies that the absolute space of phenomena, which is free of all partiality or bias and is pervasive, unchanging, and sublime, should not be sought anywhere else—as it is totally subsumed in the essential nature of a single instant of the actual nature of your own mind,[8] naked awareness. So there is no need to discover any absolute space or primordial consciousness different in their essential nature from awareness.

4. Tib. *chos kyi dbyings*, Skt. *dharmadhātu*.

5. Tib. *chos can*, Skt. *dharmin*.

6. Tib. *chos nyid*, Skt. *dharmatā*.

7. The Tibetan *pa* in *rdzog pa chen po*.

8. Tib. *sems nyid*, Skt. *cittatā*.

There are many ways of explaining the meaning of "perfection." However, in this context it is explained as signifying that all kinds of specific phenomena, including appearances and consciousness, kāyas and facets of primordial consciousness, are subsumed in one taste within the essential nature of absolute space; and since that absolute space never consists of anything beyond awareness, all crucial points are subsumed in awareness.

"Great" signifies there is nothing else to be realized or to be revealed that is higher than this indivisibility of absolute space and awareness, the ultimate mode of existence of all phenomena. Thus the jinas and jinaputras of all directions and times see nothing and reveal nothing that is superior to this.

Thus what has been primordially present, without contrivance, is the basis. Realizing one's own awareness directly, free of the intellect, [605] and familiarizing oneself with it, is the path. Taking possession of the everlasting kingdom of one's own awareness, once one is completely purified of defilements, is the ultimate fruition. Everything is perfected in the essential nature of absolute space and awareness, and this is the great indivisibility in which one's own nature is free of increase and decrease.

The supremely distinguished avenue on which disciples with faculties that are superior, [middling,] and so on may realize and actualize this method consists of the three classes of the Great Perfection. Among those, the foremost is the secret class of pith instruction, and within this there are the outer cycle, the inner cycle, the secret cycle, and the unsurpassed, ultrasecret cycle. Among those four, this here is the unsurpassed, ultrasecret one.

"Pith instruction" refers to amazing methods, difficult to evaluate with the intellect, through which great goals can be easily and swiftly accomplished with few causes and little hardship.

"Class" signifies something of great value that is manifold and extensive, beyond anything meager or small. These eighteen classes are as follows:

1. *The Root Tantra on the Reverberation of Sound* is the sovereign pinnacle atop the totality of the precious teachings of the Jina,

and it is like the door and the key to all the essential, clear light tantras of the supreme vehicle.

2. The tantra that is like a river is the *Self-Arisen Perfection* [*of Empowerment*]. [606]
3. The tantra that is like the king of mountains is *Without Letters*.
4. The tantra that is like the ocean is the *Self-Arisen Pristine Awareness*.
5. The tantra that is like the sun is the *Heart Mirror of Vajrasattva*.
6. The tantra that is like the great garuḍa is the *Six Expanses* [*of Samantabhadra*].
7. The tantra that is like a lion is the *Lion's Perfected Power*.
8. The tantra that is like a king's treasure is the *Mound of Jewels*.
9. The tantra that is like a wheel is *Beautiful Auspiciousness*.
10. The tantra that is like a sword is the *Mind Mirror* [*of Samantabhadra*].
11. The tantra that is like molten gold is *Studded Jewels*.
12. The tantra that is like a garland of ornaments is the *Pearl Garland*.
13. The tantra that is like a charming damsel displayed in a mirror is *Adorned with* [*the Jewels of*] *Identification*.
14. The tantra that is like jewels blazing with light is the *Blazing Lamp*.
15. The tantra that is like a knotted snake unraveling itself is the *Self-Liberating Pristine Awareness*.
16. The tantra that is like a child coming onto its mother's lap is the *Union of the Sun and Moon*.
17. The tantra that is like a king holding onto his territory is *Flaming Relics*. This makes seventeen.
18. The eighteenth, the tantra of the *Wrathful Protectoress of Mantra*, is like a razor.[9]

9. Though rendered variously in different texts and collections, recognizable expanded Tibetan titles of the eighteen tantras are: (1) *Sgra thal 'gyur chen po rtsa ba'i rgyud*, (2) *Sku*

The commentarial literature that explicates these properly, as well as the extremely profound and extensive pith instructions, were composed by many great vidyādharas, including the master Pramodavajra.[10] These texts now remain, without limit, in the ḍākinī realms. Some of them, as appropriate, also exist in the form of profound hidden treasures. [607] In Tibet, too, the heart quintessence[11] of the glorious, great Orgyen[12] and the Mahāpaṇḍit Vimalamitra, which had arrived earlier, is still present now. There are also numerous superior individuals who preserve this teaching, who possess outstanding quintessential views and meditation. They are beyond compare with most spiritual people. One after the other, such individuals have appeared in the past, are still present now, and will come in the future as well. Without exception they arise from the pith instruction of the guru. Therefore, beginning with the glorious Samantabhadra, the progenitor of all the jinas, the precious teachings have appeared due to the kindness of the Teacher, and all the classes of those who hold the Teaching have appeared due to the kindness of the Teaching, and this is the only way it will continue to be.

The "vessel of its vital essence" is so named because the refined, vital quintessence of the classes of Dharma just mentioned have an extraordinary distinction that makes them so profound, namely, that they may be sown easily, joyfully, and swiftly within the mindstreams of students.

*thams cad kyi snang ba ston pa dang dbang rdzogs pa rang byung chen po'i rgyud*, (3) *Yi ge med pa'i rgyud chen po*, (4) *Rig pa rang shar chen po'i rgyud*, (5) *Rdo rje sems dpa'i snying gi me long gi rgyud*, (6) *Kun tu bzang po klong drug pa'i rgyud*, (7) *Seng ge rtsal rdzogs chen po'i rgyud*, (8) *Rin chen spungs pa yon tan rin po che'i rgyud*, (9) *Bkra shis mdzes ldan rin po che'i gyi rgyud*, (10) *Kun tu bzang po thugs kyi me long gi rgyud*, (11) *Nor bu phra bkod rang gi don thams cad gsal bar byed pa'i rgyud*, (12) *Mu tig rin po che phreng ba'i rgyud*, (13) *Ngo sprod rin po che spras / sprad pa'i zhing khams bstan pa'i rgyud*, (14) *Sgron ma bar ba'i rgyud*, (15) *Rig pa rang grol chen po thams cad grol ba'i rgyud*, (16) *Nyi ma dang zla ba kha sbyor ba chen po gsang ba'i rgyud*, (17) *Sku gdung 'bar ba chen po'i rgyud*, (18) *Sngags srung khros ma'i rgyud / Bka' srung nag mo'i rgyud*.

10. Tib. *Dga' rab rdo rje*, Garab Dorjé, dates unknown. He is also known as Prahevajra.

11. Tib. *snying thig*.

12. That is, Padmasambhava.

"Pith instruction," as it appears the first time in the title,[13] indicates the supreme methods by which the profound points—regarding the sensory gateways, their objects, the vital energies,[14] and awareness—are very easy to implement and can be followed with joy. The ability to establish with direct perception that the kāyas and primordial consciousness exist right where you are is not something that can be fathomed [608] through argumentation or the intellect.

The phrase "sovereign of all" means this. The greater and lesser causal vehicles that work with philosophical definitions, as well as all the outer and inner tantras, the oral transmissions, and the pith instructions of the resultant vehicle of secret mantra, whether directly or indirectly, are none other than methods that take you toward omniscience alone. So each one does have its distinctive pith instructions. Nevertheless, this one here surpasses the others. As an analogy, no matter how many aristocrats a royal province might have, and no matter how much military strength and influence it may wield, it cannot in any way contend with the single eminent presence of a wheel-turning world emperor. In the same way, whatever methods of practicing Dharma might come below this one—even the two profound stages [of generation and completion]—cannot contend with just this unit of pith instructions belonging to the supreme vehicle of the Great Perfection; for there is nothing like this swift and joyful path to omniscience.

The "five expanses" indicate a classification of absolute space in terms of the five facets of primordial consciousness that apprehend characteristics. This includes the realm that is the primordial consciousness of the absolute space of phenomena and so on.

Their "letters" are the six seed-syllables of the six types of expanse and liberation—this being the way in which the ḍākinīs assembled the final vajra testimony of Chetsun [Senggé Wangchuk]: (1) the short *a* is

13. In Tibetan, this is the "second time" the word for "pith instructions" appears in the title (Tib. *mtshan gnyis pa'i skabs kyi man ngag ces pa*), but the translation has been adjusted to match the way the sequence of words must be rendered in English.

14. Tib. *rlung*. Depending on context, this can translate either the Sanskrit *prāṇa* or *vāyu*, but in this case seems to refer to all the inner vital energies in general.

subsumed under *a*, so [609] (2) *a* is mirror-like primordial consciousness, (3) *sha* is the primordial consciousness of the absolute space of phenomena, (4) *sa* is the primordial consciousness of equality, (5) *ma* is the primordial consciousness of discernment, and (6) *ha* is the primordial consciousness of accomplishment. The [short *a* that is subsumed under *a*] is itself held to be the absolute space of the five expanses of primordial consciousness.

Later on, when I was twenty-four years old and the contributing circumstances of the place, time, and virtue came together, a trillion ḍākinīs of the emanated entourage of the noble Pelgyi Lodröma[15] revealed their smiling faces. I was enchanted by the reverberations of the lovely melody of the six vajra letters, which are the intrinsic sound of the indestructible nāda. Thus aroused, there occurred in me a spontaneous, accurate memory of a past life. Therefore, although previously it had been sufficient to present the six vajra letters in symbolic form, out of necessity I made them into Tibetan letters and wrote them down, as was appropriate, within the first unit.

Here is a brief explanation of the reason for the fivefold classification of expanses. At the time of the ground and the path there are numerous sets of five, such as the five elements of the physical world, the five aggregates of its inhabitants, and the five sensory objects. At the time of the fruition, there are the five families [of buddhas], the five kāyas, the five facets of primordial consciousness, and the five buddha fields and so on. [610] In accordance with their individual characteristics and different functions, they appear without partiality or bias. From the very moment they appear they do not depart from the nature of the immovable, utterly supreme absolute space of phenomena, the great, vast, joyful expanse. Thus, in accordance with the mode in which the distinct, manifold phenomena of saṃsāra and nirvāṇa appear, there is the fivefold classification of expanses.

Concerning their letters: For the most part it seems as if the miracles of the methods of Secret Mantrayāna, including the forms and sounds of

15. Tib. *Dpal gyi blo gros ma*.

letters, arise solely because of temporary causes and conditions. However, in reality, they are simply specific emanations of supreme, immutable, great bliss taking on those forms. Thus the essential nature of all that is recalled in the mind, all that is presented in form, and all that is expressed in spoken words with respect to the sequence of letters included within the three units is nothing other than the great indivisibility of absolute space and primordial consciousness appearing in those ways.

"The three units" signify their division into separate sections.

Here is the meaning of the first[16] part of the title: It is not as if this extraordinary final testimony given just before the nirvāṇa of Chetsun Senggé Wanchuk, who attained the vajrakāya of the great transference, is solely something self-revealed, which arose all of a sudden. [611] Rather, it is the ultimate, distilled, exceptionally profound, essential core that synthesizes the 119 profound pith instructions and so on, which were beautifully explained by the great master Vimalamitra, the crown jewel of 500 paṇḍits and siddhas. These pith instructions in turn explain the vajra words and their meanings that have come down without break from the dharmakāya Teacher, the glorious Samantabhadra.

## B. The Homage

When this Teaching, given as [Chetsun Senggé Wangchuk] passed into nirvāṇa, was first assembled, the primordial consciousness ḍākinīs made reverent homage.[17] Here is the meaning: The actual nature of the mind of all superior, inferior, and middling beings throughout all time and space is primordially pure, without reliance upon any other causes or conditions. Its nature is spontaneous; it is the great, all-pervading, self-emergent, connate

16. Again, because sentence structure is often reversed when translating from Tibetan to English, this is the "third" part of the Tibetan title (Tib. *mtshan gsum pa'i don ni*), hence the reason for it being treated last.

17. The root text of Chetsun's revelation (Tib. *Man ngag thams cad kyi rgyal po klong lnga'i yi ge dum bu gsum pa*), on which this present text is a commentary, begins with the following line of homage: "I bow down to the deity that is self-emergent pristine awareness" (Tib. *rang byung rig pa'i lha la phyag 'tshal lo*).

clear light, never wavering from the essential nature of all the myriad threefold kāyas of the jinas. The infinite purity that forms the basis of the phenomenal world arises of its own accord in the manner of limitless circles of the maṇḍalas of primordial consciousness deities. All these are indivisible from the essential nature of a single instant of one's own pristine awareness. This all-encompassing realization, depicted as the "sole bindu," does not objectify even a trace of [612] a sign of a difference between the object to be realized and the subject that realizes. And they bow in the manner of knowing their "own face" as the nature of existence, directly perceived, without error, just as it is.

## II. The Meaning of the Text, Explained according to the Tradition of Giving Guidance in the Profound Pith Instructions

Here there are three sections: (A) giving rise to confident belief in the Dharma and guru through an account of the lineage, (B) ripening the unripened mindstreams of disciples who are suitable vessels through the supreme, profound empowerment, and (C) liberating those who have already been ripened by means of the unique and extraordinary pith instructions.

### A. Giving Rise to Confident Belief in the Dharma and Guru through an Account of the Lineage

Here there are two sections: (1) the way it appeared in the past, and (2) the prophecy about how it will appear later.

#### 1. The Way It Appeared in the Past

The dharmakāya Teacher, the original Buddha, the glorious Samantabhadra, dwells in the great abode of Akaniṣṭha in the limitless absolute space of phenomena. From within his nonconceptual, profoundly clear, originally pure mind—the vajra of space,[18] great suchness—he makes manifest the immaculate awareness and vital energies of self-appearing primordial consciousness, which dawn of their own accord. And he does so by means of that same pristine awareness, primordial consciousness. Thus he has always been pure, never having had to eliminate the many "adventitious defilements" so that they never arise again. The primordial consciousness of the dharmakāya, empty in its essential nature, never wavers [613] from perfect power as the pervasive lord of all families [of buddhas].

At the same time, the primordial consciousness of the sambhogakāya, whose manifest nature is luminosity, lights up spontaneously as the self-appearing, self-illuminating kāyas and as limitless oceans of pure realms. These then appear spontaneously to the bodhisattvas of the tenth ground, as limitless arrays of kāyas and pure realms, again and again, in an everlasting, continuous cycle.

The primordial consciousness of the nirmāṇakāya, which is all-pervasive compassion, reveals itself in every possible way, in a vast, unbroken stream of countless, immeasurable nirmāṇakāyas, in order to train everyone in limitless numbers of pure and impure realms, thereby fulfilling the various needs of disciples forever, pervasively and spontaneously.

To the sambhogakāya Teacher, the glorious Vajrasattva, the supreme family of the mind-vajra, the Teacher Samantabhadra himself directly revealed the inconceivable Dharma of the Great Perfection in the pure abode of Akaniṣṭha, such that the Teacher and the audience, their perspective and their behavior, were made indivisible.

Vajrasattva bestowed this upon the supreme nirmāṇakāya, the Vidyādhara Pramodavajra. His birthplace was the Land of Orgyen in the west, and he did not have a human father. Rather, [614] Vajrapāṇi himself came in the form of a yellow goose, and he placed the awareness of the devaputra Adhicitta, in the form of a red-and-white-colored syllable *hūṃ*,

18. Tib. *nam mkha'i rdo rje*, Skt. *ākāśavajra*. Note that this term is sometimes said to be the original given name of Pramodavajra.

in the center of the mother's heart, and from this he was born. Thus he is counted as a son of the glorious Vajrapāṇi.[19]

Pramodavajra granted the definitive secret of the complete ripening and liberation of the Great Perfection, together with the "Three Words That Strike the Crucial Points,"[20] practical instructions that were given at his passing to Ācārya Mañjuśrīmitra, a son of the Siṃhala[21] brahman class.

He [Mañjuśrīmitra] granted the complete ripening and liberation [empowerments] of the sovereign supreme vehicle, together with pith instructions on the "Six Meditative Experiences,"[22] given at his passing to the Vidyādhara Śrī Siṃha,[23] a son of the Chinese[24] householder class. To Jñānasūtra, a son of the Chinese[25] peasant class, together with the Mahāpaṇḍit Vimalamitra,[26] a son of the Kashmiri householder class, he [Śrī Siṃha] granted the Great Perfection up to and including the secret cycle, at which point Vimalamitra traveled to another region. Thereafter he [Śrī Siṃha] gave the complete, unsurpassed, ultrasecret ripening and liberation, together with the "Seven Spikes,"[27] pith instructions given at his passing, to Jñānasūtra. It is said that Vimalamitra later heard the complete, unsurpassed, ultrasecret [cycle] from Jñānasūtra, together with [615] the teachings given at [Jñānasūtra's] passing, known as "Four Methods of Resting [in Equipoise]."[28] If this is so, Jñānasūtra must also be in this lineage. Since Vimalamitra's vajrakāya rainbow body is still present now, there were no teachings given at his passing.

19. Tib. *Gsang ba'i bdag po*, lit. "The Lord of Secrets."

20. Tib. *Tshig gsum gnad brdeg.*

21. A land not far from Orgyen. Tib. *Seng ga la.*

22. Tib. *Dgongs nyams drug pa.*

23. Pronounced "Shri Singha."

24. Tib. *Rgya nag.* This may refer to Burma, rather than China.

25. As in previous note.

26. Vimalamitra appears to have lived in the eighth century CE. For a more detailed version of this biography, see http://treasuryoflives.org/biographies/view/Vimalamitra/9985.

27. Tib. *Gzer bu bdun pa.*

28. Tib. *Bzhag thabs bzhi pa.*

Vimalamitra concealed many Great Perfection Dharma treasures in Tibet, and the Nyang Kadampa Tingdzin Zangpo,[29] Néten Dangma Lhüngyal,[30] Trulku Gyalwa Zhangtön,[31] and others have already brought some of them to light. But there is no need to list this lineage here. Vimalamitra gave [the teachings] directly to Chetsun [Senggé Wangchuk].

The Teachers Samantabhadra and Vajrasattva constitute the actual "lineage of the enlightened view of the jinas." Vajrasattva transmitted to Pramodavajra the "meaning lineage blessed by the enlightened view." Then from Vimalamitra onward there is the "symbolic lineage of the vidyādharas." The manner in which he gave it to Chetsun [Senggé Wangchuk] is as explained before. Chetsun's pith instructions given at his passing, which were solicited by the ḍākinīs, are even clearer than the *Great Heart Essence*.[32] So, fortunate ones, this is something to believe in.

There exists an authentic account of Ācārya Padma[33] and Vimalamitra hearing the unsurpassed, ultrasecret [cycle] directly from Śrī Siṃha on another occasion. [616] If this is so, it accords with the lineage prayer composed by our lord, the Gentle Protector Guru.[34]

Furthermore, this is the reason why, in the *Complete Secrets of the Quintessence*,[35] no other lineage of gurus is mentioned other than the one that goes from Samantabhadra to Vimalamitra. The kāya of primordial consciousness that unifies (1) the King of Form, Vairocana, (2) the King of Feeling, Ratnasambhava, (3) the King of Discernment, Amitābha, (4) the King of Mental Formations, Amoghasiddhi, and (5) the King of

29. Tib. *Nyang bka' gdams pa ting 'dzin bzang po*, fl. mid-eighth century. See http://treasuryoflives.org/biographies/view/Nyang-Tingngedzin-Zangpo/6205.

30. Tib. *Gnas brtan ldang ma lhun rgyal*, eleventh century. This figure was also a teacher of Chetsun Senggé Wangchuk. See http://treasuryoflives.org/biographies/view/Dangma-Lhungyel/494.

31. Tib. *Sprul sku rgyal ba zhang ston*, 1097–1167. See http://treasuryoflives.org/biographies/view/Shangton-Tashi-Dorje-/8923.

32. Tib. *Snying thig chen mo*.

33. That is, Padmasambhava.

34. Tib. *Rje 'jam mgon bla ma*. This likely refers to Jamgön Kongtrul Lodrö Tayé (*'Jam mgon kong sprul blo gros mtha yas*, 1813–99).

35. Tib. *Thig le gsang rdzogs*.

Consciousness, Akṣobhya—as these belong to all the sugatas, subsumed under the three kāyas, along with their countless dances as wrathful beings, female deities, and entourages—is none other than the pervasive Lord, the sixth family, the glorious Samantabhadra. It is permissible, indeed there is a purpose, in not listing other gurus prior to the birth of the Lord of Contemplatives, Siṃheśvara,[36] as he is the supreme Heruka himself, the great exalted one who already attained the sublime state of Samantabhadra.

## 2. The Prophecy about How It Will Appear Later

Now is the time indicated by the prophecy that comes at the end of the first unit. [617] As [Jamyang Khyentsé Wangpo] explained: "In this era, which is more degenerate than the dregs, even to an individual more ordinary than the ordinary, who obviously has a multitude of faults of all kinds and only feeble virtues of any sort—to an individual like myself—the time of the Jina's activity has not passed, but is extremely powerful. Thus, at a time when the ḍākinīs' symbolic words aroused my mindstream from its depths, this inferior mind and lowly appearances were purified in their natural abode and transformed. Not even a trace remained, but everything vanished of itself. In their place there was a magnificent orb of the light of precious primordial consciousness, such that one could never tire of gazing upon it. There, a single instant of this present-moment awareness experienced itself in every way as the body, speech, and mind-vajra of the great Chetsun. Then a wonderful event occurred: The complete [empowerments of] ripening and liberation were revealed with great clarity, in a very brief time, to an ocean-like assembly of primordial consciousness ḍākinīs, karmic ḍākinīs, and mundane ḍākinīs. There was no contamination at all, whether from error in the meaning or else through missing or superfluous words. During the period after the meditative experience, [618] I wrote down letters that were like an illusion. But for thirteen or fourteen human years, I left them alone.

36. That is, Chetsun Senggé Wangchuk. The text includes both a Sanskrit rendering of, and an added play on, his Tibetan name, where Wangchuk means "lord," and Senggé means "lion." The Sanskrit name, pronounced "Singheshvara," means "lion lord."

Then, in accord with the prophecy given by the Jina, I opened the Dharma gate for the first time to Lodrö Tayépa[37] and his group of practitioners.

Thus, except for myself alone, the great vidyādharas of the past were only siddhas greater than siddhas, all of whom had attained the undefiled vajrakāya rainbow body. Over and over again they have blessed this Dharma. I think there may be value in revealing it and value in practicing it."[38]

## B. Ripening the Unripened Mindstreams of Disciples Who Are Suitable Vessels through the Supreme, Profound Empowerment

A qualified vajra-king teacher properly sows the seeds of both ripening and liberation at the same time, bestowing both the empowerment of the creative power of pristine awareness and the essential, profound instruction as the marvelous, supreme, unified method, in complete accordance with the parts of the ritual treatise, including the place, time, and requisites. This is granted to disciples who yearn for Dharma and are suitable vessels of the sovereign, supreme vehicle, by force of having trained their mindstreams with the lower paths. Or else it is granted from the very beginning to certain fortunate individuals with sharp faculties, disciples who have little clinging to this life, who have great faith and aspiration—not mere lip service—for the essential Dharma and the guru, who are without pretense when it comes to guarding their samaya, and who are not frauds that, as if they were beguiled by Māra, broadcast what is a mere semblance of view and meditation or disdain the infallible law of actions and their results. [619] Rather, they are able to apply themselves to practice in accordance with the guru's words. It is extremely important that the profound method for actualizing the

37. Tib. *Blo gros mtha yas pa*; that is, Jamgön Kongtrul Lodrö Tayé.

38. This is an expanded commentary on the prophetic passage at the end of the first unit of Jamyang Khyentsé Wangpo's root treasure text (called *The Three Units of Letters on the Five Expanses, the Sovereign of All Pith Instructions, Man ngag thams cad kyi rgyal po klong lnga'i yi ge dum bu gsum pa*, in *The Cycle of Dharma Teachings on Chetsun's Heart Essence, Lce btsun sñing thig gi chos skor*, 18–19), which begins at the letter *ma* and continues to the letter *ha*.

ultimate fruition is exacted each time, in order to ripen the crucial points in accordance with the practice tradition of the lineage gurus.

Here are the individual phases of the superior empowerment.

## *Empowerment with Elaborations*

In the version with elaborations, catalyzed by the water of the vase, one's own body, objective appearances, and all clinging to the appearances of materiality vanish in their own place. Then [the guru] arouses the vital fluids and the cakras that are masses of light, along with their letters. By this power, the grasping mind, along with its karmic energies, either ripens directly—without being eliminated—into the essential nature of naturally liberated, connate great bliss, or else a special potency for such ripening is planted in the mindstream.

## *Empowerment without Elaborations*

In the version without elaborations, the guru's bodhicitta—the vital fluid that consists of the essential drops of indestructible ambrosia—[620] dissolves into the lamp of the empty bindu that resides naturally in the cakra of great bliss at the crown of your own body of light. Your essential, vital fluid of vajra primordial consciousness, indivisible from that of the guru, greatly increases, thereby completely filling the cakras formed from the channels of light, as well as the rest of your body, down to the tips of your hairs. This awakens pristine awareness, the nature of primordial consciousness—which has itself always been perfect—in the essential nature of an inconceivable experience of bliss, luminosity, and nonconceptuality. Within that state, your own creative power, together with the activity of the vital energy of primordial consciousness, is forcefully drawn inward. Thus the light of the vital fluids, along with your body, channels, and letters, spontaneously enter and dissolve into the single taste of the great, nonconceptual, absolute space of clear light. This causes all the gross and subtle movements—which relate to the conceptualization of signs, whether good and bad—to subside, without remainder, into absolute space. You are ripened solely into uncontrived nakedness, primordially free of elaboration, which grants you the fortune to be able to take hold of the everlasting kingdom.

## *Empowerment Entirely without Elaborations*

The preliminary practices for the version that is entirely without elaboration are as follows. There is the vajra purification of the body, the *hūṃ*[39] purification of speech, and the purification of mind, which takes place through resting without focusing on any object and then rising up from that state. [621] The mind takes on the aspect of each of the six classes of sentient beings and culminates by resting in the absolute space of emptiness. Each of these is a method for severing the root basis of each [type of existence], and principally these constitute a subset of the methods for cutting the root basis of the mind. When, through this method, you are absolutely certain that all good and bad elements of the body, speech, and mind are without root or basis, you settle naturally, without contrivance, in a state of unimpeded nonobjectification, without engaging in hopes or fears about anything.

For the main event, [the guru] reveals the refracting crystal and utters the words of empowerment. These are extraordinary symbolic means for demonstrating the originally pure essential nature and the spontaneously actualized manifest nature of pristine awareness. What they symbolize is this: Due to the mystical force of the guru pointing out the enlightened view, superior disciples realize, through a single instant of pristine awareness, how it is that what is symbolized—or what is to be realized—is nothing other than one's own awareness. The essence of what is symbolized is: (1) The great absence of elaboration, where the actual nature of the mind has an *essential nature* that is empty and without identity; (2) the great, all-pervasive luminosity, where the *manifest nature* shines primordially and automatically; and (3) the great *union* of this emptiness and luminosity,

39. Pronounced *huung*, with a long *u* rhyming with the English word "who."

which were never, ever separate. So, regarding superior disciples' realization (through a single instant of pristine awareness) of how this was never beyond the identity of their own awareness; regarding the birth, in middling disciples, of a wonderful experience with respect to their own condition; and regarding the fine understanding that comes even in lesser disciples; [622] for any of these to take place, the primordial consciousness that is the intent of the empowerment is absolutely indispensable.

Then the guru strikes the crucial points of the body, of the eyes, and of the vital energy and mind. The guru seals them with *hūṃ*, thereby instilling uncontrived, natural meditation in the meaning of the view. Thus is planted in one's mindstream the fortune to be able to achieve the three kāyas swiftly, such that one can never again turn back from the path.

## *Empowerment Absolutely without Elaboration*

In the preliminary practice for the version that is absolutely without elaboration, the body is nakedly cast off. This demonstrates that the actual nature of the mind is being set free from the covering of obscurations, and reveals in a symbolic way and with an auspicious portent that absolute space and pristine awareness will be laid bare.

The upright posture of the ācārya sitting cross-legged in meditative equipoise reveals in a symbolic way that if one is never separated from a straight posture of the body while cultivating the path of the view and meditation, extraordinary experiences and realizations will naturally arise.

The disciples focusing their attention on the blue letter *a* at the guru's heart demonstrates the way in which the unborn, immutable mind-vajra of the guru is indivisibly united in one taste with the body, speech, and mind of the disciples, and it directly brings about the circumstances for that to occur.

[623] The guru utters *hūṃ* three times, and into the disciple's mindstream there descends, by forceful means, the majesty of the three vajras, whose essential nature is the three facets of primordial consciousness. All the gross and subtle elements of the disciple's body, speech, and mind are

totally absorbed into the aspect of a deep-blue syllable *hūṃ*. With the forceful sound of *phaṭ*,[40] this instantly enters into its own place, the absolute space of the three kāyas. Or, if that does not quite happen, the knots in the disciple's mind that make the mistake about subject-object duality are immediately cut. As a result, the obscurations and faults that cause body and mind to rove helplessly in the miserable places of rebirth within the three realms are dispelled. This is a method that creates the circumstances for them to be elevated to the pure realms of the three kāyas.

At that point, if you, the disciple, see your mind to bear the nature of emptiness, luminosity, and pristine awareness, then, without shifting from that experience, you should sustain uninterrupted familiarity with the realization that (1) the primordial consciousness of emptiness is "cutting through," (2) the primordial consciousness of luminosity is the "direct crossing over," and (3) both bear the essence of your own awareness. In dependence upon gaining uninterrupted familiarity with that realization, then within this very life you will take hold of your invulnerable royal throne in the essential nature of the original three kāyas, in their own place. Or else, by attaining stability in the perfection of creative power that comes when you either recognize (1) the dying process as the self-appearance of the dharmakāya, (2) the intermediate period as self-appearance of the sambhogakāya, [624] or (3) birth as the self-appearance of the nirmāṇakāya, you take hold of each of these in their own place.

Otherwise, if that does not occur, it is true that right now, outside of us, there exist those who have actually reached the manifest fruition, who are of one taste in the many dances of the infinite arrays of the ocean of pure realms. It is true that the actual nature of the mind of every being, including that of the disciples, remains in the essential nature of emptiness, luminosity, and pristine awareness. And without transgressing the manner in which this has both always been the case, and is also yet to come, it is true that all are of one taste in the actual nature of reality. There is also the truth of the profound Dharma of the Secret Mantrayāna, and the infallible

40. Usually pronounced by Tibetans as *phé*.

truth of dependent origination, by which the extraordinary methods that carry the guru's blessing will take you across the border [to the next life]. By the power of these truths, in the life following this one or else in some other lifetime, you will certainly pass through the door into rebirth within those pure realms.

During the main event, for the body, there are the three postures; for the speech, there is the gentle exhalation and inhalation of the vital energy; and then there are the three "distant lasso" ways of gazing. As for the mind, it is settled in meditative equipoise within the state where pristine awareness is indivisible from outer and inner absolute space. At that time the guru grants pointing-out instructions with the vajra words and bestows a prophecy along with [625] the seal. By this power, in accordance with each individual's mental level, each one travels to the culmination of the stages of the path of the four visions. This entails seeing, with an unmistaken, direct perception, the actual nature of the mind (uncontaminated by the defilements of vital energy and mind)—insofar as it is the naked face of the indwelling kāyas and primordial consciousness—to be the self-emergent pristine awareness, primordial consciousness, as well as the objects of the refined sense faculties. This demonstrates the unsurpassed, supreme method for taking hold of the everlasting kingdom within the inwardly luminous, original absolute space.

For the conclusion, in order to make everything firm, from the respective places on the guru's body emanate (1) bodies of the guru, (2) strings of white and red vowels and consonants, (3) deep-blue letters *a*, and (4) orbs of the five lights. These dissolve into the respective places on the disciple's body. This impresses the seal of the indivisible, indestructible, three vajras of the guru and all the jinas, along with the vajra of primordial consciousness. Thus, without a doubt, the disciple has been made into someone who has the good fortune to attain enlightenment.

In general this is the essential core from among the infinite special characteristics of this sovereign, supreme empowerment into the creative power of awareness. At this point, you should certainly know at least this much.

# 2 Shared Preliminaries to Meditation

## C. Liberating Those Who Have Already Been Ripened by Means of the Unique and Extraordinary Pith Instructions

Here there are three sections [626]: (1) the preliminaries to the profound teachings, (2) the main practice, and (3) the concluding teachings.

## 1. The Preliminaries to the Profound Teachings

Here there are also three sections: (a) the preliminaries to the meditation session, to make the mindstream a suitable vessel, (b) the shared preliminaries: the sevenfold mind training, and (c) the exceptional preliminaries: the five unique ways to accumulate [the collections] and purify [obscurations].

## a. The Preliminaries to the Meditation Session, to Make the Mindstream a Suitable Vessel

Here, furthermore, there are three sections: (i) the way to resort to solitude, (ii) settling the body, speech, and mind in their natural state, and (iii) making supplication to the guru.

## i. The Way to Resort to Solitude

The whole of the region of Tibet, from its interior to its frontiers, is a realm subdued by the supreme Teacher, the King of the Śākyas, and it is the supreme realm of Ārya Avalokiteśvara. Among the twenty-four sites at which the vīras and ḍākinīs naturally assemble, if one is to connect them to the structure of the vajra body, then this land represents the Secret Place, the Cakra of Sustained Bliss. It is an extraordinary region that is capable of bringing forth, through forceful means, both defiled and undefiled great bliss. When you have the pure vision that knows this to be so, it becomes an area in which unfavorable conditions for practice are few and favorable conditions are plentiful.

You may move about from one place to another—including cemeteries, mountain peaks, remote mountain regions, islands, or forests [627]—that cause your practice to thrive and that are free of human intruders such as enemies and thieves. Or you may stay in a single location that is conducive to Dharma. Most important is that you remain free of the causes of distraction. Whether you are there alone or with friends whose Dharma is compatible with your own, you should resort to that for as long as you live.

## ii. Settling the Body, Speech, and Mind in Their Natural State

No matter how isolated your dwelling place might be, if you pass the time with your body, speech, and mind continuously involved in negligent sloth and petty distractions, and if you are covertly engaged in reprehensible thoughts and behavior, you should be disgusted with yourself. Since that is especially detrimental, with constant, stable mindfulness, introspection, and conscientiousness, in order to achieve a meaningful foundation of practice, put a firm stop to ordinary thoughts and behavior and to fake Dharma. Determine the appropriate amount of food, clothing, and sleep; arouse your awareness and, with the special daily conduct of practicing meditation, constantly remain seated on a comfortable meditation cushion. This constitutes settling your body in its natural state.

Imagine that all the faults and downfalls accumulated by yourself and others in beginningless lifetimes, [628] and especially all the obstructing forces, as well as all good and bad conditions that would interfere with your practice of the profound path, are purified right where they are, without remainder. Dispel the residual vital energy either three times or with the ninefold expulsion. Then slow the movements of your respiration so that they are imperceptible, thereby settling your speech in its natural state.

Let go of all other good, bad, and neutral thoughts, and repeatedly cultivate the attitude of yearning for liberation by considering: "It is said that the nature of my mind and that of every other living being throughout space is primordially enlightened. But solely due to lack of realization and to our own mistake, we continually experience the numerous causes of the three kinds of suffering and their effects, which, like a dream, appear but are nonexistent. What a tragedy! Now I must swiftly strive in the methods that free us from this.

"Sentient beings who in the past, present, and future cared for me with kindness and who have been my mother are helplessly and constantly tormented by the vast and endless causes of sufferings and their effects." With this thought, repeatedly cultivate the powerful, virtually unbearable attitude of considering everyone with extraordinary compassion.

Single-pointedly and repeatedly cultivate the altruistic, extraordinary resolve and precious, supreme bodhicitta, thinking, "It is not [629] enough just to think, 'What a pity!' So I alone shall utterly dispel the causes of suffering and their effects and establish us in our own place of the kāyas and great primordial consciousness.

"The state of omniscience for the sake of others cannot possibly occur without causes or conditions. Those causes and conditions are the ultimate, unsurpassed swift path, the essence of the pith instructions on the clear light Great Perfection, which most spiritual people can rarely find. I shall practice this in accordance with the guru's teachings and the treatises of pith instructions, and I shall follow the practice to its culmination." Thinking in this way, cultivate from the depths of your heart—and not with mere lip service—the faith and devotion that come from belief in the Dharma that is to be practiced here, and in the guru who reveals this Dharma. In this way your mind is settled in its natural state.

## iii. Supplication to the Guru

"In a single instant, in the center of the phenomenal world that is the great pure realm of Akaniṣṭha, along with a vast array of the offering clouds of Samantabhadra, appears my own compassionate root guru. [630] The guru's body-vajra outshines the entire phenomenal world with the splendor of its signs and symbols. The speech-vajra reveals limitless avenues of profound and vast Dharma with the voice of Brahmā. The mind-vajra looks after all sentient beings including myself, never separated from us, with the gaze of a primordial consciousness endowed with unimaginable knowledge, love, power, and strength. The guru is radiantly present, as if perceived directly, with the essential nature of the infinite jinas of the three kāyas, all combined into one. Until we reach the essential heart of enlightenment, you alone know what is to be done. Not even in my dreams do I have any other refuge or source of hope."

Thinking in this way becomes a method of meditation in which other mental states simply cease by themselves, due to the intensity of your powerful admiration and reverence. Utter supplications according to the oral recitation,[41] and at the conclusion of this fervent supplication, imagine that

41. The recitation text written for this practice by Jamyang Khyentsé Wangpo himself, *The Mystery of Primordial Consciousness Perfected: The Preliminaries to the Great Chetsun's Profound Quintessence from Vimalamitra, Fluidly Presented as an Oral Recitation* (*Lce btsun chen po'i bi ma la'i zab tig gi sngon 'gro'i ngag 'don chu 'babs su bkod pa ye shes gsang rdzogs*, in *The Cycle of Dharma Teachings on Chetsun's Heart Essence, Lce btsun sñing thig gi chos skor*, 34), indicates that one is to begin with the famous verse:

> Come, my precious root guru, shining in glory,
> [sit atop the lotus in my heart,
> and in your great kindness take me after you;
> please grant me the *siddhis* of body, speech, and mind.]

(Note that there are numerous versions of this verse, and only the first line is quoted here in Tibetan, *dpal ldan rtsa ba'i bla ma rin po che . . .*) One is to follow this with the words of supplication: "Think of me, O precious guru, who has the essential nature of all the buddhas of the past, present, and future! Please pour out your grace upon me, to ripen and

the guru joyfully and with great love dissolves into yourself, such that the three vajras of the guru and your own body, speech, and mind are merged into one taste. Then settle your mind for a while without any modification.

These are the foundation of all the practices that follow, [631] and they are at all times extremely important.

## b. The Shared Preliminaries: The Sevenfold Mind Training

The sevenfold method of training the mind is the indispensable crown jewel of all spiritual people and does not pertain solely to this practice.

### i. Meditation on Impermanence

Each thing within the physical world and its inhabitants—what did not exist before but newly comes into existence—appears exactly insofar as its various causes and conditions have temporarily come together. For every validly existing thing, from the very next moment after it has finished coming into being, it is powerless to remain. Thus it decays, and even when something of the same type keeps arising later, in a continuum, all that has to happen is that, at the bridge between each sequential production and decay, its own result fails to manifest. Then it easily transforms into something else. So what in that is permanent and stable?

Therefore, everything that you have—including your dwelling, body, possessions, and life—is solely of the nature of impermanence. The lifespan of the people of Jambudvīpa is uncertain, and in this degenerate era there are the additional afflictions of short lifespans, a multitude of diseases, and so on. Thus it is certain that you will die soon. Earnestly meditate again and again [632] on how this resembles a water bubble buffeted by the wind, and counteract the reprehensible attitude of grasping onto things as being permanent, which is like the mental state of a lunatic. Repeatedly ponder

liberate my mindstream. Please bless me that the extraordinary realizations of the profound path may arise within my mindstream. Please grant your blessing that within this very life I may reach the final end of the supreme path of the clear light Great Perfection."

this on all occasions, both during and between formal meditation sessions, without ever being separated from the thought, until there arises a continual, uncontrived attitude of knowing what is impermanent to be impermanent. And by all means strive in methods that prevent your practice of the sublime Dharma from slipping into even the slightest bit of procrastination and spiritual sloth.

### ii. Meditation on the Way in Which Even the Pleasures of Saṃsāra Are Causes Leading to Unhappiness

Insofar as we crave and are attached to every occurrence of the pleasures of the fortunate realms (which are the result of defiled virtue accumulated in the past), we do not let go of this life. Since we are carried away solely by thoughts of aspiring for pleasure and the behaviors that accompany them, we do not accomplish any sublime Dharma at all. Each time we strive in our constant pursuits, such as subduing our enemies and protecting our loved ones, as a byproduct we accumulate numerous reprehensible vices. The result of these is that we must experience many kinds of unhappiness in this lifetime, and in later lifetimes, as much as we wish otherwise, we must experience the violent suffering of the miserable realms of existence. Therefore, the greater the fleeting pleasures of saṃsāra, the more they are a terrible, utterly worthless seduction that causes the ruin of spiritual people. [633]

As an analogy, if we are seduced by delicious food and drink mixed with poison, which are attractive in color, with a savory aroma and taste, and we eat them, as a result we must helplessly experience the agony of poisoning. When that happens, even if we feel remorse, it is difficult to remedy. Recognize the parallel. If we do not sever craving and attachment to the seductive pleasures of this life, whatever we are involved in naturally leads to terrible suffering. Meditate well on how this pattern comes about, turn your mind away from the craving and attachment of this life, and by all means strive in every way to focus your mind on the sublime Dharma.

## iii. Meditation on How There Is No Closure, No Matter How Much We Strive for Favorable Circumstances in Saṃsāra

All beings in saṃsāra from the least to the greatest strive in many ways, employing various expedient tools as means of gaining individual physical and mental well being. And yet, if what we have accumulated in the past is inadequate, it is difficult for us to have any success at all. As a result of defiled virtue, we may have a little success, but no matter how much enjoyment we have, it dwindles away until it has vanished. Then the urge to move on once again rises up powerfully as it did before, resulting in physical and mental exhaustion. With many struggles we must strive again and again, without any finality to our efforts. For apart from having to create more causes, there is never a time when there is a complete and satisfying closure. Meditate carefully on the striking similarity between this and the example of a deer tormented by thirst mistaking a mirage for water and chasing after it. Then earnestly strive in the ways of contentment by making your way of life accord with Dharma.

## iv. Meditation on the Futility of All Superficial Human Pursuits, Whether Good or Bad

For as long as we have been alive, all our past experiences, for better or worse—including joy and sorrow, felicity and adversity, progress and decline, prestige and disgrace, and the affluence and poverty of this life—have become nothing more than mere memories. At the time of death, we follow solely the maturation of virtuous and evil deeds, and there is no one at all who can help or harm us. So those individual episodes of joy and sorrow are utterly devoid of even a speck of any enduring essence or significance. [635] As an example, meditate repeatedly on the sure resemblance between this and the fleeting occurrence of good and bad dreams during a single nap. Then stop trying to seek or avoid any superficial joys or sorrows, and do not foster any hopes or fears concerning them. Instead, whatever happens, it is crucial to focus your mind in the even taste of contentment.

In summary, meditate again and again on the disadvantages of becoming obsessed with each of these pleasures of saṃsāra, the things that contribute to them, and fleeting appearances of what is good or bad. Then saturate your mindstream with the pure, uncontrived resolve to turn your mind away from them and with the desire to free the minds of others from them. This is the root of all sublime Dharma, so you must apply yourself to this repeatedly.

## v. Meditation on the Benefits of Liberation

If we reach the precious state of a śrāvaka or pratyekabuddha arhat, which is the culminating fruition of the authentic path to liberation, we are forever freed from the sufferings of saṃsāra and their causes, and we will have actualized the bountiful excellences of peace and joy. [636] Therefore we will never again return to the sufferings of this swamp of saṃsāra. For example, it is like the fact that it is impossible for a person who has recovered from smallpox ever again to be afflicted with that disease.

Moreover, the ultimate fruition that comes from proper cultivation of the Mahāyāna path is far superior even to that kind of peace and joy. Sublime liberation, or the precious state of omniscience, which is unsurpassed, supreme liberation, is like a supreme wish-fulfilling gem. It totally transcends the two extremes of mundane existence and of the peace of nirvāṇa as well as their causes, and it is endowed with the infinite, inconceivable, inexpressible excellence of mastery over the supreme interests of yourself and others, as well as permanence, all-pervasiveness, and spontaneous actualization. Let alone reaching such a supreme state, the benefits of even once aspiring to reach it cannot be calculated with a vajra tongue. So it is of the utmost importance for you knowledgeable people to make a firm resolve to cultivate diligently, until it arises in your mindstreams, an uncontrived, [637] powerful attitude of yearning to reach the state of perfect buddhahood swiftly, never abandoning this resolve even at the cost of your lives. Do not give mere lip service to this attitude, but cultivate it earnestly now while you have the freedom to do so.

## vi. Meditation on the Importance of the Guru's Practical Instructions

The extraordinary, excellent path by which the states of liberation and omniscience are accomplished is available solely due to the kindness of the Sugata, the supreme Teacher, and the countless avenues of this sublime Dharma shine without bias upon the meritorious disciples of this illumined realm. Yet even a single practical instruction from among all of these is something beyond the experience of presumptuous people with their own fabrications. If you obtain practical instructions that provide a complete synthesis of the crucial points from beginning to end from a qualified guru who is well-versed in that Dharma, you will readily understand what is truly to be practiced. So the guru's profound practical instructions are indispensable. As an analogy, this is like relying upon a fine stairway as the means to reach the roof of a mansion.

Therefore, first of all seek out and examine a qualified guru. [638] When you find one, devote yourself to that guru by means of the three services[42] and resolve to practice according to the guru's practical instructions. This is a marvelous, all-sufficient, swift path. Thus a single practical instruction of the guru is more important than a hundred or a thousand lectures that are not derived from experience. This is widely known and is also confirmed with direct experience.

## vii. How to Settle the Mind in Its Natural State, since This Method Is So Crucially Important

Simply hearing the guru's practical instructions and understanding the explanation does not liberate your own mindstream, so you must meditate. Even if you spend your whole life practicing what is a mere semblance of meditation—meditating in a stupor, contaminated with compulsive

42. These are (1) following the guru's guidance, (2) assisting the guru in any way that is helpful, and (3) offering material goods to the guru.

ideation, and taking many breaks during your sessions because you are unable to control mental scattering—no good experiences or realizations will arise. So it is important during each session to meditate according to the guru's oral guidance.

In solitude, sit upright on a comfortable cushion. Gently hold the vase breath until the vital energies settle in their natural flow. Let your gaze be vacant. With your body and mind inwardly relaxed, and without allowing the continuum of your consciousness to fade from a state of lucidity and vivid clarity, sustain [639] it naturally and radiantly. Do not contaminate it with many critical judgments. Do not be impatient with your meditation, and avoid great hopes and fears that your meditation will turn out in one way and not another. At the beginning you should have many daily sessions, each of them of brief duration, and focus well in each one. Whenever you meditate, bear in mind the words "no distraction and no grasping," and put this into practice.

As you gradually familiarize yourself with the meditation, increase the duration of your sessions. If dullness sets in, arouse your awareness. If there is excessive scattering and excitation, loosen up. Determine in terms of your own experience the optimal degree of mental intensity as well as the healthiest diet and behavior.

Excessive, imprisoning constriction of the mind, loss of lucidity due to lassitude, and excessive relaxation resulting in involuntary vocalization and eye movement are faults. It is a hindrance to talk a lot about such things as extrasensory perception and miscellaneous dreams, or to claim, "I saw a deity. I saw a ghost. I know this. I've realized that," and so on. The presence or absence of any variety of pleasure or displeasure, such as a sensation of motion, is not uniform, for there are great differences in the dispositions and faculties from one individual to another.

By settling the mind in its natural state, sensations of bliss may arise, such as pleasant physical and mental sensations, experiences of luminosity, such as the clarity of consciousness, [640] and experiences of nonconceptuality, such as the appearance of empty forms, as well as a nonconceptual sense that nothing can harm your mind, regardless of whether or not thoughts have ceased.

Whatever kinds of experiences and visions arise—be they gentle or violent, subtle or gross, of long or short duration, strong or weak, good or bad—observe their nature and avoid any obsessive evaluation of them as being one thing and not another. Let the heart of your practice be consciousness, naturally at rest, lucid and clear. Acting as your own mentor, if you can bring the crucial points to perfection, as if you were threading a needle, the afflictions of your own mindstream will be subdued, you will gain the autonomy of not succumbing to them, and your mind will constantly be calm and composed. This is a sound basis for the arising of all samādhis of the stages of generation and completion.

This is like tilling the soil of a field. So from the outset avoid making a lot of great, exalted, and pointless proclamations. Rather, it is crucial to do all you can to refine your mind and establish a foundation for contemplative practice.

Thus, for each of those seven mind trainings, cultivate bodhicitta at the beginning of each meditation session and conclude with pure prayers of dedication. Between sessions [641] make sure that you unceasingly apply the elixir of each of these practices to your own mindstream.

# 3 Unique Preliminaries to the Main Practice

## c. The Exceptional, Unique Preliminaries

There are five unique preliminary practices: (i) an exceptional way to go for refuge, (ii) generating bodhicitta, (iii) purifying obscurations, (iv) accumulating the collections, and (v) guru yoga.

## i. An Exceptional Way to Go for Refuge

The object of refuge is in the space in front of you. In the midst of an ocean of offering clouds, upon a lion throne, atop a lotus, sun, and moon seat is my root guru himself, Śrī Heruka Siṃheśvara.[43] His body-vajra is reddish-brown in color and his countenance is smiling and majestic. He is adorned with various jewel and bone ornaments, his hands are in the mudrā of meditative equipoise, and he is seated in the vajrāsana posture. His radiance is like that of the mass of light from ten million suns, and the flaming light of his vajra primordial consciousness emanates out to the ten directions. His speech-vajra proclaims the great sound of Dharma everywhere. The deep clarity of pristine awareness that is his mind-vajra is of the nature of the dharmakāya. The natural luminosity of the inner radiance of his pristine awareness is of the nature of the sambhogakāya. And the impartial, creative

43. That is, Chetsun Senggé Wangchuk. Once again, the Sanskrit name is pronounced "Shri Heruka Singheshvara."

expressions of his pristine awareness are of the nature of the nirmāṇakāya. This great being, who sends forth and withdraws the infinite, myriad objects of refuge, focuses on you intently with kind affection. [642] He perceives you directly with the eyes of primordial consciousness. Imagine him as being joyfully present. For the sake of those who go for refuge, namely, all sentient beings throughout space, sit in the presence of the guru with your body, speech, and mind showing your reverence.

Here is the way to go for refuge. The actual nature of the mind of animate beings such as yourself is said to be the primordially empty, originally pure dharmakāya. Its self-illuminating spontaneous actualization is the sambhogakāya. The appearances of the creative power of the great indivisibility are the nirmāṇakāya. Its essential nature is nondual from the objects of refuge, and it is primordially of the nature of buddhahood. However, the adventitious stains of being unconscious of your own essential nature, or the mistaken thoughts of ignorance regarding its meaning, are the root of all fear and suffering. In order to be liberated from this, with irreversible faith bring forth the conviction, "I entrust my ultimate hopes and confidence solely to you, the eternal refuge and protector. By the immeasurable power of the glory of your supreme, primordial consciousness, may we all be liberated, by forceful means, from every last stain of dualistic grasping that remains in our consciousness, through a single instant of the indwelling nature of our own mind. [643] May my mind be indivisibly unified with your enlightened mind, and please bring me to buddhahood right now, upon this very seat." Thinking this, with passionate admiration and reverence, recite and ponder the words of going for refuge according to the scriptures a hundred or a thousand times or as much as seems fit. At the conclusion, your guru merges with you, and you rest naturally in the state in which his enlightened mind and your mind are unified.

On the occasion of each of the four kinds of daily activities,[44] practice the spiritual transformation of never being separated from the vision of your guru. If at all times and in all circumstances you let the mind

44. This refers to sitting, standing, walking, and lying down.

of your guru and your own mind be indivisibly unified, and if you can keep your mind clean and without pretense, you will have synthesized the crucial points of the vows to be maintained, including the precepts of going for refuge.

## ii. Generating Bodhicitta

Recall that you have taken on the vow to generate bodhicitta at the time of empowerment. Here is the situation. Living beings called *yourself* and *others* appear to your direct perceptions as being different. The mind more and more adamantly apprehends such appearances as being truly existent, until there appears to be a differentiation of the two groups called *your side* and *their side*, together with tenacious clinging onto those reified divisions, [644] and you grasp onto true existence in accordance with those appearances. You make many outer and inner divisions, fundamentally segregating off yourself and your loved ones. For your own side you apply yourself intently to the two concerns of doing whatever is needed to find happiness and doing away with suffering. Those beings who impair the fulfillment of your self-centered desires you regard as your enemies, and you do whatever you can to harm them. With such unceasing partiality, attachment, and aversion, whatever you have done during beginningless lifetimes has turned you away from omniscience. It has propelled you to either of the extremes, of mundane existence or the peace of nirvāṇa, and it has caused your roots of virtue for the Mahāyāna to degenerate. As this attitude is like a demon of poverty that infiltrates your wealth, it is called *the demon of self-centeredness*. You must get rid of this malignant attitude and for the sake of others devote yourself to the extraordinary thoughts and deeds by which to realize omniscience.

Here is a quintessential way to cultivate that thought: "The absolute space of the phenomena that are the minds of all sentient beings throughout space—who have been my mothers and shown me such great kindness—[645] has never been other than the nature of the originally pure three kāyas. However, under the adventitious influence of appearances that are misconstrued by ignorance, tragically, these beings are constantly, helplessly afflicted by the endless miseries of the three realms of saṃsāra. I alone shall help them to see their own face as the actual nature of their minds, to familiarize themselves with that, to become totally free of the mistaken cycle of the causes of suffering and their effects, and to realize their own state of the kāyas and facets of primordial consciousness. For that purpose I shall properly enter the secret path of the supreme vehicle, the ultrasecret, unsurpassed, extraordinary Dharma of the indivisibility of the absolute space of phenomena and pristine awareness. No matter what, I shall devote myself to the skillful means necessary to proceed along that path to its culmination."

By generating extraordinary bodhicitta in that way, reciting the words of the text, and engaging in the visualization and its accompanying liturgy, meditate so that this is definitely integrated with your own mindstream.

## iii. and iv. The Combined Practice of Purifying Obscurations and Accumulating the Collections

Visualize yourself as the indwelling deity, whose form is hollow, free of all obscurations and obstructions, lucid and clear, and of the nature of light. Within your center visualize the central channel, as wide [646] as your ring finger, white on the outside, red on the inside, radiating blue light. Its upper tip is at the crown of your head and its lower tip is four finger-widths beneath your navel. Penetrating it there at the lower tip is the red rasanā channel on the right, moistened by menses, and on the left is the white lalanā channel, flowing with semen. Each of them is one-third the width of the central channel. Their upper ends come up to one finger-width beneath the central channel and emerge through the right and left nostrils, while their lower ends penetrate the central channel in the shape of the Tibetan letter *cha* (ཆ). From those three principal channels extend secondary channels, with thirty-two white channel petals from the great bliss cakra facing downward from the crown of the head, sixteen red channel petals facing upward from the enjoyment cakra at the throat, eight blue channel petals facing slightly downward from the dharma cakra at the heart, and sixty-four yellow channel petals facing upward from the emanation cakra at the navel. They all have the aspect of tubes made of lucid, clear light.

One finger-width above the point at the lower end of the central channel where the three channels converge, visualize a lotus, sun, and moon. Atop them visualize your root guru as Vajrasattva of the lotus-speech family, luminously red, wearing bone ornaments, holding a vajra and bell, and embracing his female deity, who is of his own light. [647] They sit with their legs in the vajrāsana, as the archetypal synthesis of all the jinas of the vast expanse, indivisible from the inner heat that is present in the condition of the ground. They constitute the power of reliance.[45]

With intense remorse earnestly confess and disclose all the obscurations and faults of your own and others' body, speech, and mind that have been accumulated over beginningless lifetimes. These include the downfalls of misdeeds and obscurations that are naturally wrong, as well as the faults and obscurations that come from breaking any of the three sets of precepts, and especially from a degeneration of one's root and secondary pledges. The wish that they may be cleansed and purified is the power of remorse.

The firm resolve that "I will not commit them from now on, even at the cost of my life," constitutes the power of restoration.

Pray that due to the majesty of the guru's compassion and primordial consciousness the misdeeds and obscurations that you have committed in the past, together with their habitual propensities, may be completely purified and never again arise in your mindstream. By reciting the hundred syllables twenty-one times, earnestly invoke the enlightened mindstream from the crucial point [in your inner body]. Then dispel the dead, residual energies, restrain the lower energies, and gently suppress the upper energies. [648] By so doing, flames of primordial consciousness from Guru Vajrasattva's body rise upward in a clockwise spiral, filling the navel cakra. They incinerate, cleanse, and purify all the obscurations from sexual intercourse and attachment. The tongues of flame fill the heart cakra,

45. That is, the first of the "four powers" of a classical Buddhist rite of confession.

incinerating, cleansing, and purifying all the obscurations from deep sleep and delusion. Then they fill the throat cakra, incinerating, cleansing, and purifying all the obscurations from the dream state and envy. Finally, they fill the crown cakra, incinerating, cleansing, and purifying all the obscurations from the waking state and from hatred and pride. Imagine that at the same time all the misdeeds and obscurations of all sentient beings are simultaneously incinerated, cleansed, and evacuated. When you can no longer restrain your energies, gradually expel them. Then hold them once again and maintain the visualization.

At the end of the session, release the conjoined energies,[46] and without losing the visualization or aspiration, recite the hundred syllables as much as you wish. It would be good to recite *Rudra's Heartfelt Confession* from the *Confessional Tantra*;[47] the verses beginning with "Protector, I . . ." from [649] the *Tantra of the Source of Saṃvara*;[48] or the words of Drogün Chögyal Phagpa,[49] "The roots of the enlightened body, speech, and mind . . . ," and so on; but it is all right not to. In the root verses and in the meditation manual of our Gentle Protector Guru,[50] it seems that the conjoining of the energies is not much emphasized, in which case you primarily engage in the visualization and enumerated recitations. Here, given the importance of the crucial point by which the vital energies are joined with the fire, it is not necessary to do many recitations. Either way, at the conclusion the mind of the Guru Vajrasattva is utterly delighted,

46. Tib. *rlung sbyor*. This is a formal name for such a prāṇa practice.

47. Tib. *Bshags rgyud kyi ru dra'i smre bshags*. *Rudra's Heartfelt Confession* (*Ru dra'i smre bshags kyi le'u*) is a chapter from the *Stainless Sovereign Confessional Tantra* (*Dri med rgyal po bshags pa'i rgyud*).

48. Tib. *Bde mchog mngon 'byung gi rgyud*. This is the *Mahāsambarodaya-tantra*, also known as the *Saṃvarodaya-tantra* (Tib. *Bde mchog 'byung ba'i rgyud*, though the colophon begins: *dpal he ru ka* ***mngon*** *par brjod pa'i rgyud chen po 'bum phrag gsum pa las lhan cig skyes pa '****byung*** *ba'i rtog pa las btus pa . . .*).

49. Tib. *'Gro mgon chos rgyal 'phags pa*, 1235–80. He was one of the five great patriarchs of the Sakya lineage. See http://treasuryoflives.org/biographies/view/Pakpa-Lodro-Gyeltsen/2051.

50. Tib. *'Jam mgon bla ma*. Again, this may refer to Jamgön Kongtrul Lodrö Tayé.

and with a smiling face he says, "O child of the family, all your faults and downfalls are utterly purified." With those words, imagine that absolution is granted, the guru's mind merges with your own, and you rest in meditative equipoise. That is the power of applying the antidote.

Then, for the practice of accumulating the collections [of merit and knowledge], the exceptional field of merit consists of a lotus, sun, and moon seat inside the central channel, at the hub of each of the four cakras. At the crown is the guru, as the body-vajra, male and female, white in color. At the throat [650] is the guru as the speech-vajra, male and female, red in color. At the heart is the guru as the mind-vajra, male and female, indigo in color. And at the navel is the guru as the primordial consciousness-vajra, male and female, radiant yellow in color. All are endowed with the signs and symbols of enlightenment, naked, adorned with bone ornaments, the male deity holding a vajra and bell and embracing the female deity, while sitting in the vajrāsana. All the female deities hold a cleaver in their right hands and a bhandha vessel of ambrosia in their left hands while in union with the male deity. Inside the channel petals of each cakra, as an exceptionally auspicious sign for realizing the primordial consciousness of connate bliss and emptiness by forceful means, imagine lotus and sun seats on which white, red, indigo, and yellow ḍākinīs of the absolute space of primordial consciousness, each holding a cleaver and skull-cup, dance in bliss together with their entourages. Visualize them abiding in a continuous rain of blessings.

For the exceptional offering substances, meditate as follows. Above the crown cakra, inside the central channel, is the white element that is present in the condition of the ground, refined two or three times over. Simply by bringing to mind this drop of vital essence, in the form of a luminous, white *haṃ* syllable facing upside-down, you effortlessly generate great bliss. Imagine that the ambrosia of the primordial consciousness of all the buddhas combined is on the verge of dripping downward. [651]

Offer this heartfelt supplication to the Guru Vajrasattva and his female deity beneath your navel: "May I swiftly complete the great collections of merit and knowledge and realize the state of omniscient, primordial consciousness!" Invoke their mindstreams by reciting *Mahāsukha Vajrasattva ahaṃ* a hundred times or more. Then restrain your vital energies properly, as you did before. This incites the flame of primordial consciousness from the guru's body to blaze. It blazes up through the inside of the central channel, in front of the line of gurus, and when it reaches the top, merely touching the *haṃ* causes a stream of ambrosia to descend.

When it strikes the guru and the female deity who comprise the body-vajra, together with their entourage at the crown, you delight them with the offering of ecstasy. The ambrosia that has descended from the bodies of the guru and the female deity, and all the rest, fills the crown cakra, purifying the coarse obscurations of the body and the subtle obscurations of the channels, and completing the great collections. The primordial consciousness of ecstasy arises in your mindstream, the clear light of emptiness manifests, and you become a nirmāṇakāya, indivisible with the body-vajra of appearances and emptiness.

The ambrosia then descends to the throat, [652] striking the guru and female deity who comprise the speech-vajra, together with their entourage, and they are delighted with the offering of supreme ecstasy. The ambrosia of their bodies fills the throat cakra, purifying the coarse obscurations of the speech and the subtle obscurations of the vital energies, and completing the great collections. The primordial consciousness of supreme ecstasy arises in your mindstream, the clear light of extreme emptiness manifests, and you become a sambhogakāya, indivisible with the speech-vajra that is empty of sound.

The ambrosia then descends to the heart, striking the guru and his entourage who comprise the mind-vajra, and they are delighted with the offering of extraordinary ecstasy. The ambrosia of their bodies fills the heart cakra, purifying the coarse obscurations of the mind and the subtle obscurations of the vital essences, and completing the great collections. The primordial consciousness of extraordinary ecstasy arises in your mindstream, the clear light of total emptiness manifests, and you become a dharmakāya, indivisible with the mind-vajra that is empty of thought.

The ambrosia then descends to the navel, striking the guru, his female deity, and his entourage who comprise the primordial consciousness-vajra, and they are delighted with the offering of connate ecstasy. The ambrosia of their bodies fills the navel cakra, [653] purifying the coarse and subtle obscurations of the movements [of vital energies][51] of the defiled body, speech, and mind together, and completing the great collections. Imagine that the connate primordial consciousness beyond ecstasy arises in your mindstream, the clear light of uttermost emptiness manifests, and you become a svabhāvakāya, indivisible with the supreme, immutable bliss and emptiness. Practice that repeatedly.

At the end of the session the channel petals and the ḍākinīs of the entourage dissolve into the hearts of each of the gurus. Your own body, from the ends of your hair on down—including the upper sections of the three channels, as well as the male and female gurus at the crown and throat—dissolves in the form of white light down into the guru at the heart. Your body, from the tips of your toes upward—including the lower sections of the three channels, as well as the gurus with their female deities beneath the navel and at the navel—is drawn upward in the form of red light and dissolves into the guru at the heart. Then the guru, too, instantly disappears into the absolute space of phenomena, so that you rest in meditative equipoise in an inconceivable state with no basis or foundation. When you emerge from that state, visualize yourself in the divine form of the indwelling vajra and apply yourself to the continual practice of prayers of dedication and so forth. [654]

## v. Guru Yoga

This brief summary of the two stages, in which you take the guru's blessings as the path, is similar to the main practice in which you approach

51. Tib. *'pho ba'i sgrib pa*. This is a very subtle obscuration due to the movements of the vital energy, known in Tibetan as *khu rdul rlung*, which are the vital energies of the male (*khu*) and female (*rdul*) fluids.

actualization of the guru and the completion stage in which you take hold of the actual ground.[52] When you are going to practice, expel the residual vital energies by clearing them, then rest your consciousness in its own place and meditate well. The stages of the meditation are just as the lines of the oral recitation say, which clarify the meaning of the main text. But at the end of the invitation, when you have made invocation with the Vīma mantra and the five *hūṃ* syllables, Vimalamitra arrives from Wu-t'ai-shan, and from the abode of the ḍākinīs comes Chetsun. They arrive in the form of countless indigo, white, yellow, red, and green bodies, whose essential nature is the primordial consciousness of the five expanses, and they repeatedly dissolve into the five places on both the guru's body and your own, respectively.[53]

The meaning of the sevenfold devotion is as follows.[54] Through bringing the four visions of the path to their culmination, the guru has already actualized the great kingdom of the three kāyas, which abide in their own place without ever ceasing, because they never began. The guru's mind and your own mind remain indivisible in the three aspects of their (1) essential nature, (2) manifest nature, and (3) compassion. Although right now you appear to be two, in reality you have never been joined or separated. So you bow down by encountering thus the nature of existence as your own nature.

52. Tib. *dngos kyi gzhi 'dzin*. This appears to be a play on the Tibetan word for "main practice," *dngos gzhi*.

53. According to the recitation text, one's own body has just been visualized in the form of Chetsun Siṃheśvara, and the body of one's root guru has been visualized in the form of Vimalamitra.

54. The Tibetan verses alluded to here are from Jamyang Khyentsé Wangpo's *Mystery of Primordial Consciousness Perfected* (*Ye shes gsang rdzogs*, in *The Cycle of Dharma Teachings on Chetsun's Heart Essence*, *Lce btsun sñing thig gi chos skor*, 39): *a / snang bzhi mthar phyin bla ma la / 'du 'bral med par phyag 'tshal lo / rlung sems dag pa'i mchod sprin 'bul / sdig ltung 'dus ma byas par bshags / gnyis 'dzin bral bas rjes yi rang / brjod med chos 'khor bskor bzhin du / yongs grub chen por bzhugs gsol 'debs / dge tshogs 'od gsal dbyings su bsngo/.* "Ah. I bow down to the guru who has brought the four visions to their culmination, never joined or separated. I present the offering cloud of pure energy-mind. I confess misdeeds and downfalls within that which is unproduced. I rejoice without any grasping to duality. And even as you turn the wheel of inexpressible Dharma, I beg you to remain as the great, perfected one. I dedicate the collection of virtue in the absolute space of clear light."

When your energy-mind [655] dissolves into pristine awareness, vast offering clouds of the totally pure displays of pristine awareness are offered in the mode of a self-emergent offering, which never had to be set forth. All adventitious misdeeds and downfalls are naturally released in their own place, without having to be abandoned, in the unproduced expanse of absolute space and pristine awareness, and are thereby confessed. You rejoice in the meaning of signlessness, with an attitude free of grasping to any dualities of good or bad, including self and others, realization and non-realization, and so forth. You request that the great wheel of Dharma that reveals inexpressible reality be turned, along with the profound melody of vajra speech that is the unimpeded, unceasing majesty of primordial consciousness, the displays of pristine awareness. At the same time, you pray that the great, unmoving, perfected vajra nirmāṇakāya may remain. Dedicate all the illusory, dependently related collections of virtue, in which agent, action, and object cannot be focused upon, in the absolute space of the clear light. Single-pointedly practice those devotions.

At this point you may recite the supplication to the lineage gurus according to the lines [of the recitation text], or else change accordingly the verses that go, "You who are empowered with the creative displays of pristine awareness: Śrī Siṃha, Jñānasūtra . . ."[55] The meaning of the words of the supplication in the main text[56] [656] is that upon cutting through to the original purity of the empty clear light and completing the four visions of the path of the direct crossing over to the spontaneously actualized clear light of appearance (namely, the direct appearances of the actual nature of

55. Tib. *rig rtsal dbang thob śrī seng ye shes mdo.*

56. This refers to the following lines from the root text, *The Three Units of Letters on the Five Expanses, the Sovereign of All Pith Instructions* (*Man ngag thams cad kyi rgyal po klong lnga'i yi ge dum bu gsum pa*, in *The Cycle of Dharma Teachings on Chetsun's Heart Essence, Lce btsun sñing thig gi chos skor*, 14): *'od gsal snang bzhi mthar phyin nas / rig pa mi 'gyur sku lngar bzhengs / 'ja' lus 'pho chen dwangs ma'i gzugs / 'chi med bi ma mi tra kye / bdag la thugs rjes brtser dgongs nas / mngon sum byin rlabs deng stsol cig/.* "After bringing to their culmination the four visions of clear light, pristine awareness arises in the five immutable kāyas. O, form of the refined essence, great transference rainbow body, deathless Vimalamitra, kyé! Kindly attend to me, with your compassion, and please grant me right now the blessing of what is actually here."

reality, progress in meditative experience, reaching consummate awareness, and extinction into the actual nature of reality), you manifest possession of the ultimate twofold purity.[57] From this supreme, immutable, pristine awareness, then, for the glory of your disciples you arise in the form of the five kāyas of great, primordial consciousness that dawn of their own accord.

Your precious guru, the stainless spiritual friend, is master of the "undefiled rainbow body, the great transference vajra," which is completely unknown in other traditions. It is indestructible, a natural form of the refined essence, which remains for as long as space remains, without aging, degeneration, or death. Call your guru by name, saying, "Kyé! Please think of me!" Earnestly and firmly request, "Kindly attend to me, your disciple, with the compassion of primordial consciousness, free of obscurations. In this very instant—not at some indefinite time in the future—please grant me the tremendous blessing to become actually indivisible from you, and not merely as a way of seeing it in meditation, or the like." Single-pointedly apply yourself to reciting [Vimalamitra's] mantra many times, [657] and when you are finished, again request the empowerment. Visualize receiving the empowerment in accordance with the liturgy. If you wish to do this in an elaborate fashion, by making a special offering and praise to Vimala, then after the primordial consciousness beings dissolve, you should imagine emanating from your heart offering goddesses and the bounties of offerings. Then imagine that you actually make the offerings and add the offerings and praises from *The Fine Path of Primordial Consciousness*.[58] Then offer the prayers of the sevenfold devotion, make the supplication,

57. Tib. *mthar thug gi dag pa gnyis ldan*. The purity from afflictive obscurations and cognitive obscurations.

58. Tib. *don phrin* (lit. "actual sacred deeds"). This clearly refers to *The Fine Path of Primordial Consciousness: The Mystery of the Actual Sacred Deeds, Compiled in Proper Order, Gsang ba don gyi phrin las khrigs su bsdeb pa ye shes lam bzang*, by Rikdzin Natsok Rangdröl (*Rig 'dzin sna tshogs rang grol*, 1842–1924), in *The Cycle of Dharma Teachings on Chetsun's Heart Essence, Lce btsun sñing thig gi chos skor*, 167–84. The author of this retreat manual for the Chetsun Nyingtik practice, also known as Adzom Drukpa Dröndul Pawo Dorjé (*A 'dzom 'brug pa 'gro 'dul dpa' bo rdo rje*), was a student of Jamyang Khyentsé Wangpo and a teacher of Lerab Lingpa. See http://treasuryoflives.org/biographies/view/Adzom-Drukpa-Pawo-Dorje/8574.

and receive empowerment. Finally, withdraw the guru into a subtle orb between your eyebrows.

Visualize clearly the appearance of yourself as the deity, especially focus your awareness on the subtle orb between your eyebrows, and recite the mantra. Here you may also practice the vajra recitation, in which you contemplate that the vital energies naturally enter with the sound of *oṃ*, remain with the sound of *āḥ*, and rise up with the sound of *hūṃ*. Or else you train gradually in taking this onto the path by imagining that the white, red, and indigo forms of each of the three seed syllables [enter, remain, and rise up again], followed by their sounds, respectively, or else you imagine that they do so all at once. If you become tired, or if you wish to practice emanation and withdrawal, then from the subtle orb emanate the five lights and withdraw them, in accordance with the scriptures. Then withdraw the pure physical world and its sentient inhabitants into yourself. The sequence for this withdrawal may be taken from any of the general methods cited previously. [658] At the end of the session you may make offerings and praise in accordance with *The Fine Path of Primordial Consciousness* by knowing how to make offerings to yourself with the clouds of offerings emanated from yourself. But you may skip that if you wish.

When you are practicing the sequence of withdrawal as a special way to bring onto the path the occasions when you are about to die and when you are dead, dissolve the pure physical world and its sentient inhabitants into your heart. Then funnel your own body—appearing like mind—into the subtle orb between your eyebrows. Single-pointedly concentrate your awareness on that lucid, luminous, motionless, subtle orb, and remain focused like that for a long time. That is a crucial aspect of the path when you are about to die.

Then focus intently on the syllable *a* in the absolute space of phenomena, free of conceptual elaborations, and without having to recognize that absolute space with pristine awareness, simply rest in your own nature, free of concepts. That is the yoga of the phase of death, a method for bringing death onto the path.

Then radiantly arise in the divine form of the indwelling vajra, and when the good and bad appearances of the six kinds arise abundantly as objects to your six sensory consciousnesses, do not follow after them, wondering whether or not they are truly existent and so on. The essence of the meditation when the deity and absolute space appear must be for pristine awareness to hold its own ground within you. The specifics of the appearance of the guru, the subtle orb, the vajra recitation, and [659] the emanation and withdrawal are like piling dry wood on a fire, for if you practice with clarity and stability each one will support the others. That is what it means to remain in the union of the stages of generation and completion.

To encapsulate the stage of completion, moreover, the appearance of the deity, the appearance of absolute space, and the appearances to the six kinds of consciousness that come during your meditation sessions are not established in any way beyond merely being set forth by the mind—even the mind of the one who set them forth, the one who has experiences: How is this anything other than a mere luminous appearance, which does not exist conventionally? The ultimate essential nature of that mind is the absolute space of phenomena, which transcends the objects conceived by the dualistic mind that sees consciousness and the objects of consciousness to be separate.

Furthermore, the *view* is seeing with the primordial consciousness of your own individual awareness, which nakedly perceives the nonduality of subject and object, free of conceptual elaboration, and without support. A yogin who realizes this practices the great freedom from extremes, which is the naturally luminous, nonconceptual inner space of the actual nature of the mind. The *meditation* is the achievement of the yoga—or of the stability in clarity—that comes from familiarization with such practice. The *conduct* is not to follow after good and bad objects and mental states, [660] but to gain mastery over the experience of everything arising naturally as ornaments of pristine awareness.

If you can continuously apply yourself day and night to such conduct, meditation, and view for seven days, you will simultaneously achieve the yogas of śamatha and vipaśyanā. The appearance of the deity does not obscure the essential nature of absolute space, and even if you rest in meditative equipoise in absolute space without meditating on the appearance of the deity, it will arise naturally. The signs that come when each of the ten vital energies finishes off will also arise naturally, and you will be held close and blessed by the guru, so you should meditate single-pointedly and with faith free of uncertainty.

In those ways establish a strong basis in the foundations of practice by means of the profound shared and exceptional preliminary practices. Then you must engage in the main body of the practice that is the king of the supreme vehicle of clear light.

# 4 The Generation Stage of the Guru and Cutting the Basis of Delusion

## 2. Profound Instructions on the Main Practice

Here there are two sections: (a) the devout and reverent generation stage of the guru, and (b) the unique, essential stage of completion.

### a. The Devout and Reverent Generation Stage of the Guru

In a solitary and pleasant place to practice, set out medicinal liquor, tormas, offerings, ganacakra substances, and torma offerings to the guardians, according to your resources. Firmly set the boundaries of your retreat and [661] purify your mindstream by way of the preliminary practices, as is appropriate to the circumstances and in whatever way you see fit. After that, when you begin your session at dusk, offer supplications to the guru lineage, take refuge, generate bodhicitta, and engage in practices to accumulate merit as explained in *The Fine Path of Primordial Consciousness.* Then visualize yourself as Śrī Siṃheśvara, standing up in the form of the Supreme Horse Heruka. Amidst your hair is the green face of a horse, and on your body are the ornaments of a wrathful one. You hold a cleaver and a skull-cup. Offer a torma to the bhūtas in accordance with the general custom.

On the first day it is enough for you to meditate on Hayagrīva, together with the torma offering to the bhūtas. There is no need to plant a pole for the Great Kings. Once you have set the boundaries of your retreat in accordance with *The Fine Path* and have gone as far as uttering the verses of praise, make supplications to the guru, earnestly recite the mantras, and take the empowerment. Then meditate well, primarily on the appearance of your deity. Since, apart from the two forms of the guru, there are no other objects on which to meditate, this is very simple. Recite the verses describing the meaning of the mantra, according to *The Fine Path*, and reflecting upon them, recite the root mantra. Then practice the vajra recitation, followed by the visualizations of the emanation and withdrawal. Once you have made pointed efforts at reciting the root mantra, and so on, step by step, then at the end recite the vowels and consonants, the hundred-syllable mantra, [662] and the mantra of the *Essence of Dependent Origination*. At the conclusion, make offerings and recite praises to the guru and yourself in accordance with *The Fine Path*. Then recite "The Inexpressible, Actual Confession"[59] in accordance with the *Confessional Tantra*. Then perform the ganacakra offering and supplication to the guardians according to the *Fine Path* liturgy. There is no need to recite the verses for receiving siddhis except on the last day. Again make offerings and recite praises as before, and disclose your faults. Then make three requests to the guru for empowerment and so on, engage in the visualizations for receiving empowerments, and rest in meditative equipoise upon the union of your mind and the guru's mind. Then withdraw the appearance of your deity and arise again as explained previously. Recite the prayers of dedication and auspiciousness in accordance with the liturgy. Concisely engage in meditation on the stage of completion and then enter the yoga of sleep.

In the dawn session practice the visualizations, recitations, and so on for the self-generation following the way they appear in the oral recitation for the preliminaries, as explained before. If you wish to engage in six sessions, perform an early session, a later session, and one at noon, followed by another earlier and later session, and one at midnight. If you are happy

59. Tib. *Brjod med don bshags*. This appears in the fourth chapter of the *Stainless Sovereign Confessional Tantra* (*Dri med rgyal po bshags pa'i rgyud*).

with four sessions, you don't need to engage in the two sessions at noon and midnight. Whatever you do, except for the dawn session, at the end of your recitations do the complete practice of making offerings and praises, disclosing faults, and requesting the guru for empowerment, [663] on through to the recitation of the words of auspiciousness, in accordance with the liturgy in the *Fine Path*. Since it is all right to offer the ganacakra and make supplications and offerings to the guardians only once each day, you should do so in connection with your later session or your nighttime session. Even if you spend a long time lazily counting your recitations while engaging in a mere semblance of a retreat, if the stages of generation and completion are not clear, you should be disgusted with your own mind, for there is a danger that this will act as a cause for what is not Dharma—such as overturning your faith in the Dharma! So it is important that your mind be clear and pure in each session. If you strive well, signs will appear within twenty-one days.

On the final day refresh the tormas that you set forth previously with torma substances, and in the dawn session recite *The Fine Path of Primordial Consciousness*. At the end of the recitation make offerings, sing praises, disclose your faults, request empowerment from your guru, take the empowerment, and dissolve the guru into the orb between your eyebrows. Then instantly imagine the torma as actually being Chetsun and decisively view him as being of the nature of the synthesis of all the objects of refuge. Recite the verses for receiving siddhis, and at the end raise him to the crown of your head. Touch each of the three areas [of the crown, throat, and heart], and take a small taste of the torma substances. Imagine the torma deity, who is Chetsun himself, dissolving into the center of your heart, such that you instantly and completely traverse the path of the four visions. Imagine that you thereby become enlightened in the great transference vajrakāya, achieving the great siddhi, indivisible from the actual Chetsun. [664] Arouse this conviction and rest in meditative equipoise. At this point there is no need to engage in the dissolution and remanifestation as the deity, so recite the prayers of dedication and auspicious verses in accordance with the liturgy and bring your dawn session to a close.

In your morning session practice the rest of the points in a concise way, according to the oral recitation for the preliminary practices. To make amends for defects in practice, in the place of the expiating fire offering, make effective use of the practices for purifying obscurations and accumulating merit, done together with the practice for conjoining the vital energies.[60] In your later session, after you have set forth whatever ganacakra and torma offerings you have prepared, do the recitations from *The Fine Path* in concise form. Then recite seven times the vowels and consonants, the hundred-syllable mantra, and the *Essence of Dependent Origination*, followed by the offering and praise. Perform the "Inexpressible, Actual Confession." After pointedly offering the hundred ganacakras and so forth, as well as the supplication and offering to the guardians, recite the offerings, praises, and disclosure of faults, up to the words of auspiciousness. You can also recite whatever extensive prayers of dedication and auspiciousness that you wish. Then gradually bring your retreat to an end. When the later teachings were given, I didn't recall well how to end the session according to *The Fine Path*, so I needed to ask for them again, and I took notes in the guru's presence.

## b. The Unique, Essential Stage of Completion

Here there are three sections: (i) instructions for individuals of superior faculties to achieve liberation in this lifetime, (ii) instructions for individuals of middling faculties to achieve liberation in the intermediate period, and (iii) practical instructions for individuals of inferior faculties [665] to achieve liberation in a natural nirmāṇakāya buddha field.

Regarding "faculties" in this context: The innermost essence of this profound path is the practice of the spontaneously actualized direct crossing over, so one must have no eye defects. However, among those who have faith, enthusiasm, mindfulness, concentration, and wisdom, distinctions

60. Tib. *rlung sbyor*. This refers to the prāṇa practice associated with the meditation on Vajrasattva that was described above.

of supreme, middling, and inferior faculties are made specifically in terms of the degree of one's confidence, irreversible faith, and reverence toward the essential Dharma and the guru who teaches it.

## i. Instructions for Individuals of Superior Faculties to Achieve Liberation in This Lifetime

Regarding the instructions to achieve liberation in this lifetime, there are two sections: [I] the preliminary practice of cutting the basis of delusion from the root, and [II] the main practice of letting delusion release itself and then letting delusive appearances arise naturally as primordial consciousness.

## [I]. The Preliminary Practice of Cutting the Basis of Delusion from the Root

The "basis of delusion" is that which is to be dispelled by means of the reality of the path. The cause is the reality of the origin of suffering and the result is the reality of suffering. The basis and root of both is erroneous conceptualization. The nature of existence is primordially free from all signs of conceptual elaborations, but by failing to recognize that, negative attitudes arise with which one grasps to signs. Since unfathomable, beginningless time, those mental processes have arisen adventitiously in one's mindstream and remain there continually. [666] If they are not eliminated by means of the reality of the path, they will never vanish by themselves, so it is as if they are endless. Since we sentient beings have become so habituated to these negative attitudes for so very long, it seems as if they are really there and really like that. But how could this negative attitude ever occur beyond the home of what is ultimate and free of conceptual elaboration? Or else how could it be totally cut off, as in the case where, once you have arrived somewhere very far away, you can't find your way back? Or how could it be like the case where, even if you did find a path, there would be no way for you to get back to your home for a very long time?

If you grasp well even a few of the profound methods of the pith instructions, then bad thoughts that have become serious bad habits for a very long time might more easily be able to take you home to great bliss, free of conceptual elaboration, in a single instant, within a flash. For example, it is like turning over your palm or like waking from sleep. Therefore the teachings of Śrī Kālacakra say there is a way even for those who have committed the five deeds of immediate retribution in this life to achieve perfect enlightenment in this lifetime. And treatises of the Great Perfection say there is no such thing as good or bad karma and no such thing as sharp or dull faculties. [667] But the real point is how immense are the methods of secret mantra. How could claims that are incompatible with Dharma, such as "There is no disadvantage to having tremendous false views and no advantage to having great faith," ever be true?

In such degenerate times as these there are persons who are said to be realized siddhas and great contemplatives. But I worry about a lot of them. For the most part, when people recognize thoughts disappearing due to impermanence, they have the conceit of believing they have recognized the nature of the mind. In other cases, when thoughts arise they think those are delusions, and when none arise they conceitedly think they are liberated. Some people regard all good and bad thoughts as enemies, and stop trying to cultivate any virtuous mental states. Others regard all thoughts without exception as being good and proclaim the greatness of evil mental states. With the conceit of regarding all good and bad thoughts as being displays of the dharmakāya, they indulge in perverted behavior. Whatever realization of emptiness they may have due to the view and meditation, it descends into hostile incompatibility with the infallible relationship between actions and their effects. All such errors are a great disgrace to the Buddha's teachings, and for sentient beings in this final, degenerate era this is the awful behavior of kicking a corpse. [668] Apart from those who know how to spin the wheel that will arouse demons in the mind, those who have recognized the nature of the mind and who know how to meditate reject this. Moreover, those who thoroughly investigate what is meant by "delusion" are rarer than a star in the daytime.

In short, within a mere fraction of consciousness in the mindstream of a sentient being there is no beginning or end. Not only that, but the defilements that contaminate that endless continuum are undifferentiated in aspect from those very parts of consciousness, which is why the former are called "the māras that came along from before." Since they arise in this fashion of accompaniment, they are said to be of the same nature as their host mindstream, and they are connate ignorance, and so on. However, in reality, no one has a deluded mind that is forever and inwardly present in the way that connate great bliss is never either conjoined with or separated from one's mindstream. The fundamental root of defilements can undoubtedly be severed completely, so that they never arise again, even deceptively. That which severs this root could not be anything other than the extraordinary reality of the path, which is its direct antidote. What is that reality of the path? It is extraordinary wisdom. One can engage in limitless methods, each one superior to the others, including the approach to and actualization of one's personal deity, which cause the profound and vast wisdom that comes from hearing, thinking, and meditating to arise swiftly and with ease. [669] However, in this context, if you gain just a glimpse of the actual nature of your own mind and familiarize yourself with that, powerful wisdom will arise effortlessly. If you apply yourself to these crucial points (without falling under the influence of those followers of Māra who disparage them and so on), you will dispel the darkness of your mind—including obstacles on the path, such as doubts—and the authentic path will unerringly transform into wisdom. So from the very beginning apply yourself to methods for recognizing the actual nature of the mind as your own essential nature.

However, when the coarse energy-mind obscures your essential nature, even if you try many times to fathom its empty and luminous nature, it is difficult to perceive the actual nature of the mind just as it is. This is similar to the fact that it is difficult to observe the sun if the sky is covered with thick clouds, even if one tries many times. In such cases it is necessary to rely upon siddhas with experience in the pith instructions that are in accord with the vast teachings of the jinas, regarding skillful means for stopping the flow of coarse energy-mind. In dependence upon such splendid pith instructions on any of the elaborate or concise methods of the authentic generation stage practices of the unsurpassed Mantrayāna, [670] there are numerous, extraordinary methods for experiencing the clear light as the culmination of vital energies entering, remaining, and dissolving into the central channel by way of the stage of completion. But here, without needing to resort to them, there are pith instructions for directly severing delusive thoughts, which are potent and easy to practice. If you follow them correctly, delusive thoughts, along with their karmic energies, naturally cease. When that happens, whether you recognize it or not, it is inevitable that the undeluded, actual nature of the mind will nakedly emerge. The entrance to that method is the crucial point of thoroughly investigating the basis of delusion.

In this regard there are four points: purifying the body, speech, and mind, and the crucial point of cherishing them all.

Now is the time to take to heart the meaning of the empowerment that arises from the preliminary practices of the empowerment without elaborations. So go to a very solitary place and make torma and liquid offerings to the local gods in order to dispel interferences and bring about conducive conditions. Earnestly cultivate the motivation of bodhicitta, aspiring for supreme enlightenment, and after offering sincere prayers of supplication to your guru, [671] merge your mind with the guru's. Then arise suddenly in the vajra posture, visualizing your body as a blue, five-pointed vajra, blazing with swirling flames of the fire of primordial consciousness, with sparks showering outward so that nothing can overcome you, and remain like that for a little while. Then once again sit upright and while just chanting *hūṃ*, imagine that the whole of phenomenal existence is filled with the indigo syllables *hūṃ*, radiating the five lights of primordial consciousness so they completely burst into flame. Imagine that the natural sounds of those syllables resound like a thousand simultaneous thunderclaps, and then suddenly and forcefully chant *hūṃ* for a little while. Then stop all good and bad thoughts and memories in the mind and rest evenly in a state of nonconceptuality. By forcefully reciting *phaṭ*, arouse yourself from that state and take on the bodily forms of beings of the six realms. Speak with their voices. Clearly imagine all the emotions of joy, sorrow, and neutrality embraced by their minds. As these become very vivid before your mind, recite *phaṭ*, cut off mental dispersions, and rest in a state free of mental elaborations. Then repeat those steps. During interval periods, [672] if you spontaneously adopt the bodily and verbal expressions of the six kinds of sentient beings, it is also permissible for you to intensify the experience. Do not slip into distraction, sluggishness, or fantasizing.

You should do that for one to three days as a preliminary, and then apply yourself to the actual methods for purifying your body, speech, and mind.

First is the purification of your body. Although it does not arise from any kind of body—good or bad—nonetheless, while you are alive, the clear light of pristine awareness that resides at places in the body, such as the center of the heart, can become manifest if you fully master your body through the crucial points of the path. Therefore, to carry out the vajra posture, within a dwelling or wherever you like, arrange yourself comfortably on a mat such that even if you fall over you will not be injured. Earnestly meditate with the thought "I shall strive on this path so that my body does not return to saṃsāra, but rather that I may achieve the body-vajra of a buddha!"

Pray to your guru and imagine the guru's mind merging with yours. Then, standing up, place your heels together, rise a little on your toes, press them into the cushion, and spread your knees out to the sides. Straighten the small of your back, your head, and neck, extend your elbows out to the sides, and completely press your palms together just above the crown of your head.[61] The crucial point regarding the eyes is to keep them wide open and clear. Rest your consciousness in its own nature. With force, gradually exhale and powerfully compress the regions of your body [673]

61. It seems this pose would resemble a balletic *grand plié* in first position, with arms overhead in a prayer position, so that both knees and elbows form the angles of a roughly two-dimensional vajra.

together with the breath in your belly so that you tremble a little bit. If you become dizzy or feel like you are going to pass out, do not let your awareness slip into that, but rather arouse a sense of alertness. When you cannot stand it any longer and are about to faint, then stop and rest in a state of nonobjectivity. Even if you become exhausted, strive tenaciously without becoming discouraged. This is a method for stopping the movements of the vital energies and the mind, so there is no need for a lot of visualizations during this time.

On occasion, such as at dusk, if you visualize your body as a blue, five-pointed vajra, blazing with the five lights of primordial consciousness, for the time being this will protect you from harm by obstructive beings and enflame the creative power of pristine awareness. Ultimately it has the value of enabling you to attain the immutable dharmakāya, imbued with the five facets of primordial consciousness.

Moreover, the upper central prong of a three-pointed blue vajra symbolizes the dharmakāya, and the right and left prongs symbolize the rūpakāyas, namely, the sambhogakāya and nirmāṇakāya. The lower central prong symbolizes the empty essential nature, the right prong symbolizes the luminous manifest nature, and the left prong symbolizes all-pervasive compassion. Those comprise the three facets of primordial consciousness. The unification of those prongs in the single center rod of the vajra symbolizes the way in which the three facets of primordial consciousness that are present in the ground are able to bring you instantaneously to an experiential realization of the crucial points of the paths of cutting through and the direct crossing over, combined as one. And they do so through the fresh, perfecting, pristine awareness that is the reality of the path, in the essential nature of the three resultant kāyas. [674] Understanding those symbolic meanings has the value of liberating you from the fetters of grasping to saṃsāra and nirvāṇa as being utterly separate. As you meditate in either of those two ways, you should imagine that your body and mind are totally absorbed into that vajra without leaving any trace behind.

The importance of the immutable vajra posture, together with the corresponding practice, is explained very clearly according to the very final words of the *Meditation Manual of the Primordial Consciousness Guru*,[62] so you should practice well in that way. This uncommonly auspicious bodily purification is more important and valuable than such practices as prostrations, circumambulations, sacred dances, mudrās, and exercises involving the channels and vital energies. So it is in no way something insignificant or ineffectual. This is a special, proximate cause for suspending the energy-mind, identifying the actual nature of the clear light mind, and liberating your immaculate body as an embodiment of light.

Second, here is the purification for your speech. While seated upright on a comfortable cushion, earnestly arouse the thought "In order to turn my speech away from saṃsāra and to actualize it as the speech-vajra of a buddha, I shall enter this path." With heartfelt devotion and reverence to your guru, merge your mind with the guru's mind. [675] Then visualize a tiny blue *hūṃ*, blazing with five-colored lights, at your heart, in the essential nature of your guru. Imagine this as having the essential nature of the primordial consciousness that is present in the ground of being. When your consciousness is settled in a state of equilibrium, alternately recite the sound of *hūṃ* loudly and softly. If you become bored, recite it more forcefully, with vigor. If you become agitated, invoke the song of *hūṃ* more softly and slowly in accordance with your constitution. When many such utterances of *hūṃ* are emitted from your right nostril, simply by striking the objects around you, people, dwellings, and so on, imagine that they all completely turn into *hūṃ* and constantly murmur that sound. Then let your mind emanate the syllable *hūṃ* as much as you can in all directions, so that the entire physical world and its inhabitants are transformed into the form and sound of *hūṃ*. Then they are all retracted, along with their sounds. Some are drawn inside your body by way of the left nostril, while others dissolve inside from the exterior of your body, so that your body, together with the energy-mind, totally transforms into the form and sound of *hūṃ*, without leaving even the tip of a hair behind. Then the *hūṃ* syllables are withdrawn

62. Tib. *Khrid yig ye shes bla ma*, a work by Jigmed Lingpa, *Yeshe Lama*. See also Dowman, *The Yeshe Lama*.

into the primary *hūṃ*, which withdraws into absolute space, and you rest. Continue practicing until you have a sense that whatever appears to consciousness after your meditation arises as *hūṃ*. [676]

If that does not cut off your previous tendency for reification, or if you cling to the appearances of *hūṃ*, imagine many blazing indigo *hūṃ* syllables of all different sizes being emitted from your heart as an ordinary person, all of them more powerful than meteorite vajra thunderbolts. Imagine that they utterly demolish your natural body, vital energies, mind, and habitual propensities, as well as the entire outer physical world, until finally even the *hūṃ* syllables dissolve right where they are, and all phenomena become of one taste with the great emptiness of the absolute space of phenomena. Let your awareness rest in meditative equipoise in that state, without grasping. You must continue striving in this practice until you have a sense of all subsequent appearances arising evanescently as shards of clear emptiness.

This extraordinary verbal practice is the supreme method for cutting through, by forceful means, the cords of a mind that reifies objects, and it is swifter than other practices for conjoining the vital energies—such as the vajra recitation, the great vase breathing, and so on—and it is also swifter than other verbal recitations and chanting. So you must recognize this as a proximate cause for dissolving the body and mind away like mist.

Third is the purification of your mind. While sitting upright on a comfortable cushion, [677] earnestly arouse the thought "In order to turn my mind away from saṃsāra and to actualize it as the mind-vajra of a buddha, I shall identify the actual nature of the mind." With heartfelt devotion and reverence, single-pointedly pray to your guru and merge your mind with that of the guru. With your body and mind loose and relaxed from within, without letting your mind be distracted elsewhere, consider: "Simply due to the adventitious configuration of various individual causes and conditions, and due to mutual, dependent relationships, all the limitless instances of good and bad phenomena of saṃsāra and nirvāṇa appear to be separate, in the manner of causes and effects, in all the various ways they do. However they manifest, in all possible arrays, they are all nothing more than mental projections or creations, for in reality nothing is established as real even to the tiniest degree. While the mind, too, has no existence apart from being a mere mental imputation, it clearly seems to exist, and it distinctly gives rise to one unprecedented good, bad, and neutral thought after another. Once present, they cease and vanish, constantly giving way to new ones."

You may wonder, how do these things first arise? [678] Perception occurs due to the mere confluence of the presence of an object nearby, undamaged sensory faculties, and a ceaseless flow of consciousness that can manifest appearances. But since, apart from something like illusory people and so on, which do not exist, yet clearly appear, it is impossible to determine with certainty that these emerge solely from any one cause, they are empty of causality. In the meantime, how do they remain? However long these mere appearances of nonexistent entities may seem to last, they are only facsimiles of the gestures of illusory people and so on, but in reality nothing is there. So thoughts are empty of their own essential nature. Finally, when you consider how things pass away, those adventitious conceptual fabrications that never started and are nowhere present appear to pass away, due to destructive conditions. However, just as illusory horses, elephants, and so forth do not arise again after they have disappeared, so are there no subsequent conceptual fabrications of a similar type that are the proper consequences of earlier ones, which have already disappeared. So they are empty of consequences.

Therefore, however much mere appearances that are empty of causes, consequences, and an essential nature may arise in the aspects of the birth, cessation, and abiding of a deceptive mind—or else in the aspects of its origin, location, and destination—[679] from the very moment they arise, ultimately such movements and transformations have never existed. Recognition of that is known as *realization of the actual nature of the mind.*

To the extent that you familiarize yourself with this, the impulses that are to be ended by Dharma practitioners—namely, defiled, negative thoughts of confusion, attachment, hostility, and so on—are purified, and that which is to be accomplished—namely, the stainless virtues of faith, enthusiasm, compassion, wisdom, and so on—naturally increase. Since this is infallible, if you correctly fathom it according to what is ultimate, not only will you not dismiss the dependent relationships of deceptive reality, but you will also certainly be able to practice correctly abandoning and accepting what should be avoided and adopted, respectively. Since it has to be this way, this pith instruction on purifying your mind is far more profound than striving in other practices. This is the great, unmistaken pillar of the excellent path to liberation and omniscience, and it is an indispensable method for experiencing the originally pure, pristine awareness of the Great Perfection. So fortunate people who do not veer away from this Dharma should practice it with great reverence.

Fourth is the crucial point of cherishing them all. [680] On this occasion for determining the ultimate mode of existence of the actual nature of the mind it is necessary to expel the conceptual fabrications that are to be abandoned, along with the objects to which they cling, as they have no basis and no root. In addition, as soon as you have performed the purifications of the body, speech, and mind, determine that all your efforts on any of the defiled and undefiled paths indicated, including the stage of generation and stage of completion, are not established as real in the absolute space of phenomena, the nature of existence. Thus come to rest decisively in the place where there is nothing upon which to focus.

In this way, all these activities in which you apply remedies to that which is to be abandoned, in which you negate and affirm, are merely illusory in the way that they appear. They are methods for liberating the mindstreams of unrealized—that is, deluded—sentient beings. But like the unfolding of a marvelous, illusory drama, from the very moment at which the slightest part of any such appearance has not yet stopped, it is of the same taste as a mere dance of the totally pure absolute space of phenomena and of the clear light. To know this, and to retain your mindful awareness in the manner of your own naturally settled stronghold, without wavering from the absolute space of phenomena, is like the life-force channel upholding the ultimate crucial point of the path of the Great Perfection. So, without mixing this up with other philosophical systems, strive in every way to follow your own path correctly. [681] You should practice until you have determined that the consciousness of the agent who performs those many different practices of the body, speech, and mind has no basis and no root. At the conclusion of each of your meditation sessions offer pure prayers of dedication, and even between sessions continually practice by applying firm mindfulness, introspection, and conscientiousness, without pretense, in order to sustain the flow of each of your practices.

# 5 Original Purity

## [II]. The Main Practice of Letting Delusion Release Itself and Then Letting Delusive Appearances Arise Naturally as Primordial Consciousness

Here there are two sections: [A] the practice of the original purity of the essential nature, and [B] the practice of the spontaneous actualization of your own appearances.

## [A]. The Practice of the Original Purity of the Essential Nature

The main practices of the Great Perfection entail nothing more than taking unmodified, naked, pristine awareness as the path. In the context of this ultrasecret, unsurpassed class of pith instructions, since there has never been any delusion, there is nothing to do in terms of achieving some new liberation by means of the path. Within a state of meditative equipoise upon the essential nature of primordially free pristine awareness, the method for releasing, of its accord, the energy-mind that has fallen into delusion, due to adventitious contamination by obscuring stains, is the path of cutting through. The method for experiencing one's own stainless appearances that follow upon the essential nature of pristine awareness, without ever being separated from it, [682] is the path of the direct crossing over. The latter of these two paths cannot be accurately determined by means of the cycles of outer, inner, or secret teachings,[63] and this is its distinguishing characteristic.

The first of those two paths is the practice of original purity, and here there are three sections: [1] decisive understanding by way of the view, [2] practice by way of meditation, and [3] enhancement by way of conduct.

## [1]. Decisive Understanding by Way of the View

The mystery of the mind, pristine awareness itself, without being modified by anyone, primordially without basis or root, is the great expanse, utterly transcending all signs of substantiality and devoid of conceptual elaborations. So its essential nature is said to be empty.

The manifest nature of pristine awareness is far superior to the "substrate," for the substrate consciousness, and so on, is said to be the basis for all manner of adventitious good and bad habitual propensities. This manifest nature of pristine awareness is also superior to a mind devoid of concepts, and to other ethically neutral, nonconceptual states like the five modes of sensory consciousness. Its unchanging, natural luminosity is primordially free from all the defilements of conceptuality and obscurations. From the moment it is experienced, the aspect of its unmodified, original, essential nature that cognizes in the manner of an inner luminosity is the spontaneously actualized great being that arises on its own. [683] So its manifest nature is said to be luminosity.

Rather than emptiness and luminosity being present merely in a manner of mutual interdependence, it is all-pervasively impossible for them to waver even the slightest bit from the essential nature of the one taste, primordially inseparable. The outwardly luminous primordial consciousness that is the natural creativity of the great union of pristine awareness and emptiness—unchanging and sublime—is utterly free of bias or partiality.

63. Tib. *gsang skor man chod*. The meaning is that the direct crossing over can be fathomed only in terms of the cycle of ultrasecret teachings and not the outer, inner, or secret teachings.

If you realize it, you are a buddha, and if you don't, you are a sentient being. Unceasing, it is that from which all manner of phenomenal worlds, along with all that move upon them, are able to emerge. In its basic nature, it is primordially omnipresent and all-encompassing, without being located anywhere at all. So it is called all-pervasive compassion.

All phenomena that appear as such creative expressions are distinct, without being merged together, but they are none other than the very nature of existence, the union of pristine awareness and emptiness. So the three aspects [of emptiness, luminosity, and all-pervasive compassion] are said to be the great indivisibility.

This is not an emptiness that is left over as a trace after reification has been destroyed, nor is it the clear mind of the one who understands that, nor is it something trifling like the mere union of an object that comes first and a subject that comes later. [684] The essential nature of pristine awareness, free of conceptual elaborations, which cannot be altered by anything, has always been empty. It is free of the intellect, self-emergent, inwardly luminous, and its nature is not designed by anyone. Not only have distinct things—such as objects that come first and subjects that come later—always been inseparable, but what buddha or sentient being could ever make anything empty, or make anything luminous, or join those two together? That which is unmodified, unified, and unchanging, which does not have the slightest need to be made or joined, cannot be identified by any adventitious intellect (such as one that apprehends the mere absence of true existence), let alone by an intellect that grasps onto true existence! Even if it could, what would be the use?

So even though there is not the slightest indication of something to be realized and something that realizes it, it is identified within itself. All faults of wondering about such things as what it is and what it is not are cut off naturally from within. So there is no room for vacillating uncertainty. But if this does not occur, what is the point of merely imputing the conceptual label of "original purity" on anything? The best is to realize it as it is. Middling is for there to arise a fine experience of it within yourself. At the very least it is imperative [685] to gain a resolute understanding of the secret, crucial point, which is entirely unlike other mentally contrived philosophical systems involving signs.

Moreover, if a qualified student and teacher meet, it has occurred in the past, and still takes place now, that at the time of the empowerment and such, pointing-out instructions are given as well. Even if it doesn't happen just so, then by way of this compilation of pith instructions, if those who explain and listen to the teachings, from the preliminary practices up to this point, sincerely put them into practice—and don't just give lip service to them—they will certainly gain insight with these methods. In particular, it is better to practice one short session with fine reverence and devotion for the guru than to perform other mind trainings for a long time. So, without indulging in a lot of rumination, it is certainly sufficient to practice this one method for realizing the actual nature of the mind, with a singular attitude of reverence and devotion to the guru. If you strive at all times and in all ways, there will be great benefit, with no downside whatsoever. On the other hand, if you place your hopes in what some god, demon, or old guy has to say, or in some divination, who knows what will happen?

If you spout off about there being no one who views and nothing to view, the phenomenon and the individual would be torn away from one another, so what would there be to realize? Such people definitely turn their backs on Dharma. [686] Therefore apply yourself to offering fine prayers for your authentic realization of the actual nature of the mind from now on through the rest of your life.

## [2]. Practice by Way of Meditation

From the time that pristine awareness is first recognized until you awaken as a buddha to the inner luminosity within primordial, absolute space, without modifying or contaminating awareness with any other thoughts or practices, you should practice continually day and night so that your meditation proceeds to the crucial point.

Without engaging in various physical activities of trying to change and avert things while moving about from here to there, by remaining firmly in one place, like a mountain, establish a foundation in meditation. This will later result in the body feeling relaxed and comfortable. So sit upright and rest your gaze steadily in front of you. When you silence your speech and rest your awareness without wavering, your vital energies will naturally flow freely. When you feel your awareness is becoming contaminated by a sense of laxity, forcefully direct your attention while breathing out from your mouth, and hold the vital energies on the outside until you cannot stand it any longer. When a sense of excitation arises, gently hold the vase breath and forcefully direct your energy-mind inward. "Forcefully directing your attention" [687] means immersing your energy-mind in absolute space, and in this phase of practice you may immerse your energy-mind in pristine awareness.

Since the energies and mind move together, if the vital energies are agitated, the mind will vacillate and be disturbed like the waves on the ocean. When the vital energies calm down, the mind is no longer dispersed, like the ocean free of waves. It is the vital energies that move the body and mind, so these energies are of crucial importance. During the initial practice of open presence, if you do not hold your own ground, insofar as you succumb to good and bad agitations, the power of the vital energies will increase. That impairs the intermediate practice of open presence. The disturbance of body and mind by the vital energies obscures the recognition of pristine awareness, so that realization will not come forth and meditation will be uncomfortable. So that impairs the final practice of open presence. For this reason it is important to rest your body, speech, and mind effortlessly. What is more, this final practice of open presence is the vital core of this path. The recognition—by way of understanding, experience, or realization—of the primordial nature of being, the self-illuminating, immutable inseparability of absolute space and pristine awareness, naturally arises free of all modification or contamination by the intellect. So it is imperative to fathom the depths of the practice, penetrating to the ground and root of being, [688] by engaging in such meditation alone.

If you practice even one short session in which pristine awareness is left unmodified, in the freshness of its autonomy, during that time whatever good or bad, subtle or coarse, long or short creative displays of awareness appear, do not cling or grasp to them. Don't even examine them. Rather, release them into nonobjectivity. Then there will be no place or basis for the arising of hope, or fear, or reification. Without basis, it will be impossible for anything to arise as anything other than its own natural purity, so it is fine not to engage in any judgments about the way to liberation.

Once the power of the creative displays of pristine awareness has been perfected, you achieve clarity and stability in ever-increasing ways. If, in order to achieve the culmination of irreversible stability, you meditate without being separated even for an instant from the three types of open presence, then, to the extent that you attain clarity and stability with respect to pristine awareness, all contamination by the deluded aspects of the mind—which are expressions of pristine awareness—will be purified effortlessly. Simultaneously, karmic energies will naturally be purified, the purified energy-mind will be empowered, and the defilements of the body, [689] including knots in the channels of the material body, will gradually be released. When they are completely purified, your body will be impervious to injury and so on. In short, all appearances and mental states will be naturally immersed in pristine awareness, so everything you do will arise as the authentic path, and your own appearances will come under your own power and will emerge even though you do not strive at them.

Suppose you think that because all-pervasive compassion is inseparable from the three aspects [of emptiness, luminosity, and pervasive compassion] it makes no difference whether you are looking out at the dawning of the creative displays or whether you take cutting their root basis and such as the path. But this is tantamount to seeking the branches after casting away the root. Or it is like not knowing that the elephant is inside; or even if you do know, not being satisfied with that, and then seeking its footprints outside, hoping there might be something there to help you find the elephant. This attitude leads you far from the main practice of the path.

In short, when you do not hold your ground solely by means of open presence in pristine awareness, then for the main practice of the path of cutting through itself, with what other mind will you hold it? If you think that this is similar to each of the various states of mind involved in taking emptiness as the path through the respective methods of mental investigation, constraining the vital energies, or melting into bliss, then what difference would there be between the path of the Great Perfection and other paths? [690] Not only are those other methods not on a par with open presence in pristine awareness, they are not even close! Not only that, when you waver from the creative expressions of pristine awareness, the energy-mind associated with those creative displays extends out to each of those objects. By falling under the domination of each of those negative habitual propensities and by clinging to each of their objects, how can your mind avoid becoming afflicted? If you make fine distinctions by analyzing the essential nature of pristine awareness with each moment of the conscious aspect of its creative expressions, this will also prevent you from apprehending the unmodified, natural state of pristine awareness just as it is. So rest in open presence within the freshness of pristine awareness, free of conceptualization.

Whatever meditative experiences of pristine awareness and whatever mental states arise [along the path of śamatha], due to the arousal of various vital energies, many positive and negative experiences arise, including bliss, luminosity, and nonconceptuality; powerful craving and hostility; the empty forms associated with the ten signs [of dissolution of the vital energies into the heart cakra]; as well as visions of deities and of demons. Of course there are individuals for whom these arise and others for whom they do not. When they do arise, if you follow after them, like a child who trips over stones and falls down when chasing after a rainbow, what can there be but frustration! So you must rest in the one taste of everything within pristine awareness, free of all hope and fear. [691]

Those who indulge in many hopes and fears, in joys and sorrows regarding the whole array of yogic experiences, and who talk about them to others as well, do not hold to the practice or fathom what it's about, so they show that they are bums. Of what use are they? Although you know a lot, if you don't have much to say, what great fault is there in that? Regarding the term "nonmeditation" in the Great Perfection and so on, when the nature of being is realized, if you rest in meditative equipoise in this, you don't seek after other meditations involving signs. And when you accustom yourself to such meditative equipoise and perfect your ability in it, even if you do not meditate intentionally, the benefits of meditation increase spontaneously or automatically. But this term ["nonmeditation"] does not mean that you don't practice at all. Although it is said that it is possible for some fortunate people who have trained in the past to gain realization and familiarization all at once, how could they ever do so by means of mental wandering that is not in accord with Dharma? Moreover, for all those who are said to have gained liberation, when they truly apply themselves so that there is no discrepancy between the Dharma and the individual, then such freedom arises. That is the meaning. This does not imply that if they are not liberated at that time, there is no time when they will be liberated, or that they never need to practice at all from that time forward. [692]

Therefore it is wrong to talk of "nonmeditation" while disgracing yourself by wasting your life. In accordance with the sublime masters of the past who meditated with great courage in applying themselves to the difficulties of practice, both realization and familiarity certainly come. So now, while you are healthy and have the opportunity, you should continue meditating until you die, regardless of whether or not realizations arise, and earnestly offer noble prayers that you may be so fortunate as to meditate continually until you achieve enlightenment.

## [3]. Enhancement by Way of Conduct

Although there are many types of conduct that are supportive to the view and meditation of cutting through, in brief, you must—as your foundation—avoid all unwholesome thoughts and behavior. If you strive in the difficulties of strenuous practices of body, speech, and mind other than this one, which is the consummate virtue and the extraordinary method for cutting through the flow of nonvirtue, then any movements of the energy-mind toward those objects will turn into obstacles for the stabilization and flourishing of pristine awareness. Therefore, in light of this special phase of practice, rest all positive and negative coarse movements and efforts involving the energy-mind in their naturally indwelling state, [693] and constantly engage in the conduct of resting unwaveringly in absolute space and pristine awareness. Like a king holding fast to his own domain, this conscientious conduct, as well as the secret conduct in which you take all the phenomena that appear as good or bad to be of one inseparable taste within pristine awareness, is the one perfect method. Training in this is the indispensable, essential accompaniment for the main practice. So both during sessions and between sessions gradually let go of the nine kinds of activities.[64] However, if you disdain the teachings from all the yānas regarding effortful practices involved with what is to be accepted and rejected, thinking that they are of no benefit and have no significance, it is wrong to indulge in such thoughts even for an instant. People who are not completely satisfied with this supreme, conceptually unelaborated practice alone may also occasionally apply themselves to other pure, virtuous practices of their choice between sessions.

64. Tib. *bya ba dgu sprugs*. The nine kinds of activity include the body's (1) outer activities, such as walking, sitting, and moving about, (2) inner activities of prostrations and circumambulations, and (3) secret activities of ritual dancing, performing mudrās, and so on; the speech's (4) outer activities, such as all kinds of delusional chatter, (5) inner activities, such as reciting liturgies, and (6) secret activities, such as counting propitiatory mantras of your personal deity; and the mind's (7) outer activities, such as thoughts aroused by the five poisons and the three poisons, (8) inner activities of mind training and cultivating positive thoughts, and (9) the secret activity of dwelling in mundane states of dhyāna.

# 6 Spontaneous Actualization

## [B]. The Practice of the Spontaneous Actualization of Your Own Appearances

Related to and following the previous practice, in the swift path of the direct crossing over, by which delusive appearances arise as the natural appearances of primordial consciousness, there are three parts: [694] [1] a brief explanation of the secret, crucial point of the spontaneously actualized clear light, [2] how to apply that to the path, and [3] auxiliary pith instructions for dispelling obstacles.

## [1]. A Brief Explanation of the Secret, Crucial Point of the Spontaneously Actualized Clear Light

The central road for the swift path of unsurpassed Vajrayāna, and all the steps of the stage of generation—method—consist of taking the aspect of the rūpakāya of a primordial consciousness deity as the path. By such means you principally purify the obscurations, and so on, which pertain to the body, and either in this lifetime, in the transitional phase of becoming, or else in the transitional phase of birth, you gain liberation. Reciting the mantra of each deity, along with the rest of the various practices, can be subsumed under the triad of approach, actualization, and activity. On that basis, with the profound stage of completion—wisdom—you take the mind of your personal deity as your dharmakāya path. In that way, you principally purify your energy-mind, and by so doing you gain liberation in this lifetime or in the transitional phase of dying. These are like a unitary system.

As for achieving the fruition while on the path, your kāya of primordial consciousness gradually flourishes: from the illusory body that is connected with realization of and familiarization with the approximate and actual clear light, to the union of the two while still in training, all the way to the great union of the two with no more training. This is one system of practice, and then there are the many versions of how to achieve the states of the four vidyādharas,[65] [695] each one as though more profound than the other.

Here, however, in dependence upon a splendid synchronicity of interdependence between the disciple's reverence, devotion, and so on, and an extraordinary method of introduction—the guru's blessings and empowerment—then, in accordance with the degree of your merit, you identify the sublime mystery of the mind, the actual nature of your mind as the dharmakāya. By sustaining that recognition, the impurities of your energy-mind, together with the defilements of your body, speech, and mind, are purified. In the best of cases, you reach manifest enlightenment in this life. Below that, you reach it when the clear light of emptiness dawns during the transitional phase of dying, making the state of enlightenment manifest in the great, lofty expanse, solely by cutting through to original, inner, absolute space. So even without cultivating the direct crossing over, it is possible to progress to the culmination of the path.

On the one hand, there is the intent of the tantras concerning the way to enter the direct crossing over, in which you do so after you have achieved liberation of whichever type by abiding with stability in the originally pure primordial consciousness of emptiness. On the other hand, there is a way to enter the indivisible, single taste by means of the very subtle inner luminosity: where, with respect to the spontaneously actualized manifest nature of the originally pure essential nature, the unimpeded openness of

65. Nyingma tantras describe four levels of vidyādharas, which are, in ascending order of realization, a matured vidyādhara, a vidyādhara with mastery over life, a Mahāmudrā vidyādhara, and a spontaneously actualized vidyādhara.

the aspect of cognizance that resides in the ground is the essential nature of the dharmakāya of primordial consciousness, and [696] the unimpeded openness of the aspect of appearances residing in the ground is the essential nature of the rūpakāyas. In dependence upon words, understanding occurs, and that is indicated with symbols. When, from the very beginning, the crucial points of (1) the method that makes manifest great visionary experiences of stainless, spontaneous actualization through forceful means, (2) the senses, (3) their objective fields, (4) the vital energies, and (5) awareness are all in tune, for fortunate disciples who are introduced to the appearances of light, it is impossible for such a disciple not to perceive the luminous appearances of empty form.

Although the Kālacakra system discusses pure, empty forms and their mode of appearance, apart from that it makes no reference to the vajra strands, kāyas, lamps of the empty bindus, or palaces: those appearances of light from the inner and outer pure absolute space, which have the essential nature of buddha fields. The Great Perfection tantras do not even speak of the manner in which many forms of female deities arise, let alone the need for delighting in bliss with a lady mudrā of light.[66] These are different paths: one that is effortful and the other effortless. (1) The empty forms that are signs of the vital energies, which arise adventitiously due to practices of retention on the path of skillful means, and (2) what arises as outer luminosity on the basis of methods involving the radiance of indwelling, pristine awareness, have essential natures that are different. [697] This is a fundamental point.

Therefore if disciples who directly perceive the experiential visions of the direct crossing over meditate without uncertainty, according to their guru's instructions, they will clearly see luminous displays of the indwelling kāyas and buddha fields that abide in the ground, at the center of the heart. That is known as the *citta lamp of the flesh*. The pathway of outer movement or dispersion, the crystal kati channel, is wound around by its fine, hollow, tube-like branches, called the *white silken threads*. These come

66. Tib. *'od kyi phyag rgya ma*. This is a female partner made of light, such as the mudrā of empty form discussed in *Kālacakratantra*.

to the eyes and are known as the *soft, white channel lamp*. The light channel that is the aperture for what emerges outward, whether it be open or closed, remains in openness, free of obscuration, without blocking the luminous visions. It is known as the *fluid lasso lamp*. The indwelling vital energies that make the empty, hollow, luminous channels remain straight, and that emit or activate the luminous visions there, are known as the *vital energies that are the life force of wisdom*. All of those are distinct from one another, but they are not experienced as being anything other than the primordial consciousness of the essential nature of pristine awareness. So even if you haven't previously perceived originally pure, great emptiness, due to the crucial point of the infallible truth of the actual nature of reality, [698] in this phase of taking the luminous visions as the path, you will see it as it is. This is another way into the intent of the tantras.

Forcefully directing your attention to the absolute space of phenomena, the nonconceptual, great reality that transcends the intellect, free of conceptual elaborations, together with its luminous visions and the conscious awareness of them, brings you to the culmination point of extinction, and that is the ultimate, crucial point of the path. But solely by resting in the naturally settled, essential nature of pristine awareness, you hold your ground without wavering from absolute space. Without having a superior mind and without robust familiarization, this is difficult. However, through mindful consciousness of the fresh, creative displays of pristine awareness, without conceptual investigation, let alone clinging to the luminous visions, you will naturally settle in pristine awareness. That is one way, and it synthesizes the crucial points of the principal path of cutting through.

As you gaze out with fresh, mindful consciousness toward the strands that are the creative displays of pristine awareness, this awareness is free of bias and prejudice, and it must not grasp to extremes such as the interior and exterior of the body, let alone view the luminous visions whose essential nature is that of the kāya of primordial consciousness as being made of matter. In order not to waver from the transparent luminosity of absolute space inside the lamps of the empty bindus, [699] intently focus on them with single-pointed, forceful attention, as if your eyes and vital energies were dissolving into them. If you accustom yourself to that, the more stability you gain, the more the stability of your inner pristine awareness will naturally increase. This is one way to synthesize the crucial points of the principal path of spontaneous actualization.

In any case, on the path of the originally pure essential nature, reduce yourself to nakedness, and this will bring you to the state of liberation in ultimate, absolute space. That must be experienced effortlessly. If the culmination of the four visions is not reached in this life by meditating on the direct crossing over, when the clear light of appearance dawns in the intermediate period, there are means to take that as the path. If you train your mind in those methods from now on, it will be very easy to be liberated, for there is an interval between your previous and subsequent coarse bodies. This period, before your subsequent mental body arises in the transitional phase of becoming, is the proper time at which it is very easy to connect to the basis for liberation, original purity.

The Great Perfection tantras' presentation of a buddha's self-appearing sambhogakāya made its way to Tibet, and even now there is no evidence of such a presentation in other available tantras. [700] However, only an omniscient mind knows what kinds of tantras may have existed before—whether in India or in other regions—and only an omniscient mind can fathom what kinds of presentations they may have contained. If you think that those who achieve enlightenment from other paths have no self-appearing sambhogakāya, this would seem very implausible, for it is certain that all the many, limitless arrays of the pure lands of the jinas are indivisibly of one taste. This would be like saying that the great transference vajrakāya is a characteristic unique to the culmination of the direct crossing over. Who but a buddha can fathom what a buddha knows?

Thus, ever so mysterious, spontaneously actualized primordial consciousness, the great clear light that naturally appears as the kāyas and buddha fields, uncontaminated by defilements and free of partiality, is naturally present within the being of disciples. This ultimate, swift path that is a method for taking this clear light directly into the path right now, in this instant, by way of the direct crossing over, is found nowhere else, and it is unsurpassed. So devote yourself to practicing this path with the faith and reverence that come from knowing that to be so. [701]

## [2]. How to Apply That to the Path

The way to take up the actual path into practice is as follows. You strike the crucial points of body, speech, and mind, and by means of those three crucial points, the essential nature of the clear light kāyas and facets of primordial consciousness that abide within you become direct visions during the path. These will bring you to the place of primordial extinction. The crucial points of the body are the dharmakāya posture, which is like that of a proud lion, the sambhogakāya posture, which is like a reclining elephant, and the nirmāṇakāya posture, which is the posture of a squatting ṛṣi who is meditating. Carefully study the unmistaken, personal instructions that are the innermost essence of the meaning of the tantras, and without ever moving from one of these three postures, and without succumbing to even the slightest movement, strive in this practice continually day and night.

The crucial point for the speech is to terminate all vocalization, draw the lower vital energies upward, and restrain them to an appropriate degree. Forcefully expel the upper energy from your mouth and gently hold it. [702] When you inhale again, do so very slowly, and when you exhale, do so with a bit of force, and practice this continually for a long time without distraction.

The crucial point for the mind is to singularly recognize and decisively ascertain the self-illumination and self-appearances that come from having been introduced to primordial consciousness, your own pristine awareness. Without analyzing it, rest without modification as you are brought to the ultimate state of the originally pure, absolute space of naturally present, empty, pristine awareness. Even if you haven't already realized the essential nature of pristine awareness, intensely let your mind focus on the center, or interior, of the luminous appearances in general and the vajra strands in particular, as though entering further and further into them.

Without engaging in even the slightest bit of grasping to signs involving investigation or analysis, such as hope or fear, affirmation or negation, and by letting your consciousness dissolve into them and merge with them, the vajra strands will withdraw into absolute space. Gradually practicing the method for this to occur is a sublime, crucial point.

The crucial points regarding the object, the basis of appearances, are as follows. In general, the sky should be free of dust and pollution. In particular, during the daytime the support for the dharmakāya is to direct your gaze one hand-span,[67] one cubit, or one arrow-length beneath the sun, free of clouds. At night, the support for the sambhogakāya is to direct your gaze at the center of the moon, free of clouds, and the support for the nirmāṇakāya is to direct your gaze at the center of a clear, unflickering butter lamp. [703]

Even if you don't find the objective conditions, it is important that you rely on the crucial points of the object, without ever being separated from them, until the visionary experiences arise of their own accord. Moreover, you should primarily focus on the object that accords with your psychophysical constitution, including your eyes, and for which the five-colored lights most easily arise, increase, and stabilize. There is also a tradition of meditating in a dark room with a small hole through which light enters.

The crucial points concerning the apertures by which appearances arise are as follows. The apertures by which consciousness sees visual forms are the unimpaired pupils. If, with physical visual organs that are impaired by some adventitious defect, you can't see even ordinary, nearby objects, whether large or small, then how could you ever see the visions of meditative experience? But if even those who have extrasensory vision accomplished by way of the dhyānas cannot see these visionary appearances that are beyond what appear adventitiously to the senses, then it is not necessarily the case that ordinary people lack the aperture by which to see the visions. Rather, the natural radiance of pristine awareness, from the indestructible orb in the center of the heart, comes up to the eyes through

67. This is the distance from the tip of one's thumb to the tip of one's middle finger on a widely stretched hand, equal to twelve finger-widths.

the great channel of primordial consciousness, and by that means you see directly the undefiled visions of light.

Therefore, by familiarizing yourself [704] with the dharmakāya gaze, in which you direct both eyes slightly upward, remain with your awareness focused on the vajra strands and you will see the appearances of the three kāyas during the path come to their culmination. By familiarizing yourself with the sambhogakāya gaze, in which you direct both eyes straight ahead, and then, pressing slightly downward, slowly glance to the sides, you will directly see the self-appearances of the indwelling, actual nature of reality. The karmic energies will naturally stop moving, and the essential nature of primordial consciousness will emerge and proliferate, resulting in the clear manifestation of many major and minor bindus. By familiarizing yourself with the nirmāṇakāya gaze, in which you squint while directing your gaze slightly downward, the delusive appearances of things being distinct and differentiated will cease, and you will never be separated from the appearances of the actual nature of reality that are naturally present in pristine awareness.

Thus, while practicing any of the three gazes, let your eyes come to rest naturally, without focusing them too strongly, without blinking, and without moving them around. Continue striving day and night until the luminous visions spontaneously arise even when you are not holding these gazes. [705] When luminous visions of any size directly appear in the five colors, do not waver from that gaze. If they are predominantly white, shift your eyes slightly to the right and concentrate. If they are predominantly yellow, turn your eyes upward. If they are predominantly red, turn your eyes downward. If they are predominantly green, turn your eyes to the left. If they are predominantly indigo, focus on the center and concentrate.

If the visions of light arise in vertical shapes, direct your eyes downward. If they arise horizontally, direct them back in front of you. If they are round, turn your eyes to the left. If they are rectangular, turn your eyes to the right. If they are semicircular, look upward. If they are triangular, look downward. If their design is like a mass of lines, a lotus, a pavilion, a castle, a hoop, or a swirl of bliss, focus your gaze on them without wavering. In order to stabilize the experiential visions, focus your consciousness and the pupils of your eyes single-pointedly on the vajra strands alone, and once the vajra strands have entered inside the visions of light, it is a sublime, crucial point that you try not to waver from them. [706]

In order to increase the luminous visions, slowly move your gaze up and down and from right to left. Once they have arisen in the morning, turn to the south, and once they have subsided in the evening, direct your gaze to the north. But once the visions have arisen in the morning, women should turn to the north, and once the visions have subsided in the evening, women should turn to the south. If they are unclear, focus again on the crucial points of the object and know how to adjust your gaze gradually so that the clear visions do not diminish.

In order for the lamp of the empty bindus to arise easily, let the intensity of both your eyes be equal and let your gaze be even. Since the experiential visions are objects of sensory perception, it is important that you strike the crucial points regarding the apertures by which they arise. Now those of us who use imagination as the path may occasionally rehearse a facsimile of the practice differentiating [saṃsāra and nirvāṇa],[68] but apart from those times, for as long as you meditate on the main practice of the great, supreme mystery of the direct crossing over to the clear light, in all your sessions you should remain in one of the physical postures and gently keep your eyes solely in one of the gazes without veering from it the slightest bit. [707] Cease all speech as if you were mute, and mentally avoid any investigation or analysis of the outer or inner absolute space and pristine awareness. Resting in your natural state, hold fast to the foundation of the practice.

Even between sessions move your body as little as possible, and when you move do so slowly and in a relaxed manner. Cut off all verbal articulation. As for mental inquiry, practice focusing directly, without letting your eyes wander, on the vajra strands. As for the qualities of the place to

68. Tib. *ru shan dbye ba*. This refers to *'khor 'das ru shan*, the direct-crossing-over practice of differentiating saṃsāra from nirvāṇa with respect to one's body, speech, and mind.

practice, least desirable is a low-lying region where you can't see much sky, where the views to the east and west are limited, and the high mountains to the east and west make it necessary to look upward to see the rays of the sun. If the region is a little elevated, you can see a bit more of the sky, the views to the east and west are more expansive, and if the nearby mountains are not too high, you have to look up only a little to see the sun. Such a region is okay. If the region where you live is on a mountain peak, for instance, so that you have a vast view of the sky, you can see a great distance to the east and west, and the mountains in those directions are low enough that you can see the rays of the sun by looking straight across, that is best. [708]

If your physical constitution has a prominent heat element and if you are very prone to mental laxity, you should emphasize the dharmakāya posture and gaze. If your constitution is mixed or balanced in terms of hot and cold elements and you are alternately prone to laxity and excitation, apply yourself to the sambhogakāya posture and gaze. If the cold element is dominant and you are especially prone to excitation, primarily practice the nirmāṇakāya posture and gaze.

Here is the crucial point concerning how absolute space and pristine awareness arise. The root is the inner absolute space: the originally pure essential nature of the actual nature of the mind—eternal, primordial consciousness, great emptiness, the great, primordially present, pervasive expanse, free of conceptual elaboration. The pristine awareness that is inner luminosity, the spontaneously actualized manifest nature—unconditioned primordial consciousness—dissolves without becoming dimmed. The basis for the emergence of compassion is unimpeded primordial consciousness, all-pervasive pristine awareness, which transcends all bias and partiality and which is primordially and naturally present as the essential nature of bodhicitta.

This unobstructed, naked instant of one's own self-cognizant, pristine awareness, which has the character of that essential nature, manifest nature, and compassion, utterly pervades every superior, middling, and inferior sentient being of any of the six realms, [709] every yogin who dwells on the bodhisattva grounds and paths, and every buddha endowed with the twofold purity. Its essential nature is devoid of even a trace of any variation in terms of being positive or negative, increasing or decreasing, and never for even an instant does it form or disintegrate. If anyone on the path realizes and becomes familiar with this, which has always been connately present in a manner that is sublime, unchanging, and immutable, that person will swiftly be liberated.

Ordinary people who do not realize or familiarize themselves with it will inevitably and immediately proceed helplessly into endless delusion. So the fundamental taproot, so to speak, of both liberation and delusion is the inner absolute space and pristine awareness. From that arise lucid, clear forms of light bearing various colors that are the outer manifestations of absolute space and pristine awareness. These arise abundantly as lucid objects of direct sensory perception. The radiance of pristine awareness appears as vajra strands like a horse's tail or braided threads of gold, adorned with many fine lines. Those are not established as being anything more than the mere appearance of empty forms, so they do not exist apart from absolute space. Nevertheless, if you correctly take as the path all the [710] outer and inner divisions of the lamp of the empty bindus and the lamp of the pristine space of awareness, which arise naturally in their complete luminosity, without confusion, then from the perspective of what you have not yet realized, you will not need to resort to any other method of the path for abandoning or transforming all the delusive appearances of subjects and objects that arise adventitiously. For they will naturally disappear and cease of their own accord.

It is impossible for anything to surpass the perfect dominion wielded by the essential nature of the inconceivable kāyas and facets of great primordial consciousness that are primordially present within you. This is the infallible truth of the actual nature of reality. Therefore recognize outer and inner absolute space and pristine awareness, and train in experiencing the root of existence—the inner pristine awareness endowed with luminosity, purity, and power—as being of a single, nondual taste with great emptiness: originally pure, absolute space. Immerse yourself without wavering in the vajra strands and in the bindu enclosures of the space of awareness that are the outwardly luminous radiance of pristine awareness. Take this as the heart of your practice, and apply yourself single-pointedly to familiarizing yourself with it.

Without contaminating or modifying the pristine awareness of outer and inner absolute space with any kind of analysis or reification, make it authentic practice by simply resting in your natural state. Based upon that, the modes of pristine awareness regarding outer and inner absolute space will augment each other, [711] bringing to culmination their vividness and stability, so that you are swiftly liberated in the great, primordial extinction. As a result, you will undoubtedly realize the ultimate kāyas and facets of primordial consciousness. As illustrated in *The Tantra of the Reverberation of Sound*:[69]

> The crucial points of what is direct must definitely
> accord with each of the crucial points of the body, speech, and
> mind.
> Do not let your body depart for long
> from the three kāyas.
> The practice of speech is to seal it
> in total silence.
> Establish your mind firmly in absolute space.

It further states:

> Never be parted from the pith instructions on the three crucial
> points.
> Rely on the crucial points of the apertures and the region,
> the vital energies and pristine awareness.
> Regarding the apertures, gaze in the manner of the three kāyas.
> The region must be free of obscurations.

69. Tib. *Sgra thal 'gyur ba'i rgyud.*

> Actualize primordial consciousness with gentle energy and
> awareness.

The benefits of this are explained in *Liberation through Wearing: The Tantra of the One Buddha Son*:[70]

> Position your body like a lion,
> a ṛṣi, and an elephant.
> If you do not waver from those, [712]
> your good fortune is equal to that
> of three thousand buddhas . . .
>
> Your voice, like that of a mute,
> does not express anything to anyone.
> Anyone who practices like this
> will naturally sever the dispersions and withdrawals of the
> mind . . .
>
> Rest in meditative equipoise without being parted from
> the vajra strands within absolute space.
> Anyone who practices like this
> has good fortune equal to that of
> the primordial Samantabhadra.

In particular, inner absolute space, the originally pure great emptiness, free of conceptual elaboration, which is the site of timeless liberation, is primordially of one taste, indivisible from the sole bindu of clear light—the naturally present pristine awareness—within the great, vast expanse. When you recognize this for what it is, then without ever wavering from the immutable state of naturally present lucidity and luminosity, the extraordinary, effortless, implicit wisdom of the creative displays

70. Tib. *Btags grol sangs rgyas sras gcig gi rgyud.*

of pristine awareness will arise and grow by spontaneously emerging from the expanse.

As a result, you will not succumb to the arrogance of striving to discredit other spiritual traditions or individuals, and you will not succumb to the deceitful causes and conditions that lead to the māras' doorstep, wherein you make idle proclamations about seeing gods and demons or having extrasensory perception. [713] Then your faith in, reverence for, and pure perception of both the impartial and unbiased Dharma, and sublime individuals, will grow greater and greater. This will cut through superimposition of uncertainties regarding your own special path, and by gaining the existential certainty of irreversible conviction, you will apply yourself single-pointedly to these methods so that your whole life becomes coextensive with the practice. That will be illustrated by your having great compassion for others who lack realization, have false realizations, or have partial realizations, so that you strive to benefit them in whatever way you can. You must by all means strive solely in the methods that follow in the faultless footsteps of the life stories of the vidyādharas of the past.

In the centers of the bindus of the space of awareness, which are the outer luminosity of the radiance of pristine awareness that has never been sullied with stains, the formless appears to take on form—that is, the pristine awareness that is the vital core of the essence of primordial consciousness appears as the vajra strands. Without letting this become contaminated by adventitious analysis, in order for this lucid luminosity to become unwaveringly stable, [714] if you constantly strive to immerse yourself in them totally, this will synthesize the essential nature of all the practices from the pinnacle of spiritual vehicles. However, even while disengaging from such crucial points, among contemporary practitioners of the heart essence of the Great Perfection, there are some who spend years in foolish meditation and think very highly of themselves. Some air moldy meat by making loud proclamations that are like idle, intellectual talk and foolish babbling. Wasting their lives in such ways, many ignorant people lead others away from the path while entertaining the conceit that they are performing the work of brave men. It is obvious that there are far too many such people, so this is utterly intolerable. Still, even now there may be fortunate individuals who—due to the confluence of the power of the jinas and some authentic, fine, individual karmic momentum—do not fall under the domination of the māras of envy and prejudice. For their sake, I have explained this again and again and have made these points very clear. So I ask you to do all you can to hold these ultimately profound, essential points in the center of your heart.

Thus [Jamyang Khyentsé Wangpo] spoke to us. To this point the *Tantra of the Reverberation of Sound* states further:

> The nature of the vajra strands
> purifies conceptual thought, [715]
> resulting in unmistaken enlightenment . . .
>
> For those of fortune who discover it directly,
> not even the phrase "the three realms of saṃsāra" exists;
> this severs the membrane of all three worlds.

These words make very clear how it is that the radiance of pristine awareness exists, and what the benefits are of seeing it.

If you correctly familiarize yourself with outer and inner absolute space and pristine awareness, the way that the dawning of the four visions will naturally emerge is definite. Nonetheless, since the individuals who experience them have different constitutions, and since they have superior, middling, and inferior degrees of realization and of familiarization with cutting through, [Jamyang Khyentsé Wangpo] said that there is a difference as to the sequence by which such visions will progress. Those who are extremely diligent are able to progress swiftly along the path, while those who are lazy take longer. But to explain how the visions arise, one by one, these are as follows.

First, in the direct appearances of the actual nature of reality, you directly realize inner pristine awareness, which transcends the intellect, and can sustain this easily. The *Tantra of the Reverberation of Sound* explains the luminous outer appearances of absolute space and pristine awareness:

> The direct appearances of the actual nature of reality
> definitely emerge from the apertures of the senses.
> They appear clearly in the sky free of clouds. [716]

Accordingly, from the indestructible radiance of pristine awareness at the center of the heart stems the mysterious passageway of the light channel, and it emerges at the apertures of the lasso lamp. Seeing the indistinct, luminous appearances, which are as though the same as the radiance of the basis for all arising, is the outer space of awareness. Seeing that there are many fine orbs that bear the brilliant radiance of the luminous appearances, in the manner of a proliferation, is the inner space of awareness. The lamp of the pristine space of awareness has the essential nature of a sambhogakāya pure realm. Seeing round red, orange, pale yellow, indigo, and other-colored orbs in the shape of wheels the size of a thumb joint sometimes appearing, sometimes disappearing, then appearing just two at a time, is the lamp of the empty bindus, which has the essential nature of the inconceivable palace. Luminous visions like a horse's tail, like a crystal rosary, and like golden threads are interspersed with tiny orbs emitting other tiny orbs. When you see all kinds of movements and swift vacillations inside and in between the orbs of the space of awareness, these are the vajra strands, which have the essential nature of kāyas. When they directly appear in the form of distinct luminosity and purity as objects of your refined sense faculty, they pervade everywhere, [717] overshadowing the appearances of ordinary objects. The first phase of the visions on this path lasts until (1) wherever these luminous visions lead, there they appear, and (2) the vajra strands remain for just a little while within a set of three lamps of empty bindus. Because the naked self-appearances of the actual nature of reality are directly seen in a way that transcends all analogies, symbols, reasons, words, and analysis, this is called the vision of the direct appearances of the actual nature of reality. The *Tantra of the Reverberation of Sound* states:

> The vision of the direct appearances of the actual nature of
> reality
> transcends words used in intellectual analysis.

In the past, when even great sinners died while practicing the yoga of this phase of the path, even without other factors contributing to the path, they did not take rebirth in a miserable realm of existence, even though they were heading there, but rather gained a fine rebirth in a fortunate realm of existence, where they were able to continue on the path.

Second, in the phase of progress in meditative experience, the luminous visions increase, and they separate off at about four finger-widths from the point between your eyebrows. In the space of awareness of the perceived sky appear rainbow lights, five-colored orbs arising vertically and horizontally, like a lattice in the forms of mansions of light, lotus petals, castles, [718] stūpas, checkered patterns, and so on. In the expanse of these various masses of light continually appear fivefold clusters (and more) of the lamps of empty bindus. They greatly increase in the forms of mirrors, clay cups, and small round shields, and inside these dense appearances the vajra strands of pristine awareness become increasingly stable and thick, so that their power is perfected. Solitary kāyas, appearing from the uṣṇīṣa down to the waist, arise as one and then many. Since they remain without moving, ordinary, delusive appearances gradually fade away as the self-appearances of primordial consciousness increase. When this happens, (1) outwardly, the power of the karmic energies that generate and withdraw the appearances of coarse outer objects, (2) inwardly, the power of the vital energies that operate the inner psychophysical aggregates and elements, and (3) secretly, the power of the vital energies that move thoughts toward objects all subside to the point of extinction. Consequently, all the positive and negative appearances of outer circumstances arise as aids to the yogic path.

The obsessive effort of the inner delusions of afflictive thoughts and actions no longer arises. At the secret level, pristine awareness naturally remains in absolute space, free of movement and conceptualization. If you were to die at this time, you would achieve enlightenment [719] in the transitional phase of the actual nature of reality, and from that point onward the substantial, delusive appearances of conditioned existence will no longer arise. *The Tantra of the Reverberation of Sound* states:

> Progress in meditative experience
> causes delusive appearances to subside.

Third, in the visions of reaching consummate awareness all current, impure, ordinary, substantial appearances of material things such as earth, stones, mountains, and boulders subside, and everything is totally pervaded by great visions of pure lands from the spontaneously actualized clear light. Everything that appears consists of nothing other than the nature of light. Many fivefold clusters of five-colored orbs present themselves beautifully, and inside each one are clusters of peaceful and wrathful male and female kāyas in union filling the whole of space. From their hearts, extremely fine rays of light connect with your own heart, at which point the outer environment appears as a sambhogakāya pure land. Inwardly, your own body no longer appears to you as though material but arises in the aspect of an empty form. Secretly, the movements of impure states of energy-mind cease right where they are, and pure states of energy-mind increase to the point of consummation. You gain mastery over immeasurable qualities such as extraordinary clairvoyance and other kinds of extrasensory perception. [720] If you were to die at this point, your body and mind would dissolve into rays of light and the light of primordial consciousness would enter the heart of a kāya of light, or else all the kāyas of light would withdraw into your own heart. Either way, when you transmigrate, in the transitional phase you will merge with the ground clear light, and then your coarse, defiled body, together with your habitual propensities, will be purified so that they never take birth again, and your primordial consciousness will dissolve into a mass of precious light. You will be freed from all the faults of obscurations that veil pristine awareness, and you will become enlightened in the originally pure, great expanse of inner absolute space. The tantra states further:

> The visions of reaching consummate awareness
> liberate you from inner and outer, from apprehender and apprehended, from all material things.

Fourth, regarding the visions of extinction into the actual nature of reality—outwardly the impure appearances of the environment, inwardly your body, and secretly the configurations of mental afflictions and the karmic energies that animate them—these are purified right in their own place, right in pristine awareness, and having nowhere to arise again, they are extinguished. *The Tantra of the Reverberation of Sound* states:

> The visions of extinction into the actual nature of reality
> cut the cord of the three realms of saṃsāra. [721]

The great visions of the spontaneously actualized path of primordially stainless outer luminosity are released like waves of water that are withdrawn again. When you approach natural entry into the great youthful vase kāya, the deep luminosity of the originally pure ground, it is in the nature of things that you have mastery over whatever birth you take. So if you wish to arise as an undefiled, great transference vajrakāya, your body dissolves into a mass of light and fingers of five-colored light vividly appear just from the perspective of pristine awareness. At this juncture there is no appearance of any other form of your body, and in the very instant that pristine awareness is immersed in those fingers of light you realize the quintessential, indestructible rainbow body, the great transference vajra, the undefiled embodiment of primordial consciousness.

In any case, the visions on the path, without remainder, are of the vast, great expanse, the primordial, originally pure, ultimate abode of liberation, the actual nature of your own mind, which utterly transcends all conceptual elaborations involving signs. They dissolve into the inward luminosity of subtle, great primordial consciousness and totally merge with its essential nature, free of delusion, bias, or partiality. Becoming indivisibly of one taste, [722] ultimate, eternal being imbued with the twofold purity is achieved in this lifetime. *The Tantra of the Reverberation of Sound* states:

> The visions of extinction into the actual nature of reality
> evacuate all experiential visions.
> Your body is extinguished, as well as sensory objects.
> You are naturally freed from delusive configurations of thoughts,
> beyond all words or anything to articulate . . .
>
> Having severed thus the stream of elements in the body,
> the defiled aggregates disappear,
> and enlightenment is achieved in this very lifetime.

These final three lines also show clearly how it is the case that those, such as Vimalamitra, who abide in a great transference vajrakāya are actual, perfectly completed buddhas.

Now I shall give a brief explanation of three sets of pith instructions on the stable culmination of each of the visions along the path, as well as the measure of dreams for those on that stage and the actual signs of the body, speech, and mind.

To establish a basis for the three modes of remaining without moving, with any of the three physical postures and three gazes, focus your energy-mind in absolute space and pristine awareness. When you do not drift away, absolute space and pristine awareness expand and stabilize. These pith instructions are to be cherished during the phase of the direct appearances of the actual nature of reality. [723]

The measure of the three kinds of stillness is that outwardly, due to the stillness of appearances right where they are, they do not captivate the mind, and the conditions of appearances arise as aids to the path. Inwardly, due to the stillness of the aggregates, deluded activities do not increase. Secretly, due to the stillness of the energy-mind, deluded mental states cease. These pith instructions pertain to the phase of progress in meditative experience.

The measures of these phases are determined by your dreams. At first you have only good dreams. After some time you identify them and are able to emanate and transform them. Finally, they are purified in the clear light and they stop altogether.

Signs arise in your body, speech, and mind. During the phase of the direct appearances of the actual nature of reality, your body is free of movement, your voice is free of articulate speech, and your mind is immediately purified of deluded thoughts. In the phase of progress in meditative experience, your body is free of pleasure-seeking activities, your speech becomes spontaneous, and your mind remains in a state of nonconceptuality. In the phase of reaching consummate awareness, your body cannot be harmed by the four elements, your speech naturally arises with the sweet melodies of Dharma, and your mind is freed from fear and trepidation. In the phase of extinction into the actual nature of reality, your body becomes like a rainbow or like mist, your speech becomes like the sound of an echo, and in your mind thoughts arise as nothing more than flashes of lightning. [724]

As for the key points of the three attainments: Outwardly, you attain mastery so that the appearances of the environment appear naturally as a pure land. Inwardly, your own body naturally arises as radiant light. Secretly, the afflictive energy-mind is cleared away and is mastered as primordial consciousness. These occur during the phase of reaching consummate awareness.

Here are the measures of liberation regarding the four kinds of confidence. All of the following will naturally cease during the four visions along the path: (1) the hope to achieve buddhahood from elsewhere, (2) the fear that you will not experience your own natural abode, (3) the hope that you will not return to saṃsāra after you have been liberated from it without a trace, and (4) the fear that you will have to do so (or vice versa).

Without reliance on other factors of the path, such as recognizing your dreams, if you familiarize yourself with the direct crossing over, you should know that they will arise naturally. These pith instructions on the direct crossing over are indubitable and are for people with great enthusiasm. So if you can single-pointedly strive in them, regardless of how smart you are or how good your karma is, this is the most sublime, secret path, which should be taken to heart by the wise.

## [3]. A Summary of Auxiliary Practices for Dispelling Obstacles

You can learn elsewhere, such as in the heart essence texts, the treasure teachings, and the canonical scriptures,[71] methods for dispelling eye defects and for stabilizing lucidity and clarity, [725] as well as mantras, substances, and auspicious conditions for increasing the lamps. The one, ultimate, totally sufficient auxiliary practice for dispelling obstacles is to emphasize devotion and reverence for your guru. The fundamental method that eliminates obstacles and brings you to the culmination of the path is secret practice with a partner, so you should do everything you can to strive in the following seven practices for retaining the vital energies.

First, in the manner of a bee seeking nectar, generally speaking you should recognize the remedies for what needs to be abandoned. However, in this phase of practice, the *root* of what is to be abandoned is the cognizant aspect of the mindstreams of sentient beings, without distinction. This is the prior, ethically neutral, general basis of both liberation and delusion. If you realize it, then the embodiments of buddhas and displays of pure lands will definitely arise. But if you fail to realize it, the myriad abodes, bodies, and sensory objects specific to the beings of the six realms will definitely arise. Those two [namely, the pure lands and six realms of existence] do not obscure each other. When causes and conditions come together it is suitable for nonexistent appearances to become manifest, like illusions, and the opportunity for them to arise is not stopped. When not making specific

71. Tib. *snying thig bka' gter.*

divisions, they are equal in terms of existing. But from the very time that they appear, they are also equal in being devoid of the conceptual elaborations that cannot in any way be established in reality. [726]

In this regard, since what is known as the "vital energy of the life force" also remains, it catalyzes the following. When the appearing aspect is projected outward and manifests like light, the initial mode of delusion occurs in dependence upon that, by way of the four conditions: (1) The causal condition is not recognizing them to be your own appearances. (2) With that as the dominant condition you hold them to be something other [than your own appearances]. (3) With that as the objective condition many more delusive appearances proliferate. (4) Since the consciousness that is the immediately preceding condition [for the next moment of consciousness] occurs simultaneously with those objects of consciousness, you mistake the kāya of primordial consciousness for a defiled body. Appearances of the space of awareness are mistaken for objects, and pristine awareness is mistaken for the mind. However, from the very beginning of delusion, right now, while we are dwelling in the proliferation of delusion, our alienation from the kāyas and facets of primordial consciousness doesn't really exist at all. As an analogy, even when water, under the temporary influence of a cold wind, has frozen rock-solid as what is called "ice," its nature is still nothing other than water. So it is never correct to doubt its pure nature [727] based merely on the very different good and bad ways in which it appears. Thus, if you understand this adventitious process of becoming deluded for what it is, it is impossible for you not to ascertain its direct antidote—the reality of the path—as the identification of pristine awareness and its own appearances, which is the final, ultimate view with respect to the way things are.

There are also four conditions by which you are liberated: (1) The causal condition is great emptiness, the original purity of the primordial, actual nature of the mind, which has eternally been the ultimate mode of existence of all phenomena. (2) The dominant condition is naked, naturally present, unmodified, pristine awareness. (3) The objective condition is recognizing the great indivisibility of absolute space and pristine awareness.

(4) The immediately preceding or congruent condition is that, immediately after you achieve final, total stability in the perfected power of recognizing stainless absolute space and pristine awareness, in the very next instant it is impossible for you ever to lose the realization of the essential nature of all the buddhas, who are endowed with the two boundless, eternal purities. Until that occurs, however much you may designate merely pleasing words upon the deluded aspect, if the remedy is absent, there is nowhere and no time when you can ever be liberated naturally. [Jamyang Khyentsé Wangpo] said that [728] however great or limited your learning, if those who are practicing the *Heart Essence* do not know even this, then however much they may spout off about being in the lineage of having no virtue, no vice, no view, no meditation, and no separation of day and night, in reality they are like fools.

Second, regarding the [practice of a] swallow entering its nest, if you come to certainty by cutting through all qualms regarding the essential, crucial points of the path of the *Heart Essence*, then it will be difficult for doubts to arise regarding the need to devote yourself to practice. On the other hand, if you practice with heartfelt devotion and reverence for your guru, it is also the case that doubts will vanish by themselves. So don't remain like a corpse sleeping inside your room, but by focusing your intention on the meaning of the direct perception of absolute space and pristine awareness, counteract your mental afflictions. Every time you intend for those crucial points to ripen, conditioned existence is shredded by your meditation, and when the power of the practice is perfected, it is inevitable that the very characteristics of your mental afflictions will be utterly uprooted.

Third, as for the analogy of a deer, as an aid to your practice, like a wounded deer, you should remain in solitude for the rest of your life.

Fourth, as for the analogy of a mute, [729] since there is nothing more detrimental than idle chatter in a mountain hermitage, practice remaining in silence. On occasion, even when in a crowd, be like a mute.

Fifth, if you behave like that, when you spontaneously utter sporadic, unrelated words without any hope or fear and without trying to avoid them, you will come to be known as "someone who speaks like a madman."

Sixth, when you are content to live like a dog or pig, without any preference for the quality of your food, clothing, or habitation, this is known as "the conduct in which you equalize the taste of good and bad."

Once you have perfected those six—whether in sequence or as is appropriate—when you gain stable mastery over your own pristine awareness, primordial consciousness, then having the seal of visions will occur naturally. Moreover, your pristine awareness will not be suppressed by the condition of appearances but will remain solely in its own state. But in this case, why would there be any need to patch pristine awareness onto appearances as described in the mind class teachings and so on? As long as pristine awareness holds its own ground, you will not hope for good circumstances existing out there, so you will be free of all desire and craving. Since it cannot be suppressed by negative circumstances from in here, there is no place for anger and hatred. When all aspects of objects and subjects do not arise as anything other [730] than displays of pristine awareness, that refers to the seventh analogy of a lion, known as "the conduct of gaining mastery over the phenomenal world." Apply these well to your own experience, and without pretense, engage in pure conduct appropriate to the circumstances.

Since the augmentation of the practice should definitely emerge by means of the practice itself, included here within this instruction on the main practice are the pith instructions for entering virtuous practice by a direct route. Here I will explain them in accordance with the text *The Union of Buddhas in the Four Times*.[72]

First, during the daytime, gaze at your own face: absolute space and pristine awareness. This entails practicing correctly, as explained before, with the originally pure, empty, pristine awareness, and with all the

72. Tib. *Dus bzhi sangs rgyas mnyam sbyor*. While there are many texts by the title of *The Union of Buddhas* (an abbreviation for the Skt. *Sarvabuddhasamāyoga-ḍākinījālasamvara Tantra*, also known as the *Samvara Tantra*, in the cycle of Cakrasaṃvara), this particular title appears to refer to the redaction by the Vidyādhara and Treasure Revealer, Pema Lingpa (*Padma gling pa*, 1450–1521): *Dus bzhi sangs rgyas mnyam sbyor gyi 'grel ba yang zab rin chen 'khor lo*.

spontaneously actualized luminous appearances that are its own radiance. It is good if you can spend the whole day meditating on the daytime appearances, to ripen the crucial points of the direct crossing over in accordance with the main teaching of the treatise. During the late evening and so on, or the first half of the night, if the moon is clear—or if it's not, then in reliance on a butter lamp—it is best if you immerse your energy-mind in the network of the illusory vajra king, the vajra strands of pristine awareness.

Second is the withdrawal of the senses into the crucial points at dusk. If it is the practice involving desire, [731] then when you are fit for the work of making your own body into the skillful means, then, while in the state of bliss and emptiness that emerges from relying properly on a karmamudrā, withdraw your energy-mind into a crucial point upon the sense objects. If you do so, since in this treatise it is called "relying on external ambrosia," then in general it is obviously permitted. However, it is also appropriate for you to practice thus with [the bliss and emptiness] that emerge during the preliminary phase, when you make your own body into the skillful means through blaze and descent.[73]

Third is the practice of "placing knowable things into the vase"[74] at midnight. When you are almost asleep, clearly visualize a white syllable *a*—just the vertical stroke—inside a white orb the size of a pea, one inside your heart and one between your eyebrows. The essential nature of the orbs is the indivisibility of your guru and your own pristine awareness. Single-pointedly pray to your guru that you may apprehend the clear light and fix your attention on this subtle orb. If you can apprehend it clearly, imagine that its light pervades the whole of phenomenal existence with five-colored lights. Finally, gather everything back into the orb, and without letting your mind wander elsewhere, fall asleep. If you are not comfortable meditating on two orbs simultaneously, you may focus on them alternately or primarily focus on the one at the heart. It is not that there is a syllable *a* in the middle of a flat orb; rather, meditate on a syllable *a* standing clearly and

73. Tib. *rang lus thabs ldan gyi 'bar 'dzag*. This refers to a practice of inner fire (Tib. *gtum mo*) that is "free of desire" (Tib. *chags bral*).

74. Tib. *shes bya bum 'jug*.

free of obscuration inside a spherical orb. [732] With that method you will apprehend the clear light and recognize your dreams.

Fourth, to arouse the natural luminosity of pristine awareness at dawn, at that time attend to the crucial point of the body by adopting the lion posture and clear your vital energies by stirring them with the exhaled sound of *ha*. Then, in the space one arrow-length or one cubit in front of you, visualize a lucid, radiant, white syllable *a*, blazing with five colors, which has the essential nature of your root guru, indivisible from Vimalamitra, and direct your eyes there as well. Immerse your vital energies and awareness single-pointedly in the thought of your own body and mind being merged in complete stillness with the nature of your guru's unborn mind, and focus on the syllable *a*. Having separated your awareness from defilements, when it arises lucidly and pristinely, if your awareness deteriorates from the state of the unborn mind, you will convince yourself that your guru is not there. But if you comfortably sustain pristine awareness in its natural state, all conceptual fabrications will arise as its displays and will naturally be released.

At all times and in all circumstances, here is the one crucial point to prize above all. Whatever practice you do and whatever other activities of body, speech, and mind you perform, if you do them from the luminous and pure nature of pristine awareness, all appearances and mental states will arise as ornaments of pristine awareness, like reflections of the planets and stars in the ocean. [733] And, like waves dissolving into the sea, they are perfected in a single taste with pristine awareness.

# 7 Liberation in the Intermediate Period

## ii. Instructions for Individuals of Middling Faculties to Achieve Liberation in the Intermediate Period

Here there are two sections: [I] pith instructions on the transitional phase at the time of death, which is like a child crawling onto its mother's lap, and [II] pith instructions on the transitional phase of the actual nature of reality, which is like an immutable golden spoon.

## [I]. Pith Instructions on the Transitional Phase at the Time of Death, Which Is Like a Child Crawling onto Its Mother's Lap

Here there are again two sections: [A] the merging of absolute space and pristine awareness, and [B] practical instructions on the transference of consciousness.

## [A]. The Merging of Absolute Space and Pristine Awareness

From this day forward, let your practice proceed to the crucial point by which you merge the three spaces into one. That which symbolizes *outer absolute space* is this clear, empty space around you, free of anything that could obscure or obstruct the mind from its objects. Or else it can be recognized as the ornamental sky, free of dust or clouds. In any case, that which is actually symbolized is the great expanse of the originally pure, actual nature of all phenomena, devoid of an outside or inside, absolute space that is in fact totally, radically within, and unchanging. That must currently pervade everything outside as well, but it is not present in any way that is partial or biased. Likewise, *inner absolute space*, too, simply consists of the clear, empty cavities inside the body. [734] *Secret absolute space* is nothing other than the actual nature of the mind, great emptiness, which bears the essential nature of pristine awareness.

While those are primordially of one taste, to the minds of us sentient beings it seems as though they are separate and cut off. Through the extraordinary, transformative methods of the supremely secret, royal pith instructions you merge them inseparably into one taste. Coming to know the crucial points of the path of the way things are, strive single-pointedly in merging absolute space with pristine awareness, or the meditation on threefold space.

During in-between periods, think: "I have already died. This absolute space of great emptiness, which is like the sky, is the dharmakāya clear light of the transitional phase of dying. This recognition of empty awareness, the actual nature of the mind, appears like a brook or a child. The clear light of indwelling, great emptiness, which is present in the ground of being, appears like the ocean, or a mother. These merely appear to the mind as two, but in reality when you arrive in your own state, like a mother and son, from the very beginning they have never known any difference, not even that of male and female. So I shall realize them as being indivisibly of one taste, like water flowing into water." In this way decisively form this powerful resolve. [735] If you familiarize yourself with this, it will be easy for you when you're about to die. Then when you are on the verge of dying, in accordance with your prior familiarization, forcefully merge absolute space and pristine awareness.

## [B]. Practical Instructions on the Transference of Consciousness

The way to train in the transference of consciousness now is as follows. Dwelling in the conduct of meditation, after you have completed the preliminary practices, or else have finished taking refuge and cultivating bodhicitta properly, imagine the whole of space being pervaded by the five supreme, natural nirmāṇakāya buddha fields, together with the great charnel ground, Blazing Mountain of Fire. In the center of your own luminous, empty body, visualize the central channel, the pathway of great enlightenment, having the width of a bamboo arrow and reaching straight up from your secret place to the crown of your head like a blue crystal tube. Inside the central channel, at the level of your heart, single-pointedly visualize all your energy-mind states, without exception, being synthesized in the essential nature of a radiant, five-colored orb marked in its center by a small white syllable *a*. At the crown of your head, above the central channel, inside a circular rainbow, is your smiling, gloriously kind root guru, [736] who is directly manifest—in the form of a body of light—as the great captain who will guide you along the path of the transitional phase. Earnestly offer prayers of supplication with powerful devotion and reverence, thinking: "Please lead me, also, in this very instant, to the expanse of the clear light, the great bliss of my guru's mind." Imagine that as soon as you focus your mind on the orb of your energy-mind—that which is to be transferred—it floats to the upper tip of the central channel. When it arrives there, loudly recite twice, or as many times as you wish, the syllable *hig* or *phaṭ*, and repeatedly imagine that this results in the orb dissolving gently into the heart of your guru and merging with it, as of one taste.

When you conclude your session, visualize your guru dissolving into the center of your heart through the pathway of the central channel, and imagine that you become enlightened in the essential nature of your own guru. Then rest your mind in relaxation and ease. All the buddha fields disappear, and from that state of nonobjectivity, dedicate your virtue and pray, "In all my lifetimes, without ever being separated from authentic gurus . . ."[75]

When the time comes that you are certainly dying, abandon clinging to the appearances of this life, without following after them at all, and practice the transference of consciousness as before. At the end of the session, imagine that your root guru actually departs [737] to the supreme, natural nirmāṇakāya buddha field of your choice, such as the charnel ground, Blazing Mountain of Fire, and so on. Simply by visualizing this, while in this single-pointed state of meditation, if you can meditate until your breath stops or for as long as you can, you will be unstained by vices and will be reborn in a pure buddha field. You should know that whether or not you reach liberation in the transitional phase, by practicing transference of consciousness you will not take a lower rebirth.

## [II] Pith Instructions on the Transitional Phase of the Actual Nature of Reality, Which Is Like an Immutable Golden Spoon

Once the coarse stages of dissolution during the dying process have finished, whether or not you have time to recognize the three appearances of the white light, the red proliferation, and the dark near-attainment, when the movements of all the adventitious energy-minds have naturally ceased, the essential nature of the indwelling, actual nature of the mind, the ground clear light on the occasion of the transitional phase of dying naturally arises, like the autumn sky free of pollution. However, those who do not know this crucial point of the path become unconscious and are temporarily engulfed in a state of mindlessness. Then, even when the

75. Tib. *skye ba kun tu yang dag bla ma dang / 'bral med chos kyi dpal la longs spyod cing / sa dang lam gyis yon tan rab rdzogs nas / rdo rje 'chang gi go 'phang myur thob shog//.* "In all my lifetimes, without ever being separated from authentic gurus, may I enjoy the glory of the Dharma. Having perfected the virtues of the bodhisattva grounds and paths, may I swiftly reach the state of Vajradhara."

self-appearances of the energy-awareness arise from the creative power of the clear light, which is the actual nature of the mind, they subside without one's having time to recognize them, and the delusive appearances of the transitional phase of becoming inevitably begin. [738]

At this time those who do not have the pith instructions on taking the phase of birth as the path have no alternative but to adopt a mental body of the transitional phase. If those who are familiar with the crucial points of the path of Vajrayāna—as in the immediately preceding explanation—realize the approximate clear light of uttermost emptiness without being engulfed in mindlessness when other mental processes have ceased, then, after that, they may achieve a pure illusory body without taking on a mental body of the transitional phase of becoming. However, this is not the same as the divine kāya that dawns as an appearance of the path during the transitional phase of the self-appearing actual nature of reality, which is a distinctive characteristic of the heart essence of the Great Perfection. The *Tantra of the Six Expanses* states:

> It is a mistake to assert that
> the transitional phase of the pure, actual nature of reality
> and the divine illusory body of one's personal deity are at all
> similar.

Accordingly, there is a great difference between the question of (1) whether the appearances of the creative power of the clear light are subtle or coarse, and (2) whether or not [that clear light] is contaminated by a subtle energy-mind that has stains. It is true that what surpasses the practices of the stages of generation and completion does not go beyond the actualization of the union of the two in an uncontrived divine kāya, after directly realizing the actual clear light of uttermost emptiness. Nevertheless, [739] that is still the path of training, with something left over. So you should understand further the difference between that and the great transference vajrakāya explained previously, with its various manifestations of the rūpakāya imbued with the two purities, which has nothing whatsoever left over on the path.

In this context the cessation of the triad of white light, red proliferation, and dark near-attainment is known as *consciousness dissolving into space.* At that point the naturally abiding, indwelling clear light, the primordial great emptiness, the actual nature of the mind, dawns spontaneously. The period from then until the inner radiance of its light rays proliferates outwardly is called *the dharmakāya clear light of the transitional phase of dying.* The great abode of liberation of the originally pure, absolute space of the ground of being is like a mother, and having the stable practice in this lifetime of the originally pure, actual nature of the mind is like the child. When those two are united, you recognize that with which you were previously familiar and do not move away from it, and that is called *the meeting of the mother and child clear light.* Taking hold of your royal throne without turning back from it is called *the liberation in upward openness with no intermediate period.* Having become completely liberated without any residue of anything to be abandoned, so that you are not reborn, constitutes the realization of the ultimate, fruitional dharmakāya. [740]

If you fail to take hold of the eternal kingdom of the dharmakāya in that way, the creative power of pristine awareness, wisdom, will be aroused by the vital energies of the life force, and the spontaneously actualized clear light of the transitional phase will dawn as the outer luminosity, whose essential nature is the sambhogakāya as it appears during the path. However, that too arises in the nature of original purity, so it does not move outside its own abode, as if it were arriving somewhere else. However it arises, this is known as *the clear light dissolving into the union of the two,* and various appearances orbs ripen as kāyas. Countless clusters of peaceful and wrathful male and female deities of the five buddha families, and so on, appear with even greater brilliance than on the occasion of reaching consummate awareness, together with sounds, light, and light rays. They arise spontaneously, and for as long as they arise, this is the period of the union of the two, as a specific instance of the clear light that appears in the transitional phase.

If you are not liberated at this point, the *visions of the fourfold primordial consciousness* arise as streamers of light adorned with large orbs. If you are not liberated then, the *visions of the eight portals of spontaneous actualization* arise simultaneously in the manner of compassion, primordial consciousness, lights, kāyas, nonduality, [741] liberation from extremes, portals to impure saṃsāra, and portals to pure primordial consciousness. If you are not liberated even then, you move beyond the transitional phase of the actual nature of reality and wander in the transitional phase of becoming.

In this way, the crucial point of the path by which you are liberated, from the union of the two—the self-appearing transitional phase of the actual nature of reality—up until any of the spontaneously actualized, transitional appearances arise, is as follows. Recognize whatever visions arise as being your own originally pure appearances, and without diverging from that recognition, rest in your natural state. If you come to a decisive understanding of this without any vacillating doubts, if you perfect this power without being moved by dualistic appearances, and if you achieve stability in this, the appearing aspects of the light, together with your subjective wisdom, will become of one taste in the great, originally pure, vast expanse of inner, absolute space. Without ever wavering from this state of ultimate liberation, you will hold to the fortress of the twofold purity, and this is known as *becoming enlightened by way of the sambhogakāya transitional phase.*

It would be too much to give a precise explanation of the specific ways in which these appearances arise, the criteria of becoming liberated, the days spent in meditation, the partitions between moments, and so on, and [742] a partial account would be difficult to understand. So you should learn this from the great secret treasuries of the teachings of the lord of jinas, the omniscient Longchen Rabjam. This is what [Jamyang Khyentsé Wangpo] said.

## iii. Practical Instructions for Individuals of Inferior Faculties to Achieve Liberation in a Natural Nirmāṇakāya Buddha Field

If you are unable to be liberated in the preceding great states of liberation, and the mental body of the transitional phase of becoming arises automatically, like a dream, you will be tormented by many terrifying delusive appearances, including the sound of mountains crumbling to pieces, the sound of turbulence in the ocean and great rivers, the sounds of ferocious winds and the unbearable sound of a thousand thunderclaps at once, the appearance of numerous regions, towns, dwellings, and people known to you, including living and dead friends, as well as those you don't recognize. You will be tormented by many different, indeterminate manifestations of your own body, behavior, food, drink, clothing, and so forth, as well as by various pleasant and unpleasant visions, great fire, great bodies of water, and fearsome precipices of earth and stone. Like a feather blown by the wind, you will have no control over where you go. Even if you have no refuge and no protector, you will have some minor extrasensory perception and paranormal abilities, with your body and mind that can feed on smells. For the most part [743] you will be able to remember your thoughts and behavior while you were alive, and you will continually experience a strong attraction to look for a body.

At such a time, you must recognize the appearances of the transitional phase, and you must know the ultimate refuge, your root guru, and the essence of your guru's practical instructions, which are easy to follow and very potent. At that time, like having a mighty escort, bring to mind the self-appearing, supreme, pure buddha field. It will be enough for you to have just an instant of powerful longing to go there and to hold that in mind. It is ever so important to know how to bring your body and mind to the path.

As for the buddha fields that may be your destination, in the center is the Mind-Vajra, Vairocana, in Ghanavyūha; in the east is the Body-Vajra, King Akṣobhya, in Abhirati; in the south is the Vajra of Enlightened Qualities, Ratnasambhava, in Śrīmat; in the west is the Speech-Vajra, Amitābha in Padmovyūha; and in the north is the Enlightened Activity-Vajra,

Amoghasiddhi in Karmaprasiddhi. These male deities, with their female partners, shower upon their retinues a great rain of Dharma, including the Vajrayāna. Their experience of wondrous bliss is manifestly present in the pure, supreme, nirmāṇakāya buddha fields such as Sukhāvatī, [744] whose qualities are indescribable because innumerable.

Here is the way to go there. For whatever buddha family you have special admiration and faith, this indicates some excellent residual karma for that family. So it makes no difference whether you have complete certainty regarding that family or whether you have gained a clear conviction that all of the many kāyas and buddha fields of the jinas are inseparably of one taste. Either way, pray with powerful, earnest devotion and reverence that you may now proceed to the pure land, which is your own appearance, like an arrow shot to its target, and that you may right now be caught with the hook of the impartial, unobscured, boundless compassion of your precious, root guru, whose essential nature is that of the five jina families. Simply by doing so, like waking from a dream, you will arrive in a pure land. Once you have arrived, you will be spontaneously born there in a body of primordial consciousness, replete with the major and minor marks of a buddha. You will meet with the Buddha and his retinue, hear the Dharma, receive empowerments, have prophecies revealed to you, and receive honor and consolation. On the basis of that lifetime you will become enlightened in the primordial expanse of inner absolute space.

Alternatively, [745] you may express a powerful aspiration and yearning to be swiftly led by the glorious and supreme Guru Heruka to the terrifying great charnel ground, Blazing Mountain of Fire, set above the peaceful maṇḍala of the five buddha-families, where the Teacher known as the Youthful, Powerful Warrior[76] stands as a wrathful embodiment of the omnipresent lord of the sixth buddha-family. This Great Bhairava of primordial consciousness resides together with his retinue: wrathful assemblies of vidyādharas, vīras, and ḍākinīs, pouring down a veritable rain of inconceivable Vajrayāna Dharma with a primary emphasis on the

76. Tib. *Gzhon nu dpa' bo stobs ldan*.

great methods of union and liberation. As soon as you express your wish to go there right now, visualize your mental body as a dharmodaya[77] of red light, inside of which is your energy-mind in the radiant form of a white syllable *a*. Instantly, like a flash of lightning, it melts and dissolves gently into the heart of your great, glorious guru. If you think that you have become a buddha, of one taste, inseparable from your guru, then you will swiftly achieve liberation. But it is only by the immeasurable power of blessings of the Dharma and the guru, by the power of the purity of the actual nature of reality, and by the inconceivable power of great truth that you will indubitably achieve these things. [746]

77. Tib. *chos 'byung*, lit. "source of dharmas." This refers to the ultimate source of phenomena, usually visualized in the form of an inverted tetrahedron, which serves as the foundation for most maṇḍalas in anuttarayogatantra.

# 8 Closing Advice

## 3. The Concluding Teachings

### a. Following the Profound Instructions on the Meaning of the Text, the First Part of the Concluding Teachings

Not only in this phase of practice, but in whatever practice you adopt on the path of Vajrayāna, here are the indispensable requisite conditions, as it were. If you have little faith and devotion for your guru, however much you strive on other facsimiles of paths, it will be difficult for this to be fruitful. So if you each have the authentic, powerful faith and devotion that come from irreversible confidence in your own compassionate root guru, free of the harmful thoughts of doubt, and if you do not dismiss the guru as being at your level, but rather view the guru with pure perception as an actual buddha, you will naturally find that all the desired results of the Mantrayāna, including siddhis, fall into your hands with no problem. Therefore practice in accordance with what has been taught again and again, from the past up to the present, and earnestly offer prayers of supplication.

The foundational source, as it were, of all the varieties of suffering and the unbearable vices that cause them, are these five defiled, closely grasped aggregates. Repeatedly consider that you are oppressed by them, and if your connection with them is not severed, it is the awful nature of this saṃsāra that your suffering will never be exhausted or end. So cultivate again and again a pronounced spirit of emergence, [747] aspiring for the liberation of yourself and others. Forget about the idea of proceeding on an authentic path while turning your back—for fear of suffering—on these mother sentient beings throughout space, burdened with negative karma, who have shown you such kindness. Hold firmly as the root of the path the repeated cultivation of unbearable, powerful compassion with the desire to liberate them from suffering and its causes, as if you were a person with clear vision rescuing the bewildered, downtrodden blind. Without fostering negative thoughts such as "Everyone but my guru and this Dharma is inferior and impure," strongly arouse an attitude of admiration and reverence for gurus and the [Three] Jewels in general, by way of sincere faith and pure perception for everyone. As much as you can, cut off all thoughts about inauthentic dharma and the mundane distractions of this life, which are pointless and extremely harmful.

At the beginning, if, at the very least, you draw back from negative mindsets—thinking to do this and that—from the very moment they arise, and you remain in silence without thinking about anything, [748] then mental chitchat will naturally cease. Whatever good and bad objects appear to your six senses, such as visual forms and sounds, by knowing how to let them release themselves without clinging to them, you will see how they arise as aids on your path, without your having to abandon the ambrosia of these six objects. Let your breath naturally flow through your nostrils loosely and evenly, and without either clenching your teeth or lips, or leaving them wide open, practice gentle breathing in which you hold the breath out for just a moment.

In the interim, as much as you can, apply yourself to the practice of joining the vital energies—which gives rise to precious qualities—by holding the fullness of the vase breath to a moderate degree at the level of your navel. The eyes are more important than the other senses in terms of serving as an avenue, or contributing condition, for the appearance of the outer and inner clear light. Without moving them, blinking, or fluttering your eyelashes, gaze steadily into empty space. The time for this is in the context of the crucial point regarding the three spaces, but you should do so whenever you remember. The root of those practices is this essential nature of naked, clear, uncontrived, pristine awareness. With the proper degree of intensity, continually and at all times sustain this awareness without distraction and without grasping, without ever disengaging from this practice. As much as you can, according to your means, make the ganacakra offering on days such as the tenth, twenty-fifth, fifteen, eighth, and third of each lunar month. [749]

Whatever virtue you perform, do not just let it slip away but completely dedicate it for the benefit of the teachings and sentient beings. It is very important that every time you offer a pure prayer, each one rises up greater than the last, so you fortunate ones who wish well for yourselves and others, strive as well as you can! If even once you have the opportunity to listen to, reflect upon, and investigate the boundless profundity and vastness of the qualities that distinguish the sovereign, supremely secret *Heart Essence*, as well as the specifics of the pith instructions, you have the good fortune that is difficult to find even over the course of a hundred eons. So without contaminating your mind with bad thoughts, such as seeking a great reputation, material wealth, and renown as a scholar, to the best of your ability carefully investigate the fine treatises of the canonical and treasure teachings in general, and in particular, as explained previously, investigate again and again the Seven Great Treasuries [of Longchenpa], the *Heart Essence of the Mother and the Son*, and the incomparable *Secret Treasures of the Ḍākinīs*.[78] Some people nowadays, without having taken the time to understand or fathom the teachings for themselves, clamor on as soon as they have heard a little bit. Do not be like them, casting the teachings to the wind, [750] but rather hold their profound meaning in your heart. If you retain all that has been explained, there is little danger and great benefit, but don't follow after fools who are famous. For the rest of your life, do not turn away from authentic, sublime gurus who are knowledgeable and accomplished in practice, who are well versed in the Dharma and altruistic,

78. Tib. *Mdzod chen bdun, Snying thig ma bu, Mkha' 'gro'i gsang mdzod.*

but listen attentively to each one. If you fail to do this, you will never discover the depths of the profound secret under the influence of prejudice and your own fabrications. So to apply yourself diligently to your own tradition, while not disparaging any Dharma at all, is the root of all the goodness of conditioned existence and of ultimate peace.

## b. The Time at Which One Manifests the Final Fruition, Along with a Vajra Song of Realizations, How This Was Consigned to the Treasure Custodians, and How to Make Prayers

Now I will explain the times at which those who immerse themselves experientially in such a path make manifest the great state of perfect buddhahood, which is the ultimate fruition, in their own place. In general the swift path of the Vajrayāna has the distinction of enabling accomplishment in one lifetime and so forth. Those of inferior faculties may manifest enlightenment in twelve years, those of middling faculties in three years, and those of superior faculties in six months. That depends on one's previous lives and on the degree of practice and effort one applies now, while [751] the actual fruition consists of the two sublime, supreme kāyas of perfect buddhahood. I have already explained the complete and unmistaken swift path of ripening and liberation as collected under the three units.

As for the vajra song of realizations, Chetsun has sung one beginning with the words, "É-ma! I, the idiot Seng-Wang . . ."

The one who was entrusted to reveal this treasure to fortunate disciples expressed in its entirety the innermost essence of the Great Perfection in vajra words when on the verge of death, so that we have it in the palm of our hand. These final words will appear to fortunate beings who are worthy vessels in the last phase of the final era, and by their power—not obstructed even by a long interval—those who encounter them will be directly granted the vajra words of truth, fine prayers for swiftly achieving the great transference, primordial consciousness vajrakāya equal to that of the guru.

## III. The Concluding Topic of the Final Ornament of Vajra Words, Consisting of the Advice of the Primordial Consciousness Ḍākinī

The third section from the original outline of this text, the meaning of the conclusion, is finally adorned with the vajra words of advice from the foremost lady of the primordial consciousness ḍākinīs, Pelgyi Lodröma:

> When granting an empowerment, give advice in the manner of providing pointing-out instructions. When giving teachings, give an unmistaken commentary while summarizing the sections of the material. When engaging in practice, [752] it is best for liberation through wearing to come through a firm grasp of experience. Even though you perceive the ornamental analogies, the real, great liberation through seeing comes from experience. Even though you bear in mind the meanings of various words and have the texts in hand, experience is what swiftly liberates you, so truly accomplish your aims by liberation through mindfulness and liberation through direct touch. Whoever meditates correctly, it goes without saying that they will be liberated even more swiftly than those in the past. Therefore, since this Dharma that synthesizes the profound crucial points in so few words has such incomparable qualities, the way of practicing the *Heart Essence* is easier than other methods, the meaning of its words is very clear, it is unmixed with other modes of Dharma, it includes everything that is needed, and it is free of incomprehensible verbal elaborations. That such extraordinary qualities are true to the facts has been confirmed experientially by many millions of scholars and adepts.
>
> Of course there are other sublime beings of the past who greatly prize their profound Dharmas. But with respect to this one, you can see that those who contaminate this with their own fabrications, additions, and deletions, and all those who engage in their own speculations, will fear curses that will cut short what is

> left of their lives, and the like. [753] You can also see that this has been entrusted to, or placed in the keeping of, the powerful, divine protectors, and, considering that, you may think it is better not to write about it. As for me, I have dared to propagate it, so each person may practice for themselves. If you disseminate this to others who are drawn to it and do all you can to help them connect with it, since this Dharma is appropriate for the present era, even if they have a negative connection with this, how could it not be meaningful? It is certain that even if this is not beneficial it will bring no harm, so I ask you to do your best to hold this in mind.

These infallible, authoritative, secret vajra words of truth, which were lavishly granted in their entirety to all beings with incomparable kindness, have been well received.

In this way, upon the vast pathway of the divine—the intended meaning of the unsurpassed, ultrasecret Great Perfection, the royal pinnacle of the nine yānas—the King of the Garuḍas, who is the creative display of the pristine awareness of the venerable omniscient guru, Great Vajradhara, stretches out his wings and teaches with just the edge of them. Upon the great highway that translates just that corner of his teaching, the mind's eye of a moth like myself may stretch his wings as far as he can, but it is certain he will not be able to represent even a portion of it. [754] Therefore I ask the Most Affectionate One to be so kind as to have patience with me for whatever errors there are here. By this virtue, from now until enlightenment, may I never be separated from my guru, and may it serve as a cause for him to take me ever after him as his follower.

Thus [Jamyang Khyentsé Wangpo] spoke. Moreover, I, bearing the name of the treasure revealer Lerab Lingpa, have sat among the lowest ranks of the many accomplished scholars to receive teachings from the venerable guru and have taken notes of whatever I have understood from the key points among the earlier and later profound teachings. May it all be virtuous!

# Outline of *The Vital Essence of Primordial Consciousness*

## Tertön Lerab Lingpa

### Chapter 1: The Treasure Text, Its Lineage, and Empowerment

I. The Introductory Topic of the Special Title, Together with the Homage of the Assembly of Ḍākinīs
   A. The Meaning of the Title
   B. The Homage
II. The Meaning of the Text, Explained according to the Tradition of Giving Guidance in the Profound Pith Instructions
   A. Giving Rise to Confident Belief in the Dharma and Guru through an Account of the Lineage
      1. The Way It Appeared in the Past
      2. The Prophecy about How It Will Appear Later
   B. Ripening the Unripened Mindstreams of Disciples Who Are Suitable Vessels through the Supreme, Profound Empowerment

### Chapter 2: Shared Preliminaries to Meditation

   C. Liberating Those Who Have Already Been Ripened by Means of the Unique and Extraordinary Pith Instructions

1. The Preliminaries to the Profound Teachings
    a. The Preliminaries to the Meditation Session, to Make the Mindstream a Suitable Vessel
        i. The Way to Resort to Solitude
        ii. Settling the Body, Speech, and Mind in Their Natural State
        iii. Supplication to the Guru
    b. The Shared Preliminaries: The Sevenfold Mind-Training
        i. Meditation on Impermanence
        ii. Meditation on the Way in Which Even the Pleasures of Saṃsāra Are Causes Leading to Unhappiness
        iii. Meditation on How There Is No Closure, No Matter How Much We Strive for Favorable Circumstances in Saṃsāra
        iv. Meditation on the Futility of All Superficial Human Pursuits, Whether Good or Bad
        v. Meditation on the Benefits of Liberation
        vi. Meditation on the Importance of the Guru's Practical Instructions
        vii. How to Settle the Mind in Its Natural State, since This Method Is So Crucially Important

Chapter 3: Unique Preliminaries to the Main Practice

    c. The Exceptional, Unique Preliminaries
        i. An Exceptional Way to Go for Refuge
        ii. Generating Bodhicitta
        iii. and iv. The Combined Practice of Purifying Obscurations and Accumulating the Collections
        v. Guru Yoga

## Chapter 4: The Generation Stage of the Guru and Cutting the Basis of Delusion

2. Profound Instructions on the Main Practice
   a. The Devout and Reverent Generation Stage of the Guru
   b. The Unique, Essential Stage of Completion
      i. Instructions for Individuals of Superior Faculties to Achieve Liberation in This Lifetime
         [I]. The Preliminary Practice of Cutting the Basis of Delusion from the Root

## Chapter 5: Original Purity

[II]. The Main Practice of Letting Delusion Release Itself and Then Letting Delusive Appearances Arise Naturally as Primordial Consciousness
- [A]. The Practice of the Original Purity of the Essential Nature
  - [1]. Decisive Understanding by Way of the View
  - [2]. Practice by Way of Meditation
  - [3]. Enhancement by Way of Conduct

## Chapter 6: Spontaneous Actualization

- [B]. The Practice of the Spontaneous Actualization of Your Own Appearances
  - [1]. A Brief Explanation of the Secret, Crucial Point of the Spontaneously Actualized Clear Light
  - [2]. How to Apply That to the Path
  - [3]. A Summary of Auxiliary Practices for Dispelling Obstacles

Chapter 7: Liberation in the Intermediate Period

ii. Instructions for Individuals of Middling Faculties to Achieve Liberation in the Intermediate Period
    [I]. Pith Instructions on the Transitional Phase at the Time of Death, Which Is Like a Child Crawling onto Its Mother's Lap
        [A]. The Merging of Absolute Space and Pristine Awareness
        [B]. Practical Instructions on the Transference of Consciousness
    [II] Pith Instructions on the Transitional Phase of the Actual Nature of Reality, Which Is Like an Immutable Golden Spoon
iii. Practical Instructions for Individuals of Inferior Faculties to Achieve Liberation in a Natural Nirmāṇakāya Buddha Field

Chapter 8: Closing Advice

3. The Concluding Teachings
    a. The First Part of the Concluding Teachings
    b. The Time at Which One Manifests the Final Fruition, Along with a Vajra Song of Realizations, How This Was Consigned to the Treasure Custodians, and How to Make Prayers

III. The Concluding Topic of the Final Ornament of Vajra Words, Consisting of the Advice of the Primordial Consciousness Ḍākinī

# Selected Essays on Old and New Views of the Secret Mantrayāna

གསང་སྔགས་གསར་རྙིང་གི་ལྟ་བའི་རྣམ་གཞག་ལེགས་བཤད་གཅེས་བཏུས།། །།

# Oral Instructions of the Vidyādhara Gurus

## *A Presentation of the Path of the Natural Great Perfection and Its Preliminaries*

Dharmasāra

With great reverence I bow at the lotus feet of the guru,
indivisible from the Bhagavān Mañjuvajra

In this brief presentation of the path of the natural Great Perfection there are three parts: (I) the structure of the path of the preliminary eight yānas, (II) the main practice: the way to follow the path of the Great Perfection, and (III) the way to actualize the ultimate state of the primordial protector resulting from the practice.

## I. The Structure of the Path of the Preliminary Eight Yānas

Everything that the Teacher said was taught solely for the sake of directly or indirectly bringing disciples to perfect enlightenment. All those teachings [2] are included in the two paths of ripening the streams of consciousness of disciples that have not been ripened and of liberating those that have been ripened. Without reliance upon the contributing condition of the path, it is impossible for the mindstreams of sentient beings to be ripened from the very beginning. For people whose mindstreams are unripe, the main practices of the activities of the path cannot be performed, for they are not suitable vessels of the path, and it would be like pouring water into an unfired clay pot.

So what are the criteria for a mindstream to be ripened so that it is a suitable vessel for the main practices of the path of liberation, and what is this path of ripening? Literally speaking, to be a disciple of the main practices of the liberating path of the Great Perfection, one must have "the intelligence of self-appearing pristine awareness." For that, an individual who has fully measured up to the view of a Vajrācārya must first receive the guru's blessings of the three lineages,[1] and then simply through being granted the empowerment of the creative power of pristine awareness, which forcefully elevates one to realization, one simultaneously experiences the meaning of the empowerment—naked, originally pure, pristine awareness. Upon receiving that empowerment, one transcends the contrived, effortful path of accomplishment, [3] and the clear light pristine awareness naturally spreads forth, like the taste of molasses for someone who is mute. Only by such means does one enter the path of the supreme yāna and complete the necessary antidotes. That is what is needed. Such a person must be of sharper than sharp faculties, and to become such a vajra student who has the fortune to be trained in this great mystery depends on becoming accomplished by way of the path of ripening mentioned earlier. But if even the desire to reach perfect enlightenment by progressing on the Mahāyāna path—without need for those kinds of accomplishments—doesn't arise in one's mindstream, what need is there to speak of the impossibility of reaching in this lifetime the swift path of the great mystery that aspires to the kingdom of the primordial protector by sealing progress in the Mahāyāna six perfections in the nature of connate pristine awareness?! That would be as impossible as someone who is unable to ride a horse handling an even swifter mount.

Such a path of ripening, which makes one a suitable vessel, consists of all the stages of the yānas discussed in all the teachings of the Buddha, from the Śrāvakayāna up to anuyoga. [4] However, since one is not striving for nirvāṇa,

1. These are the enlightened-view lineage of the buddhas, the symbolic lineage of the vidyādharas, and the aural lineage of ordinary individuals.

free of suffering, for one's own sake, as do the śrāvakas, one does not enter the actual path of the śrāvakas. Nevertheless, if one fails to abandon [what is abandoned] and lacks the noble qualities or the kinds of realization that are fathomed even by the śrāvakas, although one may bear an elegant name, one is inferior even to the śrāvakas. So, as the saying goes, while abandoning an inferior attitude like that of the śrāvakas, one should adopt practices like those of the śrāvakas. Just as the śrāvakas are the kind of people who escape the mundane existence of saṃsāra for themselves, so should one have the attitude of delivering not only oneself but all sentient beings from saṃsāra.

Thus the stage of the path to be practiced that is shared with the śrāvakas is as follows: The śrāvakas recognize this city of the three realms—from the pinnacle of mundane existence in the fortunate realms, down to the hells—as the conditioned suffering of being under the domination of karma and mental afflictions. Seeing it as a fiery pit and a poisonous vipers' nest, they have the attitude of wishing to definitely emerge from saṃsāra. [5] On that basis, with a fervent, urgent desire to avert rebirth with such a sense of urgency that even if their head is on fire they don't put it out, they practice the three trainings in general. Specifically, they unify their wisdom drawn from hearing, reflection, and meditation on the meaning of the nonexistence of an autonomous personal identity. Even to enter the path of the supreme yāna, the Great Perfection, one definitely needs such a special attitude and such an aspect of wisdom. Without that, in terms of one's own experience, there would be no basis for the great compassion of wishing others to be free of suffering to arise. As it is said: "If those beings have never before had that wish for their own sake even in their dreams, how could they possibly have it for the sake of others?"[2] Without that compassion, one will lack the attitude of aspiring for the Great Perfection that is aroused by it. So without progress in the Mahāyāna, the Great Perfection is impossible, just as there can be no aśoka tree[3] if there are no trees.

2. Śāntideva, *A Guide to the Bodhisattva Way of Life*, 1.24.

3. The Tibetan reads *sha ba* (deer), but it would make more sense for it to read *sha pa* (aśoka tree). This echoes a classical point from Dharmakīrti's logic, that a subset cannot exist if its general category does not exist.

Thus both that special attitude and that aspect of wisdom constitute the stage of the yāna that is shared with the śrāvakas, so they [6] have the nature of the path of ripening that makes one a suitable vessel for this supreme yāna. If one's mindstream is not ripened by this path, the desire to escape from saṃsāra will not arise, and whatever one does, it will act as a cause of saṃsāra. So one will not be freed from the greatest obstacle on the path of the supreme yāna.

Likewise, even though one refuses to enter the path of the pratyekabuddhas, one must be replete with all their excellent qualities. What then is the stage of the yāna that is held in common with the pratyekabuddhas? In addition to the attitude and faculty of wisdom of the śrāvakas that were just discussed, the pratyekabuddhas ascertain the sequence of arising and cessation corresponding to the progressive emergence and reverse order of the twelve links of dependent origination. Insofar as this understanding increases their attitude of renunciation—the wish to definitely escape from saṃsāra—this becomes the middling yāna. Moreover, they well realize not only the nonexistence of an autonomous individual but also, in terms of phenomena, the emptiness of apprehended external objects. So their engagement with wisdom is also superior to that of the śrāvakas. For that reason they are said to have faculties that are of a middling nature. Moreover, to progress on the path of the natural Great Perfection, [7] the power of one's yāna, in terms of the yearning of renunciation on the basis of [comprehending] the forward and reverse order of the twelve links of dependent origination, must be even stronger than that of the śrāvakas. As it is said, one's mindstream must be completely purified, or ripened, by the faculty of wisdom that knows the appearances of objects—which are apprehended as being external and unrelated to the substance of the inner mind that apprehends them—to lack true existence. Without that, one will not be able to stop the coarse confusion that clings to the apprehender and the apprehended as though they were totally separate from each other. Then there is no way one can realize all phenomena of saṃsāra, nirvāṇa, and the path as being unreal, like illusions. So these yānas, along with the wisdom connected to realizations of their type, constitute the two yāna stages that are held in common with the supreme yāna and what should be practiced within it, respectively.[4]

Explaining it this way enables one to recognize, principally, how progress on the path can be categorized[5] in either the yāna of the śrāvakas or that of the pratyekabuddhas, respectively, and illustrates how the distinctive attitudes by which each of them desires to emerge [from saṃsāra]—along with the types of wisdom realizations related to those attitudes—are dissimilar in the sense of being either superior or inferior. With the motivation of such an attitude, outwardly one practices [8] the ethical discipline of restraining from improper physical and verbal behavior, and inwardly one resorts in many ways to samādhi that overcomes the allures of compulsive thoughts[6] involving laxity and excitation. On that basis, by training in the wisdom that was just explained, one severs the root of saṃsāra. Moreover, śrāvakas accumulate merit by worshipping the buddhas and so on for three lifetimes and more, whereas the pratyekabuddhas achieve nirvāṇa by such practices as serving the buddhas who appear over the course of a hundred eons and more. Since both kinds of practitioners make their accumulations insofar as they achieve nirvāṇa just for their own sakes, one can apprehend the difference between the inferiority and superiority of their yānas just from that [difference in the way they accumulate merit] alone.

As for the Bodhisattvayāna, you do not enter the actual yānas of the śrāvakas and pratyekabuddhas in the way that they do, and it is not as if you must train in the kinds of paths that are common to them. Rather, the distinction of the Bodhisattvayāna is that you take your own kinds of tragic suffering in the ocean of saṃsāra's miseries and relate them to others, viewing all other sentient beings as close relatives, as if they were your own kindhearted mothers. [9] That which is worshipped is the field of merit for accomplishing perfect enlightenment, and that which is despised

4. This translation follows the version of this essay in the author's collected works, which reads *rim pa gnyis yin no*, instead of *rim pa gnyis pa* in the present collection.

5. This translation follows the version of this essay in the author's collected works, which reads *so sor 'jog pa'i*, instead of *so sor 'jug pa'i* in the present collection.

6. Tib. *rnam rtog*, Skt. *vikalpa*.

is whatever could serve as a basis for wrongdoings that propel you into the miserable states of existence. Seeing all these things, you achieve others' benefit even as you achieve your own. Recognize that the root of all wrongdoing is the hope to accomplish your own ends, whether in the past or from now on. Just as you [previously] disregarded others, [now] cast that aside and arouse the extraordinary attitude of exchanging yourself for others. Principally, this means having the distinctive attitude of wishing to proceed to the state of ultimate, perfect enlightenment for the sake of others. Such an attitude is the path, or the body of the yāna, or the central core of the natural Great Perfection.[7] Regarding the Great Perfection, primarily in terms of skillful means, there are very many superior qualities by which it is superior to other [parts of the] Mahāyāna, but in terms of the main practice of this yāna, many hundreds of scriptures and reasonings establish that the root of skillful means is this precious bodhicitta itself, which is the primary skillful means that stems from great compassion.

If, first of all, the scriptures are the basis of analysis, and reasoning is actually that which analyzes, what is this practice of the path of the Great Perfection, [10] what is to be achieved, and as a result of your striving what state do you wish to reach? Assuming that state needs to be achieved, do you focus on your own interests or on the interests of others? Distinguish between the former state to be achieved, the nirvāṇa that is the mere extinction of the miseries of saṃsāra, and what goes beyond that to fulfill the hopes of all suffering sentient beings, which is like a wish-fulfilling gem and a wish-granting tree. The former aspiration is to achieve something very inferior, so even when you reach that state, since its positive qualities are so insignificant, how could they ever result in the Great Perfection that brings you to the kingdom of the primordial protector? If the goal for which you aspire is for your own sake, such an inferior attitude will lead to an inferior and limited yāna like those of the śrāvakas and pratyekabuddhas. Even in the mundane world, if acting primarily in one's own interests is unworthy

7. This translation follows the version of this essay in the author's collected works, which reads *rang bzhin rdzogs pa chen po'i*, instead of *rang gzhan* in the present collection.

of a great individual, in the tradition of Dharma, how could that be a great yāna? The distinction of the attitude that does not bear all sentient beings as its beneficiaries and the state of perfect enlightenment as its goal is an inferior vehicle or mount, [11] like a sheep or donkey that cannot carry a great burden. There is much more that could be said, but just this will suffice for the time being.

Thus as for the vital core of the path of the Great Perfection, the means by which the fruition is achieved, and what enables one to take up the burden of the vast activities of the path that achieves such fruition, it is this precious bodhicitta that brings one to the Mahāyāna. With such a mind, whatever kind of yāna you follow toward your intended, ultimate goal, the great vow to practice made by all the bodhisattvas of the past, present, and future from within the Pāramitāyāna pertains to the six perfections themselves. In this context they constitute the structure of the path. That mind has the two qualities of aspiring to accomplish the welfare of others and to achieve perfect enlightenment. With regard to accomplishing the welfare of others and perfect enlightenment, however good a path is presumed to be, if it is unrelated to generosity and so on, it will not have the potential to ripen sentient beings or liberate one's own mindstream. [12] Like the paths of the śrāvakas and pratyekabuddhas, even if one generates a mind that is lacking [those perfections], it will be merely a positive mindset but will not lead to perfect enlightenment. To enter the path of the natural Great Perfection, not only is this the vital core of the path, but from the very beginning the distinct qualities of this attitude are indispensible for ripening one's mindstream. Without this attitude arising, even if one fills a galaxy with offerings of the seven precious substances and cultivates the wisdom of the identitylessness of the subject for a hundred eons and so on, one does not enter the Mahāyāna. As soon as it does arise, even giving a crow a morsel of food counts as a Mahāyāna activity. By the arising of this attitude alone one truly warrants the name of a bodhisattva, and if it declines, one ceases to be a bodhisattva. So this alone is the entrance to the Mahāyāna.

If one's mind is not thoroughly ripened in this general entrance to the Mahāyāna, there is no way one can enter into the specific realizations of the Mahāyāna Dharma. Likewise, if one's mindstream is not ripened by way of generosity and so on, one lacks the conduct of bodhicitta, [13] so there is no way one can proceed to perfect enlightenment. That special mind depends on the aid of conduct, and the culmination of such conduct is the meaning of completely progressing along the path. Therefore the Bodhisattvayāna is the special, vital core of the structure of the yāna of the general path of an individual who enters the path of the Great Perfection, and it is the third stage of the path for ripening, or transforming, one's mindstream. If you do not properly recognize this point, all the realizations of the Secret Mantrayāna, like a sketch of a butter lamp, do not become the authentic Mahāyāna, so they cannot perform the tasks of that path, just as a sketched butter lamp cannot dispel darkness. For that reason try to come to the certain conviction that, with the yogas of skillful means and wisdom shared with the śrāvakas and pratyekabuddhas serving auxiliary roles, the vital core of the path is precious bodhicitta. This is the indispensible entrance to the shared preliminaries of the path of the Great Perfection.

The wisdom included among the six perfections within the context of this yāna, moreover, is not [14] merely the wisdom of the śrāvakas and pratyekabuddhas. Rather, it is an exceptional wisdom that realizes the subtle lack of identity to phenomena: that all phenomena and individuals are empty of true existence, like illusions. The vital core, or the principal element, of the yāna by which one progresses on the path is bodhicitta. But the key criterion by which to evaluate progress along each of the five paths is how one brings forth an experience of the activities of bodhicitta with respect to the wisdom that realizes identitylessness, from among the six perfections.

Thus just having ripened one's mindstream through the Pāramitāyāna does not make one into a disciple of the Great Perfection per se. On the basis of progress in the six perfections, one must certainly be an individual who has an uncontrived aspiration to reach the state of perfect enlightenment and has set forth on the path of buddhahood. Even so, if not transmuted by antidotes, attachment—which is the primary mental affliction that obstructs enlightenment and the conduct of enlightenment—will not be stopped by the power of antidotes. Yet with the power of antidotes, just as even enemies can be put into service, so too mental afflictions, [15] without casting off their afflictive nature, can be generated in the nature of the path. The key that transforms mental afflictions into the path is known as the Vajrayāna. It is similar to a diamond [i.e., a "precious vajra"] because in this yāna you are invulnerable to harmful mental afflictions. That is not due solely to the power of familiarization, but rather to the profound aspects of wisdom and the powerful qualities of skillful means. It is not just that one is undisturbed by mental afflictions. Rather, like the ingestion of poison improving one's complexion, mental afflictions not only aid one on the path but are assimilated into the path.

So the power of the antidotes has a function beyond that of the general Pāramitāyāna, and that pertains precisely to abandoning the obscurations to be overcome. As such, this is a swift path for the Mahāyāna, and it is for those disciples who are of exceptionally sharp faculties. One's body, speech, and mind appear to the mind as being ordinary, and the mind, which is a secret to others, clings to these appearances. There does exist within sūtra a path by which to transmute that mind so that it bears the aspects of a buddha's dharmakāya, which remains a secret to others. Yet the unique aspect of method that *protects the mind* from the obstacle of clinging to ordinary appearances, so that the body and speech are actualized as the ultimate rūpakāya and enlightened voice, [16] brings the fruition onto the path. Thus it is called *mantra* [etymologically, "mind protector"], and that is the meaning of the precious classes of tantras, in which there are four entrances for disciples corresponding to their level of mental capacity: (1) The one that primarily emphasizes outer activities, is kṛya, or the kriyātantra; (2) the one that equally entails the practice of activities and yoga is upa, or the caryātantra; (3) the one that primarily emphasizes yoga is yoga, or the yogatantra; and (4) the one that focuses solely on yoga, without reliance on activity, is the anuttarayogatantra.

The meaning of those terms is applied in relation to the degree of emphasis they place on verbal and physical activities, including those of hygiene and so on, done in order to please the deities and to increase one's insights. In dependence upon the power of the skillful means and the distinguishing feature by which the wisdom is so profound, the Vajrayāna that takes the fruition onto the path, as just explained, is divided into four classes, principally in terms of whether or not individuals with successive degrees of spiritual acuity are able to transform attachment into the path. There are also different numbers of deity yogas and greater and lesser enumerations of the paths. [17] But just as, even within those [classes of tantra], there are some of superior and some of inferior faculties, so is it perfectly appropriate that there should be further divisions into superior and inferior. Insofar as the realizations of such Vajrayāna individuals, who are a subset of Mahāyāna practitioners, are able to abandon what is to be abandoned, they are able to transmute mental afflictions into the path. Thus they are exceptional. In terms of their achievements and the means of achieving them, they are able to bring what has an aspect in accordance with the rūpakāya onto the path as its fruition. So this is an especially swift path. It is necessary for one to be ripened in the secret continuum [i.e., tantra] of the Mantrayāna, through the infusion of potentials for these kinds of realizations or antidotes in one's mindstream. If one lacks this, the path of the natural Great Perfection, since it is the final goal of what is ultimately taken as the main event—the ultimate skillful means even amidst the Vajrayāna, endowed as it is with the greatness of the skillful means of the path of the Secret Mantrayāna—cannot stand alone by itself without relating to the interior of the earlier and later paths.

Therefore the three stages of the Vajrayāna—kṛya, upa, and yoga—hold up the path of the natural Great Perfection by greatly increasing the capacity of the mind for abandoning the mental afflictions to be abandoned [18] and for reaching the fruition to be achieved. These potentials in the mind are carried along in what has the essential nature of a single yāna at the time of the path. Thus they constitute three stages of ripening. If the power of these paths is not upwardly perfected in the mindstream, know that it will be missing on the path of the natural Great Perfection, and so you should definitely value the ripening that results from them.

There are three entrances to the class of the great yoga, anuttarayogatantra, which are also demarcated in terms of the successive degrees of the faculties of disciples: (1) mahāyoga, which primarily emphasizes the skillful means of the stage of generation regarding the aspect of appearances; (2) anuyoga, which primarily emphasizes the wisdom of the stage of completion regarding the aspect of emptiness; and (3) atiyoga, which primarily emphasizes the indivisibility of appearances and emptiness by taking pristine awareness as the path. Disciples of the great yoga with conceptual elaborations engage in approach, actualization, close actualization,[8] and so on, regarding many circles of residential maṇḍalas and their inhabitants, including the assemblies of deities of the three divine seats.[9] By so doing, this yāna of skillful means leads them to the primordial consciousness of great bliss, which refines their subtle and coarse body, speech, and mind. [19] This is mahāyoga. Disciples of the great yoga with a little bit of freedom from conceptual elaborations practice the methods of the stage of completion, in which they focus on the loci of the channels, the movements of the vital energies, and the arrays of the orbs of bodhicitta that came into being together with the formation of their bodies. By so doing, the perfect yāna of unique skillful means that forcefully leads them to connate primordial consciousness, the clear light of the union of absolute space and primordial consciousness, is anuyoga. Disciples who are greatly, or entirely, free from conceptual elaborations practice simply resting in the reality that is identified with words, which is the view of the indivisibility of pristine awareness and emptiness that has never been combined or separated. The yāna of skillful means by which one discovers the union of the kāyas and facets of primordial consciousness that are the ultimate goal to be accomplished by the path of the Vajrayāna is the Great Perfection, atiyoga. There are very

8. Tib. *bsnyen pa, sgrub pa, nye bar sgrub pa*. The two primary aspects of sādhana practice within the context of mahāyoga (*bsnyen sgrub*) are often subdivided into four branches: approach, close approach, actualization, and great actualization.

9. Tib. *gdan gsum*. Buddhas, bodhisattvas, and wrathful deities.

many things to be explained regarding those three yogas, but I will leave it there for the time being.

Now the path of mahāyoga, with conceptual elaborations, makes the body, speech, and mind serviceable and creates habitual propensities for arousing ordinary birth, death, and the intermediate period as the three kāyas. And it increases the unique potentials for the collection of merit that actualizes the rūpakāya. On the basis of the types of realization that evolve upwardly from there, [20] along the path of anuyoga, which is without conceptual elaborations, one must experience the realization of the connate clear light by focusing on the crucial points of the channels and vital energies. For someone who has ripened his or her mindstream with the two yogas, but still has no experience of realizing the clear light by the power of meditation, it will be impossible for a direct identification of naked pristine awareness to arise merely by differentiating between the mind and pristine awareness in this context [of the Great Perfection]. So one will not earn the title of being a disciple of the Great Perfection.

The foregoing accounts definitively arrange, even as they completely and accurately set forth, the essential nature, enumeration, and progression of the stages of the yānas by which one becomes a suitable vessel for the Great Perfection in this lifetime by the kindness of a knowledgeable Vajrācārya. By training in such a path in other lifetimes, the potentials for realization are implanted in one's mindstream, so even if one does not train in this lifetime, since the Vajrācārya has progressed to the heights of the enlightened view, he sows practical instructions according to one's disposition and capacity. And from the proximate cause of one's own faith, one's previous, uncompleted training for realizations is forcefully catalyzed. So there are two approaches to the Great Perfection. [21] With the eye of wisdom that has become utterly myopic, those who turn the practice topsy-turvy[10] are very wearying. Through the stages of practice of the path of the eight yānas that ripen in those ways, if one's mindstream is properly cultivated, henceforth the Dharma of the Great Perfection and the practitioner

10. Tib. *zhva dpe lham 'geb byed pa*. Lit. "wearing a hat as a shoe."

will not be mismatched. If one enters the Great Perfection like that, one will become an exceptional vessel for the direct experience of all the stages of progress along the paths of each of the yānas.

Intervening verses:

> Nowadays most people enter this Dharma
> with the hope that it will liberate them
> without having matured through the path of ripening.
> But their mindstreams will remain ordinary.
>
> Nevertheless, if one systematizes the paths of liberation and ripening
> and dispels confusion regarding the realizations of the great mystery,
> who can train these people who do not see this as an act of kindness,
> but rather become upset?
>
> The white light of hearing and reflection shines like the sun
> on the nature of the straight paths of ripening and liberation.
> With the wish that it should lead my mind to the peak of the eastern mountain,
> may my aspirations [22] be fulfilled!

## II. The Main Practice: The Way to Follow the Stages of Liberation on the Path of the Natural Great Perfection

Regarding the way to practice the unique preliminaries for settling one's body, speech, and mind in their natural states and so on, there is nothing clearer than the Great Perfection training manuals such as *The Primordial Consciousness Guru*. However, since it is important to bring forth the unmistaken meaning of the in-depth presentation of this yāna in terms of the ground, path, and fruition, I shall explain that meaning. I shall give a literal, undistorted description of the path of this yāna in terms of (A) how to enter the essential nature of the ground, (B) the stages of progress along the path, and (C) the manifestation of the fruition.

## A. How to Enter the Essential Nature of the Ground

With respect to the way to follow the path at this point, there are two ways of laying out the presentation of the ground: (1) the threefold division of the essential nature, the manifest nature, and yāna,[11] and (2) the twofold division of original purity and spontaneous actualization.

### 1. The Threefold Division of the Essential Nature, the Manifest Nature, and Yāna

Regarding the ultimate fruition to be accomplished with the practices along the path, there is the dharmakāya, the culmination of one's own welfare, [23] and the two rūpakāyas, the culmination of others' welfare. These are the sambhogakāya, which accomplishes by means of the supreme yāna the goals of those whose mindstreams have been ripened, and the nirmāṇakāya, which accomplishes the goals of those whose mindstreams have not been ripened. So it is certain that the ultimate goal to be accomplished consists of three kāyas. If there were not already a basis for accomplishing each of them, this would be like the fact that crops will not grow later when there was no soil there previously, so there must be a basis for accomplishing each one.

The basis for accomplishing the first [i.e., the dharmakāya] is the way the mind really exists, naturally free of conceptual elaboration, its *essential nature*, which is the mere absence of the object to be refuted. The meaning of this is the view of the pith instructions, free of all assertions, by which

11. This translation follows the version of this essay in the present collection, whereas the version in the author's collected works reads *thugs rje* instead of *theg*.

the origin, location, and destination [of the mind] are analyzed. That is the reality to be ascertained.

The basis for accomplishing the second [i.e., the sambhogakāya] is conscious awareness—luminous in the *manifest nature* of brilliance and vividness—that arises in dependence upon causes and conditions; empty, but not in the sense of a nihilistic void. Regarding the two—the mind and pristine awareness—in the latter there is both the aspect of cognizance and the radiance of pristine awareness. Between these two, the former [cognizance] is the dharmakāya of primordial consciousness, and the latter [radiance] is the impartial, all-encompassing ground for [24] the assembly of the teacher and retinue—not separate from one another—in the great Akaniṣṭha, which is imbued with the five certainties.[12]

The basis for accomplishing the third [i.e., the nirmāṇakāya] is this indivisible unity of the emptiness and luminosity that were just explained. From that emerge countless trillions of pure and impure nirmāṇakāyas as its creative expressions. Although they do not exist apart from the former two, they emerge from this coarse mind of the present moment and in the location of this material form that is created by the mind.

As for the term *yāna*, there is no need to attribute other labels to the basis for accomplishing the nirmāṇakāya, such as the *essential nature* and *manifest nature* corresponding to the prior two [kāyas]. In general the contributing condition for manifesting the three kāyas is the Mahāyāna. But to be specific, without wavering from the inconceivable enlightened view, free of conceptual elaborations, in which impure aspects that belong to one's own appearances are pacified within absolute space imbued with the twofold purity,[13] the emanated displays of appearances for others arise automatically, for as long as phenomenal existence continues, without reliance upon even the slightest effort. Those are the function of the great compassion that came at the time of the path, of unbearable power, [25] sealed

12. Tib. *nges pa lnga*. The certainty of the perfect teacher, the perfect teaching, the certain perfect place, the perfect disciples, and the perfect time.

13. Tib. *dag pa gnyis ldan*. The purity from afflictive obscurations and cognitive obscurations.

solely by the indwelling, essential nature of indivisible pristine awareness and emptiness. That which is called the *basis for accomplishing*, or the *basis for the arising of*, the nirmāṇakāya is presented insofar as it is a unique contributing condition, so it is imperative for catalyzing the crucial points of the path in order to bring about the welfare of others directly. But I say with approval that what is called *compassion* is not something that needs to be "discovered" as a basis to be actualized as the essential nature of the nirmāṇakāya.

## 2. The Twofold Division of Original Purity and Spontaneous Actualization

The three kāyas of the fruition can also be subsumed under the dharmakāya and rūpakāya. The basis for accomplishing the dharmakāya is the aspect of original purity, and the basis for accomplishing the rūpakāya is spontaneous actualization. First, with respect to the dharmakāya, there is (1) ultimate, absolute space imbued with the two purities, and (2) the dharmakāya of primordial consciousness, in which the following are not separate in their essential nature: (a) the meditative equipoise that is absorbed in that absolute space, like water poured into water, and (b) the postmeditative state in which one is unobstructedly aware of the appearing aspect of what is deceptive[14] without wavering from that meditative equipoise. The basis for the first is originally pure emptiness, which is pure from conceptual elaborations concerning true existence from the very beginning. The basis

14. Tib. *kun rdzob*, Skt. *saṃvṛti*. This adjective usually occurs as a modifier of one of the two kinds of reality. The Tibetan and Sanskrit adjective means "totally obscuring," for this reality totally obscures the deeper dimension of ultimate reality (Tib. *don dam bden pa*, Skt. *paramārthasatya*). "Totally obscuring reality" seems too awkward in English and also does not quite get at the meaning, since, according to Candrakīrti, it is *ignorance* that obscures the nature of the reality, not the appearances themselves. Hence the appearances are "deceptive," but for those who are deceived by the obscuring veil of ignorance, they appear to be "real." Thus they are "deceptively real" and constitute what is known as "deceptive reality."

for the second is originally pure pristine awareness, [26] which never enters the domain of karmic energies and conceptual elaborations.

Second, with respect to the rūpakāya, there is the sambhogakāya and the nirmāṇakāya, which are comprised of one's own appearances and appearances for others, respectively. As divided off from the pair of the mind and pristine awareness, the latter consists of self-emergent, unimpeded cognizance and of luminosity manifesting as the five lights that are the radiance of pristine awareness. They are the basis for the arising of the self-appearing sambhogakāya and facets of primordial consciousness. The nirmāṇakāyas emerge as its creative expressions. In this regard the term "spontaneous actualization" means that they are naturally present, without being suddenly created by causes and conditions. To understand these precisely, look to the words of a master. Whereas fools entrust themselves to books, you should entrust yourself to a master. Still, very clear writings concerning great mysteries are formidable. So if you wish to know them, it is best to cut through your false assumptions by pleasing a vajra guru.

## B. The Stages of Progress along the Path of This Yāna

This is how someone whose stream of consciousness has been elevated through having been genuinely ripened with the eight yānas should train [27] in the enlightened view that the kāyas and facets of primordial consciousness are neither joined nor separate, the liberating path that directly frees one from all subtle and coarse defects of the two obscurations. First of all, one needs to distinguish between the mind and pristine awareness. In accordance with the earlier and later omniscient ones,[15] one should explain in words the crucial points about the doors to the mind and pristine awareness, respectively—about the channels, vital energies, bases, and so on. Reaching certainty about these is extremely important. However, in general, the entrance to the path of this supreme yāna is primarily the

15. Tib. *kun mkhyen snga phyi*. That is, Longchenpa and Jikmé Lingpa (*'Jigs med gling pa mkhyen brtse 'od zer*, 1730–85).

actual empowerment,[16] without conceptual elaborations, and, specifically, the empowerment of the creative expressions of pristine awareness. When there is the coming together of the circumstances of the blessings of the unmistaken enlightened view of the vajra guru and the power of faith of the disciple—like the coming together of fire and kindling—the actual primordial consciousness that is the meaning of the pointing-out empowerment forcefully granted by the guru is unmodified pristine awareness, which is the life force of the path of this yāna.

Sitting in the posture of Vairocana, with its seven attributes, the disciple brings forth just the aspects of conscious awareness and luminosity, in which thoughts of the three times are suspended. After the blessings of the three lineages have descended through the guru, with the forceful utterance of *phaṭ*, the guru abruptly clears away the dust of coarse conscious awareness so that awareness has nothing on which to focus. [28] Then, asking, "What is the mind?" the guru draws one to recognize the essential nature of the mind. Certain knowledge of the actual nature of reality, which is empty of being established as anything and devoid of a referential object, arises unobstructedly, free of fixation. It is imbued with the power of clarity of pristine awareness, uncontaminated by configurations of thoughts. This discovery of vividly awake brilliance that is three-fourths uncoiled is the identification of naked pristine awareness. Without needing to look for the Buddha elsewhere, the dharmakāya is literally found from within your own resting place, certain knowledge arises from within, the dispensation of the three lineages is received, realization powerfully blazes forth, you see the face of the primordial protector as your own, and so forth.

Then, just as you don't look for a thief on the grasslands after he has gone to the forest, you easily proceed to the kingdom of the three kāyas by taking pristine awareness alone as your path. There are two phases to this: (1) how to naturally sustain the pristine awareness of cutting through to original purity and (2) how to take as your path the radiance of the pristine awareness of the direct crossing over into spontaneous actualization.

16. Tib. *don dbang*.

## 1. How to Sustain the Pristine Awareness of Cutting through to Original Purity

Single-pointedly cut through to the unmodified pristine awareness that identifies your own essential nature within yourself. [29] With the confidence of realization that overcomes the many thoughts that arise and pass, if you gain realization by practicing with the four methods of release, three degrees of liberation will come in sequence, what comes before followed by what comes after. Thus whatever thoughts arise, familiarity with the realization of how they release themselves right where they are comes to its full strength, just as it is said:

> Whatever moves is nourishment for the king, dharmakāya.
> Whatever thoughts arise are creative expressions of pristine awareness.

There is much that needs to be known about the four kinds of open presence and so forth in this mode of practice, but I shall not elaborate, for these are clear in the meditation manuals.[17]

## 2. The Practice of the Direct Crossing Over

If one properly acquires the confidence of realization through the practice of naturally settling the pristine awareness of cutting through, then by focusing on the crucial points of the body, speech, and mind by way of postures and gazes, appearances of the five lights of the radiance of pristine awareness will arise directly as objects of perception in the form of bindus and kāyas from pathways of the channels of primordial consciousness. In this regard there is a presentation of the four lamps. By practicing accordingly, one traverses the path of the four visions and so on, which begins

17. See, for example, Sera Khandro, *Garland for the Delight of the Fortunate*, in Düdjom Lingpa, *Buddhahood without Meditation*, 251–55. See also the next essay in this volume, by Jé Tsultrim Zangpo.

when one sees the radiance of pristine awareness appear as vajra strands, and proceeds up to the direct appearances of the actual nature of reality. [30] These topics are clear in the meditation manuals, and I shall explain them a little later on.

Now in the manner of an addendum, I shall explain the general meaning a little bit by clarifying how this is not incompatible with the sūtras and tantras[18] in general, and in particular how this is an uncommonly extraordinary path. First of all, as explained previously, the structure of the path of this supreme yāna has the nature of proceeding along the straight highway of the central practices of the six perfections with the attitude of striving for perfect enlightenment for the sake of others. So how could it be incompatible with the [Mahā]yāna? Moreover, if the mindstreams of individuals who are genuine disciples of this supreme yāna have been authentically ripened with the precious bodhicitta imbued with the two goals,[19] then the luminosity and cognizance in which thoughts have been completely cut off is not devoid of the elixir of the unsurpassed yāna, for it is impossible for [one person] to have two different streams of mental consciousness. This is definitive reasoning, for the luminosity and the cognizance that remain as a fourth part after cutting off the manifested thoughts of the three times is the continuum of the mind. [31] Thus that continuum of the mind arises in the essential nature of this supreme mind [of bodhicitta], and the way it arises is by nature unmodified. So it is impossible for it to lack the power of that mind, regardless of whether it is manifest or not.

Therefore it is wonderful to know that to sustain naturally the pristine awareness of the Great Perfection one needs the elixir of bodhicitta to bring it to the Mahāyāna. To deny that is to let one's dull intelligence liberally burst with faults. On that basis, the crucial points of the path of the outer kriyā and caryā, the inner yoga, and the two lower yogas of the secret annuttarayoga are perfected. From this point onward, on the basis of this ordinary consciousness one directly and immediately identifies and

18. Tib. *sngags*. Lit. "mantras."

19. The two goals are to serve all sentient beings and to attain perfect enlightenment.

sustains clear light pristine awareness—and not just a generality based on having heard about it[20]—without reliance on the effortful practices of the channels, vital energies, and orbs. By so doing, after some time delusive thoughts and mental constructs concerning the nature of connate pristine awareness vanish like mist into the sky, and certain knowledge arises. In terms of the general anuttarayoga, this corresponds to the fourth stage known as the actual clear light. [32] Only those authentic disciples of this supreme yāna who are utterly free of conceptual elaborations reach that realization in this tradition, without reliance on the effortful path of divine appearances in accordance with mahāyoga or the arduous practices of the channels, vital energies, and orbs according to anuyoga. The ability to settle naturally in the essential nature of pristine awareness, in which the clear light nakedly flows forth, even without the elaborations of those effortful paths, is because one has experientially ascertained the clear light by striving in the practices of the lower yānas either in former lifetimes or in this lifetime. Since one's mindstream must be ripened in that way, all the crucial points of the lower paths must be completed, for if they are not, that realization will not arise.

Therefore the assertions that "the Secret Mantrayāna is great in terms of skillful means" and that it is the "yāna of skillful means" indicate that what distinguishes it above the Mahāyāna in general is solely its skillful means. As explained previously, those skillful means are its unique methods for actualizing connate primordial consciousness and the vajrakāya rainbow body, which is of the same nature as that primordial consciousness. They are said to be the methods for reaching that accomplishment. In this regard, in each of the three yogas there are three methods: those involving conceptual elaborations, those devoid of conceptual elaborations, and those utterly devoid of such elaborations. In this present context [33] the arousal of pristine awareness as the path by means of open presence and arising-and-release is the culmination of all skillful means, and it is utterly devoid of conceptual elaborations.

20. Tib. *sgra spyi*.

If one investigates in that way, it is easy to recognize that it is necessary to complete the crucial points of the lower paths, and that is a very important point that absolutely must be known. Now, even though one understands that the Great Perfection is a swift path that is devoid of conceptual elaborations, without precise knowledge of what that means, one will mix this up with the three kinds of laziness, such as lethargy. So even if one spends a lot of time diligently sustaining the sense of luminosity and cognizance but without distinguishing between the mind and pristine awareness, there is the great danger that one will go astray without attenuating attachment and hostility in the least.

According to this tradition, the fundamental nature of pristine awareness is constricted as the mind—like fluid water being coldly constricted as ice—into the essential nature of the coarse thoughts of clinging and grasping. This is due to the emanations of karmic energies that set in motion conceptual fabrications.[21] Pristine awareness—like the fluidity that is not newly produced when the cold turns [water] into ice—is not newly created even when contaminated by karmic energies and the agitation of conceptual fabrications. Rather, it is said that self-emergent pristine awareness, which has never been joined or separated, [34] is latently present, like the nature of fluidity that is there even when water is temporarily constricted by the cold, and then manifests its nature when it melts due to fire or sunlight.

Now the way this analogy is used to illustrate the ground awareness itself, as it is held in common with the lower two inner tantras—in terms of the distinction between the indwelling mind and the adventitious mind in the condition of the ground[22]—is not appropriate to the analogy used for

21. Tib. *kun rtog*, Skt. *saṃkalpa, parikalpa*.

22. For an example of such analogies being used in the context of New Translation anuttarayogatantra, see Tsongkhapa, *A Lamp to Illuminate the Five Stages*, 390. The primary difference seems to be that there, Tsongkhapa describes the indwelling, very subtle energy-mind as being a constant property that forms the basis of designation for the stream of a sentient being from lifetime to lifetime, "like the wetness of water," whereas the body and consciousness acquired within each lifetime are adventitious, "like the heat of water." Tsongkhapa is not at all describing the coarse mind as being like a constricted or frozen form *of* the indwelling mind, in the way that the analogy described here in the context of the Great Perfection does. Note that in the anuttarayogatantra tradition, too, there is a

the pristine awareness of the Great Perfection. For the pristine awareness of the Great Perfection is referred to as the youthful vase kāya[23] imbued with six characteristics, including its superiority to the ground. Now the anuttarayogatantras generally distinguish between the coarse and subtle body, speech, and mind, and what they identify as a very subtle mind, which is synonymous with this ground awareness. However, without correctly assessing each of the three yogas in terms of their specific methods for forcefully bringing forth realization of the clear light *while on the path*, most sectarian Nyingmapas nowadays pretentiously present the three yogas and so forth in terms of the degree of subtlety of their respective recognitions of the ground. This approach does not bear analysis when scrutinized by realized individuals well versed in the textual tradition. [35] Nevertheless, if one is glib, whatever one says may be acceptable for others.

Now then, does the tradition of the Great Perfection in the Early Translation school affirm or not affirm an originally pure pristine awareness that is uncontaminated by conceptual fabrications? If it does, just as there is nothing in the essential nature of ice that is not constricted by the cold, so, relative to pristine awareness, there is no aspect of consciousness that is not generated with the identity of mind. So how could it be originally pure? Suppose you say the tradition does not affirm [original purity]. This would discard the basis for the unique, swift path that takes the clear light as the path. Regarding all cases of ice and fluid water and of the mind and pristine awareness, are they of the same nature or of different natures? Since you have become absorbed in the meaning of the primordially liberated

significant subjective difference between the indwelling mind of clear light, which already exists at the time of the original condition (or "ground"), and the connate primordial consciousness of the actual clear light that is realized by a yogi while on the path, at "the fourth stage" mentioned just above in Dharmasāra's essay.

23. Tib. *gzhon nu bum pa'i sku*, Skt. *kumārakalaśakāya*. This term is unique to the Great Perfection tradition, referring to the state of enlightenment. It is like a "vase," for, as the sole bindu, it encompasses the whole of saṃsāra and nirvāṇa, while transcending the three times. It is called "youthful," for it is not subject to aging or degeneration, and it is called a "kāya," for it is the aggregate of all the inexhaustible enlightened bodies, speech, mind, qualities, and activities of all the buddhas. Its six characteristics are that it (1) is superior to the ground, (2) appears as one's own essential nature, (3) is discerning, (4) is liberated in activity, (5) does not emerge from anything else, and (6) dwells in one's own ground.

pristine awareness of the Great Perfection, which is free of all assertions, you don't know how to say anything about any point of reference.

How do you present the mind and pristine awareness as dependently related events in terms of something that is merely established by the conventional designations of concepts? The mind is dependent upon pristine awareness, but since pristine awareness is not dependent upon the mind, it is established in dependence upon the objects of awareness. [36] While there are the distinctions of subtle and coarse with regard to the essential nature of luminosity and cognizance, the meaning of this should be understood in accordance with Gyalwé Nyugu Khyentsé Lha,[24] who said, "For the source of the river of explanation, ask Candrakīrti . . ."

Old Nyingma meditators whose ocean of experience overflows say that the nature of the mind is pristine awareness, but that the essential nature of pristine awareness is not the mind; rather it is solely emptiness devoid of any referent. This assertion is very meaningful and there is much that could be said to elaborate on it, but I shall leave it for now.

Thus, although there is an assertion of an originally pure pristine awareness that has never been contaminated by conceptual fabrications and their concomitant karmic energies, this does not falsely imply that sentient beings are buddhas or that the ground of being is clean, blissful, permanent and that there exists a self in accordance with non-Buddhist speculations. To get this right from the beginning, by way of an analogy, when water is constricted by the cold and turns into ice, although the water is adulterated by the cold, its essential nature is not. The essential nature of water is just fluid and moist, and it has never existed in the essential nature of any *other* phenomenon. [37] So its essential nature is not adulterated by the cold and ice. If ice adulterated the essential nature of water, it would be impossible for ice to melt into fluid water, for ice is of the very nature of water. For example, it is like the way that [the very qualities of] fluidity and moisture cannot turn into [the very qualities of] firmness and solidity. As for the adulteration of water, due to the confluence of water and coldness,

24. Tib. *Rgyal ba'i myu gu mkhyen brtse'i lha.*

the fluid and moist qualities that make it function as water go dormant, and with the formation of ice, water turns into ice. Therefore, the essential nature of water is not lost in the way that fire burns kindling. Rather, the manifestation of its fluidity and moisture is temporarily suspended, and since they are dormant, the essential nature of water does not cease to exist.

Likewise, if these conceptual fabrications of the three poisons, such as craving and hostility, were qualities of the essential nature of the mind, these defilements would violate its basic nature, so it would not be originally pure. But as it is, once the connate ignorance that fails to realize the nature of existence has entered, the karmic energies move in a disoriented way, so the labyrinth of unbearable thoughts proliferates. This compels the ground pristine awareness to remain dormant. Yet in the end, [38] it is speculative ignorance that conjures up adventitious defilements and their factions, and that ignorance is subsumed solely in the intellect that confuses appearances with that which does not exist. So there are a hundred reasons why the ground pristine awareness remains originally pure, forever free of defilements.

With this in mind, the originally pure ground is presented as being unadulterated by adventitious obscurations. It is very important for you to know that when you practice the path of a tradition such as this, the inner necessity that makes it a straight, swift path is that one needs to draw forth the creative power [of pristine awareness]. If you understand the presentation of such original purity to mean that adventitious defilements do not exist and they do not mingle with one's stream of consciousness, you are mistaken. The radiance or inner glow of the originally pure clear light—pristine awareness—is of the nature of the five lights that are its subtle movements, and these are explained in the lower inner tantras in terms of vital energies. In this present context, these are the basis for accomplishing the ultimate rūpakāya, the vajrakāya rainbow body. Neither these [energies] nor the dormant original purity that is empty of something other—that is, empty of adventitious defilements—[39] are transient composites manifestly constructed by karma and mental afflictions. Rather, it is said that this ground—upon which the continuum that has been formed in a stream without beginning comes into being—is the *unconditioned* continuum, the jeweled [vessel] of spontaneous actualization turned on its head. This is the ground on which the unique, effortless method of this Dharma strikes the crucial point. Is there any difference between the ground and the basis for accomplishment? The mental domain of conceptual fabrications is not the basis for accomplishing the dharmakāya, but—as when sifting gold from soil—insofar as one strikes the crucial point, it is as if it were simply the ground.

Thus, while the presentation of the ground is the same as that of the anuttarayogatantra in general, the pith instructions on distinguishing pristine awareness from the mind—without reliance on the yogas of the channels, vital energies, and orbs—differentiate between indwelling and adventitious phenomena, like separating milk from pure water. They nakedly bring forth the clear light pristine awareness from its own place, so they are not incompatible with the sūtras and tantras in general. Moreover, they have unique qualities beyond those of the lower inner tantras. On the lower levels the bases to be purified are primarily birth, death, and the intermediate period, and one meditates by taking as the path the purifying agents, [40] the three kāyas, which bear aspects similar to the bases to be purified. This here is even more profound, for without conceptual elaborations, the basis to be purified is just this mind, which is the root of all of saṃsāra and nirvāṇa. Drawing the threefold classification of its essential nature, manifest nature, and compassion, and in reliance upon effortless methods, the three kāyas are taken as the path. For authentic disciples of this supreme yāna, the purpose of taking the three kāyas as the path in accordance with the lower yānas is achieved solely by this, and it is a very blissful method.

For those reasons, whatever purpose there may be in the stage of completion of the two realities that are established primarily in terms of the similarities between oneself and the accomplishment of the dharmakāya and rūpakāya, they lead to the crucial point of the practice of cutting through in this context. Moreover, without the elaborations of an effortful path, this is the ultimate blissful and swift path. If you ascertain the essence of the path of atiyoga by correctly knowing how that is so, you will fathom the innermost depths of the Dharma. By determining whether or not your disposition and faculties accord for now [with this path], you will not be fooled by exaggerations concerning the swiftness of this path, [41] and there will be no danger of your abandoning this profound mystery based only on a lower mode of progress.

The way to progress along the grounds and paths in dependence upon such practice in a way comparable to the progression along the five stages[25] and so on in the stage of completion is explained in the following way by our sublime guru.[26] The first two visions [of the direct appearances of the actual nature of reality and progress in meditative experience] correspond to the phases of the three isolations [of the body, speech, and mind].[27] The vision of reaching consummate awareness corresponds to the third stage, the illusory body; and the extinction into the actual nature of reality corresponds to the fourth stage, the actual clear light. The vajrakāya rainbow body, in which the kāyas and facets of primordial consciousness are neither joined nor separated, is asserted to be [the fifth stage,] the union of the two. In this tradition, the primordial consciousness that extinguishes [impure appearances] into the actual nature of reality corresponds to the phase of the uninterrupted path that acts as the antidote for overcoming afflictive and cognitive obscurations without any remainder. The way that leads up this path, which can generally serve in place of the accumulations [of merit and knowledge] over three countless eons, needs to be examined according to the tradition of the great charioteer, the protector Nāgārjuna. Once one has accepted the authenticity of the meaning of the perfection of wisdom sūtras, there is no point in denying the authenticity of the meaning of the classes of tantras of the Mantrayāna. For the Jina himself prophesied in connection to the profound meaning of the yāna of each one's own awareness, [42] which is not a matter of speculation.

25. See Tsongkhapa, *A Lamp to Illuminate the Five Stages*.

26. This most likely refers to Lerab Lingpa.

27. Tib. *dben gsum*.

As for recognizing the four visions, when the actual nature of the radiance of pristine awareness—or the way conventional things actually exist—is conjoined with the contributing conditions of practice on the path, there is a method present that is suitable to arouse the rūpakāya. Since this very method also empowers the clear light pristine awareness just a little bit, pristine awareness itself appears as kāyas like empty forms. The beginning of this path that ripens pristine awareness itself into kāyas consists of bindus of the five lights and so forth at first appearing directly to one's [visual] faculty.[28] This is [the first vision], the *direct appearances of the actual nature of reality*. Meditative experiences of the visions of such facets of primordial consciousness and the bindus progress up to the point where the solitary principal deities appear, and that is [the second] vision, *progress in meditative experience*. The complete appearances of assemblies of the five [buddha] families constitute [the third vision], *reaching consummate awareness*. The extinction into the expanse, not only of delusive mental appearances but also of the appearing aspect of the clear light, without any differentiation between emptiness and awareness, free of any referential object, like mist vanishing into the sky, is [the fourth vision], *extinction into the actual nature of reality*. Those appearances of clear light are what are extinguished into the actual nature of reality, and the four visions are presented in terms of the ways the appearances of the clear light [43] successively manifest along the path. The appearances of the radiance of the clear light pristine awareness manifest as visions along the path by the power of striking the crucial point of pristine awareness itself. This is an unparalleled quality of this path. For more extensive explanations of the four visions, look to the teachings of the earlier and later omniscient ones.

In general, according to the shared manner of progressing completely along the grounds and paths, divisions are made in terms of the stages of realization of the nature of existence, adorned with the accumulations [of merit and knowledge]. However, with the skillful means of

28. I have followed the version in the author's collected works, which reads *od lnga'i thig le sogs dang por mngon sum*, rather than the version in the present collection: *od lnga'i thig le sogs dang ser po mngon sum*.

anuttarayogatantra, one needs to ascertain how to complete the crucial points of the swift path on the basis of the unique path of the rūpakāya, in a tradition that is superior to other paths. Similarly, in this tradition as well, one needs to ascertain the structure of the path on the basis of nakedly arousing appearances of the clear light, with unique methods for taking the rūpakāya as the path. I presume to have provided a somewhat sound explanation of this as a service to this system of teaching of the earlier and later omniscient ones.

The ultimate essential point in this Dharma is simply taking pristine awareness as the path, and this doesn't happen without distinguishing between the mind and pristine awareness. [44] While there are many ways of distinguishing between the mind and pristine awareness, an unmistaken, straightforward criterion has to do with whether or not one grasps the meaning of the nature of existence that is devoid of a referential object. If you take as a starting point the meaning of the four visions, and then on top of this set forth the nature of existence, this will not be devoid of a referential object. Therefore, since all of saṃsāra and nirvāṇa is constructed by the mind and has no existence apart from delusive mental appearances, everything stems from the mind. It is not that the mind is first established as a subject and then the actual nature of reality is newly brought into existence. Rather, one recognizes what it means for the mind itself not to be established as anything. It is not as if the mind gets left behind[29] and then, falling down somewhere or other, gets lost. Instead, an emptiness must arise that is as though the mind has gone into nonexistence apart from the mere label of "mind." Then, from the perspective of that certain knowledge, one is devoid of all assertions of "this" and "not that." (This is the assertion of the position of the Sakyapas.) Furthermore, one's referential object disappears. (This is the assertion of the Gelukpas.) In this context, since this is the introduction to the indispensable view, this view of the pith instructions of the Great Perfection [45] remains within the Prāsaṅgika Madhyamaka tradition.

29. I have followed the version in the author's collected works, which reads *sems bor song ba lta bu*, rather than the version in the present collection: *sems ngor song ba lta bu*.

Therefore, an explanation of the contextual etymology of the Great Perfection must accord with taking the clear light pristine awareness as the path. The teachings of the gurus are excellent, as they are presented on the basis of recognizing how all phenomena included in saṃsāra, nirvāṇa, and the path are *encompassed*[30] in the expanse of the unborn, ultimate nature of the mind. The identification of pristine awareness in this system is unlike identifications of the clear light in the anuttarayogatantras as a whole. Rather than forcefully revealing the clear light and uniting emptiness with a primordial subject and object, [here], while the domain of any type of conceptual fabrications goes dormant in the face of the subjective mind, that mind experiences the clear light and, while having no referential object, comes to know, or have pristine awareness of, the meaning of the nature of existence. On the basis of that aspect of cognizance, or of knowing, "the pristine awareness of pristine awareness" is presented as the life force of the swift path, so that is also why there are differences with reference to "bliss and emptiness" and so forth [as presented in the anuttarayogatantras].

Such emptiness from the side of pristine awareness is the actual nature of pristine awareness, and that actual nature is also empty. While devoting yourself to that way of experiencing such emptiness, [46] do not rely on appearances to the conceptual mind that follows after words. Occasionally it seems as if the term "pristine awareness" is used to refer to emptiness, but these are obviously loose accounts of experience. The indivisibility of pristine awareness and emptiness is not just an emptiness of a single entity. Rather, it is an emptiness in which all of saṃsāra and nirvāṇa is ascertained as having no existence apart from the mind, and in which the mind, too, does not exist from its own side. This is not a conceptual construct or an emptiness that is patched on, as it were. Rather, it is an emptiness of a referential object when focusing on the actual nature of the mind. Now, this is the great, uniform pervasiveness of the actual nature of reality, in which all of saṃsāra and nirvāṇa is singularly extinguished in the expanse of the

30. Tib. *gcig tu rdzog pa*. A variant translation of *rdzogs chen* ("Dzokchen") is the Great Encompassment rather than the Great Perfection.

nature of being. The "great expanse," the "vast expanse," and so forth also refer to this.

Resting in meditative equipoise in the meaning of indivisible pristine awareness and emptiness as pointed out previously does not entail a limited emptiness of a particular object, which is [like] the mere eye of a needle. Rather, one's awareness infinitely pervades the great expanse of the actual nature of reality, just as there is a limitless range of the kinds of emptiness in the perfection [of wisdom]. So if you are wondering whether this serves to perfect the power of vipaśyanā meditation, [47] know that just this does it.

## III. The Results of the Practice

When extinction into the actual nature of reality takes place, not only delusive thoughts and appearances but also the path-time appearances associated with the actual nature of reality are extinguished into the great expanse, like the temporary disappearance of the moon on the last day of the lunar month. In this way one experiences liberation in which afflictive obscurations and their seeds are abandoned. Then one achieves the vajrakāya rainbow body, and the remaining cognitive obscurations to be abandoned (which involve the subtle habitual propensities of delusive dualistic appearances) are forever extinguished, solely by sustaining once again the natural flow of realization of the indivisibility of pristine awareness and emptiness. At the very same time, one attains the [fulfillment of] one's own welfare, the dharmakāya. Then, while not wavering even a little from this dharmakāya, the tainted elements from the earlier appearances of the kāyas along the path of the clear light are extinguished. Pristine awareness is transferred over to the vajrakāya, and a continuation of that arises as the primordial protector Samantabhadra. Then for as long as the realms of sentient beings remain, you have mastery over the kingdom of the great transference rainbow body, in which [48] the facets of primordial consciousness and the kāyas (which consist of the two indivisible rūpakāyas, [the fulfillment of] others' welfare) are neither joined nor separated. These rūpakāyas remain as great treasures of benefit and joy, without ever wearying of entering into enlightened activities.

Whatever faults there may be here, of making mistakes and of revealing secrets, I reverently confess in the presence of the vidyādhara root and lineage gurus. It is difficult to make decisions regarding such profound, secret matters, so this should not be regarded unequivocally as anything more than mere seeds for analysis. With these words as the basis, one should open the gate of analysis, and I ask that you immerse yourself in the teachings of the earlier and later omniscient ones, gain certainty regarding them, and offer fine prayers of supplication. I ask that you not reveal this teaching to everyone.

This is a revision of an earlier, old memorandum by Dharmasāra to fulfill the desires of the lamas of White Conch Monastery.[31] May there be virtue! [49]

31. Tib. *dung dkar dgon pa*.

# An Ornament of the Enlightened View of Samantabhadra

## *Secret Guidance Nakedly Granted to Dispel All Misconceptions regarding the View of the Clear Light Great Perfection*

Jé Tsultrim Zangpo[1]

The unmoving ground, primordially empty, the great freedom
    from elaboration,
the spontaneously actualized reality that is illuminated by the
    unimpeded inner glow,
the all-pervasive domain in which the creative displays arise
    everywhere,
father guru, the victor, self-knowing Padmasambhava:

For the sake of all those who are bereft of a permanent dwelling,
grant your blessing that the face of the indwelling dharmakāya
    may nakedly appear,
the source that serves the needs of sentient beings who have been
    my own mother and children,
terribly afflicted by unbearable suffering,

1. Tib. *Rje tshul khrims bzang po* (1884–1957).

and firmly bound by the fetters of karma, the source of suffering.
Bless me that I may proceed along the path of the four visions.

Here is a teaching that reveals in this lifetime the enlightened view of the primordial protector, the dharmakāya, Samantabhadra, for fortunate people with supreme faculties. [50] It is the ultimate enlightened view of all the buddhas, the refined essence of all practical instructions, the king of all the tantras, and the victorious summit of all yānas. Those who wish to follow the path of the exceptionally secret Great Perfection must first properly assemble all the elements of skillful means for ripening their own mindstreams and then enter this primordial, greatly secret, sovereign path. Otherwise, if they nonchalantly disregard the preliminaries to the path and are about to engage in the practices of the main body of the path, not only will this fail to serve as a proximate cause for the actual paths, but they won't even be able to engage in the main practices. So this will serve only as a cause for their entire lives being utterly wasted.

Well then, what are the dharmas that precede the practices of the main body of this path? The root and branches of the path consist of devoting yourself to a sublime spiritual friend in thought and deed. Then, whatever you do, let it be for the Dharma, while turning away from clinging to the appearances of this life. That must precede all dharmas, so consider how this body is the basis of leisure and opportunity that is greatly meaningful and difficult to obtain. Then you should [51] arouse the thought of wishing to take the essence of this leisure and opportunity and apply yourself to the virtuous Dharma. Moreover, if you don't apply yourself to this straightaway, consider that death is certain and the time of death is unpredictable, and come to a firm decision to definitely and swiftly devote yourself to the practice of Dharma alone. Then you must have the intention to take the ultimate essence of this leisure and opportunity by practicing a dharma to attain buddhahood for the sake of sentient beings. In order for your spiritual practice to become Dharma, even though you may have the attitude of turning away from clinging to the appearances of this life, if you lack the sublime method for transforming your spiritual practice into the path to liberation—namely, an earnest sense of renunciation by which you turn away from clinging to all of saṃsāra—whatever Dharma you practice, it will not bring you to the path of liberation. Therefore it is important that you reflect on the faults of saṃsāra, arouse an earnest sense of renunciation, and diligently apply yourself to rejecting [nonvirtue] and embracing [virtue] in accordance with the karmic laws of actions and their consequences. If you do not turn away from clinging to the ways of saṃsāra, insofar as it is created by its causes, the source of suffering, then whatever virtues you practice will act as causes for saṃsāra and will not take you along the path to liberation. If you are not disillusioned with the miseries of saṃsāra, compassion will not arise for sentient beings, either, so the abandonment of clinging to saṃsāra is also very important for the Mahāyāna path. [52]

Whether or not your spiritual practice takes you along the Mahāyāna path depends on this bodhicitta, rooted in great compassion, with the aspiration to benefit others. Moreover, the vital core of the Dharma of the sūtra path of the Mahāyāna is that it be imbued with bodhicitta. So if it is necessary to generate this precious bodhicitta in the sūtra approach to the Mahāyāna path, it is even more important to generate bodhicitta on the path of secret mantra. Without doing so, whatever efforts you make on the path of the Secret Mantrayāna for your own sake, not only will this not turn into the Mantrayāna path, but it won't lead to any Hīnayāna or Mahāyāna path either! So the root of Dharma, this precious bodhicitta, is the great, central principle of the path of the Secret Mantrayāna. Therefore, inasmuch as this Mahāyāna path is profound and supreme, just so much it requires a bodhicitta that is swift and of enormous strength. So to enter this path of the sovereign pinnacle of yānas, you must strike the crucial point of bodhicitta even more than in the practice of other classes of tantra. [53]

Therefore, at the beginning of the practice of this profound path, you should generate this precious bodhicitta, take the bodhisattva precepts, strive in methods to avoid being stained by any of the bodhisattva root downfalls and infractions, and abide by the pure bodhisattva precepts. Then with sincere admiration and reverence for a guru who holds an enlightened view and bears the warmth of blessings, arouse the firm faith of conviction that never transgresses whatever teachings are granted. This surpasses the way of devoting oneself to a guru according to the sūtra tradition and even goes beyond that of the lower classes of tantras—this is the manner of guru devotion that is needed. With such admiration and reverence for your guru, by striving in the maturation of the crucial points of approach and actualization regarding your personal deity, Guru Rinpoché, if intense admiration and reverence is present, then, as a result of that reverent faith in your guru and your personal deity, Orgyen Rinpoché, the blessings of the guru and the deity will flow to your heart. And solely due to admiration and reverence, realizations of this path will arise. [54] Now in general, admiration and reverence are the leader of any path, but as Orgyen Rinpoché states, "Self-emergent pristine awareness dwells vividly in the light of admiration, reverence, and faith." Thus, this path in particular relies very heavily on admiration and reverence, so for this practice of the greatly secret path it is enormously important to strive in the cultivation of overwhelming admiration and reverence for the guru together with your personal deity.

One who is a suitable vessel, able to sacrifice his or her life for the sake of such a personal deity, guru, and this profound Dharma, should not stop striving in the shared practices explained previously. The most sublime method for becoming a suitable vessel for teaching, listening to, and meditating on the path of this Secret Mantrayāna depends on whether one's mindstream has been ripened by receiving a supreme, ripening empowerment. In particular, to become a suitable vessel for teaching, listening to, and meditating on the paths of the higher classes of tantras—that is, the two inner classes of tantras—and the supreme path of the nondual tantras, you should receive the four empowerments as taught in the authentic sources of these classes of tantras. Then, once you possess the Mantrayāna vows, properly guard against the primary root downfalls and defeats in general, and in particular [55] truly guard all the general and specific samayas such as those pertaining to the body, speech, and mind of the root guru. One who holds these pristine Mantrayāna vows should listen to a guru for how to practice regarding the unique preliminary practical instructions of this path and then train in them. Just as the ripening stage of generation must precede the stage of completion according to other traditions of hidden tantras, so in this context of the great stage of completion [i.e., the Great Perfection], you must arouse a sense of disillusionment by witnessing the miseries of the six kinds of existence below and sever all attachment and clinging to the activities of saṃsāra. And by coming to know the enlightened qualities of the buddhas above, recognize all the physical worlds and sentient inhabitants of your own and others' saṃsāra as maṇḍalas of buddhas, and thereby transform them into the path. In that way, you realize all pure and impure behavior as being like an illusion and empty of true existence. In order to turn away from clinging to true existence, you must ripen [your mindstream] by differentiating outwardly and inwardly between saṃsāra and nirvāṇa.[2]

Therefore, the practice of differentiating is called *guidance to the actual nature of the mind, self-emergent primordial consciousness.* To proceed in the extraordinary [56] practice of such differentiation of saṃsāra and nirvāṇa, you must purify the negative habitual propensities of your ordinary body, speech, and mind and then purify your body, speech, and mind by practicing the method of transforming them into the three pure vajras of the body, speech, and mind of the jinas. That must come first. By such outward and inward differentiation, you engage in the rigorous discipline of pristine awareness, and during the phase of practice that purifies your body, speech, and mind, these vigorous activities of body, speech, and mind constitute strenuous practices. Thus if you do not have a practice for releasing all such effort and then settling your body, speech, and mind in their natural states, it will be difficult to practice the effortless path. So in order to pacify all the karmic energies and conceptual fabrications, you must apply yourself to the practice of settling your physical, verbal, and mental behavior in their natural states. If you do that for a very long time, that is an effective

2. Tib. *ru shan dbyed ba*. Note that the following instructions refer to the practice mentioned by Lerab Lingpa, as cited at note 68 of *The Vital Essence of Primordial Consciousness*, above.

method for achieving stillness, but it may prevent you from being able to cut off thoughts of reification when appearances arise as illusions. So you must again strive in various activities of the body, speech, and mind, as you did before, and try to cause appearances to arise as illusions. Thus settling your body, speech, and mind in their natural states is a superb method [57] for developing stillness of the mind, and applying yourself to the practice of letting be is essential for developing the wisdom that realizes the emptiness of true existence. For a disciple who is imbued with such stillness of the mind—not disturbed by compulsive thoughts—and with the exceptional wisdom that ascertains the absence of true existence of whatever appears, it is easy for the guru to point out the dharmakāya, the primordial consciousness that is present in the ground of being. And when sustaining the recognition of pristine awareness, that too will be easy. There are many such reasons to be imbued with those qualities, so the unique preliminary practices are also very important.

Moreover, when following the instructions on purifying the mind within the context of purifying the body, speech, and mind, you must realize that all phenomena included within the outer physical worlds, as well as their inner sentient inhabitants, and both saṃsāra and nirvāṇa, are homogenously empty of true existence. In that regard, first of all, the creator of the whole of saṃsāra and nirvāṇa is this very mind of yours. This point is made in numerous sūtras and commentaries. So if you ascertain this mind of yours as being empty of true existence, simply by extending that reasoning you will ascertain all phenomena to be empty of true existence. Thus the guru will enable the disciple to discover how all phenomena depend on the mind, [58] and consequently, how the mind takes a primary role within the context of the body, speech, and mind. Moreover, a person with sharp faculties who can determine that this mind, which plays such a dominant role, cannot be established as truly existing from its own side, as something really, substantially existent, is someone who can determine the absence of true existence even with subtle reasoning, simply by having been shown partial reasons for establishing that absence. For such a person, just by force of a revelation as to whether or not the mind has any color or shape, and just by force of being taught the reasons why the mind is devoid of any [true] origin, location, or destination, that person will proceed to establish the fact that the mind lacks true existence by way of subtle reasoning that refutes a subtle object of negation. Thus, by the extraordinary power of relying on such reasoning, people with superior faculties are able to realize the emptiness of all phenomena. However, it is very important for people like us to hear and reflect upon the Madhyamaka treatises, to comprehend all the reasons that establish the absence of true existence, and to establish the nature of emptiness just as it is taught in the Madhyamaka.

These unique preliminaries to such a path are [59] the sublime auxiliaries for entering the main body of the path, just as it is so important to place a strong foundation stone for a house. However, if people nowadays are told that without the auxiliaries of the path, the excellent qualities of the main path will not arise, this makes them discouraged. Or should the speaker only show a white crow? Yet these days it is difficult to form even a sound understanding of the way to proceed along an authentic path. But if you do enter the main path by training in the practices of the auxiliaries of such a path, there is great potential for the main path to arise where it has not yet arisen and to progress where it has already arisen. Upon due reflection, I have expressed just a few thoughts, and more can be understood from other sources.

In terms of the main body of the path, the fruition to be accomplished includes both the dharmakāya and rūpakāyas of the Buddha Samantabhadra. Now in existence resting in the ground of being, there is originally pure, primordial consciousness, free of conceptual elaboration, and spontaneously actualized, luminous appearances. Together, these two are the union of appearances and emptiness. Once such a ground has manifested, [60] the ripening of this ground as the fruition depends on whether or not one is able to take the nature of existence of the ground as the path and sustain it. Taking the ground as the path and sustaining it depends on correctly identifying the nature of existence of the ground. So if the nature of existence of the ground is properly identified, your cultivation of the path will be free of error. If you do not recognize or identify existence resting in the ground of being, you will follow an errant path and your leisure will have been wasted. So it is important to identify properly the mode of existence of the ground.

To meditate by taking the ground as the path, you must unify the profound path of cutting through and the vast path of the spontaneous actualization of the direct crossing over. As for the ways of being introduced to the view, when the guru grants an empowerment of the creative power of pristine awareness, if one is a disciple with surpassingly superior faculties, then even without reliance upon the crucial points of the guru's speech and the disciple's body and so on, simply by resting in meditative equipoise together with the guru, the guru's meditative experiences and realized view will be transferred, as it were, to the disciple; the dharmakāya, pristine awareness that is present in the ground, [61] will manifest, and one will be able to rest there in meditative equipoise.

Here is the way for a disciple who lacks such sharp faculties to be introduced to the view. The disciple is shown how to adopt the crucial points of the posture and visual gaze, and while remaining like that, the guru suddenly and forcefully utters *phaṭ, phaṭ*! With melodious speech the guru asks, "Tell me, tell me, what does *hasaraka* mean?" By such ways of speaking, all the disciple's adventitious karmic energies of conceptual fabrications, together with their modified aspects, are suddenly and completely suspended; indwelling, actual primordial consciousness manifests, and one is able to rest in meditative equipoise there.

These two ways of introducing [the view]—both that which does not depend upon those crucial points and the one that depends upon them—stem from having both a disciple with prior training who possesses sharp faculties and from a guru who is imbued with blessings. So this is not something experienced by novices like us.

## Instructions for Introducing the View to Novices

With regard to novices like us, the instructions for introducing [the view] are as follows. A guru with experiential realization, as explained earlier, truly reveals how existence rests in the ground of being to a disciple [62] whose mind is filled with faith and admiration. Then the sublime method for bringing that to the state of fruition depends on truly manifesting the wisdom that realizes compassion with pristine awareness. One properly identifies compassion with pristine awareness by the extraordinary power of the unmistaken instructions for an introduction to that sacred compassion itself—which is pristine awareness. Since it is crucial to be able to do so, here is the way: First one must seek authentic stillness by gently releasing all conceptual elaborations involving investigation and analysis regarding the past, present, and future. Since the stillness that comes by force of settling the mind in that way is freshly contrived, when that stillness is suddenly disrupted with *phaṭ*, a blank nothingness is left behind as something that is not [the contrived stability of the mind] itself. From that instant, consciousness devoid of conceptual elaboration, with no object—an unmodified consciousness without any basis—arises. At that time, without diverging from that very nature, one must rest there in an unmodified, lucid manner.

This ground sugatagarbha, pristine awareness, self-emergent primordial consciousness, the indwelling, actual nature of existence, is the all-creating sovereign of saṃsāra and nirvāṇa. Subtle and vast, it is the spontaneously actualized presence of the uncontrived, self-emergent [63] enlightened qualities of the three kāyas. In a state of dissolution that is not dull, it pervades and is naturally present in all the virtuous, evil, and ethically neutral, good and bad, subtle and coarse thoughts in the mindstreams of all sentient beings. And it pervades in such a way that the actual nature of reality does not negate the existence of phenomena. However, due to the present power of all forceful karmic energies and conceptual fabrications, the constant movements of conceptual fabrications regarding whatever comes to mind, as well as whatever karmic energies may be present, cause you to abide exclusively in the nature of the substrate. Even though primordial consciousness is naturally present within you, when you fail to recognize your own nature, the primordial consciousness of unimpeded emptiness and luminosity, which is indivisible from the energy of primordial consciousness—having the nature of inconceivably many apparitions when it appears—is feeble. When that is so, once such primordial consciousness of the nondual profundity and luminosity emerges uncloaked, it is difficult to ascertain. However, when primordial consciousness is nakedly present—free of all the conceptual fabrications and karmic energies and so on, which obscure the face of primordial consciousness, pristine awareness—on occasion it is present even now, at the time of the ground. Such primordial consciousness is present [64] in the nature of all subtle and coarse configurations of thoughts, just as sesame seeds are pervaded by oil. On the basis of having been introduced by means of such primordial consciousness itself, one must identify it as such.

Well, when is one freed from the mind with its conceptual fabrications that obscure the face of pristine awareness, primordial consciousness, such that the dharmakāya, primordial consciousness, nakedly emerges? What is the nature of primordial consciousness itself? Among the majority of proponents of the Great Perfection nowadays, some, because they lack even mere conceptual understanding, primarily emphasize just remaining without bringing anything to mind. Others advocate focusing on a state of the lucid, pristine luminosity and cognizance of the mind, brought about through the practice of śamatha, uncontaminated by coarse thoughts. Still others pretentiously claim that when one recognizes and blocks each coarse thought, and then identifies each somewhat subtle thought and dwells in that state, this is the supreme view of the Great Perfection. Others assert the partless, permanent, true existence of a state that is a construct of karmic energies and conceptual fabrications involving a coarse nonconceptuality that is devoid of rough thoughts [65] and say this is the supreme view of this great secret path. There are just far too many cases of putting shoes on top of hats and scriptures! Therefore, since paths like these are unbearable for a heart of compassion to look upon, it is extremely important that you destroy your doubts.

Therefore I shall give a partial explanation of the meaning of the teachings that unite the scriptures and revealed treasures of this Great Perfection in accordance with the practical instructions of qualified gurus who correctly expound the enlightened views of the self-empowered great founders,[3] the earlier and later omniscient ones. As explained previously, without terminating all the subtle habitual propensities that activate conceptual fabrications and the three appearances,[4] the dharmakāya, primordial consciousness that is present in the ground, does not truly manifest. So when all such habitual propensities that activate karmic energies, conceptual fabrications, and the three appearances are ceasing, just as one is about to discard the aggregates of the illusory body, the stages of dissolution of the elements arise, beginning with the dissolution of earth into water. After air has dissolved into consciousness, consciousness dissolves into the appearance of light, the path of white light arises, and the thirty-three conceptualizations of hatred cease. Then that dissolves into the proliferation of light, the path of red proliferation arises, [66] and the forty conceptualizations of attachment cease. Then that proliferation dissolves into the near-attainment, the path of the dark near-attainment arises, and the seven conceptualizations of delusion cease. After that, once the near-attainment has dissolved into space, during the interval after the previous existences of one's mindstream have been withdrawn, and before the next existence has dawned, the transitional phase of the actual nature of reality arises. At that time all the subtle habitual propensities that catalyze the karmic energies, conceptual fabrications, and the three appearances are impeded inside the central channel at the heart. So at this point in time, indwelling, actual primordial consciousness, the pristine awareness that resides in the ground, manifests inside the very lucid channel of light, the golden sun of the supreme sovereign.[5]

The essential nature of such primordial consciousness is the empty clear light that is present in the originally pure ground, free of all conceptual elaboration. Its manifest nature is the spontaneously actualized, luminous

3. Tib. *shing rta chen po*.

4. Tib. *snang gsum*. The appearances of white light, red proliferation, and dark near-attainment, to be explained in this paragraph.

5. Tib. *rgyal mchog gser gyi nyi ma*.

primordial consciousness that is unimpededly present as apparitions of light. Compassion arises in all manner of ways as the inconceivable creative expressions [of pristine awareness], being of an omnipresent nature. Thus it abides in its essential nature, manifest nature, and compassion. [67]

## The Essential Nature

Its *empty essential nature* is originally pure. Here I shall explain the all-creating sovereign of saṃsāra and nirvāṇa, unconditioned, forever free, the primordial consciousness of empty clear light, by way of identifying its empty aspect. Just as *ka* is the first of the thirty consonants, clear light primordial consciousness is originally, or from the very beginning, pure and unstained by

- adventitious conceptual fabrications of the mind, including subtle and coarse afflictive thoughts, such as attachment and hatred, and
- the various impure, nonvirtuous deeds that are generated by them,
- subtle and coarse virtuous thoughts, such as faith, and
- the various pure, virtuous deeds generated by them,
- various ethically neutral thoughts and deeds such as building and other such activities, and
- the ignorance of holding that phenomena and individuals have [inherent] identities, together with the habitual propensities for such ignorance and all the motile karmic energies on which they ride.

Thus that clear light is said to be *originally pure* and *empty*. Moreover, the practices of the paths of the sūtra Pāramitāyāna and the three subsequent Mantrayāna tantras are also constructed from [68] modifications of conceptual fabrications, which are contradictory to the actual view of the unmodified essential nature of the adventitious mind. Without being stained or contaminated by the aspects of such a mind, by the subtle habitual propensities that catalyze the three appearances, by the substrate, or by the subtle karmic energies on which they ride, there is something primordially pure. So the basic disposition of that pristine awareness, primordial consciousness, has never inwardly experienced being stained by the delusions of the mind, nor has that pristine awareness, primordial consciousness, outwardly experienced being transformed into the essential nature of the mind. This is like the nature of the sky being unstained by clouds, and the basic disposition of water being unstained by dirt. In short, since the basic disposition of that clear light is primordially uncontaminated by such adventitious influences, it is said to be *originally pure.*

Furthermore, such primordial consciousness is also empty of true existence as something permanent, partless, and unitary as asserted by *tīrthikas,*[6] and it is also empty of being established as existing from its own side, as affirmed by substantialists,[7] so it is called *originally pure.* Such primordial consciousness, pristine awareness, is constantly present without being [69] vanquished or destroyed by such things as birth and cessation, death and transmigration (as the mind and individuals are), so it is also called *indwelling* and *unchanging.* As stated previously, it is not produced by karmic energies or conceptual fabrications, so it is called *unconditioned primordial consciousness.* Whatever adventitious virtuous and nonvirtuous assemblies of good and bad, subtle and coarse thoughts occur, it cannot be bound by such states of mind, and it is invulnerable regarding all states of mind and mental processes, so it is said to be *unobstructed.* Whereas the minds of animate beings fall to the extremes of virtue, evil, and ethical neutrality, this primordial consciousness, pristine awareness, does not fall to the extremes of virtue, nonvirtue, or ethical neutrality, so it is said to be *free of partiality*

6. Tib. *mu stegs pa.* Lit. "ford-maker," this designation for non-Buddhist philosophies and traditions connotes those on the steps at the edge of the river of saṃsāra, which they seek to ford.

7. Tib. *dngos smra ba.*

and the *great equality*. Pristine awareness does not turn into anything else by transforming into any type of mind, so it is called *unmodified*. Pristine awareness is brighter than a hundred suns and is uncontaminated by laxity and dullness, so it is called *self-illuminating*. Moreover, pristine awareness has no residue of the darkness of ignorance of the substrate and so on, so it is called the *clear light*. The very nature of pristine awareness is such that it cannot be divorced from great bliss, so it is also called the *connate primordial consciousness of great bliss*. Although when veiled by conceptual fabrications such pristine awareness [70] does not become manifest outwardly, nonetheless inwardly primordial consciousness ceaselessly remains luminous like a flame inside a pot, so it is called *inwardly luminous primordial consciousness*. This pristine awareness, primordial consciousness, is free of the fetters of an apprehending subject and an apprehended object and is devoid of the delusions whereby objects and subjects appear as dual, so it is called *nondual primordial consciousness that transcends the mind*.

If you mistake the mode of being of this originally pure essential nature, the basis of the path of cutting through is cast away. As an analogy, if you mistake the nature of the first consonant *ka* among the thirty consonants, you will mistake the nature of all the rest of the consonants. That is also the meaning of *original* in the attribute of original purity regarding primordial consciousness, the essential nature of which is empty. This pristine awareness, primordial consciousness, is an indwelling consciousness that is the congruent cause for the five facets of primordial consciousness that come at the time of the fruition. If you divide it from the point of view of five perspectives, it is said to be of the nature of the five facets of primordial consciousness. The essential nature of such ground pristine awareness is the primordial consciousness of emptiness that is free of all extremes of conceptual elaboration, and its fruition consists of the two kāyas for one's own fulfillment, endowed with the two purities. [71] The one consists of its actual nature—the svabhāvakāya—and the other is that which has this actual nature—the dharmakāya of primordial consciousness. Since what is similar to these two is present at the time of the ground, the primordial consciousness that has the essential nature of emptiness is called the *dharmakāya*.

## The Manifest Nature

The *luminous manifest nature* has the nature of arising lucidly as the various, pure visionary experiences, in which dwellings are the celestial palaces, and in which inhabitants are the principal deities and their retinues of myriad peaceful and wrathful deities displayed across the entire sky. These are established as the self-radiance of primordial consciousness, pristine awareness, the natural clear light. Furthermore, although this [luminous manifest nature] has the nature of being able to arise as the whole range of limitless phenomena belonging to the physical worlds and their sentient inhabitants within impure mundane existence, still, insofar as those *are not* the manifestations of impure energies and mind, all those appearances that have a part in common with the phenomena of impure mundane existence can be established as the self-radiating inner glow of the natural clear light.

In short, all visionary experiences that arise at the time when the ground appears and when the path appears are completely perfect. Furthermore, all the realizations without exception that are present at the time of fruition—including states of consciousness, experiences, mindfulness, samādhi, retention, confidence, and extrasensory perception—are [72] primordially, completely present in the essential nature of the natural clear light. They are not modified or adventitious, emerging from causes, conditions, or effortful practice, but they are rather of the nature of existence of the unmodified, indwelling, dharmakāya primordial consciousness, which is why it is called *naturally luminous primordial consciousness*.

Apart from the occasions when visionary experiences actually arise, at the time of the ground, all such perfect visionary experiences and conscious experiences of the essential nature of the natural clear light are not illuminated outwardly but are rather present as the inwardly illuminated youthful vase kāya. At the time of the path, everything that is inwardly illuminated in that way appears as outward illumination from the open aperture of the distant lasso channel, in dependence upon the actions of the mount of the clear light, those vital energies that are the life force of wisdom, which bear four limbs. Those five vital energies that are the life force of wisdom correspond to a fivefold classification of the indwelling consciousness that serves as the congruent cause for the five facets of primordial consciousness (such as mirror-like primordial consciousness and so on) at the time of the fruition. According to that fivefold classification, the number of vital energies that are the mounts of that primordial consciousness is also five, corresponding to the five facets of pristine awareness, primordial consciousness. Those five energies are called the *five subtle energies of primordial consciousness*, and their colors accord with those of the five buddha families. [73] Those energies of primordial consciousness that are mounts of the clear light are, as before, classified as five subtle vital energies, such as the life-sustaining energy of indwelling primordial consciousness and so on.

The fivefold classification of vital energies, such as the life-sustaining energy, which are presented in other hidden tantras, is also presented here, where they are called the *five coarse, adventitious energies*. In the tradition of this king of tantras, there is a twofold classification into subtle and coarse energies, namely, the five subtle, indwelling vital energies and the five coarse, temporary vital energies. The five energies of spontaneously actualized, luminous primordial consciousness, or the indwelling energies, are not coarse breaths like those that pass through the mouth and nostrils. Rather, they are energies that are indivisibly of the same essential nature as pristine awareness, primordial consciousness. Such spontaneously actualized appearances of luminosity are in part similar to the Buddha's actual sambhogakāya at the time of fruition, so they are called the *naturally luminous sambhogakāya*.

This kind of primordial consciousness of emptiness and the energy that is its mount—and just that alone—does appear in other hidden tantras of the Secret Mantrayāna as well, so there is no incompatibility in that, for they are similar. [74] However, regarding the *specific qualities* of both the mounted primordial consciousness and its mounts, the vital energies, there are many other hidden tantras that don't even mention their names. So this is a unique quality of this greatly secret Vajrayāna path, whose presentation is dissimilar to those found in some tantras such as the father tantras and mother tantras. Those who refute this have only a partial understanding of the meaning of the tantras, and they reject other tantras that seem incompatible with [their limited understanding]. They are satisfied with a merely partial understanding of the meaning of the tantras, and theirs is an expression of not having fathomed the meaning of all the tantras. So they are just revealing their own limitations.

Such different classifications of the meaning of the tantras are formulated according to the specific qualities of the disciples who are their recipients. So in reality, whatever the tantra may be, it is infallible with regard to the accomplishment of its own siddhis. That is a special quality of the Teacher, the Buddha.

## Compassion

This clear light primordial consciousness of emptiness and the spontaneously actualized luminous primordial consciousness abide with the same essential nature. The location of that primordial consciousness is the glorious amulet chamber within the center of the heart, or the supremely victorious channel of light, the golden sun. [75] The primordial consciousness entailing the union of appearances and emptiness rests without moving in the ground of being, but the compassionate creative displays of that primordial consciousness arise in all manner of ways, so *compassion pervades all phenomena*. The whole range of pure phenomena of nirvāṇa and impure phenomena of saṃsāra are mere appearances to one's own mind, and these *are* the phenomena of saṃsāra and nirvāṇa. Apart from those, there are no phenomena of saṃsāra and nirvāṇa that are established from their own side. The nature of all the conceptual and nonconceptual minds that engage with phenomena is pristine awareness, primordial consciousness. So in summary, all of saṃsāra and nirvāṇa consists of displays that arise from the creative power of one's own mind as pristine awareness, primordial consciousness.

With this in mind, the *Treasure Treatise for Accomplishing the Enlightened Mind*[8] states,

> All the various appearances of the outer physical worlds and their inner sentient inhabitants
> are apparitions that arise from one's own mind, pristine awareness.

Due to a failure to recognize pristine awareness, primordial consciousness that is present in the ground, the various appearances of the phenomena of saṃsāra arise. If that primordial consciousness is recognized, the various pure appearances of nirvāṇa arise. [76] So in reality there are no phenomena that do not emerge from the nature of existence of the ground, self-emergent primordial consciousness. So not only are all the inner pure and impure minds and mental processes creative expressions of pristine awareness, but the outer phenomena that appear to the mind also arise from the nature of that ground. So the primordial consciousness that is the union of appearances and emptiness, or the union of original purity and spontaneous actualization, which rests in the ground as explained previously, abides inseparably in its own place, in the center of the very lucid channel of light. But the rays, or cognizance, of that pristine awareness, primordial consciousness, pervade over and across all good and bad configurations of thoughts, which are its creative expressions. The manner of that pervasion is not one in which there is a pervasion between phenomena that have different essential natures, like clouds pervading the sky or water permeating soil. Rather, like moisture permeating water and warmth permeating fire, the pervasion is one in which that which is pervaded and that which pervades are of the same nature. So there are not individual natures to be apprehended, such as a mind that is not the "pervading" cognizance or a cognizance that is not the "pervaded" mind.

8. Tib. *Thugs sgrub gter gzhung.*

Nonetheless, those two are distinct from different perspectives: The luminosity and cognizance that are contaminated by contact with moving, fluctuating karmic energies are called [77] the *mind*, and the luminosity and cognizance that are not even slightly contaminated by fluctuating, moving energies are called the *aspect of cognizance*. To explain the difference between the aspect of cognizance and the mind: When cognizance comes in contact with fluctuating, moving energies, even when an object appears, that cognizance does not fuse by grasping to the object. The fusion by grasping to an object under the influence of fluctuation and movement is the essential nature of the conceptual fabrications of the mind. Once consciousness that is in contact with such energies comes under the influence of those energies, there is one aspect that is fluctuating and grasps to the object and another aspect that cannot be altered due to those energies, so it is free of grasping to the object and free of fluctuation due to thoughts. The former is called the *mind* and the latter is called the *aspect of cognizance*. Such cognizance is a ray of pristine awareness, primordial consciousness, or its aspect of cognizing. Thus pristine awareness, primordial consciousness, is present without fluctuation, as explained previously, inside the central channel of light at the heart. But the radiance, or rays, of that pristine awareness pervade all good and bad configurations of thoughts, which are its creative expressions. Therefore all manner of fluctuating thoughts, which are not themselves pristine awareness, are nonetheless pervaded by the radiance, or rays, of pristine awareness. It is, for example, like the fact that when when the sun is shining in the sky, [78] all its rays spread out to different objects and directions, and thus pervade all objects.

Such ground pristine awareness and cognizance are not of different essential natures, either, for both are of the manifest nature of the same clear light. They are solely what is not contaminated by the fluctuating, moving conceptual fabrications that come about due to fluctuating karmic energies. So they are not differentiated by way of having different essential natures. Nonetheless, the pristine awareness that is present in the ground and the cognizance that comprises its radiant rays are differentiated as being distinct from different perspectives. That which abides inside the channel of light at the heart and has never come in contact with fluctuating energies, and has therefore never experienced the arising of impure objects and appearances, is the *pristine awareness that is present in the ground*. The pristine awareness that is a creative expression of compassion, which does not fuse by grasping to various impure appearances—even though they do arise when pristine awareness comes into contact with moving, fluctuating energies—is called *cognizance*. So indwelling consciousness, self-emergent pristine awareness, which does not come in contact with fluctuating energies, is called *pristine awareness*, and that which does come into such contact is called *cognizance*. That is how they are each differentiated. Such [79] pristine awareness of all-pervasive compassion is similar to the actual nirmāṇakāya at the time of the fruition, insofar as it leads to it, so it is called the *all-pervasive nirmāṇakāya*.

## The Way to Practice by Following the Path

The path to be followed requires that you meditate by resting in the nature of existence of the ground, taking this as the path. To determine the nature of existence of the ground, one identifies and then establishes the nature of existence of the ground in order to follow the path. Moreover, following the path is the means by which one reveals the nature of existence of the ground. Then, the nature of existence of the ground that is to be determined and identified is the primordial consciousness that is the union of original purity and spontaneous actualization, which was described previously. Regarding the path by means of which this is revealed, there is both the path of cutting through to original purity, by which the radiance of pristine awareness is taken as the path, and the path of the spontaneously actualized direct crossing over, by which the radiance of light is taken as the path.

## The Path of Cutting through to Original Purity

Here I shall explain the way to follow the path of cutting through to original purity by taking the radiance of pristine awareness as the path. That which is to be practiced is the ground dharmakāya, the actual, indwelling primordial consciousness, clear light. There are many methods of practice to reveal that. [80] Other hidden tantras teach methods to stop all conceptual fabrications that prevent seeing the face of the clear light. In those methods one relies on practices involving the channels and energies in order to take the karmic energies upon which the conceptual fabrications ride (and which flow through the impure channels), and to gather both these conceptual fabrications and their karmic energies into the central channel. Those methods block conceptual fabrications and reveal the clear light. However, on this path, here, you don't need to resort to forceful methods such as focusing on the energies and channels, restraining the energies, and so on. Rather, from the outset you nakedly apprehend the nature of existence of the ground as it has been pointed out with the pith instructions of the guru. From the beginning you embrace the raw clear light itself itself and sustain it in dependence upon the guru's practical instructions. By so doing, the conceptual fabrications and karmic energies that prevent you from encountering your own face as the clear light, subtle, primordial consciousness, naturally cease, and the clear light is revealed. This special, profound method is found on this supreme path.

Well, if you wonder how you can sustain the essential nature of pristine awareness by embracing from the very beginning the raw, indwelling, actual primordial consciousness, clear light, in reliance on the guru's pith instructions, [81] it is like this. Beginners are not able from the outset to take as the path the clear light primordial consciousness, pristine awareness that has never come in contact with any of the karmic energies. However, as stated previously, the cognizance that is the radiance, or rays, of the ground pristine awareness pervades all the good and bad thoughts that arise in the present, and it is present in the nature of this mind. While the distinct thoughts that arise in the present moment are not themselves pristine awareness, their nature, or basic disposition, is pristine awareness. So you must be able to recognize that basic disposition and remain there. Therefore, the consciousness that is present in this very moment is not pristine awareness, but, as stated previously, in this present consciousness there is one aspect of the *mind*, the conceptual fabrications that have come under the influence of fluctuating karmic energies, and then there is the aspect of *cognizance* that has achieved autonomy so that it cannot be moved by fluctuating karmic energies. So if you can distinguish between those two, you can cast off the aspect of the mind, hold to that cognizance, and find that you can remain there.

Without being able to differentiate between [82] the aspect of the mind and that of cognizance, if you dwell in all states of consciousness of the immediate present with the assumption that they are all pristine awareness, this is like entrusting yourself to your enemy after mistaking your enemy for your friend. So this leaves you with nothing in this life or the hereafter. Therefore the only door you must open onto this greatly secret path is the guru's practical guidance, while never separating yourself from an experienced guru as if he were your eyes. Don't resort to just obstinately practicing stupid meditations.

Well then, what is the method for releasing all aspects of the mind of this current-moment consciousness and seeking cognizance? You can't reveal unwavering cognizance without disengaging from all subtle and coarse aspects of movement and fluctuation. So, regarding the method for revealing unwavering cognizance, while all coarse fluctuating thoughts of the mind can be stopped by practicing stabilizing meditation, it is very difficult to stop the subtle fluctuating thoughts of the mind that occur due to the power of adventitious, contrived conditions. So if they are not stopped, they will be a great obstacle to experiencing the cognizance [83] that is the primordially, naturally present, uncontrived, actual view. Therefore, to dispel all the obscurations that prevent you from encountering your own face of such pristine awareness, primordial consciousness, and since no other antidote serves as a remedy, the powerful antidote for dispelling all obstacles to seeing pristine awareness itself is simply to experience pristine awareness itself.

If you strive in the method for revealing pristine awareness itself, all subtle and coarse fluctuating conceptual fabrications will cease, and simultaneously pristine awareness will be revealed. Moreover, the ability to experience unwavering cognizance and the cessation of all subtle and coarse fluctuating, contrived, conceptual fabrications will also be simultaneous. Therefore, as for the way to terminate even subtle fluctuating thoughts, it is true that at first coarse fluctuating thoughts can be stopped with the power of practicing stabilizing meditation. But to stop subtle fluctuating thoughts that emerge due to contrived conditions, bring to mind the essential nature of the aspect of this immediate consciousness that is unmodified primordial consciousness, free of conceptual elaboration—indwelling, subtle clear light. If you are able to remain there without wavering, by the power of that, fluctuating subtle and coarse thoughts [84] that emerge in dependence upon contrived conditions will be completely cut off, and you will be able to experience unmodified, connate, primordial consciousness without impediment.

Beginners who are unfamiliar with dwelling in the cognizance of immediate consciousness are unable to remain there for more than just a brief time. When you can't remain in cognizance for more than just a short time, since you can't take unwavering cognizance as your object and stay there, you will fall under the influence of the excitation of fluctuating, moving thoughts. Even when that happens, without roving in the domain of those movements, identify the cognizance that is an aspect, or basic disposition, of all those movements of good and bad thoughts of the present. Without vigorously grasping to that cognizance, you should effortlessly, naturally attend to it, simply without slipping away from the essential nature of that cognizance and its inner glow. But when you do slip into the movements of compulsive thoughts, whatever movements of thoughts occur, identify, as you did before, [85] the cognizance that is the indwelling primordial consciousness of the nature of existence of those thoughts. If you can remain there, whatever movements of thoughts occur, you will be able to cut them off immediately. So without resorting to other antidotes for cutting off compulsive thoughts, they will be released by resting in the nature of the compulsive thoughts themselves as you did before. This is the meaning of the renowned advice for how compulsive thoughts release themselves without one's having to reject them. Orgyen Rinpoché says, "Leaving the movements right where they are, they are released as the dharmakāya."

With the method of releasing compulsive thoughts in this way, without blocking them, if you recognize the nature of existence of the thoughts as pristine awareness, dharmakāya, and rest there, that is the sublime method for dispelling roving, compulsive thoughts. However, nowadays among those who say they are meditating, some persistently engage in compulsive thoughts without seeking any method to stop them, and even when they do block thoughts, they don't stop, and that serves only to prevent their discerning mind from resting in its natural state. Others say, "one should let compulsive thoughts release themselves without rejecting them," and then they simply continue roaming about in compulsive ideation. [86] Some take pride in thinking that the best of meditations is simply recognizing whatever thoughts arise, while they apply themselves to counting thoughts. Some clear away coarse thoughts and recognize just such luminosity, cognizance, transparency, and clarity of the subtle mind and rest there. But they do not recognize the primordial consciousness that transcends the mind, so they are unable to differentiate between the mind and pristine awareness. Without knowing the meaning of the immediate consciousness discussed in the Great Perfection tantras, which state one must identify the immediate consciousness of the present moment, those teachings are lost on them.

Therefore, regarding this immediate consciousness, there are two aspects: that which is pervaded and that which pervades. There are many aspects to that which is pervaded that do not transcend the mind—including sensory consciousness, mental consciousness, and the substrate—so they are nothing more than the mind. That which pervades is the cognizance of primordial consciousness itself. So when you can experience such pristine awareness and rest there, then at that time there is no appearance of apprehended objects as being this or that, nor do you grasp [87] to them as being such. Since good and bad configurations of inner thoughts neither appear, nor do you grasp to them, you remain without wavering from the nature of the dharmakāya, the all-creating sovereign. With this in mind, Orgyen Rinpoché stated:

> Outwardly purify the appearance of apprehended objects,
> inwardly release the apprehending mind itself,
> and in between, recognize the clear light.

To be able to actualize the mind of clear light, cognizance free of fluctuating conceptual fabrications, without blocking the movements of air through the mouth and nostrils, is unique to this tradition and is nowhere to be found in other hidden tantras.

By remaining in such clear light primordial consciousness, there are three ways of achieving stability—great, small, and medium—and hence there are three ways of stopping fluctuations and movements—great, small, and medium. In reality, when you are able to remain in the clear light, indwelling, actual primordial consciousness, all movements and fluctuations of conceptual fabrications involving laxity, excitation, agitation, dullness, and so on are immediately cut off by the power of pristine awareness, primordial consciousness, which is why [88] that primordial consciousness is also given the name *cutting through*. This is like the absence of darkness when light appears. Just as the surface of the sun is never veiled with darkness, the face of the cognizance of the clear light has never been veiled by any of the deviations of the path, such as naturally present, fluctuating conceptual fabrications. Consequently, simply by attending to the essential nature of the cognizance of the present moment, all deviations of the path, including fluctuating conceptual fabrications, can be immediately cut off. That is also the meaning [of *cutting through*]. Thus, remaining in pristine awareness dispels all deviations, and by slipping into the mind, all deviations emerge.

## Methods for Releasing Compulsive Thoughts

If in the beginning the method for releasing compulsive thoughts depends upon sustaining the essential nature of the view, how do you sustain that view and how are compulsive thoughts released by doing so? In general, although there are many stages by which to sustain the essential nature of this view of the Great Perfection, a superb crucial point for doing so is to sustain the view by way of the four kinds of open presence. I shall explain them in terms of the phase of [89] meditative equipoise and the postmeditative phase of each of the four kinds of open presence.

First, there is the view that is open presence like a mountain.[9] The radiance of pristine awareness abides in the basic disposition of whatever compulsive thoughts arise. This is the essential nature of primordial consciousness, and it is at all times free of the fluctuations and movements of the conceptual fabrications of the mind, whether in saṃsāra or nirvāṇa. So that is a way of resting like an unmoving mountain, hence it is called the *view that is open presence like a mountain*. Not only is the essential nature of the radiance of pristine awareness, primordial consciousness, itself unchanging, but the stage at which the guru correctly points out the view, or the nature of existence of primordial consciousness, must be unmoved by errors. So relative to the guru as well, the *view* that serves as a cause for the pointing-out instruction is called *open presence like a mountain*. Furthermore, the best of disciples experience the view pointed out to them by the guru and it is unshakable. At the very least they must find certainty from within by way of understanding, so that they are unmoved by others' errors, their own doubts, and so on. So relative to the disciples as well, one speaks of the *view that is open presence like a mountain* as that for which certainty has been found once it is pointed out. Therefore, in the stage at which the guru points out the view (i.e., that the nature of existence of the ground is unchanging and free of fluctuation and movement), the disciple's ability to remain openly, or lucidly, and without modification in the unmistaken, unwavering meaning that is the view—without being moved by such things as one's own doubts or listening to others' opinions—is the meaning of the *view that is open presence like a mountain*.

Regarding the meditation that is open presence like an ocean,[10] you must practice by following the path according to the way you established the view of the ground. So the way to practice by familiarizing yourself with the path is as follows. The great settling of pristine awareness, the basic disposition of consciousness that remains while one adheres to the

9. Tib. *lta ba ri bo cog bzhag.*

10. Tib. *sgom pa rgya mtsho cog bzhag.*

crucial points of the posture and the gaze, not following after the past, not anticipating the future, and not dispersing to the objects of present moment thoughts, is undisturbed by fluctuating conceptual fabrications, like a slowly forming ocean. So this is called *open presence like an ocean*. Even while the essential nature of pristine awareness, primordial consciousness itself, is uncontaminated and undisturbed by fluctuating thoughts, objects and appearances arise unimpededly, but without tainting pristine awareness. This is like an ocean free of waves reflecting the various forms of the planets and stars in the sky, [91] without them being able to taint the ocean, and that is also why it is called *open presence like an ocean*. Even if random compulsive thoughts arise occasionally, and they do not remain within the nature of pristine awareness, primordial consciousness, still, you don't get lost in the nature of those thoughts but rather they dissolve into and remain in the forever free, unconditioned expanse of pristine awareness, primordial consciousness. Just as waves occasionally arise in the ocean due to the sudden movements of sentient beings and the movements of the air, but do not remain long, for they are naturally calmed and dissolve back into the expanse of the ocean, so too are adventitious thoughts calmed in the nature of unmodified primordial consciousness. The ability to rest openly, or lucidly, without modification in primordial consciousness is called *meditation that is open presence like an ocean*.

Regarding the pith instructions on open presence in conduct,[11] by striving in methods to view all appearances as emanations of pristine awareness, without forgetting the view of meditative equipoise, not only while in meditation but also during the postmeditative state, such that the inner glow of the view during meditation does not dissipate and its essential nature does not slip away, all your conduct during the postmeditative state will be imbued with that reckoning of pristine awareness and you will not fall under the influence [92] of good and bad objects and conditions. In reliance upon the pith instructions on merging the view in meditative equipoise with all your activities during the postmeditative state, you must

11. Tib. *spyod pa man ngag cog bzhag.*

lucidly remain in pristine awareness without modification. For that reason these are called *pith instructions on open presence in conduct.* If you do not possess such pith instructions for merging the view in meditative equipoise with the postmeditative period, you may try to attend to the essential nature of pristine awareness in meditative equipoise. But still, if you do not resort to antidotes for the movements of compulsive thoughts during the postmeditative state, and you stray into the nature of subtle and coarse movements instead, the view in meditative equipoise will weaken. And that will become a great obstacle to viewing all appearances as emanations of pristine awareness. So this practice of merging meditative equipoise with the postmeditative state is very important.

Regarding the fruitional open presence in pristine awareness,[12] in dependence upon the power of (1) establishing and identifying such a view, (2) resting in meditative equipoise by practicing meditation, and (3) applying the pith instructions to your conduct so that you do not fall under the influence of objects and conditions, eventually the cognizance that is the radiance of pristine awareness will dissolve into the ground. When pristine awareness is encountered within, [93] like the meeting of a mother and son, all types of energy-mind will enter the central channel, all movements through the mouth and nostrils will cease, and you will remain without modification, lucidly and firmly settled on the unmoving mountain of primordial consciousness, pristine awareness, resting in the ground that has never come in contact with karmic energies. That is called the *fruitional open presence in pristine awareness.* Such pristine awareness is the temporary, fruitional pristine awareness that is experienced from the time that it manifests due to the power of the path until you achieve enlightenment. The fruition that is the knowledge of the Buddha, Samantabhadra, is the ultimate fruition of pristine awareness.

Here is an explanation of how to apply those four kinds of open presence to a single meditation session. While in meditative equipoise, the view to be sustained, which is pointed out by the guru, is the view that is open

12. Tib. *'bras bu rig pa cog bzhag.*

presence like a mountain. The practice of naturally sustaining without modification the essential nature of the view, just by not letting it fade away, free of fluctuating movements, is the meditation that is open presence like an ocean. When such practice is sustained, even when fluctuating thoughts occasionally do come up, then by the power of the pith instructions on seeking the king, pristine awareness [94] (which is the nature of existence of all fluctuating thoughts), all the activities of conceptual fabrications will be released into primordial freedom. Those are the pith instructions on open presence in conduct. If you allow all such activities of distracting conceptual fabrications to release themselves and attend to them as continuous displays of one forever free, unconditioned cognizance, you have found freedom from compulsive thoughts and have found the fruitional cognizance that is to be sustained. Dwelling again in cognizance after compulsive thoughts have arisen and resting there without modification is that which is called *fruitional open presence in pristine awareness*.

Among all such types of open presence, the latter ones arise in dependence upon the earlier ones. Once you have come to a decisive understanding of the view that has first been pointed out, if you do not rest in that view, you will not be able to sustain it for a long time through meditation that repeatedly rests in that view. If you don't gain familiarity by cultivating the view for a long time, you will not acquire the powerful antidotes to be relied upon as a means to prevent you from falling under the influence of objects and conditions such as compulsive thoughts. If you do not acquire the powerful antidotes to be relied upon for familiarizing yourself with the path so that you don't fall under the influence of compulsive thoughts, objects, and conditions, [95] you will not rest without wavering in pristine awareness after completely cutting off compulsive thoughts as soon as they arise. And you will not experience the subsequent ground pristine awareness following the gradual dissolution of the radiance of pristine awareness. If you can firmly rest in the prior phases of open presence, you will be able to rest firmly in the latter phases. By way of those four kinds of open presence, due to the power of sustaining the view, the ways of releasing compulsive thoughts will arise.

To explain the ways of releasing compulsive thoughts in terms of identifying the essential nature of the way to release such thoughts, there are four ways. And relative to individuals' level of faculties, there are three ways of releasing compulsive thoughts. Thus, the four ways—in terms of the essential nature of the way to release such thoughts—are as follows.

There is a way to release compulsive thoughts that relies upon the mode in which the ground exists—that ground that is the nature of existence of pristine awareness itself, the self-emergent primordial consciousness that is luminous and subtle. This first method of release has the nature of *primordial freedom*, so it arises as what was always already released.

The ways to release compulsive thoughts by familiarizing yourself with the path, when taking the ground as the path and sustaining it, are as follows: Insofar as there is a way to release compulsive thoughts in dependence upon the practices [96] of the path, the second way of releasing them, namely, *self-release*, and the third way, *naked release*, both occur. The first way of releasing them depends on the nature of existence of the ground, and the second and third ways of releasing them depend upon the period during which one practices the path.

What is the essential nature of the freedom that is such release of compulsive thoughts? The freedom that is this so-called *release* is a kind of freedom that depends on your own essential nature. So the fourth way of release arises as the *freedom from extremes.*

First, in dependence upon the mode of existence of the ground, which is pristine awareness, the primordial consciousness of clear light itself, the way to release compulsive thoughts has the nature of primordial freedom. So the first way of release arises as primordial freedom. The mode in which the essential nature of the ground primordial consciousness itself exists has never been stained or obscured by any of the subtle or coarse karmic energies or conceptual fabrications, so it is unconditioned primordial freedom that is unchanged by the delusions of dualistic grasping. Hence that primordial consciousness is presented as *forever free.*

When you take the ground as the path and sustain it by familiarizing yourself with the path, [97] in dependence upon the practices of the path, the second way of releasing compulsive thoughts, namely, self-release, and the third, naked release, both occur. Regarding the first, self-release, when you firmly rest in the view after recognizing the view of the ground, then even when random, fluctuating thoughts suddenly arise on occasion, you do not fall under their influence. Without forcefully blocking them and without seeking other antidotes to compulsive thoughts, then as explained previously, if you identify and remain in the primordial consciousness that is present in the nature of the existence, or in the basic disposition, of the movements of the good and bad thoughts themselves, then those moving thoughts will be released within the basic disposition of those thoughts themselves. So that is called *self-release.*

Second, regarding naked release, by the power of familiarizing yourself with such practices of the path and with the methods for releasing compulsive thoughts in their own basic disposition, then eventually, even if thoughts arise once in a while, from the first moment of the arising of the thought to the second moment, it is not as if the stream of thoughts was stopped from the first instant. Rather, without remaining any further than when the movement of a thought merely pokes out its head, or than when the movement of a thought merely lets it head appear naked, [98] their presence is released into the unmodified, forever free nature of primordial consciousness. That is one reason for calling this *naked release.* Moreover, since that way of positing naked release can also be set forth as a specific instance of the way in which one explains self-release, there is a second way of positing naked release. This entails nakedly perceiving the nature of existence, suchness, without fixating on reifying any of the good or bad objects and appearances that arise while on the path of meditative equipoise. From the first moment they appear, objects and appearances are free of all elaborations concerning true existence, hence they are free of elaboration, the nature of existence of suchness—just as it is. Without forsaking this essential nature, you leave them just as they are. Thus it is said that they are *nakedly released.*

That which is called *release* in the three ways of (1) primordial release, (2) self-release, and (3) naked release entails resting in reliance upon the mode of being of the essential nature of "freedom" itself, so the fourth way of release is freedom from extremes. The basic disposition, or the nature of existence, of compulsive thoughts is free from the eight extremes of conceptual elaboration regarding signs. These extremes include an origination or a cessation, a going or a coming, a being unchanging or an annihilation, a unity or a diversity, that could truly exist. [99] So this is called *freedom from extremes.*

## Stages of Development in Practice

Furthermore, regarding the ways of releasing compulsive thoughts, there is (1) the way of releasing them for individuals of inferior faculties who have gained just a little familiarity with the practices of the path, (2) the way of releasing them for individuals of middling faculties who have gained a middling degree of familiarity with the practices of the path, and (3) the way of releasing them for individuals of sharp faculties who have gained great familiarity with the practices of the path. These three ways of releasing are not identified in terms of the sharp, middling, and dull faculties of individuals with different mindstreams. Rather, the three ways of releasing compulsive thoughts emerge due to the stages of small, middling, and great familiarity that a single individual's mindstream has with respect to the practices of the path.

First, regarding the way of releasing conceptual fabrications for an individual with dull faculties and with no more than a little familiarity with the path, release arises with a recognition of thoughts that is like meeting someone with whom you are already acquainted. This is the way of release when the power to abide in the view of the ground is weak and the power of conceptual fabrications is strong. So at first, even though you are sustaining the view of the ground [100] and remain there, when fluctuating movements and agitated mindfulness occur due to sudden thoughts, you fall under their influence and wander off. Then, once you recognize that you have fallen under the sway of such thoughts and have wandered off, you regard this as a fault, you identify the view in which you dwelt previously, you devote yourself to mindfulness and introspection to sustain that view again, and you remain in that view. That is the first way of release. As an analogy, if someone you knew traveled abroad and you didn't meet him for a long time, it would be difficult to recognize him afterward. But since you did know him earlier, it's not that you wouldn't recognize him at all. Though you have recognized pristine awareness, due to the fact your consciousness is falling under the influence of movements, you don't quickly recognize its essential nature. But following the time when you were under the influence of conceptual fabrications, you recognize pristine awareness and rest there again.

Next, regarding the way of releasing compulsive thoughts for an individual with middling faculties who has not progressed beyond a medium degree of familiarity with the path, the self-release of thoughts is like the knots made by a snake releasing themselves. While following the path, [101] when you take as the path the mode in which the aspect of pristine awareness actually exists and sustain that, then even though the movements of thoughts arise from time to time, those thoughts cannot interrupt and distract you away from the essential nature of pristine awareness. If you do not attend a bit tightly and continuously to pristine awareness with mindfulness, you will be prone to becoming distracted away from the essential nature of pristine awareness, and that will interfere with your remaining in pristine awareness. Thus, by focusing a bit tightly on its essential nature, you will firmly hold to pristine awareness' own place, and thoughts will be released without their having any power over you. Just as lines drawn in water disappear as soon as they are made, even though thoughts arise, they are released without being able to remain long. And just as it is easy for knots in a snake's body to unravel, so is the release of thoughts easy when the strength of conceptual fabrications and pristine awareness is equal.

Finally, regarding the way of releasing conceptual fabrications for an individual with sharp faculties who has great familiarity with the path, compulsive thoughts are of no benefit and no harm, like a thief entering an empty house. This way of release is one in which mindfulness is firmly established in the castle of pristine awareness. Even if ordinary, random thoughts arise, [102] not only do you not become distracted by falling under their influence, but you are not even prone to becoming distracted by them. At that point, the way of release occurs when the power of pristine awareness is great and the power of compulsive ideation is weak. Just as there is no fear of losing anything in an empty house or that a thief will get something there, so in this way of release there is no fear of losing pristine awareness or of being carried away by movements.

Regarding the way to maintain mindfulness in those phases, at the beginning, even if novices try to focus their mindfulness and sustain it, compulsive thoughts will interrupt and distract them. However, as explained previously, even when that occurs, with mindfulness they should bear in mind the aspect of pristine awareness without forgetfulness and again rest in pristine awareness. After some time, when they are resting in pristine awareness, as thoughts come along and they focus their mindfulness and rest in pristine awareness, those thoughts will be released without being able to overpower them. When mindfulness is slack, thoughts will again fluctuate and arise. Whether or not they will be released depends on whether or not you are able to remain focused in pristine awareness. [103] So during this intermediate phase, the crucial point is to focus mindfulness and attend to the essential nature of pristine awareness.

Finally, when you can remain in pristine awareness without losing the potency of mindfulness, whatever thoughts arise, they cannot cause pristine awareness to waver. So in this phase you must have a special kind of mindfulness with which to attend to the essential nature of pristine awareness. In these three phases of the beginning, middle, and end, the way to maintain mindfulness is not by deliberately holding on to the aspect of pristine awareness. Rather, you maintain a mindfulness that just bears in mind, without forgetfulness, the aspect of the mode in which pristine awareness actually exists. By so doing, eventually you will experience the ground pristine awareness. Then, in the face of that pristine awareness, there will come an extraordinary mindfulness, and such mindfulness is called *effortless, naturally settled mindfulness.*

During these three phases of the ways of release, there occur three ways of releasing compulsive thoughts by way of inferior, middling, and supreme ways of maintaining mindfulness. Whatever thoughts arise, without letting your mindfulness waver from the mode in which pristine awareness actually exists, you must with mindfulness bear in mind that alone and remain there. [104] As explained previously, that is the meaning of the phrase "When thoughts arise, observe their nature." Regarding the way in which this mindfulness is mindful of pristine awareness, it is not that the mindfulness that is being mindful and the pristine awareness of which you are mindful are different, as if they were two targets that stand on their own. Rather, like remembering yourself, without forgetting the essential nature of the clear light pristine awareness, when you bring this to mind and remain there, that is the meaning of the phrase *sustaining pristine awareness with mindfulness*. While remaining in the essential nature of pristine awareness, it is very important that you truly ascertain the mode in which the aspect of naturally settled, pristine awareness exists and rest there without deliberately holding on to it with the thought "I must attend to the essential nature of pristine awareness."

Such stages within the ways of releasing compulsive thoughts arise in dependence upon the practice of the four kinds of open presence, which are stages of practice within the path of attending to the essential nature of pristine awareness. When do all those stages of releasing thoughts arise relative to the degree of sharpness of one's faculties? They arise from the time you are able to remain in cognizance until cognizance dissolves into pristine awareness. [105] The best way of releasing thoughts occurs when thoughts have not totally stopped, but when they bring no benefit or harm. The essential nature of pristine awareness that is to be sustained at this time is the radiance, or cognizance, of pristine awareness. But this is not the experience of the pristine awareness that rests in the ground, in which all manner of fluctuating conceptual fabrications have naturally ceased and the face of pristine awareness nakedly comes forth. The type of sustaining here is one in which you sustain pristine awareness after meditating upon it, but it is not as though you sustain pristine awareness after *seeing* it. This is the phase of meditating on pristine awareness, but not of seeing pristine awareness. Therefore, this is just the path of accumulation in this tradition, but the primordial consciousness of vipaśyanā in this path has not yet arisen.

When there is such familiarity, eventually the radiance of pristine awareness dissolves into pristine awareness, and the movements of karmic energies are withdrawn into the absolute space of phenomena. When that happens, the energy-mind dissolves into the absolute space of phenomena and the pristine awareness that is present in the ground is revealed. Then, once pristine awareness manifests, that is when it is seen directly. At that time [106] you progress to the path of preparation according to this tradition, and the primordial consciousness of vipaśyanā also arises.

Regarding the method for drawing the energy-mind into the absolute space of phenomena, you don't need to rely on familiarizing yourself with focusing on the vital energies and channels or with retaining the vital energies as in other hidden tantras. Rather, from the outset, when you take pristine awareness, primordial consciousness, itself as the path and sustain that, all facets of the mind of conceptual fabrications cease, as explained before. When the mind ceases, the karmic energies that are the mounts of that mind naturally cease as well. So all energy-minds dissolve into the absolute space of phenomena at the heart. Even without holding the mind in the center of the cakra around the central channel, by the power of remaining in the essential nature of pristine awareness, primordial consciousness, without letting go of it, the ground pristine awareness manifests. Then the resting place of the ground pristine awareness, primordial consciousness, is the center of the channel of light inside the central channel at the heart. So all energy-minds dissolve into pristine awareness itself, which is the union of appearances and emptiness in the center of the central channel of light.

The experience of indwelling, actual primordial consciousness that comes in dependence upon this supreme path, and the experience of indwelling primordial consciousness that comes in dependence upon working with the channels and vital energies as in the path of other hidden tantras, [107] are similar only in that they are the clear light, indwelling primordial consciousness. However, there is a great difference between the two in terms of the greater or lesser strength of that clear light primordial consciousness, and in terms of whether or not one acquires its power. As for the clear light primordial consciousness that is experienced in dependence upon the path of other hidden tantras, since you do not familiarize yourself by remaining in the clear light after stripping down to its naked essence from the outset, the strength that comes by relying upon the ground pristine awareness that manifests itself through this supreme path remains weak and you do not acquire its power. Regarding this supreme path, from the time that you first meditate on pristine awareness, seek the radiance, or rays, of the ground pristine awareness, and take that clear light as the path. By repeatedly familiarizing yourself with that, when such ground pristine awareness is actually experienced, it will come with increased power.

On the basis of that ground pristine awareness, the wisdom that realizes emptiness awakens as an exceptional, unmodified, self-emergent wisdom. Eventually, when the meaning of the nature of existence, emptiness, is directly realized by this wisdom, without being interrupted by even subtle conceptual elaborations of dual appearance, [108] that is the path of seeing according to the tradition of this path, and that is the ārya path. Therefore, in order for the unmodified, self-emergent wisdom that directly realizes emptiness to arise, it relies upon and must be preceded by the unmodified, self-emergent wisdom that realizes emptiness as the essential nature of the ground pristine awareness, which arises at the time of the path of preparation. In order for the effortless wisdom that realizes pristine awareness to be empty from its own side to be aroused, it must be preceded by its skillful means, the practice of the union of pristine awareness and emptiness in which emptiness and pristine awareness are united while meditating on pristine awareness on the path of accumulation. If the crucial points of the practice of uniting pristine awareness and emptiness have not matured, the wisdom that realizes the emptiness that is the essential nature of pristine awareness will not emerge as an exceptional, unmodified, self-emergent wisdom.

Therefore this method of uniting pristine awareness and emptiness, called *uniting pristine awareness and emptiness*, is not the meditation on emptiness according to the Pāramitāyāna by which emptiness is analyzed with many kinds of reasoning. Here, to simply remain without thinking about anything and without abiding in the meaning of emptiness [ascertained] by refuting the subtlest object of negation [109] is not the method of sustaining the union of pristine awareness and emptiness, either. Contrary to the assertion of some people, once you have identified the domain of outer, empty space, to focus your mind on that is not the meaning of merging absolute space with pristine awareness, nor of merging pristine awareness with emptiness. Just attending to pristine awareness alone, without meditating on emptiness, entails sustaining the essential nature of pristine awareness, but it is not the uniting of pristine awareness and emptiness.

What then is the meaning here of uniting pristine awareness and emptiness? It is like this. When you dwell in cognizance and achieve stability, you must settle in a meditative equipoise in which cognizance is naturally merged, as if disappearing, into the essential nature of the absolute space of emptiness itself, that which transcends thought, articulation, or being an object of conceptual elaboration, and which is the way the nature of pristine awareness abides. If you remain in cognizance simply without abandoning the sphere of empty absolute space that is the nature of existence of such pristine awareness, and sustain that, you are both sustaining cognizance and remaining in the absolute space of emptiness. So that is also the meditation where you meditate on both pristine awareness and emptiness simultaneously. When you experience and remain in the subjective cognizance that reveals the absolute space of emptiness as its object, [110] if it is deliberately held with the thought "This is emptiness," the mind is not transcended. So even though emptiness is sustained, cognizance will not be sustained.

Therefore you should loosely rest pristine awareness in the nature of the empty absolute space of cognizance and remain there without modification. That must be a stabilizing meditation alone, without analyzing the object of negation. This must lead to the ascertainment of emptiness by way of stabilizing meditation, without reliance upon rational analysis regarding the absence of an object of negation that is either one or many, and so on. For that to happen, you must first ascertain how connate self-grasping holds to the very subtle object of negation, as taught in the Madhyamaka Prāsaṅgika tradition. The omniscient Longchenpa states that all the reasons used to refute that must lead to the ascertainment of an emptiness that is determined through the authentic logic presented in the Madhyamaka treatises. Moreover, the emptiness presented in many treatises of the Great Perfection scriptures and revealed treasures is just like the emptiness asserted according to the Prāsaṅgika tenets. [111] Thus the reasons used to determine the absence of origin, location, and destination, within the pith instructions used to establish that the mind is empty of true existence, given when granting experiential instructions, actually determine the emptiness of all phenomena. In short, with the unification of appearances and emptiness—the emptiness of any phenomena that could exist from its own side, and the conceptually designated, or merely nominal, merely apparent nature of all phenomena—the side of emptiness does not refute the side of appearances and the side of appearances does not refute the side of emptiness. Thus you must gain a pristine ascertainment of how emptiness is the meaning of dependent origination and how dependent origination arises as the meaning of emptiness.

So, as explained previously, after you have been given teachings on differentiating the mind and pristine awareness, and you are attending to the essential nature of cognizance and have achieved stability there, you must analyze and determine cognizance, too, as being unreal and empty, without its being apprehended as truly existent or substantial. That is the analysis of such pristine awareness itself as being emptiness, and although it is not the meditation that unifies pristine awareness and emptiness, it is meditation on the emptiness of the nature of existence of pristine awareness. Thus it is the *emptiness* to be united within the union of pristine awareness and emptiness. [112]

## The Way to Practice Meditative Equipoise upon Uniting Pristine Awareness and Emptiness

As explained previously, without needing to analyze the empty absolute space of the nature of existence of pristine awareness, you should merge cognizance with the essential nature of the empty absolute space of cognizance, and without modification attend to the sphere of undifferentiated emptiness and cognizance. When you can do that, you have found the union of pristine awareness and emptiness. So, as for the place where pristine awareness and emptiness are united, you do not need to analyze freshly the emptiness of the nature of existence of pristine awareness, but by the power of your previous analysis, you simply recall the empty absolute space of the nature of existence of pristine awareness, and this will lead you to ascertain that empty absolute space. Then you should rest this cognizance in the nature of that empty absolute space and sustain that without modification. This is the meaning of *uniting absolute space and pristine awareness*.

By the power of familiarizing yourself with this, eventually the radiance of pristine awareness will dissolve into pristine awareness, and the ground pristine awareness will be revealed. Then that will arouse the exceptional wisdom that realizes the fact that the ground pristine awareness is empty of existing from its own side. In this phase [113] of uniting pristine awareness and emptiness you are sustaining something that is of the same type or has a similar aspect to the primordial consciousness an ārya has while in meditative equipoise, free of grasping to pristine awareness and emptiness dualistically, as though subject and object were different. Therefore it is the proximate cause for that meditative equipoise of an ārya.

The reason why pristine awareness and emptiness must be united in this way is that by merely experiencing pristine awareness alone, but not meditating on the fact it is empty of being awareness, the root of mundane existence cannot be cut. Also, while just the pristine awareness that is present in the ground is experienced during the transitional phase of the actual nature of reality, such pristine awareness does not reveal emptiness and so there is no realization of it. Thus, since in that case there is no contradiction between your mode of apprehension and grasping to true existence, the root of mundane existence is also not cut. So the mere experience of the ground pristine awareness cannot cut the root of mundane existence, which is grasping to true existence. The ground pristine awareness that is experienced during the transitional phase of the actual nature of reality by sentient beings who have not entered the path neither grasps to true existence nor does it apprehend the absence of true existence, so it is ethically neutral. With this point in mind, the later omniscient one[13] referred to it as *unawareness*.

Therefore, everywhere in both sūtra and mantra is agreement that the one direct antidote for ignorance (that is, grasping to true existence, which is the root of karma and mental afflictions) is the wisdom of realizing emptiness alone. For practitioners of the Great Perfection, too, the realization of emptiness is of the utmost importance, as stated in the *Tantra of the Reverberation of Sound*:

> Things appear because they do not exist, and they are empty
> because they appear.
> Those are the elements of the union of appearances and
> emptiness.

Zilnön Zhepa Tsal[14] also states:

> Who achieves liberation without realizing emptiness?
> Without the Great Perfection, how can emptiness be realized?
> Apart from myself, who praises this?

The king of jinas, Longchenpa, also states, "All these outer displays of appearances are not the mind. The assertion that they are apparitions of the mind teaches that all phenomena are merely apparitions, or appearances,

13. Jikmé Lingpa.

14. Tib. *Zil gnon bzhad pa rtsal*, a secret name of the Great Fifth Dalai Lama.

of the conceptual mind. So it shows that they are empty of existence from their own side."

That being the case, those who say that, by cultivating the view of the Great Perfection, meditation on emptiness is not needed are claiming in effect that cultivating the view of the Great Perfection entails not practicing the path of the union of emptiness and appearances. So the aspects of skillful means and wisdom [115] are split apart, and this is tantamount to saying that meditation on the nature of existence of pristine awareness—empty absolute space devoid of thought and articulation—does not cut the root of mundane existence, does not eliminate the two obscurations, and does not achieve the two kāyas. So what could be more detrimental than this great denigration of the view of the Great Perfection?! Thus to engage in the practice of cutting through, it is also extremely important to hear and contemplate the meaning of emptiness.

Meditation on emptiness by uniting pristine awareness and emptiness according to the tradition of this path and meditation on emptiness according to the path of the Pāramitāyāna are alike simply in that they are meditations on emptiness. But for however many countless eons you familiarize yourself with emptiness on the path of the Pāramitāyāna, it is not even close to a hundredth or a thousandth of just an instant of meditation on the absolute space and pristine awareness of this profound path. There is no comparison between the two. Furthermore, you should know that while there is no difference in terms of the quality of the object, emptiness, being better or worse, there is a difference according to the subject, pristine awareness, or the primordial consciousness that is to be experienced. Whether you attend to the essential nature of pristine awareness or engage in the practice of the union of pristine awareness and emptiness, all karmic energies and conceptual fabrications must cease. In order to [116] stop them, you must abandon the nine kinds of activity of the body, speech, and mind.[15]

15. Tib. *bya ba dgu sprugs*. See note 64 in *The Vital Essence of Primordial Consciousness*, above.

To abandon these, you should remain alone, without companions, while dispensing with (1) the outer activities of the body, including subduing your enemies and taking care of your friends, and all activities such as farming at home. You must dispense with (2) all inner activities of the body, including prostrations, circumambulations, and austerities. You must abandon (3) all secret activities of the body, including sacred dances and mudrās. Abandon (4) all outer activities of the speech, including mundane, delusional chatter, and gossip. Abandon (5) all inner activities of the speech, including chanting, recitations, and vocal practices. And abandon (6) all secret activities of the speech, including mental recitations and vajra recitations. Abandon (7) all outer activities of the mind, including ordinary, delusive thoughts. Abandon (8) all inner activities of the mind, including all virtuous mental states such as faith and compassion. And abandon (9) secret activities of the mind, including all stages of analytical meditation such as the stages of generation, completion, and holding the mind. Practicing stabilizing meditation alone, you should attend to the essential nature of pristine awareness, as explained previously, and unite pristine awareness and emptiness.

If you fail to do so, activities of the body and speech will increase the karmic energies, and [117] the mind will increase the karmic energies not only with negative thoughts but even with positive ones, for they are of the nature of fluctuating conceptual fabrications. So all analytical meditations increase the karmic energies and obstruct the pacification of the energy-mind. Therefore the necessity of abandoning the nine kinds of activity and engaging in stabilizing meditation alone is a unique way of sustaining practice on this path.

A method for enhancing or exercising the creative power of the view from such meditative equipoise is as follows. While in meditative equipoise, strive in the practices of attending to the essential nature of pristine awareness and of unifying pristine awareness and emptiness. Then, even during the postmeditative state, recognize all appearing phenomena of the physical world and its sentient inhabitants as displays of pristine awareness, primordial consciousness. Avoid all situations that give rise to such things as desire, craving, and anger in dependence upon impure phenomena, increase the creative power of the primordial consciousness of meditative equipoise, and realize all phenomena as naked pristine awareness.

While that method does not entail realizing all phenomena to be pristine awareness itself, whatever phenomena appear, [118] they all emerge from the capacity of the creative power, or potential, of the one pristine awareness. By realizing that there is not even one phenomenon that does not emerge from the creative power of pristine awareness, you realize that every single phenomenon that exists is solely a display emerging from the creative power of pristine awareness. If that is realized, then even during the postmeditative state the essential nature of the primordial consciousness of meditative equipoise will not be lost. So the creative power of pristine awareness will be exercised and you will realize that all phenomena are simply apparitions of pristine awareness. Once you have fathomed that among all phenomena, not even a single one truly exists from its own side, doubts will be cut off, so this is the best method for finding certainty regarding emptiness. Therefore this is also the foremost method for exercising the creative power of the primordial consciousness of meditative equipoise in which pristine awareness and the emptiness of pristine awareness are unified. Such experiential knowledge—the primordial consciousness of cutting through to emptiness—is a method for actualizing the mind of Samantabhadra, the dharmakāya, at the time of the fruition.

## The Path of the Spontaneously Actualized Direct Crossing Over

Here is the way to follow the path of the spontaneously actualized direct crossing over, taking the radiance of light as the path: Once you have the capacity that comes from achieving stability in the primordial consciousness of cutting through, then, in dependence upon visionary experiences [119] involving the four visions and six lamps of the practices of the path of the direct crossing over, spontaneously actualized aspects of those appearances are taken as the path. Then, at the point of extinction into the actual nature of reality, by the power of augmenting the subtle body that has the indwelling nature, just as rust erodes iron, all the impure aggregates and elements—including coarse, adventitious karmic energies and coarse channels—disappear into the body of refined light; and the rūpakāya of the Buddha Samantabhadra, the rainbow body of the vajrakāya, is attained. Then the two precious rūpakāyas effortlessly, eternally, pervasively, greatly, spontaneously fulfill the needs of sentient beings.

Therefore, on this path such adventitious, coarse channels, orbs, and vital energies are something to be purified without striking the crucial points of the channels, orbs, and vital energies as is done in the stage of completion of the other hidden tantras. So all the appearing aspects of the spontaneously actualized, subtle, indwelling channels, orbs, and vital energies, which are not even mentioned in other hidden tantras, are primordially present, and it is those that are taken as the path. In comparison to this path, the stage of completion of the other hidden tantras does not entail striking the crucial points of the subtle, indwelling channels, orbs, and vital energies, so that is not the "great stage of completion." This path [120] is superior even to the stage of completion of the other hidden tantras, so it is given the name the *great stage of completion*.

Other hidden tantras require that one strike crucial points of the coarse channels, orbs, and vital energies. Thus since at the second stage, the stage of completion, one strikes crucial points, the channels, orbs, and vital energies must be made serviceable for that work, and as a method for bringing them to ripening, the first stage, the stage of generation involving deity yoga, must precede the second. But that is not needed here. The reason for this is that the purpose there is to purify the coarse channels, orbs, and vital energies, while here we have the sublime pith instructions for taking all the luminous appearances of the subtle, indwelling channels, orbs, and vital energies as the path. The reason why the coarse aggregates and elements disappear and are refined into the body of light, moreover, is that when the power of the subtle, indwelling body comes to its full strength, the adventitious, impure aggregates and elements are extinguished and are refined into the body of light. Many such extraordinary, unique features do not appear in other classes of tantras. There are many points to be explained about the way to progress on the path of the four visions and so on, in dependence upon the crucial points of the body, [121] speech, and mind, and the six lamps, on the path of the visionary experiences in the direct crossing over, but I shall leave it at that for the time being.

To summarize again the way of cutting through to sustain the essential nature of pristine awareness: With the view of the ground of being, take as your basis the identification of the primordial consciousness of the nature of existence that manifests during the transitional phase of the actual nature of reality. You must gain certainty that what has the nature of the primordial consciousness that is identified within yourself, and that alone, is the mode of being of every state of consciousness of the present moment, and you must ascertain an aspect of this present-moment consciousness as the primordial consciousness of the dharmakāya itself. On the basis of that decisive certainty, with mindfulness you must recall pristine awareness, primordial consciousness, and whatever thoughts course through, you must rest again in the essential nature of that pristine awareness, primordial consciousness, and let them be released with confidence.

Suitable disciples who have admiration and reverence should receive these unique secret teachings on the practice of this supreme path of the greatly secret atiyoga from an experienced guru. But these should not be explained or presented immediately upon meeting, like a dog coming across a chunk of lung meat. [122] So people like us, who are lacking in practice of the profound view and who lack the wisdom of experience, are not worthy to listen to or teach a path such as this. However, I think it is difficult to find someone who, in dependence upon the rays of compassionate enlightened activity of a qualified guru, has gained certainty regarding this supreme path, the pinnacle atop the views of the greatly secret paths, and who engages in the activities of revealing it by way of teaching, debating, and composition. Nowadays, when for the most part the faults of those who presume themselves to be teachers have come to fruition, it is difficult for this advice to be transmitted through their hearts—this advice that dissects the crucial points of practice in response to the auspicious conditions of irreversible faith and admiration for this supreme path having been assembled on the part of those requesting it, and which makes fine distinctions regarding what is and is not the case, thereby overcoming the dangers of false speculation and repudiation. It is like the saying of the paṇḍit Butön:[16]

> If you teach in accordance with the Dharma, Tibetans arise as
> your enemy.
> If you teach what is not Dharma, that will be in conflict with the
> Dharma.

In this era when we have arrived at that point, even if others were to count me as a fool, it would be best to hold to the discipline of not speaking at all. However, [123] I have spoken for the sake of spreading and enabling all the general and specific aspects of the precious teaching of the Jina to flourish, and in order to place imprints in myself for this Dharma.

> A ho!
> The primordially empty, originally pure nature of existence
> is devoid of signs of the apprehended and the apprehender
> appearing as two.
> Naturally present, it is self-emergent primordial consciousness
> itself,
> empty of the extremes of effort, striving, rejection, and
> acceptance.
> That is the very meaning of being free from the extremes,
> without conceptual elaborations.
> It is not something experienced as an object of conceptual
> fabrications, not something with elaborations.
> The clarity of this unimpeded self-illumination
> is unstained by the suffocating darkness of delusion.
> The face of Samantabhadra, primordial consciousness itself,

16. Tib. *Bu ston rin chen grub* (1290–1364).

is realized if you free yourself from the web of conceptual
constructs.
The view of the dharmakāya, the vast expanse,
is everywhere present, with no outside or inside.
This vital essence, the very quintessence, of the mind of
Samantabhadra,
is free from the biases of falling to extremes.
This view that has no need for causes or results
is free from the extremes of striving in virtue and [avoiding] vice.
The actual nature of the mind has always been the Buddha,
and that contradicts a path in which you apply antidotes to reject
things and to be rid of obscurations.
To rely upon amassing the two collections anew
contradicts the nature of the union of enlightened body and
mind. [124]
The suchness of self-illuminating primordial consciousness,
unobscured by dualistic conceptual fabrications,
is not realized through what appears to a mindset involving
conceptual elaborations.
It is seen while resting in self-illumination free of elaboration.
Train in the path of open presence, without modification.
Attend to the displays of self-liberating primordial consciousness.
From the self-illuminating, unimpeded primordial consciousness
emerge the six dharmas of Samantabhadra's way of liberation.
These profound and secret vajra words,
hard to explain without difficulty and swiftly
by those who are chained with intellectual hopes and fears,
are stated in the *Disclosure of What Was Hidden*:[17]
"The scorn of the ḍākinīs and lords of the Dharma is not turned
back.
Let the guardians of this greatly secret, supreme path

17. Tib. *Gab sbas mngon byung.*

look after disciples who are suitable vessels
and drink the heart-blood of charlatans with no samayas."

In response to the repeated requests of Ven. Örgyen Rigdzin,[18] this *Ornament of the Enlightened View of Samantabhadra: Secret Guidance Nakedly Granted to Dispel All Misconceptions regarding the View of the Clear Light Great Perfection* was given to him by the madman Tsultrim Zangpo, who had taken upon the crown of his head the dust from the feet of many qualified gurus, those whose mindstreams are rich in experiential realizations. This was uttered in whatever way came up at the time—as an addendum to an explanation of the *Guide to the Middle Way*[19] and the *Letter to a Friend*,[20] [125] from the hermitage of the Dharma Isle of Spontaneous Clear Light,[21] at the base of the Royal Hermitage, the "Tree Where *Vāḥ* Dissolves."[22] May this virtue act as a cause for the teachings of the supreme yāna atiyoga to be spread in a hundred directions without ever diminishing.

Virtue, virtue, virtue
It is of highest importance to guard the seal of secrecy. [126]

18. Tib. *Btsun pa o rgyan rig 'dzin.*

19. Tib. *Dbu ma 'jug pa*, Skt. *Madhyamakāvatāra*, by Candrakīrti.

20. Tib. *Bshes spring*, Skt. *Suhṛllekha*, by Nāgārjuna.

21. Tib. *Dben gnas lhun grub 'od gsal chos gling.*

22. Tib. *vāḥ: thim shing rgyal ba'i dben gnas kyi zhol.*

# Oral Instructions of the Wise

## *Questions and Answers regarding the Views of Mahāmudrā, Mahāsaṇdhi*[1] *and Madhyamaka*

Lozang Do-ngak Chökyi Gyatso Chok[2]

I reverently imagine the venerable Mañjughoṣa,
the compassionate guru, indivisible from all the glorious jinas,
on the lotus at the center of my heart,
bearing the marks of the intelligence that sees all displays [of
phenomena].
In order to offer honest answers to the questions posed
by noble individuals with good fortune who are applying
themselves to practice,
with few words, I shall give a little explanation of the categories
of Mahāmudrā, Mahāsaṇdhi, and Madhyamaka
in accordance with the oral lineage of my gurus.

To synthesize all the divisions of the innumerable gateways of the sublime Dharma taught for the sake of disciples by the Jina, who possesses both skillful means and great compassion, they can be included within the two paths of the sūtras and tantras. To classify them more extensively, in terms of the view, there are four schools of philosophical tenets, [127]

1. Tib. *Rdzogs pa chen po*, commonly translated as the Great Perfection.

2. Tib. *Blo bzang mdo sngags chos kyi rgya mtsho mchog* (1903–57).

and there is an excellent threefold classification of yānas in terms of the scope of the intention for engaging in practice. Nowadays in this Land of Snows, the three great teaching traditions of Mahāmudrā, Mahāsaṇdhi, and Madhyamaka more or less subsume the precious teachings of the Sage, and the glorious majesty of their blessings is present as a field of merit for living beings. Mahāmudrā and Mahāsaṇdhi are each regarded principally as the ultimate, great vajrayoga that does not differentiate between separate realizations of the skillful means and wisdom that belong to each of the great anuttarayogatantras of the New and Old Translations schools of Mantrayāna.

## Madhyamaka

Madhyamaka is, by way of wisdom, the pinnacle of the schools of philosophical tenets. By following the definitive collections of sūtras that proclaim the absence of inherent nature to be the profound nature of existence, it is the superlative view drawn from realization. This is not merely a contextual claim, but is said to be the one view of all the sūtras and tantras by [masters] of the old tantras, such as Rongzom Paṇḍita[3] and the great omniscient Longchen Rabjam. This is also asserted by many countless scholars and adepts of the new tantras, principally including the Sakya Mahāpaṇḍita, the venerable Tsongkhapa, and his two spiritual sons [Gyaltsab Jé and Khedrup Jé].[4] [128]

The nature of this view is stated by the omniscient Rongzom Chökyi Zangpo:

> The statement "As long as conditions are immediately present,
> their effects do not appear"
> does not falsely repudiate anything,
> so I do not see it as a case of repudiation.

3. Tib. *Rong zom paṇḍita*. That is, *Rong zom chos kyi bzang po* (c. 1012–88).

4. Gyaltsab Jé Darma Rinchen (*Rgyal tshab rje dar ma rin chen*, 1364–1432) and Khedrup Jé Gélek Pelzang (*Mkhas grub rje dge legs dpal bzang*, 1385–1438).

In the dependent origination of causes and effects,
apart from mere appearances,
the phenomena of causes and effects are not established as real.
So I do not see it as a case of false superimposition.
Even if the reality that is devoid of false repudiation and
superimposition
is established in some other way,
by following the definitive teachings,
reality arises in my mind like this.

The great Indian paṇḍit [Atīśa] Dīpaṃkara Śrījñāna also praised it [i.e., the Madhyamaka view], and his praise is marvelously well expressed. The omniscient lord of speech also wrote in a similar vein in his *Seven Great Treasuries* and the *Three Types of Comfort and Ease.*[5] Mañjughoṣa Sakya Paṇḍita Kün-ga Gyaltsen Pel Zangpo[6] also stated in *A Clear Differentiation of the Three Codes*[7] that if in the Secret Mantrayāna there were something superior to the Pāramitā view, that view would have to be something *with* elaboration! [129].

In *A Guide to the Way of the Mahāyāna*,[8] Rongzom states that the view of the inner tantras of the Secret Mantrayāna is not the Madhyamaka view. However, during the period of the early dissemination of the Buddhist teachings [in Tibet], Śāntarakṣita and his principal spiritual son, Kamalaśīla, did not differentiate between the Prāsaṅgika and Svātantrika [interpretations of the Madhyamaka view], but rather took the Yogācāra Svātantrika [interpretation] as the basis of their view. This, then, is the basis for the *Notes on the View* by Ācārya Yeshé Dé,[9] and so on. This view is in part similar to what Maitrīpa means when he states, "It is not endowed

5. Longchenpa's *Mdzod chen bdun* and *Ngal gso gsum*.

6. Tib. *Kun dga' rgyal mtshan dpal bzang po* (1182–1251).

7. Tib. *Sdom gsum rab dbye*. For this particular reference, see Sakya Paṇḍita Kün-ga Gyaltsen, *A Clear Differentiation of the Three Codes*, 129, v. 255.

8. Tib. *Theg chen tshul 'jug*.

9. Tib. *Ye shes sde*, a great translator and direct disciple of Padmasambhava, who lived from the mid-eighth to early ninth centuries.

with aspects, nor is it lacking in aspects . . . ," so there is no contradiction. The incomparable followers of the Riwo Geden[10] agree with the above. This accords with the words of the venerable father, our Gentle Protector Guru:[11]

> For as long as your understanding of the infallible dependent
> origination of appearances
> and of emptiness, free of philosophical assertions,
> appears to be separate,
> you have still not realized the enlightened view of the Sage.
>
> Eventually, when simultaneously, and without alternating,
> simply upon seeing the infallibility of dependent origination,
> that ascertainment destroys all reification of objects,
> then the analysis of the view is complete.
>
> Moreover, when appearances dispel the extreme of existence
> and emptiness dispels the extreme of nonexistence, [130]
> and when you know how emptiness arises as cause and effect,
> you will not be carried away by views that grasp to extremes.

His great follower, the omniscient guru Jamyang Zhepé Dorjé,[12] also makes the very important point, "Apart from this, there are only coarse and subtle extremes of eternalism and nihilism."

Regarding the merely partial statement by Rongzom above, it appears there is no clear proof that this represents the ultimate Madhyamaka view that is the Prāsaṅgika, the tradition that is utterly without a philosophical stance.[13] So how are we to establish Rongzom's assertion as referring to the

10. Tib. *ri bo dge ldan*, a synonym of the Geluk school.

11. Tib. *yab rje 'jam mgon bla ma*, referring here to Tsongkhapa. The quotation is from the *Three Principal Aspects of the Path*, Tib. *Lam gyi gtso bo rnam gsum*.

12. Tib. *'Jam dbyangs bzhad pa'i rdo rje* (1648–1721).

13. Tib. *rab tu mi gnas pa'i lugs*.

Prāsaṅgika? In *A Guide to the Way of the Mahāyāna*, [Rongzom] says that the Mādhyamikas' assertion of correct deceptive realities[14] with the analogy of King Anantayaśas is something amazing and ridiculous. Since he emphasizes the view of the two realities being indivisible insofar as everything is merely imputed, you should also understand that there is a distinction in his teaching between subtle and coarse objects of refutation when refuting false superimpositions and repudiations.[15]

According to the traditions of the omniscient Longchenpa and Rongzom regarding both sūtra and mantra, there are no differences in the nature of how [131] the view realizing emptiness is apprehended or ascertained. So, regarding sūtra and mantra respectively, there are no differences in the degree of subtlety of the object negated by this view. However, just as there is no difference in the states of meditative equipoise of higher and lower ārya bodhisattvas, but there are differences in the ways they sustain their ascertainment [of emptiness] during the postmeditative state, likewise, in sūtra and mantra respectively, there are contexts for teaching the view in different ways that are higher or lower in terms of enhancing the power of the realization of emptiness. In short, regarding what is known as "Madhyamaka," the *Fundamental Treatise on the Middle Way*,[16] which comments on the meaning of the entire original, definitive collection of sūtras, has views that are held in common with the Yogācārins, supplemented by those that are unique [to the Madhyamaka]. Teachings on the way to practice are found in both the *Four Hundred Verses*[17] and *A Guide to the Middle Way*,[18] and on the basis of these three—the *Fundamental Treatise on the Middle Way*, *Four Hundred Verses*, and *A Guide to the*

14. Tib. *yang dag kun rdzob*, Skt. *satyaṃ saṃvṛti*.

15. Since "correct deceptive realities" and a distinction "between subtle and coarse objects of refutation" are philosophical points unique to what was later termed the "Svātantrika" view of Madhyamaka, this seems to be Lozang Do-ngak Chökyi Gyatso's way of demonstrating that Rongzom was not writing about the Prāsaṅgika view. Hence when Rongzom wrote that the "Madhyamaka view" was not the same as that of the inner tantras, he could not have been referring to the Madhyamaka Prāsaṅgika interpretation.

16. Tib. *Rtsa ba shes rab*, Skt. *Mūlamadhyamakakārikā*, by Nāgārjuna.

17. Tib. *Bzhi brgya pa*, Skt. *Catuḥśataka*, by Āryadeva.

18. Tib. *Dbu ma la 'jug pa*, Skt. *Madhyamakāvātara*, by Candrakīrti.

*Middle Way*—the essence of the Mahāyāna path is set straight in a unified way. The later omniscient one [Jikmé Lingpa] asserts in his *Vajra Songs*,[19] "By embracing the Great Mother Perfection of Wisdom, the experience of the glorious protector Ārya Nāgārjuna arose. For the source of the river of explanation, ask Candrakīrti." To gain freedom from saṃsāra, this definitive view is indispensable. The glorious Candrakīrti writes:

> Apart from the tradition of the venerable Ācārya Nāgārjuna,
> there is no way to [132] pacify those who are outside.

## Mahāmudrā

The definitive Mahāmudrā is a tradition of the New Translation school of secret mantra, and it is taught in two traditions, Sūtrayāna and Mantrayāna. Insofar as it is imbued with the wisdom that realizes emptiness, all its practices are sealed with the quality of being antidotes to mundane existence. In this sense the view of the sūtra tradition has also been said to be Mahāmudrā. However, although the meaning of *mudrā* [i.e., "seal"] is complete there, the omniscient guru Jamyang Zhepé Dorjé has stated that this lacks the meaning of the *mahāmudrā* [i.e., "the great seal"].

The Mantrayāna tradition of Mahāmudrā concerns the definitive clear light, and regarding emptiness there are also ways to apply the term "lady seal."[20] When engaging in this kind of Mahāmudrā meditation, śamatha is achieved by focusing on the mind, such that one seeks the view on the basis of meditation. In dependence upon this śamatha, the mind is settled with the aspect of things as they are, once one has correctly determined the birth, cessation, and abiding of the mind as being without identity. In general there are two stages by which to augment both settling the mind and vipaśyanā. Specifically, in the tradition of [133] Marpa, Milarepa, and Gampopa there is the method of identifying the essential nature of the

19. Tib. *Rdo rje'i mgur.*
20. Tib. *phyag rgya ma.*

mind in dependence upon *caṇḍālī*.[21] So something like that is also called "Mahāmudrā." In the Geden [i.e., Geluk] tradition, Paṇchen Lozang Chökyi Gyaltsen[22] wrote a root text and autocommentary on the unique form of Mahāmudrā passed down according to the oral lineage of the [Tibetan] mahāsiddha Dharmavajra and his spiritual son [Sangyé Yeshé].[23]

The fundamental source of these teachings traces back to Naropa and Maitrīpa, and in particular it is said that the translator Marpa cut off misconceptions regarding the view of Mahāmudrā on the basis [of the teachings he received from] Maitrīpa. Maitrīpa's teacher, known as Advayavajra,[24] or Avadhūtipa, wrote many works under the Dharma name Amanasyakara, and they are the apex of Mahāmudrā treatises and practical instructions. They are also the fundamental source for all the Nyingma treatises by paṇḍits and siddhas. "Amanasyakara" has the meaning of "nonmentation,"[25] and highlights the importance of drawing forth the power of nonconceptuality. Scholars say that due to confusion on this point, here in Tibet the two traditions of Mahāmudrā and Mahāsaṇdhi—known as the "Amanasika" Great Seal and the Chinese tradition of the Great Perfection—were greatly contaminated by [134] the Hvashang view and meditation, in which one blocks mentation [altogether].

To draw a clear distinction here, there is a difference between blocking all thoughts of reification and blocking all good and bad thoughts, but I shall not elaborate. The milestones for progressing higher and higher in one's realization of this Mahāmudrā path consist of the four stages of yoga: single-pointed, freedom from conceptual elaboration, one

21. Tib. *gtum mo*. A meditative practice designed to bring forth realization of emptiness, with a side effect of generating intense heat arising from the navel cakra. It is described in *The Vajra Essence* of Düdjom Lingpa as "great, empty awareness, devoid of activity, the fire of primordial consciousness, the union of bliss and emptiness, which blazes as a display of the power of the five facets of primordial consciousness" (156).

22. Tib. *Paṇ chen blo bzang chos kyi rgyal mtshan* (1570–1662), who was a direct disciple of Sangyé Yeshé (*Sangs rgyas ye shes*, 1525–91).

23. For further reading on this lineage in the tradition of Tsongkhapa, see Willis, *Enlightened Beings*.

24. Tib. *Gnyis med rdo rje*.

25. Tib. *yid la mi byed pa*, Skt. *amanasikāra*.

taste, and nonmeditation. Those seeking an expanded presentation on this renowned topic in the Kagyü tradition should consult [the writings of] Ngomi.[26] Those who are drawn to the Mahāmudrā approach are well advised to look at the root text on Mahāmudrā called *The Highway of the Jinas*.[27] In the Mahāmudrā lineage from Marpa, Milarepa, and Gampopa the ultimate view is only Prāsaṅgika, but occasionally appearances are identified as the mind. Scholars claim that the phrase "identify the actual nature of the mind as empty" is an identification and view common to the Cittamātrins, so one cannot determine for sure that it is unique to the Mahāmudrā view alone.

## Mahāsaṇdhi—The Clear Light Great Perfection

The ultimate view of the unique class of tantras of the Early Translation school of secret mantra is the heart essence of the siddha and ācārya Pramodavajra, which is a sublime Dharma of pith instructions for those with exceptionally sharp faculties and good fortune. There is no clearer instance of this Dharma language—from the perspective of the New Translation school of Mantrayāna—than in the *Oral Instructions of Mañjuśrī* from the Guhyasamāja tradition of Jñānapāda[28]:

> The general form of primordial consciousness—the Great Perfection—
> is the immaculate body of the Great Vajradhara.
> The ultimate fruition is the sole Buddha.

Here in Tibet there is the lineage of pith instructions from the Mahāpaṇḍita Vimalamitra and the Mahācārya of Orgyen, Padmasambhava, which

26. Tib. *Rngo mi.* See also the chapter "The Four Stages of Yoga" in Karma Chagmé, *Naked Awareness.*

27. Tib. *Rgyal ba'i gzhung lam*, by Paṇchen Lozang Chökyi Gyaltsen.

28. Tib. *Ye shes zhabs*, also known as Buddhaśrījñāna. The formal Sanskrit name of this text is *Dvikramatattvabhāvanā-nāma-mukhāma*, or *Oral Instructions on How to Meditate on the Very Reality of the Two Stages.*

flows in a stream through the gradual succession of their fortunate followers. But the three internal classifications within this Dharma, namely, the mind, expanse, and pith instruction classes of teachings, have each brought countless numbers of fortunate disciples to liberation, in which their coarse aggregates disappeared into minute particles and so on. This secret path of the Vajrayāna is undeniably amazing. Among the four cycles of secret pith instructions on this path, the cycles of the heart essence pith instructions of the ultrasecret class are [136] the ultimate Great Perfection pith instructions that reveal all the hidden meanings. The earlier and later omniscient ones and others declare those to be the profound, swift path for accomplishing the indivisible kāyas and facets of primordial consciousness.

Both the earlier and later omniscient ones assert that the view of the heart essence pith instructions on the identification of appearances as the mind, and so on, is not at all in accord with the Cittamātra method. The lord of sages, Rongzom, also states that the tradition of [Svātantrika] Mādhyamikas who assert correct deceptive realities is not suitable as the view and meditation of the Great Perfection. So the view of this Dharma is established solely as the Prāsaṅgika. In this regard the great treasure revealer Trang-go Terchen Sherab Özer[29] states:

> The view of cutting through severs the membrane of the source
> of mundane existence.
> The meditation of the direct crossing over perfects the strength
> of the three kāyas.

As stated, there are these two—cutting through and the direct crossing over—and they are both unique paths of this tradition for experiencing the dharmakāya and rūpakāya in dependence upon the ground and the appearances of the ground. The correct articulation of the essential nature of this path is this: with the intelligence that understands the self-appearances of

29. Tib. *'Phrang mgo'i gter chen shes rab 'od zer,* better known as Trengpo Tertön Sherab Özer (*'Phreng po gter ston shes rab 'od zer,* 1518–84). See http://treasuryoflives.org/biographies/view/Sherab-Ozer/8964.

pristine awareness, disciples who are entirely free of conceptual elaboration rest in the nature of existence of the [137] unmodified essential nature of the mind in this very life and are able to sustain this. Sealing that with the mudrā of arising and release,[30] they overcome the poison of the fetters of compulsive ideation by transcending them in their own place. The great innovater of this tradition, which is the vajra pinnacle of the supreme yāna, the omniscient Dharma king, famously emphasizes the great importance of differentiating the mind from pristine awareness.

The way to progress in the four visions on the path and to arise as a great transference rainbow body by way of the spontaneous actualization of the appearances of the ground is a very special, unique characteristic of the wondrous pinnacle of the yānas, atiyoga. The wise who have not fallen to any extreme, but have gained thorough mastery regarding the definitive meaning, declare this to be a very difficult and astounding topic.

Many paṇḍits and siddhas of Tibet affirm that the ultimate view of Mahāmudrā, Mahāsaṇdhi, and Madhyamaka converge on the same point. In his *Prayer on the Definitive Meaning of Mahāmudrā*[31] the venerable Karmapa Rangjung Dorjé[32] offered this supplication:

> This freedom from mentation is Mahāmudrā.
> Freedom from extremes is the great Madhyamaka.
> The synthesis of this [138] is called Mahāsaṇdhi.
> May we acquire the confidence of realizing all meanings with one knowledge.

In his *The Highway of the Jinas: A Root Text on the [Precious Geluk-Kagyü] Mahāmudrā Tradition*, the omniscient Paṇchen Lozang Chökyi Gyaltsen writes:

30. Tib. *shar grol.*
31. Tib. *Nges don phyag rgya chen po'i smon lam.*
32. Tib. *Rje karma pa rang byung rdo rje'i zhabs* (1284–1339).

The amulet box, connate union,
the fivefold, equalizing taste, and the four letters,
pacification, severance, the great perfection,
the teachings on the middle-way view, and so on
may each be named in various ways,
but when they are analyzed by scholars who are knowledgeable of
the scriptures and reasoning pertaining to the
definitive meaning and by experienced yogins,
they are found to converge on the same view.

The great vidyādhara Jikmé Lingpa writes in his *White Lotus Supplement to the Pith Instructions*: "Heh, heh! The radical absence of a philosophical position of Madhyamaka is here. The transcendence of the intellect of Mahāmudrā is here. The primordial purity of Mahāsaṇdhi is here. What will the great demons who have no ground and no root do once they have entered the heart of the yogin? They will not stick around!"[33] There are many teachings of paṇḍits and siddhas that accord with this.

While there are many such traditions of teaching, [139] if we are to encapsulate their crucial points it would be as follows: The unsurpassed entry point to the view, which gathers a hundred streams under one bridge of a great summary for how to follow the path, is the presentation of the stages of the path for individuals of three capacities as taught by the glorious Lord Atīśa Dīpaṃkara. Thus it is correct to practice this with great effort, as stated by the great treasure revealer Sherab Özer:

The meaning of all the teachings of the Jina
by which fortunate states of existence are achieved
comprises the path for individuals of small capacity.
The meaning of all the kinds of Dharma articulated
so that one might strive in methods for achieving liberation

33. Tib. *Man ngag gi rgyab rten pad ma dkar po.*

comprises the stages of the path for individuals of middling capacity.
May they achieve the freedom of having definitely emerged from mundane existence!
The methods for swiftly achieving the state of omniscience
consist of the two forms of the Mahāyāna: the causal and fruitional vehicles.
All the teachings spoken thus, without exception,
comprise the stages of the path for individuals of great capacity.

The omniscient Khyentsé also stated that one should practice according to the protector Atīśa's *Lamp for the Path to Enlightenment*,[34] which is the outer framework for all the teachings in general, or else the inner core of the path held in common by all the yānas. As *The Stairway to Liberation: A Guide to the Meaning of the Seven Preliminary Mind Trainings*[35] states: [140] "Regarding this presentation for individuals of the three capacities: A vidyādhara with mastery over life[36] took rebirth in the form of a celibate monastic, and in order to spread the teachings—in the form of the three classes of scriptures and the realizations pertaining to them—he, the glorious Lord Dīpaṃkara, revealed the *Lamp for the Path to Enlightenment*. In this way his work was complete, and there was nothing extraneous. Nevertheless, since [some] thought that in essence it was no more than a way of listing the subjects of Dharma language in forward and reverse order, it was less well-known within the circles of the Early Translation school." In the *Praṇidhana for Accomplishing Words of Truth*[37] the enlightened prayer made there is similar in content.

34. Tib. *Byang chub lam gyi sgron ma*. See Sonam, *Atisha's Lamp for the Path*.

35. Tib. *Sngon 'gro sems sbyong bdun gyi don khrid thar pa'i them skas*, by Jikmé Lingpa Khyentsé Özer.

36. This is the second of the four stages of vidyādharas.

37. Tib. *Bden tshig grub pa'i pra ṇi dhana*. Found in the *Collection of Recitations from the Treasury of Teachings of the Great Secret [Tantras] of the Early Translation School, Gsang chen snga 'gyur ba'i bka' gter zhal 'don phyogs bsgrigs*.

Now amidst all this, for an ordinary person like myself all the paths of the sublime Dharma are blocked by the harmful fantasies of grasping to this life and thinking I will live forever. Thus, at the beginning, to inspect whether or not I will be able to subdue such bad thoughts is even more profound than any of these three: Mahāmudrā, Mahāsaṇdhi, or Madhyamaka!

In brief, whatever the practice may be, it is very important to meditate according to the stages of the path in relation to the level of your own mindstream. In his *Treasure of Wish-Fulfilling Jewels*,[38] the omniscient Dharma king Longchen Rabjam states:

> Just as children and adults have different food, [141]
> their Dharma too differs in nature.

This point is also discussed in detail in the commentary. It was also emphasized by the perfectly awakened Buddha in the *Sūtra of the Ten Wheels of Kṣitigarbha*:[39]

> Foolish, unintelligent, lazy people
> do not persevere in the two yānas.[40]
> So they do not come to bear the wheel of the Mahāyāna,
> and they are not vessels suitable for the vast Mahāyāna . . .
>
> If they don't have the power to drink a stream
> how could they ever imbibe the great ocean?
> If they can't accustom themselves even to the two [lower] yānas,
> how will they be able to train in the Mahāyāna?

Accordingly, the great Kadam spiritual friend Drolungpa[41] writes:

38. Tib. *Yid bzhin mdzod.*

39. Tib. *Sa yi snying po 'khor lo bcu pa'i mdo*, Skt. *Kṣitigarbhadaśacakra-sūtra.*

40. These refer to the Śrāvakayāna and the Pratyekabuddhayāna.

41. Tib. *Gro lung pa.*

The ultimate yāna is the supreme yāna,
but one gradually progresses by way of the two yānas.
Great fools who reject them and embrace the Mahāyāna
do not find the same benefit, and this causes tremendous
degeneration for the Sage's teachings.

The straight line that demarcates the authentic path from its false imitations is explained by the venerable Rangjung Dorjé:

By way of the fundamental meaning of the two realities, free of
the extremes of eternalism and nihilism,
and by means of the supreme path of the two collections, free of
the extremes of false superimposition and repudiation, [142]
may we encounter the unmistaken Dharma
by which the fruition of our own and others' well being is achieved,
free of the extremes of mundane existence and of peace.

Just that is what is needed. Emphasis on the importance of this gets redundant, so please bear it in mind. Nowadays the *Treasury of the Absolute Space of Phenomena*[42] stands alone with its high Dharma terminology, and there's a real danger of people pretending to have realization. The practices for the complete teachings of the Jina are clearly found in the *Treasuries* and their commentaries, in the *Mind in Comfort and Ease*,[43] and in the commentaries of the great founders, so it would be good to look at these again and again.

May we realize the Madhyamaka view, free of extremes,
assisted impartially by both appearances and emptiness

42. Tib. *Chos dbyings mdzod.* One of the seven treasuries of Longchen Rabjam. For an English translation, see Longchen Rabjam, *The Precious Treasury of the Basic Space of Phenomena.*

43. Tib. *Sems nyid ngal gso.* See His Holiness the Dalai Lama, *Mind in Comfort and Ease.*

in accordance with the elucidation of the Mother [Perfection of
Wisdom Sūtras] by Nāgārjuna,
and further explained by Candrakīrti.

May we engage in the meditation of the Mahāmudrā,
which is like the sky of nonconceptuality that cancels
the clouds of mentation and grasping to signs,
in accordance with the tradition of Saraha, Maitrīpa, Marpa,
Milarepa, and Gampopa.

May we achieve enlightenment by means of atiyoga, [143]
the path of the great clear light that chases after pristine
awareness alone,
which perfects the creative power of the nine yānas of the Early
Translation school,
the supreme heart essence of Vimalamitra and Padmasambhava.

When crossing the border with the momentum of such fine
prayers,
should we acquire sufficient confidence in the infallibility of
dependent origination
that it will let us practice the sublime Dharma in all our
lifetimes,
this life of leisure and opportunity will have proven to be
meaningful.

These *Oral Instructions of the Wise: Questions and Answers regarding the Views of Mahāmudrā, Mahāsaṇdhi, and Madhyamaka*, which have been assembled from hearing various teachings of the wise, were requested by Lama Pema, that diligent practitioner who grounded his practice atop the Dharma foundation that lies below great empowerments. I have placed the feet of numerous spiritual friends and scholars of the New and Old Translation schools on the crown of my head. I, Lozang Do-ngak Chökyi

Gyatso, a sick old monk who has been blessed with the name of a great bodhisattva, who—though I have heard many teachings on the Dharma of the supreme yāna—bears the reflection of a Buddhist bhikṣu, with little experience, have composed this and offer it here.

May there be virtue! [144]

# Heart Essence of the Vidyādhara Elders of the Early Translation School

## *A Brief Explanation of the Meaning of the Root Mantra of Vajrakīlaya*

Kunzang Zhepé Dorjé[1]

O, paṇḍit of paṇḍits, Gentle Protector, King of the Dharma!
O, siddha of siddhas, Lord of Secrets, Lerab Ling!
Even once I achieve enlightenment, still,
I will offer you reverence with the crown of my head.
With few words I shall distinguish between the profound and vast meanings.

Among the three classes of tantric scriptures belonging to the Old, Early Translation school of secret mantra, there is within the class of Mahāyoga both the scriptural collection of tantras and the collection of texts for actualization.[2] Within the latter, there are five groups of actualization texts for the supramundane body, speech, mind, qualities, and activities of a buddha, and three groups for the mundane accomplishments, making a

1. Tib. *Kun bzang bzhad pa'i rdo rje*. This is of course the same author who went by the names of Dharmasāra and Lozang Do-ngak Chökyi Gyatso, above.

2. Tib. *sgrub sde*, i.e., the collection of sādhana practices.

total of eight great classes of actualization texts. Among these, in accordance with the enlightened view of the *Four Ways of Incineration*[3]—[145] that swift, profound method of binding, found within the cycle for actualizing the sacred stake of enlightened activity—there is the fourteen-syllable root mantra [of Vajrakīlaya].

To give just a brief account of the syllables so that they are not forgotten, *oṃ* is the opening of the mantra. In the common language [of mantra] it is an auspicious expression having the connotation of protection. In the tradition of the unique Secret Mantrayāna, it is said to symbolize the nature of the indivisibility of the three kāyas, by way of the three sounds *a*, *u*, and *m*. The *Vajra Peak Tantra*[4] states that by reciting this just once while bearing its meaning in mind, vast merit is accumulated. Just as kindling is turned to ashes by the power of fire, this is like the blazing bonfire of a path of skillful means that incinerates the kindling of adverse obstacles that would prevent one from experiencing the state of the definitive Vajrakīlaya. The one who grants this is Vajrakīli, that is, the four Vajrakīlayas. The action is *kīlaya*, which means *achieved with the phurbu*, or *striking with the stake*. Those who are struck with the action of incineration are *sarvavighna*, or all obstructors.[5]

As for the way that they are struck: That to which they are liberated is indicated with *vaṃ*, the definitive Great Mother, the actual nature of reality, the expanse of absolute space that is emptiness, which is symbolized by placing[6] as a seal the circle [146] that is an emanation of Vajravārāhī, Dorjé Phakmo. Alternatively, the individuals who are liberated are *vighnāḥ*, for which the first letter is *va*. With that first letter one recalls one's samaya to

3. Tib. *Thal 'byin rnam pa bzhi*.

4. Tib. *Rdo rje rtse mo*, Skt. *Vajraśekhara-mahāguhya-yogatantra*.

5. Tib. *bgegs*. This refers to beings among the eighty thousand types of demons that obstruct the path to liberation; they are primarily viewed as being mere projections of thoughts of ego-grasping, craving, and attachment.

6. The Tibetan verb for "placing" here is the same as the word translated elsewhere in this essay as "striking": *'debs/gtab*.

liberate them into the real nature of the sign, through its orb[7] that has no sides or corners, [and represents] the actual nature of the obstructors, who lack an inherent nature. With the syllable *hūṃ*, one invokes Vajrakīlaya, whose three secrets[8] are indivisible. Then, in order to effect the actual liberation, *phaṭ* means "Burst apart!" or "Incinerate!" To explain this a bit more precisely, there are four incinerating Vajrakīlayas: (1) the kīlaya of pristine awareness, primordial consciousness, (2) the kīlaya of immeasurable compassion, (3) the kīlaya of ultimate bodhicitta, and (4) the symbolic, physical kīlaya.

The first is explained to be an extraordinary, profound wisdom that directly realizes the great dharmakāya itself, the equality that is praised extensively in all the sūtras and tantras, the meaning of all-pervasive suchness, symbolized by space, which is free of the conceptual elaborations of the four extremes. It realizes the nature of existence of knowable entities, as represented by phenomena and individuals, which is not experienced, just as it is, by most classes of ordinary people. [147]

The second refers to attending to the realms of sentient beings, who are destitute and tormented by suffering, relating this to your own experience of not wishing to suffer, and then desiring, without partiality, that all sentient beings throughout space may be free of suffering. It also refers to the uncontrived attitude of wishing to protect them from suffering.

The third refers to the profound yoga[9] of indivisible skillful means and wisdom, in which the three realms arise arranged as the three maṇḍalas of Vajrakīlaya—a pure physical world and its sentient inhabitants. The condition that brings this about is the radiance of the primordial consciousness that comes from meditative equipoise upon the suchness of the actual nature of reality, aroused in the aspect of great compassion. This is the unsurpassed, definitive kīlaya, which is presented as bodhicitta due to its equivalence with the enlightenment that is the ultimate attainment.

7. This refers to the small circle, or *anusvāra*, atop the letter *vaṃ*, combining the "*va*," which is the initial for the obstructors, and the bindu, which represents their ultimate nature.

8. Refers to the enlightened body, speech, and mind.

9. Tib. reads *rnam sbyor*, but should read *rnal sbyor*.

In accordance with the tantras of this cycle and the explanations in their commentaries, the fourth refers to a physical kīla, with all the requisite characteristics, that is the symbolic hand implement of the personal deity. It is accomplished as something imbued with power, and then blessed, via the three components of the material substance, the mantras, and the samādhi.

Whatever [148] those kīlayas strike, they incinerate every kind of obstructor. The kīlaya of pristine awareness, primordial consciousness, strikes all knowable entities subsumed by "phenomena" and "individuals" and incinerates the legions of obstructors that include the two types of self-grasping, along with the eighty-four thousand groups of enemies that arise from them—the mental afflictions and the three poisons, along with all the habitual propensities for them. That is the first incineration.

At that time, the Vajrakīlaya that is pristine awareness, the primordial consciousness of the nature of existence, is Vajrakīlī, "the one who strikes with the kīla." The destruction of all conceptual elaborations that grasp to signs is the kīlaya, which is "striking with the kīla." The two kinds of self-grasping to be severed are the *sarva-vighna*, the thorns of conceptual elaborations regarding dualistic appearances, which are ripped out, and they are the roots of all obstructors. In the space that you think of as the circle that strikes a seal upon the *vaṃ* (བཾ), you invoke the great majesty of *hūṃ*, and *phaṭ* is the actual syllable that pulverizes them to the point of incineration. The remaining [kīlayas] follow suit.

The kīlaya of immeasurable compassion strikes immeasurable sentient beings throughout space, without any sense of partiality, and it incinerates all that obstructs the emergence of immeasurable altruism, such as self-centeredness and the yearning to achieve peace and happiness just for oneself, [149] which would involve focusing on lesser intentions that are greatly deplored everywhere in the Mahāyāna. That is the second incineration.

The kīlaya of bodhicitta strikes all the outer physical worlds, which currently appear as ordinary, and all their inner phenomena, that is, the sentient beings who inhabit those worlds, and completely expels all obstructors, namely, the appearance of things as impure and the clinging to that appearance, along with the karmic energies that activate such appearances and the clinging to them. And it consecrates the three realms of mundane existence as the city of Vajrakīlaya. That is the third incineration.

The symbolic, physical kīlaya strikes all foul enemies and obstructors, namely, the ten fields of destruction,[10] including those who destroy the teachings of the Buddha and those who denigrate the profound mysteries of the Mantrayāna. Forcefully putting an end to evil obstructors, namely, thoughts and actions that are harmful to oneself and others, it is the glorious skillful means of the Vajrayāna for liberating evildoers. To cleanse oneself and others is the fourth incineration.

The first three incinerations primarily liberate your own mindstream by means of realization, while the final one liberates the mindstreams of others by means of compassion. Moreover, this is the incomparably sharp power of the great secret for swiftly perfecting [150] the two collections [of knowledge and merit] solely in terms of the unsurpassed path of great yoga. So if you strive in the yoga of the deity and mantra of Vajrakīlaya in this way, it will become a bounty of all wonders.

The meaning of *liberation* is stated in a tantra:

> The samaya to liberate out of compassion
> is not about killing or suppression.

Accordingly, it does not refer to ordinary killing and suppression. Rather, with the condition of *kṛta* [i.e., done, accomplished] added to the root *tṛī*—which means "to swim" and "to liberate"—it makes it into a name.[11] In the same way, it refers to something like "liberation" when one has

10. Tib. *bsgral ba'i zhing bcu*. Those who engage in (1) destroying the teaching, (2) despising the Three Jewels, (3) robbing the possessions of the Saṅgha, (4) abusing the Mahāyāna, (5) threatening the bodies of gurus, (6) holding vajra siblings and friends in contempt, (7) creating obstacles to spiritual practice, (8) being utterly devoid of mercy and compassion, (9) lacking samayas and vows, and (10) holding false views concerning actions and their ethical consequences.

11. This may refer to some form of the Sanskrit *tāraka*, or "liberator," from which the name of the deity Tāra is derived, though the exact grammatical reference is not clear.

crossed over a river by oneself or when being liberated by someone else. Likewise, regarding the practices of union and liberation,[12] these are not to be understood merely as sexual intercourse [lit. "impure behavior"[13]]. Rather, the union and liberation that arise from the glorious skillful means of the unsurpassed Mantrayāna refer to applying the elixir of the skillful means of actual realizations to the poison of the negative acts of intercourse with women and of killing, thereby transforming them into the elixir that cleanses oneself and others. So it is very important to analyze whether or not those practices refer to [151] the term and referent of "sexual intercourse."

Through being struck with the symbolic, physical kīlaya, the enemy is terminated. However, in accordance with the tantra cited above, it seems one must say "this is not killing," for it is rather a kind of nurturing. The meanings of the words the "kīlaya that liberates" and the "kīla with which the kīlaya strikes" are explained in the *Paradigms of the Roots*:[14] "Kīla refers to the act of cleansing."

Regarding the former [i.e., *kīla*], since it is said in *Definitive Teachings to Sarasvatī on the [Verbal] Roots*,[15] "Ikraśtasra[16] is pure"; one utters "ikra" [*sic*: *ikāra*, i.e., the letter "i," making it *kīli* instead of *kīla*]. Regarding the latter [i.e., *kīlaya*], the *parasmai* [best] man of the *pañcamā* [five] is the one in the middle; it seems this is after one utters the word *hi*,[17] so this is something to be examined. It is true that for "obstructors" it says "*vighnaṃ*," but I wonder whether one should utter the *-am* indicated by the second circle on top [i.e., *anusvāra*].[18]

12. Tib. *sbyor sgrol*.

13. Tib. *mi tshangs spyod*.

14. Tib. *Byings mdo*.

15. Tib. *Dbyangs can mar byings nges par brtan* [*sic*: *bstan*] *pa*.

16. The Tibetan spelling of the intended Sanskrit word here may be corrupt.

17. Pronounced "hee."

18. Grammatically, such an ending would make the case accusative: *sarva-vighnān* (or *vighnam* in the singular), as it does appear in many other Sanskrit mantras. The Tibetan in this edition always includes a nasalizing *anusvāra* at the end of this word (though with a short *a*), even when referring to it in the nominative. Perhaps this is the doubt raised by the author with respect to the proper pronunciation of the fourteen-syllable mantra itself.

In terms of common appearances, by devoting himself to this supreme deity, Padmasambhava, the king of jinas, dispelled all obstacles in Yangleshö in Nepal and gave the appearance of achieving the supreme siddhi of Mahāmudrā. Thus, since he provides great auspiciousness and blessings for his followers, the legacy for this deity is achieved by the power of great merit. So you should apply yourself [152] by all means to the divine mantra of this supreme deity.

By constantly holding to be inseparable from the innermost stamens
of my heart's flower:
The vital essence of the profound and secret, unsurpassed Dharma,
the enlightened activity of the four incinerations of the kīla,
and the supreme pith instruction of those who have become vidyādharas
of the Early Translation school,
by this supreme path, may we be liberated as realized beings.
And may we progress to the highest of the four kinds of vidyādharas,
liberating those who remain untrained by the great kindness of compassion,
and achieve the supreme state of Vajrakīlaya.

This *Heart Essence of the Vidyādhara Elders of the Early Translation School: A Brief Explanation of the Meaning of the Root Mantra of Vajrakīlaya* (that supreme deity of enlightened activity) was composed by this old monk of the Mantra tradition, Kunzang Zhepé Dorjé, so that it may not be forgotten. He has the good fortune to have pondered well the ripening and liberation offered by this Dharma, which he received from both that Gentle Protector, Vajradhara, who declares the *Fearless Lion's Melody of the Profound and Secret Vajra Song of Manifest Enlightenment in the Four*

*Incinerations*[19] and from Padmasambhava's Great Regent, who wields mastery over all things in the profound, hidden treasures of the kīla of enlightened activities.[20] May there be virtue! [153]

19. Tib. *Thal 'byin bzhi la mngon par byang chub pa'i zab gsang rdo rje glu yi mi 'jigs seng ge'i sgra dbyangs.*

20. Tib. *'phrin las phur pa'i zab gter la 'dod dgur dbang bsgyur ba'i padma'i rgyal tshab chen po.* This refers to Lerab Lingpa.

# A Blazing Sun of Brilliant Faith That Dispels the Darkness of Misconceptions

## *In Praise of the Greatly Secret Teachings of the Early Translation School*

Kunzang Zhepé Dorjé

May there be victory for the fine tradition of the Early
Translation school teachings,
that secret, profound, vital essence of the minds of all the jinas,
the path of ten million families of siddhas, each endowed with
the eight qualities of mastery,[1]
the supreme quintessence drawn from churning the ocean of
sūtra and mantra.

O, Mañjughoṣa, you who bear the pretense of the saffron robes;
O, Lord of Mysteries [Vajrapāṇi], in the guise of a siddha;
O, Avalokiteśvara, who in manner of the protector of the earth,
is the friend guiding us along the stream of this fine tradition;

1. Tib. *dbang phyug brgyad*: the qualities of (1) subtle form, (2) coarse form, (3) lightness, (4) pervasiveness, (5) authentic achievement, (6) utter clarity, (7) stability, and (8) being able to fulfill desires.

since you accomplished the power of the glorious bodhicitta
aspiration
toward the noble source of Dharma,
therefore, with your blessings in a hundred rays of blazing light,
dispel the darkness in the hearts of the fortunate!

In the Dharma lotus that is the land of the realized ones,[2]
the adornments of Oḍḍiyāna and the like, [154]
the essential nectar of honey—the secret treasures of the
ḍākinīs—
and the sweet taste of the fine tradition that unites the two:
É-ma! They remain without increase or diminishment
within the great vital essence of the teachings of the Lord of
Sages,
in this land of Jambudvīpa, according to the experience
of the garland succession of accomplished vidyādharas.

The way to drink the great ocean of Dharma of the three yānas
that cools the tormenting heat of the two obscurations,
is in the one gulp of the nine stages:
such complete teachings of the Buddha are rare.

The eight steps of the supreme yāna teachings
for realizing the culmination of the Dharma, ultimate
bodhicitta—
by striving to enter the stages of practice—
are the glorious wealth of merit possessed by the fortunate ones.

Accomplish the spectacle pleasing to the jinas,
the four kinds of reality in forward and reverse order, and

2. This refers to India.

the precious jewel of the teachings of the Lord of Sages,
the path of dependent origination.

Holding the wealth of precious bodhicitta—the entrance to
the great path of ten million jinaputras
who have the fortitude to bear the weight of the two goals—
is the royal treasure of this tradition.

Within the kingdom of the supreme yāna,
in the great marketplace of Dharma,
the goods of working for others
laid out upon the wondrous balsam
are the greatest goods of all.

On the nondual road [155] toward the gateway to peace,
the three families[3] strike the great drum
of the epic story about the lack of a self:
this is the unsurpassed way to empower a king.

The forms realized by "clarity and the profound"[4]
do not appear within the splendor of the white light of the causal
yāna;
the sun of the teachings on the fruition illuminate these forms,
and perfects this exquisite tradition as an ornament upon the sky.

The kriyās of austerities and hygiene,
the caryā in which activities and yoga come in equal proportion,
and the yoga for those primarily attracted to yoga,

3. Tib. *rnam gsum rigs pa*. This likely refers to the three Buddha families of Vairocana, Amitābha, and Akṣobhya.

4. Tib. *zab gsal*. This refers to the yoga of the indivisibility of emptiness and appearances that is unique to the fruitional yāna, or Vajrayāna.

are the three yānas that serve as the station platform
steps leading to this supreme yāna.

The unsurpassed path from among the four kinds of tantra
is approximated by the three yogas,
so that the assemblies of ten million fortunate ones who practice mantra
proceed to Akaniṣṭha and there accomplish this unsurpassed teaching.

By primarily holding to skillful means pertaining to appearances,
one progresses along the path of the four kinds of vidyādharas.
The Mahāyoga is in general the tradition for proceeding to the pinnacle of accomplishment in this lifetime,
and there are eighteen tantras,
eight great classes of accomplishment, and so on, there.

The hundred rivers of the greatly secret Dharma
carry the jeweled sands of the two accomplishments.
Likewise, when the throngs of siddhas of Jambudvīpa
perfect in their vital essence all the mantras of knowledge
for actualizing the two goals, [156]
it will be difficult to measure the treasure of this Dharma.

The elixir of the greatly secret Dharma is the best method
at the beginning for transforming the iron elements
of birth, death, and the intermediate period
into the golden jewels of the three kāyas.
Wherever there are sublime places for accomplishment,
even all these assemblies of vīras become intoxicated
with the play of the dance of spiritual discipline,
and are carried away by the music of great bliss.

The entrance for those of exceptional fortune
is the path of clear light that is devoid of stages and exertion.
By means of the anuyoga of the union of absolute space and
primordial consciousness,
a hundred experiences of wisdom's bliss issue forth.

Therefore, by taking the door that conceals great bliss
in the minds of vīras and ḍākinīs
to be just the hand implement itself,
it cannot appear before the estimation of intellectuals.

However, those who are not lacking in merit
and who proceed with admiration to the sublime
will find a little wealth, and the blessings
just according to their share.

Therefore, what immature person can withstand
the waves of the ocean of this amazing Dharma
that appear by way of the
three transmissions of this supreme yāna?

The sūtras, the apparitions, the mind class, and so forth,
the Dharma treasury of tantras, oral transmissions, and pith
instructions,
divided according to three types—[157]
What else is there apart from these fine traditions?

The time has come for enlightened activity to train sentient
beings,
and this treasury of inexhaustible Dharma
that is sealed by the mudrā of Padmasambhava
brings forth unequaled great excellence.

As a dispensation for the assemblies of vidyādharas
who frolic in this realization of great bliss,
the fountain of Dharma flows forth abundantly,
for this tradition has a hundred secret doors.

The supreme entrance for those who encounter nonconceptually
the vajra of the mind, free of conceptual elaborations,
is this very tradition,
for it completely opens the door.

Therefore, without blunting the edges of the vajra—
this illuminator of the teachings—
go directly to the lofty space of the sky,
which is adorned solely with the understanding of an ārya.

Nevertheless, the assembly of vidyādharas,
in the manner of a royal empowerment of this supreme yāna,
pound the summer drum of the secret teachings
to split open the heads of the throngs of māras.

With a hundred blazing light rays of the spectacular Dharma
the jeweled chest holding the secrets in the minds of a hundred
siddhas
binds the crowds of ten million fortunate ones seeking Dharma
to the direct lineage of supreme siddhas.

Focusing on effortless open presence
in the primordial purity of ground pristine awareness
is the path of the clear light that cuts off conceptual fabrications.
This is the swift path, [158] the foremost of all.

The greatly secret, miraculous methods of postures and gazes
for experiencing the spontaneously actualized fluctuations
of the radiance of pristine awareness as embodiments of

primordial consciousness are a wonder of wonders.

When one sounds this great drum of the Dharma
of the two realities, which are the supreme secrets,
what intelligent person would listen to that other
ordinary drumroll of chatter about union?

Through the greatness of the method devoid of effort,
the extraordinary melody of this teaching
draws fine experiences to one's mindstream,
and the sound of its being played with the fingers of the wise
brings joy to fortunate hosts of vidyādharas
in countless times and places.

In accompaniment with this vajra song,
one is lifted to the top of the nine greatly secret yānas.
É-ma-o! The wondrously profound and vast ocean of Dharma!
The wealth of all you could ever hope for, come to luscious
ripening!
The dwelling-place for all the hosts of fortunate nāgas!

What reflective person would not have faith in this?
For as long as the ocean of this fine tradition
flows forth on the earth of those who have merit,
the hundred rivers of teachings from these snowy mountains
will unceasingly yield healing medicine.

May all the jinas and jinaputras
grant the blessings of their enlightened view to the world,
and may the vīras and ḍākinīs always [159] blaze
in the thousand rays of glorious light
of the truth seen by their sacred gaze
that looks upon this teaching.

Without its ever being covered with the mud
of false superimpositions and repudiations,
may I alone preserve it by myself
as the one ornament of merit for the world.

This brief praise—*A Blazing Sun of Brilliant Faith That Dispels the Darkness of Misconceptions*—was spontaneously uttered for the precious teachings of the greatly secret Early Translation school. By means of the oral transmissions that have ripened within the great unelaborated maṇḍalas of the supreme yāna, it was set down in writing at Namgyal Geden[5] by the one called Kunzang Zhepé Dorjé. He is a reflected image of a vidyādhara, who has received the many kindnesses of the supreme, secret Dharma from vajrācāryas with the supreme vision of holders of the vidyāmantra of the lotus—those including the great treasure revealer, the venerable siddha Orgyen Lerab Lingpa, and the holy lips of Khalong Yangpa Tsel,[6] that venerable king of the Dharma who is indivisible from the lord of jinas, Padmasambhava. By setting it forth thus, may there be no false superimposition or denigration of the essence of the teaching itself, and may that teaching always spread everywhere in all directions. May virtue increase! [160]

5. Tib. *Rnam rgyal dge ldan*.

6. Tib. *Mkha' klong yangs pa rtsal*. This refers to Patrül Namkha Jikmé (*Dpal sprul nam mkha' 'jigs med*, 1888–1960), of Dzachukha, a son of Düdjom Lingpa and of Akyabza Kalzang Drönma.

# A Jeweled Mirror of Pure Appearances

## *Establishing the Unity of the Views of the Old and New Translation Schools of the Secret Mantrayāna*

Lozang Do-ngak Chökyi Gyatso Chok

Namo Guru Mañjughoṣāya

O, Mañjughoṣa, who achieved the inner force of incomparable
bodhicitta,
to train living beings with tales of the profound,
coming in the forms of jinaputras throughout the realms of the
ten directions—
you are the treasure of intelligence, performing the dance of a
spiritual friend.

I pay homage to the sublime, supreme guides:
to the masters of the teachings—
Padmakara, and the omniscient Tsongkhapa—
who are inseparable from that lord and father [Mañjughoṣa],
and to the leader of the flock of paṇḍits, appearing in the two
forms
of Rongzom and Longchenpa, and the rest.

It may be true that there are no differences with respect to the
shared yānas,
but in some cases the way of expressing the philosophical tenets
within each tradition of teaching—
split across the Earlier and Later Translation schools of Secret
Mantrayāna—
does appear to differ; nonetheless there is a way to see it as a
crucial point of enlightened intent.

I have glimpsed this a little bit, and to acquaint my mind with it,
[161]
and in order to elucidate difficult points through the necessary
implications of scriptures and reasoning—
since indeed anything that creates discord around the teachings
of the Jina displeases me—
this cowherd shall play his flute in the empty valley.

Among the many precious teachings of the Jina, which are the source of benefit and joy for all beings of this Cool Land [of Tibet], there are primarily the teachings of the Nyingma Secret Mantrayāna of the Early Translation school, from the first spread of the teachings, and the fine traditions of the old and new Kadam, from the later dissemination. In particular, as stated in the *Book of Kadam*,[1] "The final, extinct embers of teachings will be reignited by the one known as Drakpa."[2] In accordance with that prophecy, there is the great tradition of the incomparable Mount Gedenpas.[3] So the life force of the precious teachings of the Sage remains in these two great traditions. Even as that is the case, here, under the influence of present times, and as a result of the degeneration of views,

1. Tib. *Bka' gdams gleg bam*. See Thupten Jinpa, *Wisdom of the Kadam Masters* and *The Book of Kadam*.

2. Tib. *grags pa*. This refers to Lozang Drakpa, the personal name of Tsongkhapa.

3. Tib. *ri bo dge ldan pa*. Lit. "Those of the Mountain of Virtue," which refers to the Gelukpa lineage.

different perspectives and practices are seen to be in competition with one another, while it is very rare for them to be properly set forth by way of scriptures and reasoning. Since there have been too many biases introduced into the Jina's teachings, it may be that the precious teachings have been weakened, but since my own inborn and acquired [162] analytical powers are very feeble, I am incompetent to do anything for the Jina's teachings.

Nevertheless, through the compassion of being taken into the care of many sublime and authentic spiritual friends, I have seen the transmission of the enlightened view that comes down to us in the earlier and later teachings to be utterly unified in its intent. In order to shut the door to the karma of rejecting the Dharma (or any other deed that would be of a status equal to it)—as though casting out the darkness of prejudice—and in order to nurture faith and reverence toward the Jina's teachings without bias, and in order to increase pure vision, I will crack open the door of scriptures and reasoning that represent a way of presenting the ground, path, and fruition that is accepted in common. But I make supplication to all scholars, saying, "Please assist me with your unbiased discernment, without feeling this is unbearable, like a poisonous snake smelling deer musk."

First, regarding the way in which the essential nature of the *ground* abides: The unequaled Mount Gedenpas say that, as for the innovator of the tradition of the definitive, ultimate, profound view, it is only the protector Nāgārjuna, because he was prophesied to be the great elucidator of the teachings of the yāna realized individually by each tathāgata's own awareness.[4] In accordance with the interpretations [163] of Indian paṇḍits such as Lord Atīśa and Maitrīpa, in their commentaries on [Nāgārjuna's] views, Buddhapālita, Śāntideva, and Candrakīrti are regarded as incomparable masters. So principally the profound view is sought by following them. Likewise, this is also the case from the perspective of the Early Translation school of Secret Mantrayāna. The earlier omniscient Dharma

4. Tib. *de bzhin gshegs pa so so rang rig gi theg pa'i bstan pa.*

king, Longchen Rabjam, wrote in his commentary to the root text of the twelfth chapter of his *Treasure of Wish-Fulfilling Jewels*:[5]

> Now the presentation of the tradition of the Prāsaṅgika Madhyamaka, which is the pinnacle of the philosophical Buddhist Mahāyāna, is the essential meaning of the ultimate view of the Jina:
>
> The Prāsaṅgika view cancels all conceptual elaboration.
> All phenomena are dependently related events,
> emptiness devoid of inherent nature—
> the two realities: illusion, and the freedom from extremes itself—
> it is thus that the phenomena of the path and the fruition can come to their culmination.
>
> The unmistaken teachers of the view of the Sage, the Bhagavān, are the Prāsaṅgika Mādhyamikas. The initial founder of this tradition, prophesied by the Bhagavān in *The Great Drum Sūtra*,[6] the stainless sun of ārya wisdom [164] who dispelled the darkness of false views, is our Protector, Nāgārjuna. The commentators to the meaning of his six collected treatises on reasoning[7] include Āryadeva, Buddhapālita, Bhāvaviveka, and Candrakīrti. Among them, Ārya Candrakīrti, of indomitable wisdom and compassion, truly fathomed the enlightened view of the Ācārya [Nāgārjuna] and composed the "meaning commentary" to the *Fundamental Treatise on the Middle Way*[8] entitled *A Guide to the Middle Way*, and the "word commentary" entitled *Clear Words*.[9] With these

5. Tib. *Yid bzhin rin po che'i mdzod.*

6. Tib. *Rnga bo che chen po'i [le'u'i] mdo.* This refers to the *Mahābherīharaka-sūtra.*

7. Tib. *rigs pa'i tshogs drug.*

8. Tib. *Rtsa ba shes rab*, Skt. *Mūlamadhyamakakārikā*, by Nāgārjuna. See Nāgārjuna, *The Root Stanzas of the Middle Way*; and Tsongkhapa, *Ocean of Reasoning.*

9. Tib. *Tshig gsal*, Skt. *Prasannapadā.*

> compositions there rose the sun of the Prāsaṅgika Madhyamaka, the ultimate view of the Buddha in this world, dispelling the darkness of false views.

Sayings such as the assertion that Nāgārjuna is the founder of the Prāsaṅgika school refer to what is the common ground between the founder of the Madhyamaka and the Prāsaṅgika school, but the specific founder of the Prāsaṅgika school is clearly Candrakīrti, for Longchen Rabjam states here that the one who caused the sun of the Prāsaṅgika to rise in our world was Candrakīrti. The later omniscient one, [165] Vidyādhara Jikmé Lingpa, makes a similar assertion in his *Songs of Meditative Experience*:[10] "By embracing the Great Mother Perfection of Wisdom, the experience of the glorious protector Ārya Nāgārjuna arose. For the source of the river of explanation, ask Candrakīrti."

1. The venerable guru, the great Tsongkhapa, differentiated between the Svātantrika and Prāsaṅgika in terms of whether or not they assert the existence of subjects of argument that can appear in common to both parties, and so forth. Thus Tsongkhapa pushed open the great door to the path of reasoning, which makes fine divisions among the excellent explanations of Indian paṇḍits—not previously well-known in Tibet—regarding the distinction between the two methods of refutation: (1) that which turns an opponent back through an absurd consequence, and (2) that which presents an autonomous line of reasoning. In an abbreviated way, the omniscient Dharma king [Longchenpa] had also explained the two groups in terms of whether or not they assert that things can exist through characteristics of their own. To cite from the continuation of the previously quoted twelfth chapter of the *Treasure of Wish-Fulfilling Jewels*:

> To summarize the unmistaken meaning of those treatises: Since nothing can be established in its basic essence as having any nature, and since all assertions entail clinging to true existence,

10. Tib. *Nyams mgur.*

> (1) if the tradition of those who profess things to exist by nature [166] were to accept our scriptures, that would be contradictory. And (2) insofar as, within the scriptures of those who affirm the existence of potent entities, they [i.e., our scriptures] are refuted by well-known valid perceptions, then, after such refutation, there is no philosophical position to ascertain according to an autonomous line of reasoning [i.e., a *svatantra*]. As it is said:[11] "Suppose I had some thesis; then I would have this fault. But since I have no thesis, I am the only one who has no faults." Understanding it in this way, I will set it forth here.

As for this way of having no assertions, some early factions asserted that Mādhyamikas generally don't have any assertions at all, but this is not what is meant, for the difference between making and not making assertions will be clarified below. Without fixating one-sidedly on whether or not there are assertions—as with peacocks and purity[12]—one can assert or not assert in a deceptive way. It is said that ultimately there is no analysis as to whether or not one can make an assertion, but deceptively there are times to assert and not to assert. This is also stated, for as the same text [the *Treasure of Wish-Fulfilling Jewels*] says:

> When debating and when taking the ultimate as an object, there is no assertion that the appearance has no nature whatsoever, nor is there an assertion that the basic disposition does have one. For these are not things about which one can make an assertion. In the aftermath of reaching a path,[13] when taking conventional things

11. This famous quotation is from Ārya Nāgārjuna's *Ending All Debates*, Skt. *Vigrahavyāvartanīkārikā*, Tib. *Rtsod pa bzlog pa'i tshig le'ur byas pa*.

12. This may be a reference to the classical example by which peacocks can eat that which is normally impure—that is, what is poison for other forest animals—and instead transform it into the brilliant colors on their feathers. Here the analogy would seem to be that if one can use assertions wisely, while understanding their deceptive nature, one can still do something useful with reasoning. The reference, however, may be more obscure than this.

13. Tib. *lam rjes thob pa*. That is, after one has emerged from meditative equipoise in the realization of emptiness.

> as an object, then, as explained in the sacred teachings, one recognizes them, with all their multiplicity, as being merely configurations of dreams and illusions. Then, even that [realized] one can also analyze, and contemplate, and teach to others. Having made a distinction based on seeing what is to be taken up and what is to be abandoned, one engages in the two collections [of merit and knowledge] as the path of the middle way. And there is still the need to achieve the two kāyas as a result.

These and other topics are precisely explained. Likewise, the commentary *Dispelling Darkness in the Ten Directions*[14] states:

> The Svātantrika Mādhyamikas declare that all phenomena appear deceptively, but if they are analyzed, they are asserted to be ultimately devoid of inherent nature. The Madhyamaka *Two Realities*[15] states:
>
> > If it is analyzed with reasoning,
> > what appears in this deceptive way is never found.
> > That not finding is what has real meaning,
> > the primordially existent actual nature.
>
> The Prāsaṅgika Mādhyamikas assert that whether or not they are suitable to be analyzed, in every case phenomena are devoid of all assertions, for conceptual elaborations are utterly put to rest. The *Guide to the Middle Way* states:
>
> > I do not accept even as something deceptive
> > the way that you assert other-powered things to be real. [168]

14. Tib. *Phyogs bcu mun sel.* A commentary on the *Guhyagarbha Tantra* by Longchenpa.

15. Tib. *dbu ma bden gnyis.* The full title of this work by the Indian paṇḍit Jñānagarbha (Tib. *ye shes snying po*) is *A Verse Commentary on the Two Realities,* Skt. *Satyadvaya-vibhaṅga-kārikā,* Tib. *Bden pa gnyis rnam par 'byed pa'i tshig le'u byas pa.*

Thus [Longchenpa] clearly draws the distinction between the [Svātantrikas and Prāsaṅgikas] in terms of whether or not they assert the existence of things that have their own characteristics, in the way that the substantialists do.

2. Since, between the Svātantrika and Prāsaṅgika, there is such a difference in the object of negation, the venerable great being [Tsongkhapa] takes the Prāsaṅgika tradition to be the ultimate view of the Sage, and does not assert even the slightest elementary particle as being established through characteristics of its own or from its own side. Likewise, the definitive view of the three inner tantras of the Early Translation school of Secret Mantrayāna emphatically affirm that phenomena are not established through any nature of their own. *A Garland of Pith Instructions on the View*[16] by the great Ācārya [Padmasambhava] states:

> In this regard, the realization [of things] as a single continuum is this: (1) Insofar nothing at all arises ultimately, phenomena are not separate individuals, and (2) deceptively, according to the characteristics of an illusion, they are not separate individuals, either. That which does not arise, itself appears as an illusion that appears to be multiple, like a moon in water, and it can also perform functions. And the illusion itself has no essential nature. Since it never arose, then it is without division, both as something deceptive and ultimately, so one realizes it to be of a single continuum.[17]

Now [Padmasambhava] is giving this explanation by citing the root line from a sūtra that must be explained, namely, "All phenomena are empty of essential nature itself." [169] The two instances of this word "itself," [in the explanation, show that] here it is a word that refutes existence through inherent characteristics, as in the cited section of the *Sūtra Requested by*

16. Tib. *Man ngag lta ba'i phreng ba.*

17. Please note that both printed Tibetan editions of this text read *rgyu gcig pa rtogs pa'o* in this last line, but since the opening line was *de la rgyud gcig par rtogs pa ni*, it is clear that the entire discussion was meant to be about a "single continuum," not a "single cause."

*Kāśyapa*,[18] where there is a refutation involving a clear distinction. The great Rongzom states that the meaning of the two realities being indivisible is not merely that they are of one essential nature. Rather, it must refer to an extraordinary understanding of the two realities gained by having refuted the subtle object of negation. Moreover, in *A Guide to the Way of the Mahāyāna* this great translator Rongzom explains how to refute the subtle object of negation, namely, existence through inherent characteristics, as follows:

> If one does not affirm that phenomena are meant to be established as real, then how is it that all deceptive phenomena are fundamentally alike? As an analogy, when one sees a rope as a snake, the rope is correct, while the snake isn't there at all. The mind that sees it as a rope is a correct cognition, while the mind that sees it as a snake is a mistaken cognition. If it is mistaken, it is incorrect. Therefore, things do not exist as they appear to that mind, so that mind will not obtain the actual nature of the thing. Rather, it is merely imputed as something else. [170]
>
> Then if the rope itself is carefully investigated, it is seen simply as a collection of numerous parts, such as strands of grass and fuzz. When the mind that thinks the rope is solely a coiled entity dissolves, the mere assembly of parts is actually there. The rope and the snake are not at all fundamentally alike. The mind that sees it simply as an assembly of parts is a correct one. The mind that sees the rope is similar to the mind that saw the snake, insofar as it is mistaken. Then, when the strands of grass and fuzz are carefully investigated, they are seen simply as a collection of particles. When one realizes that even the composite grass and fuzz are not established, the referent and the cognitive process are entirely as before.
>
> Then, when the particles themselves are divided up by the intellect, one realizes that the particles themselves are not

18. Tib. *'Od srung gis zhus pa'i mdo*, which is the forty-third chapter of the *Ratnakūṭa Sūtra*.

established. When one sees the presence of just the emptiness that is the absence of form, the referent and what appears to the mind are entirely as before. Then, when emptiness is investigated, even that which is called *empty* is merely projected upon some entity, and if the entity itself is not established, then emptiness isn't either. So what is empty? What phenomenon is empty of what? By whom was it emptied?

When one realizes [171] the nonexistence of everything that is to be established, all referents are fundamentally the same in that they do not exist. All states of mind are fundamentally alike in that they are mistaken. All mistakes are fundamentally alike in that things are not as they appear. There is a fundamental similarity in the impossibility of obtaining the actual nature of that which is not as it appears. If one cannot obtain any actual nature, then there is no fundamental dissimilarity between the definition of a state of mind and the definition of a referent.

When one first sees it as a snake, fear—that is, aversion—arises. Then, when it is seen as a rope, the conceit of casting off aversion arises, and a mentality of attachment emerges. Then, when the cognition of the rope passes, attachment for the coiled rope is left behind, and attachment for just the collection of numerous [parts] arises. For as long as one doesn't turn away from the view of reification, there will be no end to the states of mind in which attachment and aversion arise and are cast off. Nonetheless, with respect to the characteristics of a referent, if they are simply unestablished as a substance that has been set forth correctly, then one cannot establish them as being fundamentally *unlike* any substance that is set forth temporarily.[19] Except for the case where one

19. Tib. *re zhig par bzhag pa'i rdzas*. That is, a merely labeled "substance" such as the "snake," or "coiled rope," or "grass and fuzz," or "particles" that are temporarily established, but then overcome through further analysis. It seems the point is that if nothing can be established perfectly, really, correctly, or absolutely (and all of these are meanings of the single Tibetan term, *yang dag par*), with characteristics of its own, then nothing can ever be established as being fundamentally different from any one of those layers of temporarily

> does not denigrate mere appearances, all characteristics are fundamentally alike. [172]

As is stated in the line "When neither an entity nor a non-entity remains before the mind,"[20] the point of contact upon which you were focusing as an object dissolves, and that which is dissolved stands as an acting cause.[21] So fresh-minded followers of the New and Old Translation schools, please look at this with keen intelligence and dispel the darkness of prejudice. Rongzom's way of refuting the existence of inherent characteristics in this teaching, together with the analogy, is very clear. Although there is more to quote on this subject, I must restrain myself for fear of verbosity. If followers have hopes for the definitive view and meditation, they should know the value of fine explanations.

On the same theme, the thirteenth station of the great omniscient [Longchenpa's] *Treasury of the Supreme Yāna*[22] states:

> It is similar to the rope. When the rope is also investigated, each individual strand of fuzz can't perform the function of binding, but without subjecting it to such investigation, their collection does bind. Likewise, if misleading appearances and mistaken grasping are both investigated, they are found to have no basis and are empty of any essential nature. If they are not investigated, it seems as if the mind, and the mistaken object that appears to it, are what bind one's own awareness. From the time something appears

established labeled entities mentioned in the example. In this sense all phenomena are the same, even though they may show up as variegated appearances.

20. This is a quotation from the ninth chapter of Śāntideva's *Bodhicāryāvatāra*. See Śāntideva, *A Guide to the Bodhisattva Way of Life*, 9.34.

21. Tib. *dmigs pa'i gtad so zhig pa zhig la byed rgyu yin 'dug pas*. The language here is a reference to the tenth verse of Tsongkhapa's *Three Principal Aspects of the Path*, and to Tsongkhapa's well-known explanation that, as a unique feature of the Prāsaṅgika view, a dissolved thing, or a destroyed thing (Tib. *zhig pa*) still has causal efficacy. Hence the present author is making another comparison between the Old and New Translation schools with this oblique sentence.

22. Tib. *Theg mchog mdzod*.

as bound, [173] it had no bonds, and further, once something appears to be freed, since that which binds had no characteristics of its own, there is no freeing. It is as the *Matrix of Apparitions*[23] states:

> By whom is one ever bound? There is no binding
> and there is nothing to be bound.
> With no binding, there is no release.
> This is the Dharma of the Buddha:
> primordially spontaneous and perfectly complete,
> because it has been taught, there is much rejoicing.

Thus the discussion of the striped rope being like a snake suggests that the following is the meaning of the glorious Candrakīrti's presentation of the three characteristics:[24] Upon *other-powered* phenomena that emerge as dependently related events, this deceptive mode of appearance is posited as having an inherent nature, which is nothing but a false superimposition, or *imagined construct*, of a snake upon a rope. And being something like a rope is *thoroughly established* upon a rope, according to the way in which the primordial consciousness of meditative equipoise sees.

Furthermore, the vajra words that appear in the volume on the visionary meditative experiences of the great omniscient [Longchenpa], his *Precious Treasury of the Absolute Space of Phenomena*,[25] state:

> In the essential nature of pristine bodhicitta
> there is no observed object or phenomenon of observation.

23. Tib. *sgyu 'phrul*. This is presumably a quotation from the *Guhyagarbha Tantra*, whose full title in Tibetan is *Dpal sgyu 'phrul drva ba gsang ba'i snying po de kho na nyid nges pa*. For a translation and study of this tantra see Lama Chönam and Sangye Khandro, *The Guhyagarbha Tantra*.

24. That is, the three characteristics taught in the scriptures usually associated with the Cittamātrin system, but here interpreted according to Candrakīrti's Prāsaṅgika view: Tib. *gzhan dbang, kun brtags, yongs su grub pa*, Skt. *paratantra, parikalpita, pariniṣpanna* (according to the sequence mentioned here).

25. Tib. *Chos dbyings rin po che'i mdzod*.

There is not even an atom of what is observed or the observation.
There is no mind that meditates and not the slightest object of meditation.
There is neither practice nor anything to be practiced; they are nondual. [174] Since they are spontaneously actualized,
there is not even an atom of anything to be accomplished.
There are no stages of progress in phenomena that don't exist,
and there has never been a path of perfections to follow.
Since the clear light has already been actualized as the great bindu,
there is no dispersal or withdrawal of thoughts, no generated maṇḍala,
no mantras, recitations, empowerments, or samayas.
There is no gradual withdrawal and such to focus upon, and there is no stage of completion.
Regarding the primordially present kāyas and facets of primordial consciousness,
there are no composite phenomena, nor cause and effect that emerge from adventitious conditions.
If these existed, there would be no self-emergent primordial consciousness.
Because of compositeness there is destructibility, and
the phrase *unconditioned spontaneous actualization* indicates some contamination somewhere.
Thus in the essential nature of ultimate space
there is a transcendence of causality and the ten kinds of nature do not exist.[26]
The genuine, ultimate nature of the mind is without effort or accomplishment.

26. Tib. *rang bzhin bcu*. These are the view, meditation, samayas, enlightened activity, maṇḍalas, empowerments, purification of the ground, progress along the path, purification of obscurations, and primordial consciousness.

> Seek the knowledge that pacifies all conceptual elaborations of
> existence and nonexistence.

The *Treasury of the Nature of Existence*[27] is very clear in the way it repeats the refutation of each of the four—nonexistence and the rest—and then tightly encapsulates the crucial points. Recognize the utterance of the inconceivable dohas, with their vajra words about great meditative experience of the dharmakāya and emptiness, which appear in the *Seven Treasuries*, the *Three Cycles of Comfort and Ease*,[28] and so forth, as a way to refute the subtle object of negation. And I ask those of fresh minds, in both the New and Old Translation schools of the present, to rest in the nature of pure appearances without breaking the lineage of the dharmakāya.

3. In this way the great venerable guru Tsongkhapa does not accept even an elementary particle to be established from its own side—as that would be the object to be refuted. At the same time, in accordance with the words of Mañjughoṣa, namely, that "the aspect of appearances should be cherished," he does not refute mere appearances. As he states, "Appearances are infallible dependently related events . . ." Likewise, in the Early Translation school of the Secret Mantrayāna as well, mere appearances are not refuted, as stated in *A Garland of Pith Instructions on the View*: "That which does not arise, itself appears as an illusion that appears to be multiple, like a moon in water, and it can also perform functions." The omniscient, great translator Rongzom also states:

> The statement "As long as conditions are immediately present,
> their effects do not appear"
> does not falsely repudiate anything,
> so I do not see it as a case of repudiation.
> In the dependent origination of causes and effects,

27. Tib. *Gnas lugs mdzod.*
28. Tib. *Ngal gso skor gsum.*

apart from mere appearances,
the phenomena of causes and effects are not established as real.
So I do not see it as a case of false superimposition.
Even if the reality that is devoid of false repudiation and
superimposition
is established in some other way,
by following the definitive teachings,
reality arises in my mind like this.

Likewise, the great omniscient [Longchenpa] also states in the [*Precious*] *Treasury of the Absolute Space of Phenomena*:

In the enlightenment of pristine awareness, devoid of movement
and change,
the world of appearances of samsāra and nirvāṇa arise, with
nothing to reject or affirm.
In the face of the yoga that is devoid of apprehended or
apprehender,
laughter bursts forth with amazement that this doesn't exist but
still appears.
Nothing exists as an appearance, yet still dawns as various
appearances.
Nothing exists as empty, yet uniformly pervades the center and
periphery.
There is no apprehender nor apprehended, yet we each cling to
ourselves.
There is no fundamental ground, yet lifetimes appear as a
sequence.
There is nothing to refute or affirm, yet we embrace joy and reject
sorrow.
How ridiculous that when we look outward there is the
appearance of living beings!

> Since there is grasping to what is unreal as real, it seems as
> though it was real . . .

And further on:

> In this milieu there is no striving at activities involving cause and
> effect,
> and there is no view to be meditated upon, and so forth.
> But since all the myriad dances of the worlds of appearance
> dawn from the wanton striving itself, which comes from a milieu
> other than that
> which expresses the mode of refutation—in which center and
> periphery are nondual—
> I beg you never, ever to say that cause and effect do not exist.
> [177]

4. Just as the venerable great being [Tsongkhapa] accepts that every presentation of samsāra and nirvāṇa—which are mere appearances such as this—is something merely imputed, as a name only, so too advocates of the Early Translation school of Secret Mantrayāna affirm that if something is established as a basis, then it is necessarily something imputed. The Nyingma tantra known as the *Sūtra of the Synthesis of Pristine Awareness*[29] states:

> Then the Mahāsattva declared, "O great assembly, know that all phenomena are merely symbols, conventions, and imputations. All imputed phenomena are not located anywhere, outside or inside. No phenomenon has any basis for its label, and all phenomena are devoid of the conventions that are imputed upon them."

29. Tib. *rnying rgyud kun 'dus rig pa'i mdo*. Belonging to the anuyoga class of Nyingma tantras (*rnying ma rgyud 'bum*, Toh. 829), the title sometimes appears as the *Rdo rje kun 'dus rig pa'i mdo*, which is still an abbreviation of a very much longer title.

Moreover, in accordance with the seventy-fifth chapter of his general *Synthesis of the Enlightened View of the Sūtras*,[30] the sūtra commentary by Nubchen [Sangyé Yeshé][31] entitled *Armor against Darkness*[32] asserts the following:

> Relative to the ground, there is no autonomous going, so since it is the concepts of clinging that appear, there is only imputed existence . . . One may object, "Well, if something can appear from nothing, then the horns of a hare and a sky flower should also come forth." In terms of the saying "Whatever is the basis for imputation with names does not exist, but is established through imputation, formation, and creation," [178] what sort of whole basis can there be for the imputation of different things that belong to reality as it is?
>
> Here is the meaning of "all characteristics being without characteristics," "everything with aspects being devoid of aspects," and "the origin of all speech being inarticulate": Since nothing is singled out, it is devoid of any kind of aspect. Therefore, upon a spontaneously actualized cause that has no essential nature, it appears according to the way one thinks about it, and is formed, or established, according to the way one imputes a label upon it. So it is not like the horns of a hare.

Although the basis of designation has no inherent nature, a label is imputed in dependence upon appearing phenomena. The object of imputation is understood, and it is established as being able to accomplish its function. [The above citation] well explains how, in that way, although the referent

30. Tib. *mdo dgongs 'dus*. This appears to be an abbreviation for a gradually redacted Nyingma work, originally authored by Nubchen Sangyé Yeshé in the ninth century: *Sangs rgyas thams cad kyi dgongs pa 'dus pa'i mdo'i dka' 'grel mun pa'i go cha lde mig gsal byed rnal 'byor nyi ma*.

31. Tib. *Gnubs chen sangs rgyas ye shes*.

32. Tib. *mdo 'grel mun pa'i go cha*. See the full title of this single work, just above in note 30.

[of the imputation] does not exist by its own characteristics, it doesn't have to be nonexistent like the horns of a hare. Regarding the very subtle boundaries at which one postulates conventions, understand how Nubchen is also of one mind and of one voice with the venerable guru Tsongkhapa. I request today's advocates of the New and Old Translation schools who have fresh minds not to give in to sectarianism within the Jina's teachings merely on the basis of the colors of ceremonial hats!

The third chapter of the [*Glorious*] *Matrix of Apparitions: The Secret Essence* [*of the Definitive Nature, Just As It Is*][33] states: [179]

> All phenomena are merely imputed as names.
> The Teacher authentically revealed them
> by imputing them as names and words.
> The revealed names and words have no substantial reality.

*Dispelling Darkness from the Ten Directions*[34] comments on that passage with great clarity:

> All phenomena subsumed within the world of appearances of samsāra and nirvāṇa are not established in reality but are nominally designated. A sūtra states: "Subhūti,[35] it is said that all phenomena are merely symbols and merely imputed, but they are not authentically established by their own essential nature." If you ask by whom are they imputed: The Buddha, teacher of gods and humans, without having refuted mere appearances, and in accordance with the objects of deceptive reality, taught for the time being by designating with names and words things such as *saṃsāra* and *nirvāṇa*, the *aggregates*, *elements*, and *sense-bases*.

33. Tib. *Sgyu 'phrul gsang ba snying po*. Again this refers to the root tantra for the whole of Mahāyoga, commonly known as the *Guhyagarbha Tantra*. See note 23 above.

34. Tib. *Phyogs bcu mun sel*. Longchenpa's commentary on the *Guhyagarbha Tantra*.

35. Tib. *Rab 'byor*. A personal attendant of the Buddha and one of his main disciples.

The purpose here is for the mind to realize the way in which objects actually abide. At the very moment in which one indicates something by designating it with a noun, there is no real thing within that noun. At the time when one utters "space," that very noun has no established existence within the domain of space, and the noun "space" does not exist within the body or mind either. Since one cannot find the noun "space" anywhere, there is no substantial entity and there is no recognition of one. Since that itself is indivisible from the referent of "space," all phenomena are designated with nouns, but you should know them as the nature that is not established as the referent of any word.

Regarding the mind, the *Precious Treasury of the Absolute Space of Phenomena* states:

> How ridiculous! This clinging to that which is
> without basis and whose nature is like a dream,
> as though it were a *saṃsāra* and *nirvāṇa* that
> had characteristics of their own!
> Everything is a great spontaneous actualization of
> Samantabhadra,
> which is unmistaken, causes no mistake, and never becomes
> mistaken.
> Mundane existence is merely nominal, transcending the extremes
> of existence and nonexistence . . .
>
> Great pristine awareness, primordially and spontaneously
> self-emergent,
> is not liberated, does not liberate, and will never become
> liberated;
> and in the past, which is also merely nominal, it has never
> experienced liberation.
> It will never turn into experience, and it has never been bound . . .

It is true that it makes sense to perform actions with respect to that which is merely imputed with a name in this way. To this end, the nineteenth section of the *Treasury of the Supreme Yāna* states:

> All the various outer appearances, together with inner, adventitious thoughts, and the objects appearing to the six faculties, are nonexistent, and apart from mere clear appearances, in reality there is nothing outside or inside. [181] Like hairs in the vision of someone with cataracts, and like illusions, hallucinations, and apparitions, although they appear to the mind, from the very time they appear, know that they transcend the extremes of existence and nonexistence.
>
> From the side of appearances, however they are designated, there is no contradiction. Let them be, let them not be, let them exist, let them not exist and yet appear, let them be empty, let them be mistaken, let them be free, let them be good, let them be bad, let them be the mind, let them be something else.
>
> However they are designated, from the side of emptiness, they are empty of that way in which they were designated, from the outset. That which is designated is the mind; the mind is nonexistent, and since that which is nonexistent has no designator, all is just like the activities in a dream, like the actions of an illusion.

Statements about how, even with no inherent nature, still, being this and not being that, existing or not existing, freedom, error, and so on, make perfect sense, as well as statements that strongly emphasize that the way things are as mere appearances—which have never tasted existence within objects—is similar to the appearance of hairs and so forth, are all crucially important. The *Fundamental Treatise on the Middle Way* states:

> Wherever emptiness is fitting,
> there everything will be fitting . . .

And this is exactly the meaning of the statement in [Nāgārjuna's] *Commentary on Bodhicitta*:[36]

> Once knowing [182] that phenomena are empty,
> one who adheres to cause and effect
> is more amazing than amazing,
> more wondrous than wondrous.

Moreover, in his accounts of King Ramaṇa's two sons, Balé and so forth, together with their analogies, Rongzom, the lord of paṇḍits, excellently taught in great detail how actions make sense for illusion-like phenomena that have no inherent nature. So it's really a shame not to look at his teachings.

5. In terms of what mistaken and unmistaken minds find, respectively, as the defining characteristics of the two realities, the Early Translation school also affirms what the venerable great being [Tsongkhapa] recognized. For the great omniscient [Longchenpa] affirms that the primordial consciousness of meditative equipoise[37] that belongs to the three kinds of āryas[38] is that of an unmistaken mind that establishes the ultimate. Minds that are contaminated by ignorance and its habitual propensities are mistaken minds that establish what is deceptive. [Longchenpa's] *Treasury of Philosophical Tenets*[39] states, "According to the Prāsaṅgika Madhyamaka tradition there are three [aspects]: (1) the distinction between the mistaken mind and unmistaken mind, (2) the way of classifying the realities as two, which relies upon each of those [minds], and (3) the way to cut through conceptual elaborations by means of consequential reasoning." [183] He enlarges on those points at length, but out of fear of verbosity I shall not quote it here.

36. Tib. *Byang chub sems 'grel*, Skt. *Bodhicittavivaraṇa*. This text appears in the tantric section of the Tengyur, with the other works on the *Guhyasamāja Tantra* attributed to Nāgārjuna.

37. Tib. *mnyam bzhag ye shes*, Skt. *samāhitajñāna*.

38. That is, ārya-śrāvakas, ārya-pratyekabuddhas, and ārya-bodhisattvas.

39. Tib. *Grub mtha' mdzod*.

In accordance with the view of *A Guide to the Bodhisattva Way of Life*,[40] the great omniscient [Longchenpa] explains the characteristics of the two realities in terms of whether or not they are the experiential object of a direct perception involving dualistic appearances. The *Treasure of Wish-Fulfilling Jewels* states:

> The defining characteristics of deceptive reality are qualities that are not beyond the objects of the intellect, and they do not withstand analysis. The definition of ultimate reality is that very thing that transcends the intellect, where all things have disappeared. It is not that they withstand analysis, for that has already ceased.

He states that here the meaning of transcending the intellect is that it is not directly perceived as an object of conceptual fabrications involving dualistic appearances, while the ultimate is an object of each [ārya's] own individual awareness. This is in order to dispel qualms raised as to whether, since it is the *intellect* belonging to each one's individual awareness,[41] the ultimate is also not beyond the intellect. The *Treasure of Wish-Fulfilling Jewels* states: "If you wonder, 'But each one's individual awareness and intellect are the same,' that is true for one who is confused about terminology. However, in this context the *intellect* refers to conceptual fabrications."

Therefore "primordial consciousness [184] has no object," "the actual nature of reality is not an object," "the ultimate is not within the scope of the intellect," and so on. To comment on such statements according to some of the older sages, while we have the beverage of ambrosia of the teachings from our own tradition of the omniscient [Longchenpa], would be to partake of the dust from the spittle of "others' claims." Nonetheless, as for the fact that some statements about "primordial consciousness having no object" do exist, these are said in the manner of how one should rest

40. See Śāntideva, *A Guide to the Bodhisattva Way of Life*, 9.2: "This reality is recognized as being of two kinds: deceptive and ultimate. The ultimate is not within the scope of the intellect. The intellect is called deceptive."

41. Tib. *so so rang rig gi blo*.

in meditative equipoise on just the meaning of having ripped out the way in which one had been clinging to mistaken conceptions of the negated object, *without* turning that into a phenomenal object established through active discernment. This is what it means for that which dawns in the face of the sacred gaze as a simple absence[42] to be grounds for instilling fear in novices.

6. Just as the venerable great being [Tsongkhapa] affirms that this division of the two realities is a numerically definitive classification that excludes any other category, so too the omniscient [Longchenpa] Drimé Özer affirms this. As he writes in the *Treasury of Philosophical Tenets*:

> The fourth point regards the definitive enumeration. Once you have ascertained that being free of conceptual elaborations and not being free of them stand in direct contradiction to one another, and once you have refuted the possibility of there being any third alternative to affirmation or negation, you will have ascertained them as being definitely two. In one sense, all objects are posited in reliance upon a subjective state of mind, [185] so subjects that have not reached the final end are mistaken states of mind, while those that have reached the final end are unmistaken states of mind. There is nothing beyond these two. The phenomena of saṃsāra are mistaken objects, while the actual nature of reality is an unmistaken object, so they are set forth as two with respect to the mind. As stated in *A Guide to the Middle Way*, "Since all things are seen as either real or false . . ."

[Longchenpa] explains this by quoting further. Thus if we have members of the Nyingma Secret Mantrayāna who assert that there is some third option, which is some "knowable thing that neither exists nor does not exist," and so on, since this is an obscuration to the meaning of our system, it is an embarrassment.

42. Tib. *med dgag*.

7. The great spiritual innovator of this Land of Snows asserts that in reality there is no distinction between correct and false amidst deceptive realities within the framework of the two realities. Likewise, this assertion is readily apparent in the traditional presentations of the view within the three classes of inner tantras of the Secret Mantrayāna. The great omniscient Rongzom clearly states this in his *Guide to the Way of the Mahāyāna*, citing the Svātantrika Mādhyamikas' statement that "they may be similar insofar as they appear, but since they can either perform functions or cannot perform such functions . . ." As for the position that since a pot can perform its function of holding water, whereas a reflected image of the pot cannot, they are thus posited as correct and wrong deceptives: Rongzom explains extensively how this is unreasonable, as though ripping out from its root the idea that "it carries water." Taking the analogy of King Anantayaśas, he describes this as astonishing and hilarious. The same text states:

> Ultimately, all phenomena have put to rest every sort of elaboration. Just as one cannot establish at all anything that is to be established, this grasping to the very defining characteristics of "correct deceptives," as if they were the substance of what is to be abandoned and what is to be taken up, is an extremely inappropriate grasping. Indeed it is cause for astonishment!

Furthermore, [Longchenpa's] *Commentary Dispelling Darkness from the Ten Directions* states: "Upon analysis, both what is correct and what is wrong are equal in appearing, but when they are scrutinized, they are the same in the sense of being unestablished in reality. From this very moment, all worlds of appearances in saṃsāra and nirvāṇa remain equally present, without any distinctions." He explains that a face and its reflection are equally unestablished from their own side, so this distinction between correct and wrong is unreasonable.

Candrakīrti and the venerable Tsongkhapa affirm that when relying upon a mundane perspective, there is validity to the division between what is correct and what is wrong in the sense that some things warrant the labels of "truth" and "falsehood." The great omniscient [Longchenpa] also affirms this. [187] The *Treasure of Wish-Fulfilling Jewels* states:

> In accordance with the conventional terms of "true" and "false" that worldly people use with respect to what is deceptive, then as an auxiliary to understanding terminology, correct deceptives are forms, sounds, smells, tastes, tactile sensations, and mental events that appear as appearing objects to the six unimpaired faculties. Wrong deceptives include distorted appearances, hallucinations, and the hairs [for a person with cataracts] that appear due to some damage. As *A Guide to the Middle Way* states, "The six unimpaired faculties . . ."

And [Longchenpa] quotes further. *The Treasury of Philosophical Tenets* explains the distinction between correct and wrong in accordance with what is widely regarded—or not so regarded—as real in the mundane world.

8. Considered primarily from the perspective of the subjective state of mind, Svātantrika treatises explain two kinds of "ultimate," according to whether the conceptual elaborations of dualistic appearance have or have not been reversed: classifiable and unclassifiable ultimates.[43] The venerable great being [Tsongkhapa] also affirms this idea. There is also a way of dividing these two types—of the actual and the designated ultimate, or of the classifiable and the unclassifiable ultimate[44]—according to whether or not conceptual elaborations of what is to be negated have been completely blocked or not. Rongzom's commentary to *A Garland of Pith Instructions on the View* states that whether the object is "classifiable" or not is distinguished according to [188] whether it is the object of a mind

43. Tib. *rnam grangs dang rnam grangs ma yin pa*, Skt. *paryāya* and *aparyāya*.

44. Please note that although this represents the exact order in which these alternatives appear in the Tibetan, according to most presentations (and indeed according to the way Lozang Do-ngak Chökyi Gyatso explains it just below), the "classifiable" seems to correspond to the "designated" and the "unclassifiable" to the "actual" ultimate.

that has or has not[45] cut off the various limitations of conceptual elaborations. Furthermore, something is the first [i.e., classifiable] insofar as it is that which is indicated by the words that categorize the ultimate according to something like the eighteen kinds of emptiness. And something is the second [i.e., unclassifiable] if it is the lack of inherent nature that is the pacification of all conceptual elaborations.

The great omniscient [Longchenpa] asserts that being empty of inherent nature—empty of what is negated—is the unclassifiable ultimate, whereas the knowledge, free of conceptual elaborations, which *realizes* that, is the classifiable ultimate. *Dispelling Darkness in the Ten Directions* states:

> Since the ultimate transcends the intellect, there are no divisions with respect to its essential nature. However, to divide this a little in terms of the mind: The fact that phenomena are empty of any essential nature of their own is the ultimate of the basic condition. A sūtra states, "Subhūti, it is like this. If some people praise the domain of space and others denigrate it, it is neither elated nor depressed. Likewise, all the tathāgatas state that the one ultimate essential nature of phenomena is of the nature of peace. Other tīrthika wandering ascetics[46] teach it as something permanent and immutable, but in authentic suchness[47] there is no bifurcation." [189] But the *mind* that arises free of conceptual elaborations, due to a yogin's meditation on that reality, is called the *classifiable ultimate*: "Refutation of arising and the rest, moreover, . . ."[48]

45. Again, it appears that in this particular presentation the mind that "has not" cut off conceptual elaborations would correspond to what it means to be a "classifiable" ultimate, whereas a mind that "has" done so would correspond to "not" being classifiable.

46. Tib. *kun tu rgyu*, Skt. *parivrājaka*.

47. Tib. *de bzhin nyid*, Skt. *tathatā*.

48. This is a quotation from Jñānagarbha's previously mentioned *Verse Commentary on the Two Realities* (Skt. *Satyadvaya-vibhaṅga-kārikā*, Tib. *Bden pa gnyis rnam par 'byed pa'i tshig le'u byas pa*). In the Degé Tengyur edition, the verse continues: "Refutation of arising and the rest, moreover, / since in accord with what is correct, we accept [as an ultimate]" (*skye la sogs pa bkag pa yang / yang dag pa dang mthun phyir 'dod /*). Tsongkhapa also

And [Longchenpa] continues the quotation. Therefore, while the ways of articulating the divisions of the ultimate are at slight variance, they point to the same thing.[49] Now among the followers of both the omniscient Longchenpa and Rongzom, if there are those who assert that the lack of inherent nature is "a nominal ultimate and a definitive instance of what is deceptive"[50] and so on, then without having seen these teachings of the two omniscient ones, they insert a discrepancy among the tenets of some earlier sages. But the venerable, great Tsongkhapa, the great Rongzom, and the omniscient Ngak-gi Wangpo[51] [Longchenpa] all have a single view with respect to the fact that the very emptiness that comes from having refuted existence through inherent nature—the *object* that comes from having completely refuted what was to be negated—is the unclassifiable ultimate. So it is also extremely uncomely when there are Nyingmapas who maintain, with respect to "lack of inherent nature," that it is a conceptual elaboration spun off from an extreme view of nihilism! For then they are denigrating the definitive, vajra dohas, such as the *Treasury of the Absolute Space of Phenomena*. [190]

quotes and comments on this verse (in a slightly different Tibetan translation) when discussing the two kinds of ultimate in his commentary on Ārya Nāgārjuna's *Fundamental Treatise on the Middle Way*, called the *Ocean of Reasoning* (Tib. *Rigs pa'i rgya mtsho*). Although Jñānagarbha's text was categorized as Svātantrika, it is nonetheless *the* classical source for both Tibetan masters regarding this particular topic.

49. Indeed, the point seems to be that in the work of Rongzom, Longchenpa, and Tsongkhapa, it is always the "unclassifiable" ultimate that involves the pacification of all conceptual elaborations, while specifically in the passage quoted from Longchenpa, it is the *mind* that arises *with respect to* what is free of all conceptual elaborations that is the "classifiable" ultimate.

50. It is important to note that this exact phrase appears in Tsongkhapa's own explanation of this topic in his *Ocean of Reasoning*, when he describes the classifiable ultimate in terms of a state of mind that ascertains the lack of inherent nature, even while the conventional basis of refutation still arises to one's perceptions as a dualistic appearance. (The phrase itself, however, may date to an earlier treatise of the Svātantrika tradition from which this division derives.) If the phrase had been turned around by some to say, on the other hand, that "the lack of inherent nature" *itself* was only a "nominal ultimate," then, as Lozang Do-ngak Chökyi Gyatso points out, this would be a complete misunderstanding of the subtle distinctions with respect to the subject state of mind that is made by all three masters cited here.

51. Tib. *Kun mkhyen ngag gi dbang po.*

To the majority of contemporary Nyingmapas, I make this plea: *Do not*, having discarded the great path of identitylessness—which is regarded by all Buddhists as the distinguishing feature of what is profound—go on to hold as the pith [of the path] mere luminosity and cognizance, and merely [sit there] without attending to anything at all, without identifying anything as being this or not being that, as being existent or nonexistent, and so on. Rather, it is correct for you to abide in accordance with the teachings that stem from the principal early tantric treatises on the stage of generation, the stage of completion, and the Great Perfection.[52]

9. The venerable guru [Tsongkhapa] and the great omniscient [Longchenpa] do not have different views regarding the assertion that these two realities are of the same essential nature but are logically distinct. The eighth section of the *Treasury of the Supreme Yāna* states:

> It is merely a verbal expression that the essential nature of appearances, insofar as they are deceptive, is spontaneous actualization, and that the essential nature of emptiness, insofar as it is ultimate, is original purity. Since those two have no separate substances, they are not distinct as individuals. They are of the same essential nature but are logically distinct. It is like there being no contradiction between the fact that insofar as someone is a brahman, he is a man, and insofar as he has taken vows, he is a renunciate.

10. Furthermore, they are of one view regarding the fact that when one sets forth the ultimate by way of an analogy, it has the identity of that which is not found, no matter how much one searches, just as, if one looks at the sky with eyes that are not contaminated by cataracts, [191] one does not see anything at all. The nineteenth section of the *Treasury of the Supreme Yāna* states:

52. Tib. *mdo sgyu sems*. These refer, respectively, to the *Compendium That Synthesizes the Enlightened View of All the Buddhas* (Tib. *Sangs rgyas thams cad kyi dgongs pa 'dus pa'i mdo*), the *Guhyagarbha Tantra* (Tib. *Dpal sgyu 'phrul drva ba gsang ba'i snying po de kho na nyid nges pa*), and the eighteen tantras of the mind class (Tib. *sems sde bco brgyad*).

In this way, when you investigate, or search, in many ways as to whether your own mind transcends being one thing or separate things, you do not find anything. This is the realization of the meaning of original purity, the actual nature of reality, with your faculty of wisdom.

The *Precious Treasury of the Absolute Space of Phenomena* states:

> In the face of the yoga that is devoid of apprehended or
> apprehender,
> laughter bursts forth with amazement that this doesn't exist but
> still appears.

The eighteenth chapter of the *Treasure of Wish-Fulfilling Jewels* states:

> These various appearances of what is deceptive
> are like illusions, the moon in water, emanations, and reflections.
> They have no inherent nature, and when any appearance is
> investigated carefully,
> it is found to have no root basis or substantial reality.
> So they are empty like space, free of characteristics.
> Without investigating them, they are like various entertaining
> illusions.
> They arise as dependently related events from habitual
> propensities for being mistaken,
> just like the appearances induced by datura.[53]

11. They are also of one view regarding the analogy for what is deceptive, which compares it to the appearance of hairs to a person

53. *Datura* is a genus of nine species of poisonous vespertine flowering plants belonging to the family Solanaceae. Ingestion of this plant typically produces effects similar to that of an anticholinergic delirium (usually involving a complete inability to differentiate reality from fantasy).

with cataracts. [192] This can be understood from the previously cited quotations. Furthermore, the twenty-first section of the *Treasury of the Supreme Yāna* states:

> Apart from being appearances in the face of one's own mistaken mind, these clear manifestations in the expanse—including the various outer appearances, the white and red visions, physical worlds, their sentient inhabitants, and the five elements—are not established either as substantial entities of the external world nor as substantial entities of the inner mind. Know that they have no basis, they are empty apparitions, nonexistent, while bearing the nature of clear appearances, like the hairs seen by someone with cataracts, like dreams and illusory apparitions.

Therefore the paṇḍits of the Early Translation school repeatedly speak of deceptive phenomena as appearing yet nonexistent, and as empty reflections. This is totally in accord with the statement of Ācārya Candrakīrti:[54]

> Suppose you investigate the essence that is wrong:
> those hairs and the like seen by force of cataracts—
> someone with pure eyes sees the very identity of that same
> thing—
> so in the same way you should understand the very nature of
> what is.

And this presentation of the final, definitive sense in which the two realities are indivisible [193] is of the utmost importance.

12. This very emptiness is not something adventitious in the sense of being newly fabricated by the intellect. Rather, the great omniscient [Longchenpa] affirms that it is of a nature that is indwelling, unconditioned, and primordially free. Apart from mere differences in the conventions of

54. Verse 29 from the sixth chapter of Candrakīrti's *Guide to the Middle Way*.

doctrinal language, the venerable great being [Tsongkhapa] also affirms a sense that is in full accord with this. As he offered in this prayer:

> May we totally reject all false and perverse views—
> which, after we had become frightened by the profound meaning of the nature of existence,
> have held as supreme a trivial emptiness fabricated by the intellect—
> and may we realize all phenomena as being empty from the very beginning.

13. The venerable great being [Tsongkhapa] also affirms, in accordance with the teachings in [Candrakīrti's] *Clear Words* and [Bhāvaviveka's] *Lamp of Wisdom*,[55] that what is to be proven by reasoning that analyzes the ultimate is a simple negation. In general, proponents of the Early Translation school of Secret Mantrayāna also accept the definitions of the two types of negation,[56] which the venerable [Tsongkhapa] set forth rigorously in many of his fine works, citing Indian treatises over and over again. The great Rongzom Paṇḍita writes in his *Guide to the Way of the Mahāyāna*:

> All negations [194] can be subsumed under two types: simple negations and complex negations. A simple negation is just the negation of the existence of something, without implying the affirmation of anything else. In this way one clears away someone's lack of understanding, a wrong understanding, or a simple uncertainty, thus negating what was only something imagined in the first place. It does not point to anything else. For instance, if one says, "There's no pot," this does nothing more than overcome the idea that there is a pot. It does not point to a place that has no

55. Tib. *Shes rab sgron me*, Skt. *Prajñā-pradīpa-mūlamadhyamaka-vṛtti*.
56. That is, simple negations (*med dgag*) and complex negations (*ma yin dgag*).

> pots and so forth. Likewise, if one says, "There is no person," this does nothing more than overcome the idea that a person is there. It does not point to the existence of aggregates that are devoid of a person. You can apply this to all the other cases.
>
> What is a complex negation? It is something that negates one thing while pointing to another. Here the phrase "there is the lack of a pot" leads one to understand that there is someplace that has no pots. Similarly, if one says, "there is the lack of a person," this points to there being aggregates that are devoid of an individual. Therefore a simple negation simply abolishes someone else's philosophical position, whereas [195] a complex negation does more than just that, for it also affirms one's own position.

This statement of definitions in terms of the two kinds of negation is in accord with the explanations given by the venerable great being [Tsongkhapa], in which he cites the treatises of the great founders. From the perspective of the primordial consciousness belonging to the meditative equipoise that realizes the nature of existence, there is just a sheer emptiness that is the negation of the object projected falsely by a mistaken mind, without affirming anything else. So the absence of conceptual elaboration that is apprehended by the primordial consciousness belonging to one's own individual awareness[57] is just a simple negation entailing the mere refutation of the object of negation, as explained above.

The eighth section of the *Treasury of the Supreme Yāna* states (while citing the *Tantra of Great Auspicious Beauty*):[58]

> Relying on the isolated sense in which all is originally pure, neither established as entities, nor as having signs, the statement goes from "there is no awareness; there is no lack of awareness; there are no buddhas and no sentient beings" up to "nothing is

57. Tib. *so so rang rig gi ye shes.*

58. Tib. *Bkra shis mdzes ldan chen po'i rgyud.*

> established and nothing can be focused upon." This is revealed solely in terms of what is negated, while setting aside anything that could be affirmed.

Thus the twofold classification of negations has to do with whether something else [196] is or is not implied in the wake of refuting the object of negation. This is affirmed in the treatises of the Indian paṇḍits, and here in Tibet it is affirmed by Rongzom and Longchenpa, as well as by the Gentle Protector Guru [Tsongkhapa], and his two spiritual sons [Gyaltsab Jé and Khedrup Jé], all with one view and one voice. When identifying the nature of existence of phenomena, there is nothing to affirm beyond the mere refutation of that which is falsely superimposed by the mistaken mind. If there were, those masters of wisdom agree that this would imply the error in which conceptual elaborations have not been cut off. So there is no disagreement about whether emptiness is a simple negation.

However, nowadays many readers belonging to the Old and New schools perceive a simple negation as a fault. This shows that they don't understand the meaning of a simple negation. Since wise scholars understand the fact of the matter clearly, once they have perceived this they can present definitions of the two types of negation in many ways that are similar. But in terms of their followers, there are some who get the point and others who do not. The lord of paṇḍits, Jamyang Mipham Namgyal,[59] states in his *Lamp of Certainty*[60] that the actual nature of reality is a simple negation. The saying of the two Minling brothers,[61] namely, that it is a complex negation, is stated with the intent of approaching it from another point of view and does not refer to what is just emptiness itself, isolated in

59. Tib. *'Jam dbyangs mi pham rnam rgyal ba* (1846–1912), better known as Ju Mipham Gyatso (*'Ju mi pham rgya mtsho*).

60. Tib. *Nges shes sgron me*.

61. Tib. *smin gling sku mched*. This refers to Terdag Lingpa Gyurmé Dorjé (*Gter bdag gling pa 'gyur med rdo rje*, 1646–1714) and Lochen Dharmaśrī (*Lo chen dharma shrī*, 1654–1717/18).

its own sense.[62] [197] There is much to be analyzed here, but out of fear of verbosity I shall leave it at that.

14. In his commentary to *A Guide to the Middle Way*, Candrakīrti draws on many scriptural citations and reasons to emphasize that the śrāvakas and pratyekabuddhas must realize that same actual nature of reality, and Tsongkhapa and his two spiritual sons agree. In the lineage of the Early Translation school, however, the shared system of explanation presented according to the tradition of the great abbot [Śāntarakṣita] and his spiritual son [Kamalaśīla] indicates that they do not realize it. However, the omniscient Ngak-gi Wangpo [Longchenpa] states that the unique, definitive view of the three classes of inner tantras must accord with the glorious Prāsaṅgikas. So this establishes that one must affirm that the śrāvakas and pratyekabuddhas realize the subtle identitylessness of phenomena. Moreover, in the writings of the master scholars Rongzom and Longchenpa there are very many explanations of how it is that, without the view that the nature of existence lacks any inherent nature, the mental afflictions cannot be abandoned. These prove this point as well. The need to distinguish between saṃsāra and nirvāṇa in terms of realization versus lack of realization [of the actual nature of reality] is widely known, in accordance with many of the Buddha's teachings. So the affirmation, within this unique system of explanation, that śrāvakas and pratyekabuddhas realize emptiness, is irrefutable. [198] Out of fear of verbosity I shall not elaborate.

15. The venerable great being [Tsongkhapa] asserts that there is no basis that can be established that will withstand logical analysis, but some early scholars confuse the meaning that is found by logical analysis with what can withstand logical analysis, resulting in their claim that ultimate reality can withstand analysis. In his *Treasury of Philosophical Tenets*, the omniscient king of Dharma [Longchenpa] repeats what these early scholars say, but in his discussion of the definition of ultimate reality in his *White Lotus* commentary to the *Treasure of Wish-Fulfilling Jewels*, he refutes that

62. Tib. *rang ldog*. This means the conceptual isolation of a thing itself, understood as the opposite of all that it is not.

it could ever withstand analysis. So he arrives at the same position as the venerable Tsongkhapa. I shall not elaborate.

16. Proponents of the Early Translation school, including the great omniscient [Longchenpa], are in total agreement with the assertion of Candrakīrti and the venerable Tsongkhapa that the minds of sentient beings who reify what is deceptive are mistaken. The *Treasury of Philosophical Tenets* states:

> The "false seeing," or mistaken state of mind, refers to ordinary individuals whose "eyes" are blinded by the habitual propensities for ignorance. So, just like the insistent belief that cataracts and falling hairs are real objects, what is mistaken appears as the various [199] pleasures and sorrows of the six kinds of beings, including their abodes, possessions, and so forth. All these aspects of an apprehender and what is apprehended (which have arisen through dependent relationships); the aspects that appear as a physical world, its sentient inhabitants, and so forth, which are shared in common with those who have achieved the attainment subsequent[63] to reaching a [bodhisattva] bhūmi; as well as the two types of mind that consist of (1) the direct sensory perception of mere appearances, and (2) the inferential knowledge by which one [causally] infers fire and so on: all these appear in reliance upon encountering an aspect of what is deceptive. But in that regard, what is deceptive can further be posited in two forms: (1) what stems from unimpaired faculties of sight and so on, and (2) what stems from impaired faculties.

Furthermore, in accordance with the teachings in the root text and commentary to *A Guide to the Middle Way* on the manner in which birth from other entities is unreasonable, even conventionally, the venerable guru [Tsongkhapa] offered many arguments for how to refute birth from

63. Tib. *rjes thob.*

another, such that they steal the hearts of scholars. These are presentations of the great founders' subtle reasonings that were previously unknown here in the snowy land [of Tibet]. The omniscient Drimé Özer [Longchenpa] also did not accept birth from other entities, even as something conventional. And in his commentary to the *Treasure of Wish-Fulfilling Jewels*, in the place where he is refuting the autonomous [reasoning of the Svātantrikas], he states:

> Therefore, even though things appear to arise from the appearances of causes and conditions as dependently related events, [200] it is incorrect to assert that they arise solely from another. For if a birth from something else could be established conventionally, then a birth from itself would also turn out to be established!

There he shows that it is fundamentally the same, in terms of being reasonable or unreasonable, whether things are to arise from themselves or from something else. Also, the discussion of Svātantrika in the *Treasury of Philosophical Tenets* begins with the classification of knowable entities according to the two realities, and further states that what is proven with reasoning that analyzes the ultimate is a simple negation.

Likewise, proponents of the Early Translation school of Secret Mantrayāna take the position of refusing to accept reflexive awareness. This is true, first of all, because there is the imperative to "seek the source of the river of explanation" in Candrakīrti, and second, because in his own commentary to *A Guide to the Middle Way*, Candrakīrti refutes reflexive awareness extensively. Then there is the fact that reflexive awareness could not possibly prove anything to be truly or substantially existent, because one cannot accept even an atom that could really exist in the way that it appears. Finally, this is true because in the presentation of what is conventional there is no need to seek any referent of the imputation or any apprehending valid cognition apart from just the mere appearances.

Although there is no clear place where Rongzom and Longchenpa explicitly affirm that something that has ceased is a functioning thing, they must certainly accept it. This is true, first, because it is our own position that Candrakīrti gives a detailed proof of it, and, second, because [201] within the tradition that presents all phenomena as being merely designated, there is no harm in affirming that something that has ceased is a functioning thing. There are many proofs for the necessity of affirming this. Therefore, with regard to the idea of something that has ceased being a functioning thing, do not act as though you have seen a bad portent, but rather you must accept it with an upright mind. Although there is much more to say, I fear this would go on too long.

17. They are also of one view and one voice with regard to the fact that deceptive, conventional phenomena are established in an unerring way by valid cognitions, and principally by the omniscient valid cognition that knows the entire range of phenomena. This is true because the great omniscient [Longchenpa] states, in his *White Lotus* commentary,

> Since [the Buddha] knows infinite knowable phenomena, [the Buddha] "sees all things." Since great compassion is infinite, when [the Buddha] gazes upon all worlds, then even within the space taken up by a single mustard seed, limitless realms of physical worlds and their sentient inhabitants appear. In this way their needs are fulfilled . . . In even the space inside just the eye of a needle appear innumerable realms of the physical worlds, along with their sentient inhabitants who have accumulated karma in common. The gaze of primordial consciousness engages them all and serves their needs. [202]

18. In this way, there is no lack of harmony in the intended views of the New and Old Translation schools regarding their decisive presentations of the two realities as the *ground*. In particular, the saying that is repeated over and over again in Dharma language—that the final mode of the definitive view is that the two realities are indivisible—is the intended view of Candrakīrti's three great commentaries. The venerable guru [Tsongkhapa]

comments on this in his two "Great Commentaries,"[64] in the great and small vipaśyanā [sections of his two *Treatises on the Stages of the Path*], and elsewhere. Apart from the conventions of expression that he uses, the aim of his intended view comes down to exactly the same point.

This is true for the following reasons: When determining the ultimate, [Candrakīrti] refutes the object of negation, namely, the possibility of anything being established from its own side. So then there is no deceptive thing left over with characteristics of its own—as the Svātantrikas would have it. When positing what is deceptive, he posits the presentation of saṃsāra and nirvāṇa as having a labeled existence,[65] designated solely by the names of what are merely labeled, mere appearances. Therefore, since the object of negation has been refuted directly, there is no extra ultimate anywhere else. In this sense, saying "the two realities are indivisible" splits off even from the main avenue of the middle way, which establishes what is to be established absolutely, through reasoning that is autonomous [i.e., svātantrika] in a conventional way. This proves Candrakīrti's intended view to be unique.

Speaking to this, the eighteenth chapter of the *Treasure of Wish-Fulfilling Jewels* states:

> First, cherish knowledge of the nature of existence. [203]
> Although there are many forms, on account of the many yānas,
> the essence of what is ascertained is indivisible reality.
> This is the secret treasure-house of all the buddhas.
> Its nature is clear light, primordial consciousness.
> From beginningless time, its nature is free of conceptual
> elaboration.

64. Tib. *ṭik chen*. These are the *Ocean of Reasoning: A Great Commentary on Nāgārjuna's Mūlamadhyamakakārikā* (Tib. *Rtsa shes ṭik chen*) and the *Illumination of the View of the Middle Way* (Tib. *Dbu ma dgongs pa rab gsal*).

65. Tib. *btags yod*, Skt. *prajñapti-sat*. Across many different schools of Buddhist thought, this is a term frequently opposed to Tib. *rdzas yod* (Skt. *dravya-sat*), or what would be a substantial existence.

Like the sun in the sky, it is spontaneously actualized and
unconditioned.
Since it is primordially present in the nature of pristine purity,
appearances and emptiness—indivisible—are neither established
nor eliminated; they neither come nor go.
It severs the deceptive aspect and transcends differentiated objects.
Since it transcends the two realities that are designated, all
conceptual elaborations are put to rest.
Indivisible reality is neither established nor not established.
From absolute space, appearances and emptiness are nondual in
nature,
so it is said that reality is also indivisible . . .

These are empty of nature and without identity;
this itself is the way they abide.
Therefore, they are called *ultimate*;
and insofar as that appears, it is deceptive.
When appearing, its birth and the rest are not established;
so that is its nature, and reality is indivisible . . .

An errant mind that conceives it any other way than this
is utterly confused about the meaning of the nature of existence.
[204]

In this context, to think that because something is not found through rational analysis it must be posited as nonexistent, and is therefore a nihilistic vacuity, is said to be an unfortunate, denigrating view that strays far from the door to the whole of the Mahāyāna. By saying that "not being found by a reasoning consciousness does not mean nonexistence,"[66] it is stated that the way of abiding of the empty clear light, which is realized in dependence upon what is *not* found by a reasoning consciousness—even

66. This is a close paraphrase of a sentence explicitly quoted from Tsongkhapa in the explanation that follows.

without making a direct verbal distinction between "not existing inherently" and "nonexistence"—is the ground from which all the good qualities of a buddha arise. Insofar as it has spontaneously actualized qualities, this primordially, spontaneously actualized ground of being is said not to be a nihilistic vacuity that is nothing whatsoever. Furthermore, it may be true that when analyzing time, elementary particles, and so forth, the "not finding" is said to be a provisional meaning that overcomes grasping to things with qualities as being real. But that is not to say that we do not accept *as emptiness* what remains when you have disproven, with a reasoning consciousness, a mistaken mode of insistent belief. This is true based on all that has been quoted previously and because it is stated:

> Thus, even though it appears, saṃsāra is not established as real.
> So the absence of inherent existence is the ultimate absolute space,
> and since there are no phenomena to be classified as individually distinct
> it is taught that saṃsāra and nirvāṇa are indivisible and equal . . .

[205] Therefore the intent of the statement that it is a provisional meaning is this: If one relies just upon what is apprehended in the face of what a reasoning consciousness ascertains, this is not the ultimate that is the opposite of all conceptual elaborations. Since this is grounds for a great deal of confusion, it must be analyzed carefully. The *White Lotus* states, moreover: "It seems that nowadays there are very few who have this understanding of the way existence abides." And in this regard the great venerable Tsongkhapa says, "Not being found by a reasoning consciousness and the absence of inherent existence do not mean nonexistence." With this one statement he unravels all refutations.

Nowhere else does one find such a mode of explanation, with its wonderful precision, but this does not mean that it is meaningless to draw distinctions by way of the qualities of the spontaneous actualization of the ground of being. So one really needs to know how these views are identical. Although there is much more to say in this regard, I fear this will go on too long, so, since it suffices merely to show the door for unbiased, discriminating people, and however much one elaborates for foolish, biased people, nothing is accomplished, I'll keep this short. *A Guide to the Way of the Mahāyāna* also [206] praises the view of the indivisibility of the two realities, and the meaning is exactly what is stated here. But I shall not elaborate.

As for the way to progress along the *path*, they are of one view and one voice about the fact that the essential nature of the path has two stages corresponding to the two realities for achieving the two kāyas. This is true insofar as the *White Lotus* commentary states:

> In dependence upon deceptive reality, you practice skillful means for accumulating merit by way of the six perfections and so forth. In dependence upon wisdom for the accumulation of knowledge, you meditate on the meaning of the ultimate clear light, primordial consciousness . . .
>
> Once you have stopped everything—merely stilling the mind, not thinking about anything at all, and so on—since you then require an authentic path in which both skillful means and wisdom are integrated into the two accumulations, insofar as you lack these, you stray outside this teaching. If you desire enlightenment, know that you must turn away from such things. So this is my advice: look to the sūtras and tantras and abandon the rest.

19. They are also very much in agreement [207] regarding the fact that there is not just one path, but rather many paths, and that disciples must practice after having ascertained the proper number and sequence of steps that are in accord with their own dispositions and faculties. The *Treasure of Wish-Fulfilling Jewels* states:

> Just as there are different foods for children and adults,
> so is their respective Dharma also different in nature . . .
>
> Then, explain in the manner of guiding them step by step.
> By so doing, they will understand the sequence of the yānas.
> Excellent qualities will increase, they will become fearless,
> and being free of error, view and conduct will become integrated.
> But if you fail to explain in this way, it is a limitless fault.
> When one is bereft of higher and lower, earlier and later stages,
> the general tradition of the Teachings will gradually degenerate,
> and fearful, small-minded people are thrown off by false views.
> Not knowing the sequence of stages, they don't realize the depths,
> they show contempt for virtue as being conditioned,
> and in making false superimpositions and repudiations they err
> with regard to cause and effect.
> Not knowing what to accept and what to reject, they are
> confused about the meaning of knowable things.
> They abandon the Mahāyāna aspiration and compassion,
> and their view of emptiness misleads the faithful to miserable
> states of existence.
> Saying there's nothing to be done, they indulge in ordinary
> activities,
> and they divulge secrets to those who are unripe.
> Because of these many faults, explain the stages of the yānas.

Its commentary explains at great length, including the following:

> If one topic were enough, it would be pointless for the Buddha to teach so much, [208] so that is not the case. Nowadays many people say it is enough to recognize the awareness of the present moment, and there's no point to there being many teachings. If that were enough, there would be no need for the Buddha's other teachings. But in fact this single-pointed awareness of the present

moment must depend precisely upon listening [to teachings] and upon guru yoga, so they refute themselves with their own words. Therefore, since whatever remedy is applied to the mind at the beginning, in the middle, or in the final stages is the most profound for the moment, one is advised to teach them in that way.

20. How could there be any inconsistencies regarding the ultimate *fruition* of practice, namely, manifesting the state of the two kāyas? The *Treasure of Wish-Fulfilling Jewels* states:

> The fruition of such pure meditation
> is the culmination of all that has been abandoned and all that
> has been realized, namely, the kāyas and facets of primordial
> consciousness.
> Like the sun and moon free of clouds,
> since one is free of all obscurations from the elements,
> with "enlightenment," spontaneously actualized qualities appear . . .

In this way it is affirmed that one thoroughly achieves one's own goal: the one hundred and forty-four stainless qualities of the dharmakāya, and so forth, which are the sublime perfection of purity, bliss, permanence, and identity. [209] Simultaneously, one serves the needs of sentient beings by remaining until saṃsāra is emptied, in the form of a sambhogakāya imbued with the five certainties and adorned with the newly perfected signs and symbols, who enters effortlessly into the identities of every kind of nirmāṇakāya, all for the sake of others.

To reiterate:

> Once you have obtained this great ship of leisure and
> opportunity,
> you may have found the good fortune of being able to take up
> whatever you want
> from the various manifestations of the wish-fulfilling cow—

that precious wealth of the unbiased teachings within the Land of Snows—
but if you then discriminate between yourself and others with regard to the authentic path,
or make pretense of pure appearances with respect to all that is both pure and impure,
then the cataracts of ignorance have stolen away from the eye of intelligence your share of the correct view,
and all of you are greatly to be pitied.

Alas! You may have witnessed the sun—
the profound teaching of the Jina—rising in the sky of merit,
but since you lacked the ability to greet it with the eyes of discernment
it is the hallucinated appearances of wrong conceptions that dawn instead.

You who are unable to carry the vast burden of serving others' needs—
carried by the āryas of all three yānas, whose Dharma eyes are free of dust—
can you see [210] the one taste of this unbiased enlightened view
in the absolute space of peace, utter refreshment for those worn out by conceptual elaborations?

How sad! While near-sighted people, starved of uncontaminated food,
exhaust the empty bowls of their minds
in partisan debates between our side and your side,
the exalted beings dream in the one expanse of enlightened view.

Alas! How sad! This demon of the mental afflictions
wreaks destruction at every opening,
and under the guise of bringing benefit, it lodges in the heart.
When will we have the fortune to conquer this sworn enemy?

The expanse of space—the profound view of the ocean of sūtras
and tantras—
is illuminated by the hundred thousand suns of eloquent
explanations
that play in all directions through the light rays of scriptural
quotation and reasoning;
who would cast away this fine tradition of the Virtuous?[67]

On the faces of the golden mountain of practice lineages
are the jewel gardens of the nine yānas, which accomplish the
two goals,[68]
and what is more, there are the exceptional jewels of the three
kinds of yoga.
Who would not take delight in the precious realm of the Early
Translation school?

A single primordial consciousness, moved by the methods of
great love,
dances forth a matrix of apparitions in order to benefit others.
They appear as the splendor of the teachings in the Land of
Snow:
among these three forms of nirmāṇakāya,[69] what is there to
accept or reject?

67. Tib. *dge ldan lugs bzang,* that is, the Geluk tradition.

68. That is, one's own and others' well being.

69. That is, Avalokiteśvara, Mañjuśrī, and Vajrapāṇi.

What maintains the borders of our snow mountains is nothing
but this sublime Dharma;
[211] and if the rules to uphold it are not contained within our
own tradition,
then saying the Three Jewels that pervade all of space
are combined in a single object of refuge, is merely a turn of phrase.

It may be that I have achieved pure vision toward all the
teachings
of this Land of Snow, where the supreme yāna has spread since of
old,
but there is no error if I insist on believing that the measure of an
explanation
is the authentic path: without sectarianism and without
divisions.

When you do not experience appearances and emptiness as
separate within the ground,
then on the path you will join as a pair the practices of the two
collections;
and in the fruition, this seal of accomplishing the two goals
is the great weighing balance that separates what is authentic
from what is fake.

Even if experience of all these things does not arise,
since this pure understanding that comes merely from hearing
and thinking
is due to the kindness sustained by our venerable father
[Tsongkhapa]—an actual buddha—
I will revere him until enlightenment.

I have no wisdom stemming from my former lives,
and my studies even in this lifetime have been very meager.

So for whatever is explained falsely here,
I offer my heartfelt confession to the sages of the New and Old
Translation schools.

By this virtue of explaining the view and practice without bias
through analysis of the authentic path in this way,
in all my lifetimes may I never abandon the Dharma, [212]
and may this serve as a cause for always encountering the pure
Dharma.

With our eyes opened by the sun of the fine explanations of the
Virtuous,
and with the jewels of the teachings from the greatly secret Early
Translation school,
may we plant the victory banner of practicing according
to the mind that realizes the priceless value of authentic Dharma.

With a variety of skillful means
spread throughout myriad realms,
Mañjuvajra reveals the definitive meaning
with holy discourse on the profound.
Until there is no one left in mundane existence,
may we join the flock of the chorus,
to sing of the way things really are.

And even then, may I always remain
the servant of every one
of those illusory emanations
of the primordial consciousness
of our Protector,
and in particular may I remain
the servant of that Lord of the Family
upon whom my flower of merit fell.

With this *Jeweled Mirror of Pure Appearances*, I have briefly explained how the incomparable Mount Geden[70] tradition and the Early Translation school of the Secret Mantrayāna assert the same enlightened views. This reflection of a Śākya[71] monk named Lozang Do-ngak Chökyi Gyatso has had the fortune to touch the feet of Jampel Rolway Lodrö Pel Zangpo,[72] a manifestation of the youthful Mañjuśrī, the essential nature of the wisdom of all the jinas of the past, present, and future; of Lozang Pelden Tenzin Nyendrak Pel Zangpo,[73] who is of the nature of the love that is Avalokiteśvara; and of Lerab Lingpa Rinpoché, who is the Lord of Secrets,[74] the very embodiment [213] of sacred power and ability. And I have had the good fortune to press my head to the holy feet of many other spiritual friends of the Mahāyāna. I have written primarily for the sake of increasing my own unbiased faith and wisdom, but also with the intention of benefiting some people with fortune equal to my own, who look with hope to my teachings. Therefore, may those emanations of the three different bodhisattvas grant their blessings. I have written while enjoying a celebration of the faith in which one brings to mind the Three Jewels, from this beautiful garden adorned with meadows and flowers, in the vicinity of the Tsuk-lag-khang[75] on Glorious Melodic Hill,[76] which was established as medicine to revive the teachings and living beings. May what is written here increase all virtue and goodness.

Virtue! [214]

70. Tib. *ri bo dge ldan*. Once again, a synonym of the Geluk school.

71. That is, a monk in the lineage of the Śākya clan, the family of the Buddha Śākyamuni.

72. Tib. *'Jam dpal rol ba'i blo gros dpal bzang bo* (1888–1936), known as Amdo Geshé (*A mdo dge bshes*).

73. Tib. *Blo bzang dpal ldan bstan 'dzin snyan grags dpal bzang bo* (1866–1928), known as Drakkar Geshé (*Brag dkar dge bshes*).

74. That is, Vajrapāṇi.

75. Tib. *gtsug lag khang*. That is, a temple in which sacred images and scriptures are kept.

76. Tib. *Dpal ldan snyan mo ri*. The site of Pel Nyenmo Ri Namgyel monastery, in Darlak, in the Tibetan region of Golok. See http://treasuryoflives.org/biographies/view/Amdo-Geshe-Jampel-Rolpai-Lodro/5897.

# An Offering Cloud of Ambrosia on the Path of Reasoning

## *A Discourse Showing, through Sound Logic, That the Innermost Intent of Scholars from Both the Old and New Translation Schools Is Unified within the Prāsaṅgika System*

Lozang Do-ngak Chökyi Gyatso Chok

In the vast expanse of the sky of intelligence,
a hundred thousand light rays from the sun and moon of the two kinds of knowledge spread forth,
and the great creative power of the dharmakāya's enlightened view is complete
in the venerable lord of Dharma [Tsongkhapa]. I offer reverence with the crown of my head at his lotus feet.
To dispel darkness from the minds of those who see
the distinct teachings that maintain the supreme yāna within the Early Translation school,
as being contradictory—in the aspects of view and practice that derive from the ground—to what is there [in Tsongkhapa's system],
I shall shine forth the light of sound logic. [215]

Now when beginners seek the view of the supreme yāna,
they should rely mainly upon the six collected treatises on reasoning
of our glorious protector, Ārya Nāgārjuna,
in order to discover the middle way that is the definitive meaning.
This is (1) because one will not discover it by the power of one's own intellect,
and (2) because the Lord of Nāgas [Nāgārjuna] himself was prophesied by the Jina's own speech as the one who would explain the definitive meaning,
and also since [Nāgārjuna] refuted with reasoning the idea that anything could be established as real.
Although the tradition of Nāgārjuna appears as two,
the view as held by the principal tantric treatises of the stage of generation, stage of completion, and the Great Perfection[1]
can only be ascertained according to the way the glorious Candrakīrti explained the view:
(1) because, with an exceptional form of negation, he thoroughly refuted the possibility of inherent characteristics, and
(2) because he posited saṃsāra and nirvāṇa insofar as they are mere designations.

1.

The very difference between Prāsaṅgika and Svātantrika[2]
is that the Prāsaṅgika does not accept autonomous reasoning,

1. Tib. *mdo sgyu sems*. See note 52 in *A Jeweled Mirror of Pure Appearances*, above.

2. For the poetic turn of phrase here to make sense, as it does naturally in the Tibetan, one must keep in mind that Prāsaṅgika (Tib. *thal 'gyur ba*) roughly means "leading to an absurd consequence" and Svātantrika (Tib. *rang rgyud pa*) roughly means "following autonomous reasoning." So Lozang Do-ngak Chökyi Gyatso is pointing out that each group directly disagrees with the form of reasoning the other espouses.

whereas Svātantrika asserts that simply leading someone to an
absurd consequence
has not refuted your opponent's insistent belief that things are
real.
Moreover, in [Bhāvaviveka's] *Lamp of Wisdom*, [216] whether or
not there exists a subject matter that appears in common to
both parties
is determined according to whether the object to be refuted is
coarse or subtle.
Since the cross-examination in [Candrakīrti's] *Clear Words* has
witnesses, it is reasonable.[3]
In sum, both the omniscient [Longchenpa] and the Dharma lord
[Tsongkhapa], as well as others,
say that the difference lies in whether or not one accepts the
existence of inherent characteristics,
since that is the singular crucial point.

2.

If you reach the final end, the way in which the profound abides,
not even the slightest substantiality or inherent characteristic
exists;
for those are repudiated by three reasonings, and by the fact it
would contradict scripture, as a fourth.
Now this is true (1) because [if inherent characteristics did exist]
it would follow that the meditative equipoise of an ārya
would itself destroy functioning things,

3. That is, the point appears to be that since Candrakīrti—as well as the scriptures that he enlists in his arguments—stands as witness to Bhāvaviveka's arguments (even when Candrakīrti disagrees with them), something has still appeared in common to two parties, thus making the arguments valid even by "autonomous reasoning" standards. It seems to be a debating tactic for showing that Candrakīrti has satisfied his opponent's standards of reasoning, even while attempting to prove that opponent wrong, using Candrakīrti's own standards of consequence reasoning.

(2) because what is deceptive would be able to withstand analysis with reasoning,
(3) because a real arising would never have been refuted, and finally
(4) because, according to [Candrakīrti's] commentary, it would contradict the scriptural passage
where *Requested by Kāśyapa*[4] states that
"emptiness does not *make* all phenomena empty," and so on.

3.

Nevertheless, the side of appearances is of great importance.
Rejecting saṃsāra and taking up nirvāṇa, progress along the grounds and paths,
with the enormous efficacy of acting to benefit others, and so on;
if these are to be equal in strength to the accumulation of knowledge,[5]
then proceed to perfection without finding them in objects.
Since the door through which one apprehends with certainty
the basis upon which they are established [217] is indeed hard to find,
the profound view is difficult, they say.

4.

It makes perfect sense that the side of appearances should, moreover,
be merely imputed with words and concepts, projected from this side—onto what is over there;

4. That is, the *Sūtra Requested by Kāśyapa* (Tib. *'Od srung gis zhus pa'i mdo*), which is the forty-third chapter of the *Ratnakūṭa Sūtra*.

5. Tib. *ye shes tshogs*.

because no matter how much you go to look for the referent of
the label,
apart from merely projected imputations, you will never find it.
Since this is stated over and over again, in the majority of the
sūtras and tantras,
and since it is what it means to exist by mere convention,
you should certainly seek to accept it.
The great master from Nub[6] also said
that phenomena are merely imputed with names, but dispelled
the argument that they would then turn out to be like the horns
of a hare.
And he invited those of intelligence to taste upon their tongues
the stream of libation
poured from the vase of sūtras and commentaries:
this great ambrosia of the Dharma of profound meaning.
"The lantern for followers of the Early Translation school
consists of the letters of the root tantra—the *Glorious Matrix of*
*Apparitions*—arranged in a circle,
but still you must find certainty on the basis of their message":
this is what scholars of the Early Translation school say—just
look!

5.

If something is the nature of existence, then it would be
contradictory for you to be mistaken toward that which you
have met directly;
and it would be contradictory for ordinary people to be
unmistaken toward that which establishes the false way in
which things appear. [218]

6. That is, Nubchen Sangyé Yeshé.

Therefore it makes perfect sense for the two realities to be set
forth, respectively, by unmistaken and mistaken states of
mind;[7]
this is the glorious, unsurpassed tradition of Prāsaṅgika.

6.

On the one hand, being misleading and not being misleading are
contradictory,
and also determining through elimination and determining
through inclusion
are mutually exclusive;
so with regard to reality and falsehood
a third alternative is impossible.
The twofold classification of reality is definitive,
and in order to divide up the treasure house of the two
collections,
all phenomena are divided through the doorways of the two
realities;
this is the Middle Way tradition, the supreme vehicle.

7.

Regarding what is deceptive, there are both faces and
and their reflections,
and they are alike in that the referents of the imputations are
unfindable.
With respect to objects, correct and false would make no sense—
this accords with the one voice of Rongzom and Longchenpa.
However, you may retort, "Relative to a mundane perspective,
between a horse and an illusory horse,

7. That is, deceptive reality is set forth by a mistaken state of mind and ultimate reality is set forth by an unmistaken state of mind.

there is a difference merely in whether one grasps it as real."
This is affirmed by early and later scholars,
but since these are deceptive, there is nothing correct.
So according to our own Madhyamaka tradition,
it makes sense for there to be neither correct nor false deceptives.

8.

There are two types of ultimate: that which is classifiable and that which is not classifiable,
divided according to whether conceptual elaborations of appearances have or have not been cut off, [219]
and they are yet again known as the actual and the designated [ultimate].
This is the account of [Bhāvaviveka's] *Blaze of Reasoning*[8] and similar texts.
Since there does exist the distinction between an ultimate encountered by ordinary beings and that encountered by āryas,
this is entirely in accord with the sayings of the great founders.
If at this point you wonder just whether the application might be incorrect,
"since it was explained in Svātantrika treatises"—
this is inconclusive, which is a consummate reason,
and in the absence of any other reason to support it,
you should cast that thought aside.
If you wish to strike the great drum of discourse that transcends the intellect,
with the stick of scriptural sources and reasoning,
then seek the knowledge of how to encounter the ultimate,

8. Tib. *Rtog ge 'bar ba*, Skt. *Tarkajvāla*.

both that which is classifiable as such and that which cannot be
classified.

9.

If the two realities are neither the same nor different from one
another, then it would be contradictory for them to exist.
But if they do exist, yet it were unsuitable for them to be either
one or many, you have blown away your reason.
Therefore, intelligent people, open your eyes
to the assertion of the omniscient Drimé Özer [Longchenpa]
that they are logically distinct but are of the same essential
nature.
You wonder whether, if something is asserted in the Svātantrika
treatises,
it must be incorrect in the Prāsaṅgika tradition,
and if something is affirmed by Geluk scholars,
it is not the tradition of the Early Translation school.
Although one wears a hat on one's head,
if, because *they* do so, then in our tradition
we were to wear [220] it on our feet,
wouldn't that be better?
Therefore, if something is undamaged by reasoning—
whether in the higher or the lower [schools], or anywhere at all—
yet without it ever having been examined, there remains a
frightful excess of sectarianism,
we have transgressed even the ways of the world.

10.

To illustrate the ultimate with an analogy,
*A Guide to the Middle Way* states that
just as someone without an eye disease

doesn't see falling hairs,
all that is needed
is for what is unmistaken and always indwelling to have
eliminated,
without trace, the poison of what is focused upon
when the thorns of attachment and hatred rise up.
For that which lacks inherent nature, while being imputed from
afar,
the final way in which the two realities are indivisible—
in which it makes perfect sense to reject what is afflicted and take
up what is totally pure—
is a distinction without room for censure.
Isn't this the fundamental reason
for a hundred thousand paṇḍits of both the New and Old
to affirm that the glorious Prāsaṅgika tradition
is the pinnacle of all philosophical tenets?

11.

Therefore the great distinction that makes this
analogy for what is deceptive so profound is that it
illustrates through the appearance of falling hairs to someone
with an eye disease
the mode in which what is only false exists. [221]

12.

Since this mode of emptiness is the nature of existence,
it is not fabricated by the intellect.
Since everything is alike in this regard, what could be trivial
about it?
It is the all-pervasive, original nature of existence.

13.

Since the essential nature of that emptiness
is established upon no more than the expulsion of a mistaken form of insistent belief,
it makes sense for it to be a simple negation
because a simple negation is merely the refutation of an object to be negated.
Those who are not satisfied with merely discrediting what the mistaken mind believes
still cling to the process of affirmation as best.
Since they feel it is not enough to abandon mistakes, it would seem there must be something else.
On the other hand, if abandonment of the mistake still did not occur
when you refute the object of your insistent belief,
it would follow that you would have to abandon the mistaken state of mind
by way of its *essential* nature, even as you pulled out the thorn.
Proceed without confusing nonexistence and simple negation.
There is no logical inconsistency in emptiness being a simple negation.
This is recognized in the Prāsaṅgika and Svātantrika treatises.

14.

By way of three reasonings and seven scriptural citations,
the autocommentary to *A Guide to the Middle Way* proves
that śrāvakas and pratyekabuddhas realize this actual nature of reality,
so there's no need to tire yourself about this point.
If they have properly identified the root of saṃsāra, [222]

then this proves along the way that arhats who have abandoned
saṃsāra
have also realized this meaning.
So why trouble yourself debating about it?

15.

Since the referent of imputation is not found when it is sought,
it does not withstand analysis, and since it does not,
the reality of emptiness is found with an analytical kind of knowing.
"Not withstanding analysis" and "the meaning that is found
with analytical reasoning" are not at all the same.
O smart ones! It is certain that this unprecedented path of
reasoning, with its hundred petals,
was born from the pond of Mañjuśrī's mind
in that garden of textual traditions,
as a feast for the eyes of intelligent people
to be thoroughly appreciated through its fine explanations.

16.

Since whatever appears to the minds of sentient beings
who encounter what is deceptive
seems to be real,
because they are contaminated by habitual propensities
for things to appear as dual,
it is certain that they are only mistaken.
Without going about claiming that the indwelling fortress of
what is unmistaken
is simply luminous and empty,
seek to realize the basic disposition of the reality that is the fact
that whatever appears to be real is not real.

If that is the case, even the reflexive awareness that substantialists
say is not contaminated by the appearance of being dual [223]
is not appropriate in this context,
so take on the task of analyzing in this way.
If it makes sense that all of saṃsāra and nirvāṇa are merely imputed,
then it's wearisome to invoke the ritual of substantially existent
reflexive awareness as the primary means for knowing
the basis of what is to be accepted or rejected.

Upon analyzing the conventional realities that are established by
a nonanalytical, connate mind, the notion of
reflexive versus extrospective awareness is found to be contradictory.
So the hypothesis of reflexive awareness makes no sense.
Although reflexive awareness doesn't exist, look here
for a rebuttal to complaints about whether it would make sense for memory to work.
And it should be easy for the intelligent to understand
that this is not merely a refutation of its existing ultimately.[9]

The manner in which that which has ceased is an entity
is not clearly presented in the treatises of the Old Translation school,
but scholars of the Old Translation school must accept this,
for it is proven by the glorious Candrakīrti.

Insofar as they say that it is unsuitable for that which has ceased to be an entity,
what the lower philosophical tenet systems are focusing on

9. The point being argued here is that reflexive awareness (so defined) does not exist at all, even conventionally, not merely that it does not exist ultimately.

is the part of an entity that would be the referent of the
imputation "that which has ceased."
This is not found, nor will it ever be reached.
It is like the fact that you will also never find the prime example
of a vase that has ceased
within its basis of imputation.

If it is enough to establish something solely as an entity,
then why wouldn't it be enough to establish it as something
ceased?
The presentations that the substantialists concoct—
of holds,[10] the substrate,[11] and so on [224]—
are unnecessary in this tradition.

If one determines that the teachings on actions and their results
make sense,
something that has ceased is enough to produce its own results,
and nothing beyond that is required.
Some people who don't understand this reasoning say that
"if it were produced by something that had ceased, it would not
be karmic action."
If, while not being able to establish any action that had ceased,
one could find that which had ceased, then it would be okay to
say this.
But if something is, on the one hand, that which has ceased, then
isn't that which has ceased
nondual with the essential nature of that which has ceased?
That action dawns by way of being established
with no more than the name of having ceased.
This is the mystery of the philosophical position that what has
ceased is an entity.

10. Tib. *thob pa*, Skt. *prāpti*.

11. Tib. *kun gzhi*, Skt., *ālaya*.

This is difficult to understand, O, you of fresh minds.

Even if space were to be filled with things that have ceased,
this illustration of an absurd consequence is grounds for laughter.
If space were filled with composed things that had ceased,
would it follow that the destruction of that would fill space too?
Suppose it were filled; then there would be no doubt as to
whether there was room or not,
and then how could there be any disproof?
If it were like that, then not only would things that had ceased be
entities, but they would have to be physical—oh!—
yet my intellect doubts whether even in the Sāṃkhya treatises
such a connate, coarse idea is affirmed—
that anything that dawns before the mind dawns in the
abstraction of something physical.

While phenomena lack any inherent nature, an action that has
ceased
brings forth its own consequences.
This way of ascertaining actions and their consequences [225]
is not shared with the lower [tenet systems].
Know how to arrive there, and try to respect it.

By the magical force of the same logical point,
birth from something else is refuted, so there's no other choice.
Wouldn't it be good to set aside for the time being
inconclusive speculations that have not determined the meaning
of the treatises?
There is no avoiding the consequence that a seed and a sprout do
not rely
on anything else that could exist from its own side,

but if a cause could become a result without anything relying on
anything,
it would follow that darkness could arise from fire.

17.

Although no phenomenon exists from its own side,
it is true that all are simply nominal conventions.
If that is acceptable, then why couldn't omniscient valid
cognition
establish all conventional phenomena?
The notion that this lack of existing from its own side
implies utter nonexistence
is a lyric of a mind that does not comprehend.
How sad that it's widely sung as erudition!
Since the false appearance—which is contaminated by habitual
propensities
for ignorance about the way things appear—is a mistake,
and since there is no other disproof for the part that merely appears,
it is no contradiction for the latter to be established with valid
cognition.

Since the fact of whether or not things are established
conventionally
depends on a conventional state of mind,
this twofold classification of things
is not invalidated by a conventional state of mind.
Ultimately, [226] it is impossible for conventional phenomena
to be established with valid cognition,
but since they are not presented in terms of the ultimate,
there is no contradiction.

Since (1) that which is mistaken, even conventionally, and
(2) that which is not mistaken with respect to convention
are not the same, things are established conventionally with valid cognition,
and that is not invalid.
You might say that if the two realities are divided up like that,
they become like the two antlers of a deer.
But buddhas, too, classify the two realities,
and this was a statement affirmed by Nāgārjuna.

18.

Regarding all these points, everyone belonging to the
New and Old Translation schools presumes to be followers of the glorious Candrakīrti,
and they pretend to adhere to the Prāsaṅgika view.
This path is opened only with a hundred colors of reasoning.
If there are owls of false views who fly about in the dark,
not seeing the path of reasoning laid clear in the sunlight,
then I beg you to sound out the conch-pipe signaling contradictions,
and O! to let your debating rosary blaze once again, leading the way to reasoning.

Step by step, the intellectual levels of the four philosophical schools
are progressively more profound, like the variegated designs on fine satin;
and in the end they come down to the vidyā mantra, which expels the poison
of what is focused upon when the thorns of attachment and hatred rise up. [227]

And if one lacks the eyes of intelligence to distinguish, without confusion,
the line between subtle and coarse regarding the measure of the object of negation
in the Prāsaṅgika and the Svātantrika schools,
one will not see the actual nature of profound wisdom;
so it is crucially important to analyze with care all the textual traditions.
As for the way to analyze them, one must integrate the words with the meanings
of the treatises by the great founders in general,
and in particular, of the great commentaries by Candrakīrti and so on.
But what will come of it if you just speak on the basis of whatever dawns to your own mind?

Rational people who climb up the straight stairway of reasoning
and enjoy the celebration of the Sage's teachings
in the vast palace of the definitive Dharma,
reach every kind of happiness, right there in the palm of their hands.
There is no success if one just follows the means—the paths of the profound and the vast—
separately, without integrating them,
for they are both necessary to achieve the goal of the two kāyas.
So ascertain the two stages of the path that correspond to the two realities!

19.

In accordance with the pith instructions of Maitreyanātha,
the tradition of Atīśa for following the paths of individuals of three different capacities,

is variously demarcated in terms of their essential nature,
number, and sequence.
Here all the profound, crucial points of the Dharma from the
sūtras and tantras
belonging to the supreme yāna are complete,
so the essence of practice is like clarified butter. [228]
Drink it well, and make the offering of your practice.

20.

In practice such as this,
the goals of both oneself and others
are intimately connected within the perfectly bountiful path and
its fruition;
thus both will be accomplished swiftly and with ease.

Even if the water of this honestly sought path of reasoning
turns into ambrosia for a hundred fortunate devas,
for those pretas of the class whose karmic obstacles spawn from
misconceptions,
it will be difficult for the physical fortitude of the Dharma to
become restorative food for them.
Nevertheless, so that the crescent moon of my own intelligence
may eventually increase, and for the sake of some discerning
people,
I have drawn this straight line of the path of reasoning, pointing
toward the scriptural sayings.

By the virtue of straightening out crooked, uncomprehending
minds,
may the Jina's teachings in general and the tradition of the
profound view—

the fine legacy of Nāgārjuna—spread to the ends of space, in all
directions.
May all beings who are tormented by the illness of grasping to
extremes
be forever healed with the medicine of the perfection of wisdom.

Henceforth, in the string of all my future lives,
may the deity of the saffron hue,
the deity of the wisdom wheel,
who with his sword of reasoning
severs my crooked misconceptions,
ever turn toward me
with his smiling eyes of joy.
Then, may the pond of my intelligence long overflow, and
may [229] the hundred thousand jewels of the profound view
be gathered into a mountain for graceful delight in the Jina's
teachings,
and thus may this festival for the rapture of the fortunate spread.

I was asked to write this *Offering Cloud of Ambrosia on the Path of Reasoning: A Discourse Showing, through Sound Logic, That the Final Assertions of Scholars from Both the Old and New Translation Schools Are Unified within the Prāsaṅgika System* by Lama Gyatso, the one astute in analysis, of the Willow Encampment,[12] who raises the victory banner of the Dharma belonging to the Old Translation school of the Secret Mantrayāna, and who, having been purified by the vinaya discipline that is the root of the teachings, has become a mainstay for the precious teachings of the Jina. I delayed in writing it out, but recently that Ācārya and Holder of the Vinaya, Jikmé Könchok of Peyul Darthang,[13] told me that

12. Tib. *Lcang ma'i sgar.*

13. Tib. *Dpal yul dar thang.*

the connections to scripture that I had made previously weren't enough to prove my point. In reliance upon what he said, and with the intention to increase my own intelligence and that of others with similar fortune, this reflection of a Śākya monk, known as "the servant who pleases our Gentle Protector Guru, with the intelligence to please Mañjuśrī, and who is of a class with the pride of Brahma's sons,"[14] who has taken to the crown of his head the lotus feet of that one who is in reality Mañjughoṣa, Jetsun Dampa Khalong Yangpa Tsal,[15] [230] has composed this piece in a place near the Tsuk-lag-khang on Glorious Melodic Hill, called Khachö Keutsang.[16] May there be virtue! And may it be of service to the precious teachings of the Jina. *Jayantu*!

Laying bare to the core a hundred delusive, deceptive designs
created by the mind,
I have faith in the Great Perfection that holds the everlasting
kingdom
of the perfect dharmakāya, which evenly pervades
the one expanse of reasoning.

I'm deeply saddened with the presumption that a still mind that is
infatuated with clinging to the luminosity and emptiness of
the mind is the enlightened view of the Buddha, the Great
Perfection,
without its bursting even one fault of delusion.

I take delight in the spectacle of the clear light Great Perfection
of the rainbow body in which the kāyas and bindus are ripened

14. Tib. *'Jam mgon bla ma dgyes pa'i 'bangs 'jam dpal dgyes pa'i blo gros tshangs sras snyem pa'i sde.*

15. Tib. *Mkha' klong yangs pa rtsal.* See note 6 in *A Blazing Sun of Brilliant Faith*, above.

16. Tib. *Mkha' spyod ge'u tshang.*

as the creative power of primordial consciousness that binds the
fluctuating karmic energies
in the power of the lucid space of awareness, emptiness, and
configurations of thoughts.

I'm exasperated with the "Great Perfection" that anchors one in
the depths of saṃsāra,
and in meditation that stirs up the sediment of
hope and fear regarding visions of gods and demons
in the darkness of delusion.

Aho! How difficult it is [231] to realize with experiential valid
cognition
the face of the clear light Great Perfection!
But if one reads such fine teachings as those of the *Seven Great
Treasuries*
and *Three Cycles of Comfort and Ease*, analytical realization is easy.

I think it is difficult to discover the ultimate Dharma of the
Great Secret
with just a handful of pointing-out instructions
and collecting a smattering of words said by others.
Alas, what is this pattern of people nowadays?

In the vast space that is the discernment of sūtras and tantras
appears the supreme yāna, the face of one's own pristine
awareness of the Great Perfection.
The unprecedented sun shines with unborn sunlight.

Not having studied it in the past nor in the present,
while salivating at the pretext that it is easy,
such beggars, without Dharma, in the kingdom of the dharmakāya
presume to rest blissfully in comfort and ease—what a laugh!

In the pit earnestly dug by bodhicitta in the tradition of the early
scholars, including Rongzom and Longchenpa,
brews the intoxicating wine of realizations that are the
fermentation of
the grape juice of realization about the nature of existence.

Aho! While drinking it, the ordinary mind soars in the
joyful, expansive space of the dharmakāya.
Upon the extinction of activities—the dispersion and
withdrawal of the energy-mind—
one proceeds to the kingdom of the spontaneous actualization
[232] of ultimate benefit for oneself and others.

Alas! Nowadays the muddy water of attachment and hatred
is symbolically given the name of "the ambrosia of the Great Secret"
in the water bowl of merely stilling a churning mind,
and this is taken to be the meditation of resting in one's own
nature.

How sad! While congealing one's mindstream in meditation,
the mist of the virtuous Dharma evaporates away,
the habitual propensities for revolving in the three realms are
catalyzed again,
and the intense exhaustion of rebirth proliferates.

Aho! Now, without pointing out the faults of others, I pray that
this legacy of the lineage of the Omniscient One and his spiritual
sons
may preserve the eternal kingdom of Samantabhadra
as the universal splendor for pathetic beings who are our old
mothers.

Virtue!

# Glossary

This glossary lists key terms in English, Tibetan, and Sanskrit found in the works included in this volume. Many definitions are derived from the texts themselves. Additional sources include the following:

Buswell, Robert E., Jr., and Donald S. Lopez, Jr. *The Princeton Dictionary of Buddhism*. Princeton, NJ: Princeton University Press, 2014.

Dudjom Rinpoche. *The Nyingma School of Tibetan Buddhism*. Boston: Wisdom Publications, 1991.

Duff, Tony. *The Illuminator Tibetan-English Encyclopaedic Dictionary*. Kathmandu, Nepal: Padma Karpo Translation Committee, 2014.

Keown, Damien. *A Dictionary of Buddhism*. Oxford: Oxford University Press, 2003.

Rangjung Yeshe Wiki—Dharma Dictionary at http://rywiki.tsadra.org/index.php/Main_Page.

*Abhirati* (Skt., Tib. *mngon par dga' ba*). Lit. "higher joy," this is the buddha field of Akṣobhya in the eastern direction.

*absolute space of phenomena* (Tib. *chos kyi dbyings*, Skt. *dharmadhātu*). The expanse of all phenomena in saṃsāra and nirvāṇa. This does not refer to space in the reified, Newtonian sense, but rather to an ultimate dimension of space out of which all manifestations of relative space-time and mass-energy emerge, in which they are present, and into which they eventually dissolve. Likewise, all manifestations of relative states of consciousness and mental processes emerge as displays of primordial consciousness, which according to the Great Perfection tradition has always been indivisible from the absolute space of phenomena.

*ācārya* (Skt., Tib. *slob dpon*). An accomplished teacher, especially of Dharma.

*accumulations, two* (Tib. *tshogs gnyis*, Skt. *dvisambhāra*). The twofold accumulations of merit (Tib. *bsod nams*, Skt. *puṇya*), which culminates in the achievement of the form (Tib. *gzugs sku*, Skt. *rūpakāya*) of a buddha, and of wisdom (Tib. *ye shes*, Skt. *jñāna*), which culminates in the achievement of the mind (Tib. *chos sku*, Skt. *dharmakāya*) of a buddha.

*Akaniṣṭha* (Skt., Tib. *'og min*). Lit. "unsurpassed," the buddha field of Samantabhadra, in which every being finally achieves supreme enlightenment.

*ambrosia* (Tib. *bdud rtsi,* Skt. *amṛta*). Lit. "deathlessness" or immortality, this is one result of spiritual practice and also refers to sacramental substances.

*anuttarayogatantra* (Skt., Tib. *bla na med pa'i rnal 'byor*). Unsurpassed yoga tantra, which includes both the stage of generation and the stage of completion.

*anuyoga* (Skt., Tib. *rjes su rnal 'byor*). The "subsequent yoga," or the spiritual vehicle that corresponds to the stage of completion, following the mahāyoga.

*approach and actualization* (Tib. *bsnyen sgrub*, Skt. *sevāsādhana*). The two primary aspects of sādhana practice, particularly within the context of mahāyoga. These are often subdivided into four branches: approach, close approach, actualization, and great actualization.

*ārya* (Skt., Tib. *'phags pa*). A being who has gained direct realization of ultimate reality.

*āryabodhisattva* (Skt., Tib. *'phags pa'i byang chub sems dpa'*). A bodhisattva who has gained direct realization of ultimate reality.

*asura* (Skt., Tib. *lha ma yin*). A titan, or demigod, whose existence is characterized by aggression and conflict with the devas.

*atiyoga* (Skt., Tib. *shin tu rnal 'byor*). The "extraordinary yoga," which is equivalent to the Great Perfection, the highest of the nine spiritual vehicles.

*awareness* (Tib. *rig pa*, Skt. *vidyā*). The basic act of cognizing. See also *pristine awareness.*

*Bhagavān* (Skt., Tib. *bcom ldan 'das*). Lit. "Blessed One," an epithet of the Buddha. The Tibetan term has the connotation of one who has overcome all obscurations, is imbued with all excellent qualities, and who has transcended saṃsāra.

*bindu* (Skt., Tib. *thig le*). (1) An orb of light. (2) The red and white essential drops of vital fluids within the body, included within the triad of channels, orbs, and vital energies. (3) The dot or small circle above Tibetan and Sanskrit syllables such as *hūṃ* (ཧཱུྃ). (4) The "sole bindu" is the one dharmakāya, which is replete with all the qualities of the buddhas and which encompasses the entirety of saṃsāra and nirvāṇa.

*blessing* (Tib. *byin rlabs,* Skt. *adhiṣṭhāna*). (1) Powerful realization or empowerment that is experienced in connection with a lama or a physical place or object associated with a realized being. (2) Consecration of an inanimate object or substance.

*bodhicitta* (Skt., Tib. *byang chub kyi sems*). (1) Lit. "awakening mind," it is described as having two relative aspects called aspirational and engaged, along with its absolute, ultimate aspect. The nominal cultivation of aspirational bodhicitta means wishing to achieve enlightenment in order to liberate all sentient beings in saṃsāra. Bodhicitta is called engaged when one actually practices with this motivation to achieve buddhahood. (2) In Vajrayāna, the red and white bodhicittas are the female and male regenerative fluids, which are composed of the red and white bindus. (3) In the Great Perfection, bodhicitta is the primordial, originally pure ground, which pervades the whole of saṃsāra and nirvāṇa.

*bodhicitta, ultimate* (Tib. *don dam byang chub kyi sems*, Skt. *paramārtha bodhicitta*). In the Great Perfection, the realization of ultimate bodhicitta is the actualization of identitylessness as the play of the consummation of saṃsāra and nirvāṇa, free of activity and conceptual elaboration. Precious bodhicitta subsumes all authentic realities and is the ultimate source of all phenomena; it manifests the wisdom of realizing identitylessness, liberating the three realms of saṃsāra as the play of the three kāyas.

*bodhisattva* (Skt., Tib. *byang chub sems dpa'*). A being in whom bodhicitta arises effortlessly and who devotes himself or herself to the cultivation of the six perfections in order to achieve enlightenment for the benefit of all beings.

*Bodhisattvayāna* (Skt., Tib. *byang chub sems dpa'i theg pa*). The spiritual vehicle of the bodhisattvas, in which one seals saṃsāra and nirvāṇa with bodhicitta.

*brahman* (Skt., Tib. *bram ze*). In the caste system of India, a member of the priestly class who engages in pure conduct, partakes of pure food, and is seen to have virtuous attitudes.

*buddha* (Skt., Tib. *sangs rgyas*). Lit. "awakened one," an enlightened being in whom all mental afflictions and obscurations are dispelled and all excellent qualities brought to perfection.

*buddha field* (Tib. *sangs rgyas kyi zhing khams*, Skt. *buddhakṣetradhātu*). Lit. "buddha field realm," this is a "pure realm," which is brought forth spontaneously from a buddha's enlightened mind.

*buddha nature* (Tib. *sangs rgyas kyis rigs*, Skt. *buddhadhātu*). The primordially pure, essential nature of the mind, equivalent to awareness, which is none other than the dharmakāya, but which may be regarded provisionally as one's capacity for achieving spiritual awakening.

*cakra* (Skt., Tib. *rtsa 'khor*). A "wheel" of channels through which vital energies course. The fivefold classification of the cakras includes the cakra of great bliss at the crown of the head, the cakra of enjoyment at the throat, the dharma cakra at the heart, the cakra of emanation at the navel, and the cakra of sustained bliss at the genital region.

*caryātantra* (Skt., Tib. *spyod rgyud*). The "performance tantras," in which one practices so that one's view and conduct will become nondual. The practice of such tantric systems corresponds with upāyayoga.

*channel, central* (Tib. *kun 'dar ma, rtsa dbu ma*, Skt. *avadhūti, madhyamā*). The central of the three main channels that run vertically through the core of the subtle body, and that serve as conduits for the vital energies and the bindus, or subtle drops of vital fluid. It is said that when the vital energies flowing in the two side channels enter, stay, and dissolve in the central one, the yogi's perceptions of reality shift significantly, allowing for higher and higher realizations of emptiness and all-pervasive compassion.

*channel, life-force* (Tib. *srog rtsa*). The channel in the heart through which flows the vital energy of the life force.

*citta lamp of the flesh* (Skt., Tib. *tsitta sha'i sgron ma*). The "lamp" located at the heart and included among the six lamps discussed in the teachings on the direct crossing over.

*cittamātra* (Skt., Tib. *sems tsam pa*). The Mind Only school of Indian Buddhist thought, which is known for asserting that appearances are not other than the mind.

*clear light* (Tib. *'od gsal*, Skt. *prabhāsvara*). The illuminating nature of pristine awareness.

*cleaver* (Tib. *gri gug*, Skt. *karttṛkā*). A curved flaying knife.

*conceptual elaboration* (Tib. *spros pa*, Skt. *prapañca*). Conceptual constructs such as those regarding existence, nonexistence, birth, and cessation. This term can also refer, without negative connotation, to the use of the imagination in a ritual of empowerment or advanced practice of tantra. Note the progressive sequence of empowerment "with elaborations" (Tib. *spros bcas*), "without elaborations" (Tib. *spros med*), "entirely without elaborations" (Tib. *shin tu spros med*), and "absolutely without elaborations" (Tib. *rab tu spros med*). Alternatively, the middle two can rendered as "devoid" or "free of conceptual elaborations," and "utterly free" or "utterly devoid of conceptual elaborations," respectively.

*connate* (Tib. *lhan skyes*, Skt. *sahaja*). Lit. "born together at the same time," this term is used in various contexts for that which is natural or spontaneous, whether referring to a process as it occurs within cyclic existence or referring to exalted spiritual qualities that emerge as part of the path beyond cyclic existence (as in "connate primordial consciousness").

*consciousness* (Tib. *shes pa*, Skt. *jñāna*). The basic experience of knowing, cognizing, or being aware.

*consciousness, conditioned* (Tib. *rnam par shes pa*, Skt. *vijñāna*). The clear and knowing qualities of the mind that emerge in the aspect of the object and are bound by reification. See also *primordial consciousness.*

*creative displays, creative expressions* (Tib. *rtsal*). Effulgences or manifestations, such as the creative displays of primordial consciousness.

*crystal kati channel* (Tib. *rtsa ka ti shel*). Among the six lamps, a single channel, one-eighth the width of a hair of a horse's tail, with two branches that stem from inside the heart, curve around the back of the ears, and come to the pupils of the eyes.

*cutting through* (Tib. *khregs chod*). The first of the two major phases in the practice of the Great Perfection, aimed at gaining direct, sustained realization of the original purity of pristine awareness.

*ḍākinī* (Skt., Tib. *mkha' 'gro ma*). A highly realized female bodhisattva, who manifests in the world in order to serve sentient beings. The Tibetan term means a female "sky-goer," referring to the fact that such beings course in the expanse of absolute space.

*deeds of immediate retribution, five* (Tib. *mtshams med pa lnga*, Skt. *pañcānantarya*). Actions with such negative karmic force that upon death the perpetrator is reborn immediately in hell, bypassing the intermediate period: patricide, matricide, killing an arhat, maliciously drawing the blood of a buddha, and causing a schism in the Saṅgha.

*deity* (Tib. *lha*, Skt. *deva*). Within the context of Buddhist Vajrayāna, this refers to an enlightened being who is manifest within a maṇḍala, or secret, pure abode.

*deity, personal* (Tib. *yi dam*, Skt. *iṣṭadevatā*). The enlightened manifestation, or embodiment, chosen as one's primary object of refuge and meditative practice.

*delusion* (Tib. *'khrul pa, gti mug*, Skt. *bhrānti, moha*). Principally the delusion of reifying oneself and other phenomena, which acts as the root of all other mental afflictions. Note that in the essays in part 2 of this volume, the Tibetan word *'khrul* and its variants are more often translated as "mistaken" or "mistake," since this is more appropriate to the Madhyamaka context there.

*delusive appearances* (Tib. *'khrul snang*). The reified appearances of phenomena that arise on account of delusion.

*deva* (Skt., Tib. *lha*). A "god" within saṃsāra, who experiences great joy, extrasensory perception, and paranormal abilities, but who suffers greatly when faced with death.

*devaputra* (Skt., Tib. *lha'i bu*). The son of a deva within saṃsāra.

*Dharma* (Skt., Tib. *chos*). Spiritual teachings and practices that lead one irreversibly away from suffering and the source of suffering and toward the attainment of liberation and enlightenment.

*dharmakāya* (Skt., Tib. *chos kyi sku*). The "enlightened embodiment of truth," which is the mind of the buddhas.

*dharmapāla* (Skt., Tib *chos skyong*). Dharma protector. This may be a worldly being oath-bound to protect the Dharma and sentient beings (*'jig rten pa*) or a wisdom deity who is an enlightened manifestation of compassion (*'jig rten las 'das pa*).

*differentiating saṃsāra and nirvāṇa* (Tib. *'khor 'das ru shan*). The direct-crossing-over preliminary practice of differentiating saṃsāra from nirvāṇa with respect to the body, speech, and mind.

*direct appearances of the actual nature of reality, vision of the* (Tib. *chos nyid mngon sum gyi snang ba*). The first of the four visions that arise in the course of the direct-crossing-over practice.

*direct crossing over* (Tib. *thod rgal*, Skt. *vyutkrāntaka*). The second of the two phases of the practice of the Great Perfection, which is aimed at realizing the spontaneous manifestations of the dharmakāya.

*display* (Tib. *rol pa*, Skt. *lalita*). The manifestation of reality unfolding as a "dance" or "sport."

*element of phenomena* (Tib. *chos kyi khams*, Skt. *dharmadhātu*). See *space of awareness*.

*embodiment* (Tib. *sku*, Skt. *kāya*). See *kāya*.

*emptiness* (Tib. *stong pa nyid*, Skt. *śūnyatā*). The absence of true, inherent existence with respect to all phenomena. Emptiness itself is not to be reified.

*energy-mind* (Tib. *rlung sems*). A term based upon the idea common to many presentations of anuttarayogatantra and the Great Perfection, namely, that the subtle and very subtle vital energies run in tandem with consciousness (*rlung sems 'jug pa gcig pa*), or that both are of the same essential nature, understood from different points of view (*ngo bo gcig ldog pa tha dad*). The pair of energies and mind are frequently referred to by a single compound term. In general this refers to the karmic energies and conditioned mind, but since there is sometimes reference in Great Perfection texts to a purified energy-mind, or in anuttarayogatantra texts to the indwelling, very subtle energy-mind associated with the clear light, it seems the same term can also refer to the energies of primordial consciousness.

*enlightenment* (Tib. *byang chub*, Skt. *bodhi*). Spiritual awakening.

*ethically neutral* (Tib. *lung ma bstan*, Skt. *avyākṛta*). A characteristic of all phenomena that are not by nature either virtuous or nonvirtuous.

*experience, visionary* (Tib. *nyams snang*). In the context of the Great Perfection, this usually refers to the four visions of the direct crossing over.

*extinction into the actual nature of reality* (Tib. *chos nyid zad pa*). The fourth and final vision on the path of the direct crossing over, in which all phenomena dissolve into the absolute space of phenomena.

*extremes of conceptual elaboration, eight* (Tib. *spros pa'i mtha' brgyad*, Skt. *aṣṭānta*). The eight philosophical assertions of origination, cessation, existence, nonexistence, coming, going, diversity, and unity.

*gaṇacakra* (Skt., Tib. *tshogs 'khor*). A ceremony in which one makes ritual offerings to awakened beings.

*garuḍa* (Skt., Tib. *bya khyung, mkha' lding*). The mythical king of birds, like a great eagle.

*Ghanavyūha* (Skt., Tib. *stug po bkod pa*). Lit. "compact display," this is the buddha field of Vairocana in the central direction.

*glow, inner* (Tib. *mdangs*). The natural glow (*rang mdangs*) of awareness, which is transcendently present in the ground and expresses itself as self-emergent, indwelling primordial consciousness.

*goals, two* (Tib. *don gnyis*). The goals for oneself and the goals for others. Alternatively, the two goals are to serve all sentient beings and to attain perfect enlightenment.

*Great Perfection* (Tib. *rdzogs pa chen po*, Skt. *mahāsaṇdhi*). Dzokchen, or *atiyoga*, the pinnacle of the nine vehicles transmitted by the Nyingma school. The clear light absolute space of phenomena, having no center or periphery, from which all phenomena of saṃsāra and nirvāṇa spontaneously arise as creative displays.

*ground of being* (Tib. *gzhi*, Skt. *āśraya*). The ground of the whole of saṃsāra and nirvāṇa, which is the dharmakāya. This Tibetan term is sometimes translated as "the condition of the ground" when referring to that which exists in the natural state, even without relying upon practice of the path.

*grounds and paths* (Tib. *sa lam*, Skt. *bhūmimārga*). The stages of attainment and the paths that lead to them. There are five sequential paths culminating in the liberation of a śrāvaka, five culminating in the liberation of a pratyekabuddha, and five bodhisattva paths culminating in the perfect enlightenment of a buddha. According to the sūtra tradition, there are ten āryabodhisattva grounds. According to the Great Perfection tradition, there are twenty āryabodhisattva grounds, followed by the culmination of the twenty-first ground.

*guru* (Skt., Tib. *bla ma*). A spiritual teacher or mentor who leads one to the state of liberation and spiritual awakening.

*Hīnayāna* (Skt., Tib. *theg pa dman pa*). Lit. the "lesser vehicle" of Buddhist theory and practice, aimed at one's own liberation. This includes the śrāvakayāna and the pratyekabuddhayāna.

*identitylessness* (Tib. *bdag med*, Skt. *nairātmya*). Selflessness or a lack of inherent identity. There are two types: (1) the identitylessness of persons, and (2) the identitylessness of phenomena.

*indwelling* (Tib. *gnyug ma*, Skt. *nija*). That which has remained naturally within oneself from the very beginning (without beginning) and abides continuously. It can also be translated as "fundamental" or "innate."

*instruction, pointing-out* (Tib. *mdzub khrid*, *ngo sprod pa*). An introduction to the nature of the mind.

*instruction, pith* (Tib. *man ngag*, Skt. *upadeśa*). A succinct and powerful practical instruction, coming from the experience of the guru and the lineage.

*instruction, practical* (Tib. *gdams ngag*, Skt. *avavāda*). Quintessential guidance in spiritual practice, which synthesizes the teachings of the buddhas into specific practices for specific individuals according to their needs.

*intermediate period* (Tib. *bar do*, Skt. *antarabhāva*). The interval between death and one's next rebirth, which includes two of the six transitional phases, namely, the transitional phase of the actual nature of reality and the transitional phase of becoming.

*introspection* (Tib. *shes bzhin*, Skt. *saṃprajanya*). The mental faculty by which one ascertains how the mind is functioning, which is crucial to all forms of meditation.

*Jewels, Three* (Tib. *dkon mchog gsum*, Skt. *trīratna*). The objects of refuge, which are the Buddha, Dharma, and Saṅgha.

*jina* (Skt., Tib. *rgyal ba*). Lit. a "victorious one" who has conquered cognitive and afflictive obscurations; an epithet of a buddha.

*jinaputra* (Skt., Tib. *rgyal ba'i sras*). Lit. "son of the victorious ones," an epithet of a bodhisattva.

*jñānasattva* (Skt., Tib. *ye shes sems dpa'*). A "primordial consciousness being" whom one invites and with whom one merges inseparably in the practice of the stage of generation.

*karma* (Skt., Tib. *las*). Actions defiled by mental afflictions, especially the delusion of self-grasping.

*Karmaprasiddhi* (Skt., Tib. *las rab rdzogs pa*). Lit. "perfection of excellent deeds," this is the buddha field of Amoghasiddhi in the northern direction.

*karmic energy* (Tib. *las rlung*). A vital energy that courses through the body and is propelled by one's previous karma. See also *prāṇa*.

*kāya* (Skt., Tib. *sku*). An aggregate of spontaneously actualized facets of primordial consciousness and qualities of enlightenment, designated as a composite body.

*kīla* (Skt., Tib. *phur ba*). A sacred, three-edged, ritual dagger that may be used as an object of devotions such as prostrations, offerings, and circumambulations, and is also used in various esoteric rituals.

*kriyātantra* (Skt., Tib. *bya rgyud*). The "action tantras," which are practiced by not confounding one's pure vajrayāna behavior with ordinary, impure conduct.

*lalanā* (Skt., Tib. *rkyang ma*). The left channel among the three principal channels that run vertically through the torso and up into the head.

*lamp, fluid lasso* (Tib. *rgyang zhags chu'i sgron ma*). In the direct-crossing-over terminology, this is the lamp of the eyes, which are fluid and are able to apprehend objects far away, as if they were caught with a lasso. This lamp is like the flowers of a tree that has the citta lamp of the flesh as its root and the hollow crystal kati channel as its trunk. The term "fluid lasso lamp" is collectively given to all three, which are known as the three lamps of the vessel.

*lamp of the empty bindus* (Tib. *thig le stong pa'i sgron ma*). The appearance of the five quintessences (of the five facets of primordial consciousness) in luminous spherical forms called bindus.

*lamp of the pristine space of awareness* (Tib. *dbyings rnam par dag pa'i sgron ma*). The pristine expanse of the sole bindu inside the citta lamp of the flesh, which is the space of awareness, in which the bindus and vajra strands appear.

*lamps, six* (Tib. *sgron me drug*). The three lamps of the vessel—namely, the citta lamp of the flesh, the hollow crystal kati channel, and the fluid lasso lamp—and the three lamps of the vital essence—namely, the lamp of the pristine space of awareness, the lamp of the empty bindus, and the lamp of self-emergent wisdom. (The last is not mentioned explicitly in the texts included in this volume.)

*lineage of the jinas, enlightened view* (Tib. *rgyal ba dgongs pa'i brgyud*). The honorific term for "mind" denotes the jinas' view of reality. The lineage is so designated because the minds of all the buddhas of the three times are of one taste in the absolute space of phenomena.

*lineage of ordinary individuals, aural* (Tib. *gang zag snyan khung gi brgyud*). The lineage in which the practical instructions arise naturally in verbal transmission as an entrance to the disciples' paths, like filling a vase.

*lineage of the vidyādharas, symbolic* (Tib. *rig 'dzin brda yi brgyud*). The lineage in which the symbolic signs of the actual nature of reality, the treasury of space, are spontaneously released, without reliance upon the stages of spiritual training and practice.

*Madhyamaka* (Skt., Tib. *dbu ma*). The Middle Way, the higher of the two Mahāyāna schools in the sūtra system. This in turn is composed of two traditions of interpretation: the Svātantrikas (Tib. *rang rgyud pa*), who espouse the efficacy of an autonomous line of reasoning for demonstrating that phenomena are not truly existent, and the Prāsaṅgikas (Tib. *thal 'gyur ba*), who claim that the only type of argument that can instill authentic understanding of emptiness is one that leads to an absurd consequence, or a kind of *reductio ad absurdum*.

*Mādhyamika* (Skt., Tib. *dbu ma pa*). A follower of the school of Madhyamaka.

*Mahāmudrā* (Skt., Tib. *phyag rgya chen po*). The "great seal," which is a synonym for emptiness, the absolute space of phenomena. Also refers to a system of practice designed to lead to the realization of emptiness with the very subtle mind of clear light.

*mahāsiddha* (Skt., Tib. *sgrub chen*). A "great adept," who has accomplished mundane and supermundane abilities and realizations.

*Mahāyāna* (Skt., Tib. *theg pa chen po*). The "Great Vehicle," by which one proceeds to the state of the perfect enlightenment of a buddha in order to liberate all sentient beings.

*mahāyoga* (Skt., Tib. *rnal 'byor chen po*). The "great yoga," which is perfected by realizing the nondual reality of the deity and one's own appearance. This typically corresponds to the stage of generation in anuttarayogatantra.

*maṇḍala* (Skt., Tib. *dkyil 'khor*). A symbolic representation of the world, which is ritually offered. A representation of the pure abode of a deity.

*mantra* (Skt., Tib. *sngags*). Sanskrit syllables, words, or a series of words imbued with special symbolic significance or spiritual blessings.

*māra* (Skt., Tib. *bdud*). A demonic force that manifests as grasping involving hopes and fears.

*meaning, definitive* (Tib. *nges don*, Skt. *nītārtha*). The meaning of ultimate reality, which does not have to be interpreted further.

*meaning, provisional* (Tib. *drang don*, Skt. *neyārtha*). The symbolic, relative, or contextual meaning, which has to be interpreted further, as opposed to the definitive, ultimate, or absolute meaning.

*meditative equipoise* (Tib. *mnyam bzhag*, Skt. *samāhita*). Undistracted, even placement of the mind upon its object for as long as one wishes, culminating in the achievement of śamatha.

*mental process* (Tib. *sems byung*, Skt. *caitta*). A mental process that arises in conjunction with consciousness, by means of which one engages in various ways with the objects of apprehension.

*mentation* (Tib. *yid*, Skt. *manas*). A mental function of every sentient being that serves as the basis for the emergence of all discursive thoughts and that transforms thoughts into the objects of all appearances.

*mind* (Tib. *sems*, Skt. *citta*). Within these texts, this usually refers to the dualistic awareness that clings to appearances, conceptually observes its own processes, and arouses pleasure and pain through intellectual fabrications and the acceptance and rejection of virtue and vice.

*mind, actual nature of the* (Tib. *sems nyid*, Skt. *cittatā*). Pristine awareness, the *sugatagarbha*.

*mindfulness* (Tib. *dran pa*, Skt. *smṛti*). The mental faculty of attending continuously, without forgetfulness, to an object with which one is already familiar.

*mode of existence* (Tib. *gnas tshul*). How things actually are, in contrast to their mode of appearance (Tib. *snang tshul*).

*mudrā* (Skt., Tib. *phyag rgya*). A seal or imprint, such as a ruler's insignia on a decree. A gesture symbolizing some form of enlightened activity. In tantra, the female partner of a male deity.

*mundane existence* (Tib. *srid pa*, Skt. *bhava*). The cycle of existence in which one is propelled from life to life by the force of mental afflictions and karma.

*nāda* (Skt.). The subtlest aspect of sound, represented by the vertical wavy line placed above Tibetan and Sanskrit syllables such as *hūṃ* and *vaṃ* in special contexts.

*natural liberation* (Tib. *rang grol*). Lit. "self-liberation" or "self-release," this may also be translated as "release itself" or "natural release." When there is no grasping, thoughts and afflictions are naturally liberated without any need for antidotes, interventions, or outside forces.

*nature* (Tib. *rang bzhin*, Skt. *prakṛti*). The quality or feature of some phenomenon, such as the mind, whose nature is luminosity.

*nature, essential* (Tib. *ngo bo*, Skt. *svabhāva*). The fundamental nature of a phenomenon, as in the case of awareness being the essential nature of the mind. This can also refer to emptiness, as the ultimate essential nature of any phenomenon, such as the mind.

*nature of being* (Tib. *yin lugs*). The "way it is," synonymous with *nature of existence.*

*nature of existence* (Tib. *gnas lugs*, Skt. *tathātva*). The fundamental mode of existence of all phenomena, which is emptiness. This is often contrasted with the way things appear (Tib. *snang lugs*).

*nihilism* (Tib. *med par lta ba*). A doctrine that denies the possibility of objective knowledge, meaning, values, or morality.

*nirmāṇakāya* (Skt., Tib. *sprul pa'i sku*). An "emanation embodiment" of the sugatagarbha that may appear anywhere in the universe in order to benefit sentient beings, with four types: living-being, teacher, created, and material nirmāṇakāyas.

*nirvāṇa* (Skt., Tib. *mya ngan las 'das pa*). Spiritual liberation, in which one is forever freed from delusion and all the other mental afflictions, which are what give rise to suffering.

*obscuration, afflictive* (Tib. *nyon mongs pa'i sgrib pa*, Skt. *kleśāvaraṇa*). The coarse obscurations that consist of manifest mental afflictions and their seeds, which are abandoned on the path of meditation, after the path of seeing the nature of reality directly.

*obscuration, cognitive* (Tib. *shes bya'i sgrib pa*, Skt. *jñeyāvaraṇa*). The subtle mental obscurations that impede the achievement of omniscience, specifically the habitual propensities for the mental afflictions and for phenomena appearing as though they had inherent existence.

*obscurations, two* (Tib. *sgrib pa gnyis*, Skt. *āvaraṇa dvitidhaḥ*). The afflictive and cognitive obscurations, which prevent one from reaching nirvāṇa and from achieving the omniscience of a buddha, respectively.

*one taste* (Tib. *ro gcig*, Skt. *ekarasa*). The third of the four stages of Mahāmudrā meditation. The empty nature of all phenomena of saṃsāra and nirvāṇa: equally nonexistent, equally pure, naturally arising from the expanse of the ground, and not established as anything else.

*Pacification* (Tib. *zhi byed*). A system of practice introduced into Tibet in the twelfth century by the Indian bodhisattva Phadampa Sangyé.

*palace, inconceivable (celestial)* (Tib. *gzhal yas khang*, Skt. *vimāna*). The "conceptually immeasurable abode" of a deity.

*Pāramitāyāna* (Skt., Tib. *phar phyin gyi theg pa*). The "vehicle of the perfections," namely, the path of the Mahāyāna that is based in the sūtra teachings on the six perfections, which are the foundation for the Vajrayāna, based on the teachings of the tantras. Since the Vajrayāna is actually subsumed within the Mahāyāna, the term Pāramitāyāna is often used to distinguish a practice of the perfections that does not include tantra.

*parinirvāṇa* (Skt., Tib. *yongs su myang ngan las 'das pa*). The complete enlightenment of a buddha, manifesting outwardly as death.

*perception, extrasensory* (Tib. *mngon par shes pa*, Skt. *abhijñā*). Exceptional modes of perception that arise along the path to enlightenment.

*perfections, six* (Tib. *pha rol tu phyin pa drug*, Skt. *saṭpāramitā*). Generosity, ethical discipline, patience, enthusiasm, meditation, and wisdom.

*poisons, five* (Tib. *dug lnga*). Delusion, hatred, pride, attachment, and envy.

*prāṇa* (Skt., Tib. *rlung*). Vital energy, known as "winds" or energy currents in the body. See also *karmic energy* and *vāyu*.

*pratyekabuddha* (Skt., Tib. *rang sangs rgyas*). Lit. "solitary buddha," a person who is committed to his or her own individual liberation by solitary practice.

*precious substances, seven* (Tib. *rin po che sna bdun*). Ruby, sapphire, lapis lazuli, emerald, diamond, pearl, and coral. An alternate list includes lapis lazuli, gold, silver, crystal, kakkatana, red pearl, and iron.

*preta* (Skt., Tib. *yi dvags*). A spirit whose existence is dominated by insatiable hunger, thirst, and craving.

*primordial consciousness* (Tib. *ye shes*, Skt. *jñāna*). The manifest state of the ground, which is self-arisen, naturally luminous, and free of outer and inner obscuration; this is indivisible from the all-pervasive, lucid, clear expanse of the absolute space of phenomena, free of contamination. The word is used in many contexts within Buddhist literature, where it can also simply refer to a timeless kind of knowing, free of conceptual elaboration, which realizes emptiness.

*primordial consciousness of the absolute space of phenomena* (Tib. *chos kyi dbyings kyi ye shes*, Skt. *dharmadhātujñāna*). The self-emergent essential nature of the pure ground, which is primordial great emptiness, and which subsumes all phenomena of saṃsāra and nirvāṇa.

*primordial consciousness of accomplishment* (Tib. *bya ba sgrub pa'i ye shes*, Skt. *kṛtyānuṣṭhānajñāna*). Primordial consciousness by which all pure, free, simultaneously perfected deeds and activities are accomplished naturally, of their own accord.

*primordial consciousness, discerning* (Tib. *so sor rtog pa'i ye shes*, Skt. *pratyavekṣaṇajñāna*). Primordial consciousness that unimpededly discerns the displays of pristine awareness, which knows reality as it is and perceives the full range of all phenomena.

*primordial consciousness of equality* (Tib. *mnyam pa nyid kyi ye shes*, Skt. *samatājñāna*). Primordial consciousness of the equal purity of saṃsāra and nirvāṇa in great emptiness.

*primordial consciousness, five facets of* (Tib. *ye shes lnga*, Skt. *pañcajñānāni*). Mirror-like primordial consciousness, discerning primordial consciousness, primordial consciousness of equality, primordial consciousness of accomplishment, and primordial consciousness of the absolute space of phenomena.

*primordial consciousness, mirror-like* (Tib. *me long lta bu'i ye shes*, Skt. *ādarśajñāna*). Self-illuminating primordial consciousness, which is of a lucid, clear nature, free of contamination, and allows for the unceasing appearances of all manner of objects.

*primordial consciousness, three facets of* (Tib. *ye shes gsum*). This refers to the empty essential nature, the luminous manifest nature, and all-pervasive compassion as the threefold division of primordial consciousness, or pristine awareness, as it resides in the ground, and can thus be actualized, through practice, into the three kāyas of a buddha.

*pristine awareness* (Tib. *rig pa*, Skt. *vidyā*). The eye of great, all-pervasive primordial consciousness that comprehends saṃsāra and nirvāṇa as being totally subsumed within great enlightenment, which entails a natural liberation in the absolute space of the ground—the great purity and equality of saṃsāra and nirvāṇa.

*pristine awareness that is present in the ground* (Tib. *gzhir gnas kyi rig pa*). The all-pervasive, fundamental nature of awareness, which is equivalent to the dharmakāya.

*progress in meditative experience* (Tib. *nyams snang gong 'phel ba*). The second of the four stages on the path of the direct crossing over, in which all appearances during and after meditation transform into displays of light and rainbow bindus with ever-increasing clarity, until finally all ordinary appearances vanish and dissolve into continuous, omnipresent displays of visions of light.

*propensities, habitual* (Tib. *bag chags*, Skt. *vāsanā*). Mental imprints accumulated as a result of previous experiences or actions, which influence later events and conduct.

*proximate cause* (Tib. *nyer len gyi rgyu*). A proximate, or substantial, cause of a phenomenon is a prior phenomenon that actually transforms into the subsequent phenomenon that it produces, as a seed transforms into a sprout.

*radiance* (Tib. *gdangs*). The natural luminosity of pristine awareness.

*rainbow body, great transference* (Tib. *'ja' lus 'pho ba chen po*). The highest form into which the aggregates of a practitioner of the Great Perfection path can be liberated upon reaching perfect enlightenment. As Lerab Lingpa describes it at [721], the physical "body dissolves into a mass of light and fingers of five-colored light vividly appear just from the perspective of pristine awareness." See *vajrakāya* (Tib. *rdo rje sku*).

*rasanā* (Skt., Tib. *ro ma*). The right channel among the three principal channels that run vertically through the torso and up into the head.

*reaching consummate awareness* (Tib. *rig pa tshad phebs*). The third of the four stages on the path of the direct crossing over, in which the entire universe appears to be totally pervaded with rainbow light and blazing fire, and everything appears as bindus in which the five families of male and female peaceful and wrathful divine embodiments appear in union.

*realities, two* (Tib. *bden pa gnyis*, Skt. *satyadvaya*). The pair of deceptive reality and ultimate reality.

*reality, the actual nature of* (Tib. *chos nyid*, Skt. *dharmatā*). The essential nature of all phenomena, which is emptiness.

*reality, conventional* (Tib. *tha snyad bden pa*). An aspect of deceptive reality or a synonym for it, emphasizing the way that a phenomenon is established through a name that is agreed upon by common users.

*reality, deceptive* (Tib. *kun rdzob bden pa*, Skt. *saṃvṛtisatya*). Lit. "totally obscuring reality," or that which is perceived through the veil of ignorance. This refers to ordinary phenomenal reality, which is obscurational in the sense that it appears in a manner contrary to its mode of existence and thereby obscures the nature of ultimate reality. Hence the appearances are "deceptive," yet for those who are deceived by the obscuring veil of ignorance, they appear to be "real." Such reality is typically established by a state of mind that is mistaken toward appearances, but buddhas can also establish deceptive appearances, without being mistaken toward them, through the omniscient primordial consciousness that perceives the full range of phenomena. In general, however, the way things appear (*snang lugs*) is the basis of delusion, while the nature of existence (*gnas lugs*) is the basis of liberation.

*reality, ultimate* (Tib. *don dam bden pa*, Skt. *paramārthasatya*). Lit. "the highest meaning of reality," which is trustworthy and not misleading, that is, emptiness. It is established by an unmistaken direct perception, free of conceptual elaboration.

*realization* (Tib. *rtogs pa*). Direct insight into some fundamental aspect of reality. In the context of the Great Perfection, this refers to the subtle, exact knowledge of how all appearing phenomena are nonobjective and empty from their own side, culminating in the decisive knowledge of the one taste of great emptiness—the fact that the whole of saṃsāra and nirvāṇa naturally arises from the expanse of the ground and is not established as anything else.

*realms, sentient beings of the six* (Tib. *'gro drug*). This usually refers to beings born into one of the six domains of the desire realm, whether those of the gods, asuras, humans, animals, pretas, or hell beings.

*realms, three* (Tib. *khams gsum*, Skt. *trīdhātu*). The desire, form, and formless realms.

*reflexive awareness* (Tib. *rang rig*, Skt. *svasaṃvitti*). This refers specifically to a type of self-awareness posited by the Mind Only school of Indian Buddhist thought. According to this idea, there would be a part of awareness that is simultaneously turned inward, and aware of itself, in the very same moment that another part of a unitary moment of awareness was turned outward to perceive something else. It is an idea that is refuted by the Madhyamaka Prāsaṅgika tradition.

*ṛṣi* (Skt., Tib. *drang srong*). An accomplished contemplative.

*rūpakāya* (Skt., Tib. *gzugs kyi sku*). A form embodiment of an enlightened being, including nirmāṇakāyas and saṃbhogakāyas.

*sādhana* (Skt., Tib. *sgrub pa*). A matrix of meditative practices designed to purify the mind, accumulate merit, and draw the practitioner closer and closer to a realization of the unity of one's own body, speech, and mind with that of one's personal deity.

*samādhi* (Skt., Tib. *ting nge 'dzin*). Meditative concentration.

*Samantabhadra* (Skt., Tib. *kun tu bzang po*). Lit. "all good," with many meanings, depending upon the context: (1) the name of a particular bodhisattva who is one of the eight principal bodhisattva disciples of the Buddha Śākyamuni, (2) a synonym for buddha nature in general, (3) a synonym for the dharmakāya, in the form of the primordial Buddha Samantabhadra, from whom, according to the Nyingma tantras, the diverse buddha bodies emanate and from whom the higher tantric lineages arise. As such, Samantabhadra is also the result attained through the Great Perfection practice of cutting through.

*śamatha* (Skt., Tib. *zhi gnas*). An advanced degree of meditative concentration, in which attentional stability and vividness have been developed to the point that one can fully engage in the cultivation of insight, or vipaśyanā.

*samaya* (Skt., Tib. *dam tshig*). A commitment or vow made to the buddhas as represented by one's vajra guru.

*sambhogakāya* (Skt., Tib. *longs spyod rdzogs pa'i sku*). The "full enjoyment embodiment" of an enlightened being, which is accessible only to āryabodhisattvas and buddhas.

*saṃsāra* (Skt., Tib. *'khor ba*). The cycle of existence, perpetuated by compulsively taking rebirth due to the power of one's mental afflictions and karma.

*saṅgha* (Skt., Tib. *dge 'dun*). Technically, the assembly of āryas, but more generally the congregation of Buddhist practitioners.

*Secret Mantrayāna* (Tib. *gsang sngags kyi theg pa*). The spiritual vehicle of the tantric, esoteric teachings.

*self-appearing* (Tib. *rang snang*). Manifesting from itself, a characteristic of primordial consciousness. Also translated on occasion as "your own appearances."

*self-emergent* (Tib. *rang byung*). Emerging from itself, a characteristic of primordial consciousness.

*self-grasping* (Tib *bdag tu 'dzin pa*, Skt. *ātmagrāha*). Grasping to an inherently existent identity of persons or things.

*self-illuminating* (Tib. *rang gsal*). A characteristic of the sharp vajra of wisdom, the experience of the spontaneously actualized essential nature.

*Severance* (Tib. *gcod*). A meditative practice established in Tibet and Bhutan by Phadampa Sangyé's main disciple, Machik Lapdrön (1055–1149), in which you imaginatively offer up your entire being as a means to realizing the empty nature of all phenomena, severing all clinging to the appearances of the three realms and realizing that all gods and demons are none other than your own appearances.

*siddha* (Skt., Tib. *sgrub thob*). One who has accomplished one or more siddhis.

*siddhi* (Skt., Tib. *dngos grub*). A supernormal ability or achievement. The supreme siddhi is the perfect enlightenment of a buddha, while the eight common siddhis include (1) the siddhi of celestial realms, the ability to dwell in celestial realms while still alive; (2) the siddhi of the sword, the ability to overcome any hostile army; (3) the siddhi of medicinal pills, the ability to become invisible by holding blessing pills in your hand; (4) the siddhi of fleet-footedness, by which you can walk around a lake in an instant by wearing boots you have blessed; (5) the vase siddhi, by which you can create a vessel that renders inexhaustible anything you put inside it—food or money, for example; (6) the siddhi of yakṣas, the power to make yakṣas your servants; (7) the siddhi of ambrosia (Skt. *amṛta*), which gives you a lifespan as long as the sun and the moon, the strength of an elephant, and the beauty of a lotus, and makes you feel as light as cotton wool whenever you arise from your seat; and (8) the siddhi of the balm of clairvoyance, which, when applied to your eyes, allows you to see things beneath the earth, such as treasures and so on.

*sign* (Tib. *mtshan ma*, Skt. *nimitta*). An object grasped by the conceptual mind.

*signs and symbols of enlightenment* (Tib. *mtshan dang dpe byad*). The thirty-two excellent signs and eighty symbols of a supreme nirmāṇakāya buddha.

*skull-cup* (Skt. *kapāla* or *bhanda*, Tib. *thod pa*). A ritual vessel made from the top portion of a human skull.

*space* (Tib. *dbyings*, Skt. *dhātu*). On the relative level this refers to the space of awareness (Tib. *chos kyi khams*, Skt. *dharmadhātu*), which in its primal manifestation is the substrate (Tib. *kun gzhi*, Skt. *ālaya*). On the ultimate level it refers to the absolute space of phenomena (Tib. *chos kyi dbyings*, Skt. *dharmadhātu*), which is synonymous with emptiness.

*space of awareness* (Tib. *dbyings*, Skt. *dhātu*). The Tibetan term *dbyings* can mean the relative "space of awareness," when it is not an abbreviation of *chos kyi dbyings*, or the "absolute space of phenomena." The term *space of awareness* may be regarded as identical to the term *element of phenomena* (Tib. *chos kyi khams*, Skt. *dharmadhātu*), which denotes the range of phenomena that can be perceived by the mind and is one of the eighteen elements (Tib. *khams*, Skt. *dhātu*) commonly cited in Buddhist phenomenology.

*spontaneous actualization* (Tib. *lhun grub*, Skt. *anābhoga*). The spontaneous emergence of qualities and activities from the dharmakāya, the realization of which is the central aspect of the practice of direct crossing over.

*śrāvaka* (Skt., Tib. *nyan thos*). Lit. "hearer," a disciple of the Buddha who is committed to his or her own individual liberation by following the path set forth by the Buddha.

*Śrāvakayāna* (Skt., Tib. *nyan thos kyi theg pa*). The spiritual vehicle of the śrāvakas, which is perfected by realizing personal identitylessness.

*Śrīmat* (Skt., Tib. *dpal dang ldan pa*). Lit. "endowed with glory," the buddha field of Ratnasaṃbhava in the southern direction.

*stage of completion* (Tib. *rdzogs rim*, Skt. *utpanna-* or *niṣpannakrama*). A Vajrayāna system of practice, corresponding to anuyoga, which is based on the practice of the stage of generation and which utilizes that which is already "complete" within the human body—namely, the channels, orbs, and vital energies—in order to bring about realizations of indivisible great bliss and emptiness and to manifest the indwelling mind of clear light joined with the illusory body.

*stage of generation* (Tib. *bskyed rim*, Skt. *utpattikrama*). A Vajrayāna system of practice, corresponding to mahāyoga, in which one's own body, speech, and mind are regarded as displays of the vajra body, speech, and mind of one's personal deity. As a result of such practice, one achieves stability in one's own awareness, ordinary appearances and clinging are transferred to the nature of buddha fields, and one's body, speech, and mind are transformed into the three vajras.

*stūpa* (Skt., Tib. *mchod rten*). A reliquary that holds sacred objects, such as the remains of an enlightened being; its form symbolizes the mind of a buddha.

*substantialism* (Tib. *dngos por lta ba*). The view that phenomena exist by their own inherent natures, prior to and independent of conceptual designation.

*substrate* (Tib. *kun gzhi*, Skt. *ālaya*). A vacuous, immaterial, nonconceptual state experienced in deep, dreamless sleep, when one faints, and when one dies, and in which appearances to the mind are impeded.

*substrate consciousness* (Tib. *kun gzhi rnam shes*, Skt. *ālayavijñāna*). An ethically neutral, inwardly directed state of consciousness, free of conceptualization, in which appearances of self, others, and objects are absent.

*suchness* (Tib. *de bzhin nyid*, Skt. *tathatā*). The ineffable reality of emptiness; the ultimate nature of all phenomena.

*suffering* (Tib. *sdug bsngal*, Skt. *duḥkha*). The unsatisfying nature of saṃsāra, the reality of suffering, consisting of blatant suffering, the suffering of change, and existential suffering.

*sugata* (Skt., Tib. *bde bar gshegs pa*). Lit. "well-gone one," an epithet of a buddha, meaning one who has gone to the far shore of liberation, fulfilling one's own and others' needs by achieving perfect enlightenment.

*sugatagarbha* (Skt., Tib. *bde gshegs snying po*). The essence, or womb, of the sugatas; synonymous with "buddha nature."

*Sukhāvatī* (Skt., Tib. *bde ba can*). Lit. "land of bliss," this is the buddha field of Amitābha in the western direction.

*sūtra* (Skt., Tib. *mdo*). Discourses attributed to the Buddha but not included among the tantras.

*svabhāvakāya* (Skt., Tib. *ngo bo nyid kyi sku*). The "natural embodiment" of the buddhas, which is the one nature of the dharmakāya, sambhogakāya, and nirmāṇakāya.

*tantra* (Skt., Tib. *rgyud*). A thread or continuum. A scripture belonging to the class of Vajrayāna Buddhism, as opposed to the exoteric teachings of the sūtras. Many of these scriptures are also attributed to the historical Buddha (as in the case of the *Guhyasamāja* and *Kālacakra Tantras*) or to later emanations of the buddhas.

*tathāgata* (Skt., Tib. *de bzhin gshegs pa*). Lit. "one who has gone to (or arrived at) suchness," an epithet for a buddha.

*tenet system* (Tib. *grub mtha'*, Skt. *siddhānta*). The final, stated position of a school of thought or of an individual practitioner.

*tertön* (Skt., Tib. *gter ston*). A revealer of treasures (Tib. *gter ma*, pronounced *terma*) hidden by great masters of the Great Perfection tradition for the benefit of future generations. See *treasure revealer*.

*thoughts, compulsive* (Tib. *rnam rtog*, Skt. *vikalpa*). Ordinary, dualistic thoughts concerning the objects of saṃsāra.

*torma* (Tib. *gtor ma*, Skt. *bali*). A ritual offering cake in which the nutritive essence of the universe is synthesized and which acts as a source of all desirable things.

*transference* (Tib. *'pho ba*, Skt. *saṃkrānti*). Transference of consciousness. According to the Great Perfection, the unsurpassed transference is the realization of the pristine domain of the absolute space of phenomena, the sugatagarbha.

*transitional phase* (Tib. *bar do*, Skt. *antarabhāva*). Any one of the six transitional phases of living, meditation, dreaming, dying, the actual nature of reality, and becoming. See also *intermediate period*.

*transitional phase of becoming* (Tib. *srid pa bar do*). The dream-like intermediate period immediately following the transitional phase of the actual nature of reality, in which one is on the way to one's next rebirth.

*treasure revealer* (Tib. *gter ston*). A highly realized being who reveals Dharma teachings concealed in the physical world or in the nature of mind. See *tertön*.

*tulku* (Tib. *sprul sku*, Skt. *nirmāṇakāya*). A realized being who is either firmly on the path to enlightenment or who has already achieved enlightenment and becomes incarnate for the sake of the world.

*union of the two* (Tib. *zung 'jug*, Skt. *yuganaddha*). In anuttarayogatantra, this refers to the indivisible union of the primordial consciousness that is the actual clear light with the illusory body that arises from the extremely subtle vital energies upon which that mind of clear light rides. There are two forms: the union of the two while still in training (Tib. *slob pa'i zung 'jug*), in which one is an āryabodhisattva, but not yet a buddha, and the union of the two with no more training (Tib. *mi slob pa'i zung 'jug*), which is at the level of a completed buddha.

*vajra* (Skt., Tib. *rdo rje*). A symbol of ultimate reality, with the seven attributes of invulnerability, indestructibility, reality, incorruptibility, stability, unobstructability, and invincibility.

*vajra guru* (Skt., Tib. *rdo rje'i bla ma*). A spiritual mentor who is qualified to lead one in the practices of Vajrayāna.

*vajra strands* (Skt., Tib. *rdo rje lu gu rgyud*). Lit. "vajra lamb-strands," alluding to the appearances of grazing sheep, this refers to the radiance (*rig gdangs*), appearance (*rig snang*), or display (*rig rtsal*) of pristine awareness.

*Vajrācārya* (Skt., *Tib. rdo rje slob dpon*). Lit. "vajra master." A qualified master of Vajrayāna who grants empowerment, gives formal explanations, and offers pith instructions to a qualified student of the Vajrayāna. See *vajra guru.*

*vajrakāya* (Skt., Tib. *rdo rje sku*). Lit. "vajra embodiment," a term with which *great transference rainbow body* is often combined. It emphasizes the indestructibility and incorruptibility of such an embodiment—the fact it will never again undergo a transference of consciousness—whereas *rainbow body* emphasizes its illusory appearance as light of five colors. See *rainbow body, great transference.*

*vajrāsana* (Skt., Tib. *rdo rje skyil krung*). Lit. the "vajra posture," but refers to what is more commonly known in English as the "full lotus" seated posture, with the left foot on the right thigh and the right foot on the left thigh.

*Vajrayāna* (Skt., Tib. *rdo rje'i theg pa*). The vehicle of esoteric Buddhist teachings and practices aimed at bringing one swiftly to the state of enlightenment.

*vāyu* (Skt., Tib. *rlung*). Usually refers to one or all of the five primary and five secondary subtle energies that course within the body of a human being in the original condition. The term *prāṇa-vāyu* sometimes refers specifically to just one of the five primary energies, the "vital energy of the life force" (Tib. *srog 'dzin gyi rlung*), though the word *prāṇa* alone can also be used more generally.

*vice* (Tib. *sdig pa*, Skt. *pāpam*). A nonvirtuous karma, or misdeed, that ripens as misery and adversity in this or future lifetimes.

*vidyādhara* (Skt., Tib. *rig pa 'dzin pa*). A "holder of knowledge" who has ascertained the nature of pristine awareness. Nyingma tantras describe four levels of vidyādhara. According to Düdjom Lingpa, in ascending order of realization, they are the matured vidyādhara, corresponding to the vision of the direct appearances of the actual nature of reality and the first āryabodhisattva ground, known as Very Joyful; the vidyādhara with mastery over life, corresponding to the vision of progress in meditative experience and the fifth āryabodhisattva ground, Difficult to Cultivate; the Mahāmudrā vidyādhara, corresponding to the vision of reaching consummate awareness and the eighth āryabodhisattva ground, Immovable; and the spontaneously actualized vidyādhara, corresponding to the vision of extinction into ultimate reality and the tenth āryabodhisattva ground, Cloud of Dharma. Note that this differs, however, from the presentation of the correspondences between bodhisattva grounds and the levels of a vidyādhara given by Dharmasāra in this volume.

*vinaya* (Skt., Tib. *'dul ba*). The teachings concerning rules and discipline of the Buddha's disciples.

*vipaśyanā* (Skt., Tib. *lhag mthong*). Lit. "superior vision," contemplative insight into fundamental aspects of reality, such as impermanence, suffering, nonself, and emptiness.

*vīra* (Skt., Tib. *dpa' bo*). Lit. "heroic being," one who shows great courage in not succumbing to mental afflictions and in striving diligently in spiritual practice. A highly realized male bodhisattva who manifests in the world in order to serve sentient beings.

*vital energy*. See *prāṇa* and *vāyu*.

*vital essence* (Tib. *bcud*). The vital core of phenomena such as the five elements.

*wisdom* (Tib. *shes rab*, Skt. *prajñā*). In general this refers to the faculty of discerning intelligence. More specifically in these contexts, it refers to the knowledge that determines everything included in the phenomenal world of saṃsāra and nirvāṇa as being empty, identityless, and nonobjective, such that all appearances and mental states are gradually extinguished in the space of awareness.

*yakṣa* (Skt., Tib. *gnod sbyin*). One of the eight classes of haughty, nonhuman beings who cause harm to human beings.

*yāna* (Skt., Tib. *theg pa*). A vehicle for spiritual practice leading to varying degrees of spiritual liberation and enlightenment.

*yānas, nine* (Skt., Tib. *theg pa dgu*). The nine spiritual vehicles include the three leading away from suffering—śrāvakayāna, pratyekabuddhayāna, and bodhisattvayāna; the three outer tantras evoking pristine awareness with austerities—kriyāyoga, upāyayoga, and yoga; and the three inner tantras—mahāyoga, anuyoga, and atiyoga.

*yidam* (Tib. *yi dam*, Skt. *iṣṭadevatā*). Personal deity.

*yoga* (Skt., Tib. *rnal 'byor*). Lit. "yoke," a meditative practice involving the mind and body. One of the six higher yānas of kriyāyoga, upāyayoga, yoga, mahāyoga, anuyoga, and atiyoga.

*yogatantra* (Skt., Tib. *rnal 'byor rgyud*). The "yoga tantras," according to which one practices by recognizing the profound view as being of greatest importance.

*yogin* (Skt., Tib. *rnal 'byor pa*). A man who is adept in the practice of yoga.

*yoginī* (Skt., Tib. *rnal 'byor ma*). A woman who is adept in the practice of yoga.

*youthful vase kāya* (Tib. *gzhon nu bum pa'i sku*, Skt. *kumārakalaśakāya*). This term is unique to the Great Perfection tradition, referring to the state of enlightenment. It is like a "vase," for, as the sole bindu, it encompasses the whole of saṃsāra and nirvāṇa, while transcending the three times. It is called "youthful," for it is not subject to aging or degeneration, and it is called a "kāya," for it is the aggregate of all the inexhaustible enlightened bodies, speech, mind, qualities, and activities of all the buddhas. Its six characteristics are that it (1) is superior to the ground, (2) appears as one's own essential nature, (3) is discerning, (4) is liberated in activity, (5) does not emerge from anything else, and (6) dwells in one's own ground. Alternately, according to the dictionary *Bod rgya tshig mdzod chen mo* (p. 2432), this refers to the awareness of Samantabhadra, which is of the oceanic nature of the kāyas and facets of primordial consciousness, with six qualities: (1) externally luminous consciousness is withdrawn into itself, and the great, internally luminous, original absolute space of the ground appears to itself; (2) it transcends the ground; (3) it differentiates; (4) it is liberated upward; (5) it arises from nothing else; and (6) it dwells in its own place.

# Bibliography

**Tibetan Texts Translated** (to which bracketed page numbers correspond)

Tertön Lerab Lingpa (*gter ston las rab gling pa*, 1856–1926). *The Vital Essence of Primordial Consciousness: An Essential Synthesis, Fluidly Presented as a Commentary, of Practical Guidance on the Great Chetsun's Profound Quintessence from Vimalamitra, the Three Units of Letters on the Five Expanses, the Sovereign of All Pith Instructions, a Vessel of the Vital Essence Taken from among the Classes of Pith Instructions on the Great Perfection. Rdzogs pa chen po man ngag sde'i bcud phur man ngag thams cad kyi rgyal po klong lnga'i yi ge dum bu gsum pa lce btsun chen po'i bī ma la'i zab tig gi bshad khrid chu 'babs su bkod pa snying po'i bcud dril ye shes thig le*. In *The Cycle of Dharma Teachings on Chetsun's Heart Essence, Lce btsun sñing thig gi chos skor*, 599–754. Darjeeling, India: Taklung Tsetrul Rinpoche Pema Wangyal, 1985. An alternate edition of this entire collection, with an introduction by Matthieu Ricard, is *Lce btsun snying thig gi chos skor*. Delhi, India: Shechen Publications, 2004.

Dharmasāra (aka Lozang Do-ngak Chökyi Gyatso Chok, *Blo bzang mdo sngags chos kyi rgya mtsho mchog*, aka, Kunzang Zhepé Dorjé, *Kun bzang bzhad pa'i rdo rje*, 1903–57) and Jé Tsultrim Zangpo (*Rje tshul khrims bzang po*, 1884–1957). *Selected Essays on Old and New Views of the Secret Mantrayāna. Gsang sngags gsar rnying gi lta ba'i rnam gzhag legs bshad gces btus*. Dharamsala, India: Namgyal Monastery Education Assembly, 2009.

**Other Primary Texts Consulted**

Dharmasāra. *Collected Works of Do-ngak Chökyi Gyatso* (1903–57), vols. 2–3. *Snyan dgon sprul sku gsung rab mdo sngags chos kyi rgya mtsho'i gsung 'bum legs bshad nor bu'i snang ba*. Chengdu, China: Si khron mi rigs dpe skrun khang, 2006.

Jamyang Khyentsé Wangpo (*'Jam dbyangs mkhyen brtse'i dbang po*, 1820–92). *The Mystery of Primordial Consciousness Perfected: The Preliminaries to the Great Chetsun's Profound Quintessence from Vimalamitra, Fluidly Presented as an Oral Recitation. Lce btsun chen po'i bi ma la'i zab tig gi sngon 'gro'i ngag 'don chu 'babs su bkod pa ye shes gsang rdzogs*. In Tertön Lerab Lingpa, *The Cycle of Dharma Teachings on Chetsun's Heart Essence,* 33–42.

———. *The Three Units of Letters on the Five Expanses, the Sovereign of All Pith Instructions. Man ngag thams cad kyi rgyal po klong lnga'i yi ge dum bu gsum pa*. In Tertön Lerab Lingpa, *The Cycle of Dharma Teachings on Chetsun's Heart Essence,* 3–30.

Jé Tsultrim Zangpo. *Rdzogs pa chen po'i khrid yig kun bzang dgongs rgyan*. In *Collected Works of Tsultrim Zangpo* (1884–1957). 8 vols. *Sprul sku tshul khrims bzang po'i gsung 'bum*, vol. *kha*. TBRC scanned block print: W1PD26799.

Rikdzin Natsok Rangdröl (*Rig 'dzin sna tshogs rang grol*, 1842–1924). *The Fine Path of Primordial Consciousness: The Mystery of the Actual Sacred Deeds, Compiled in Proper Order. Gsang ba don gyi phrin las khrigs su bsdeb pa ye shes lam bzang*. In Tertön Lerab Lingpa, *The Cycle of Dharma Teachings on Chetsun's Heart Essence,* 167–84.

**English-Language References**

Anālayo Bhikkhu. *Satipaṭṭhāna: The Direct Path to Realization*. Birmingham, UK: Windhorse Publications, 2004.

Dowman, Keith. *The Yeshe Lama: Jigme Lingpa's Dzogchen Atiyoga Manual*. CreateSpace Independent Publishing Platform, 2014.

Düdjom Lingpa. *The Heart of the Great Perfection.* Vol. 1 of *Düdjom Lingpa's Visions of the Great Perfection.* Translated by B. Alan Wallace. Edited by Dion Blundell. Boston: Wisdom Publications, 2016.

———. *Buddhahood without Meditation.* Vol. 2 of *Düdjom Lingpa's Visions of the Great Perfection.* Translated by B. Alan Wallace. Edited by Dion Blundell. Boston: Wisdom Publications, 2015.

———. *The Vajra Essence.* Vol. 3 of *Düdjom Lingpa's Vision of the Great Perfection.* Translated by B. Alan Wallace. Edited by Dion Blundell. Boston: Wisdom Publications, 2015.

Gampopa. *Ornament of Precious Liberation.* Translated by Ken Holmes. Boston: Wisdom Publications, 2017.

His Holiness the Dalai Lama. *The Meaning of Life.* Translated and edited by Jeffrey Hopkins. Boston: Wisdom Publications, 1992.

———. *Mind in Comfort and Ease: The Vision of Enlightenment in the Great Perfection: Including Longchen Rabjam's Finding Comfort and Ease in Meditation on the Great Perfection.* Edited by Patrick Gaffney. Foreword by Sogyal Rinpoche. Translated by Matthieu Ricard, Richard Barron, and Adam Pearcey. Boston: Wisdom Publications, 2007.

Jigmed Lingpa, Vidyādhara. *Yeshe Lama.* Translated by Lama Chönam and Sangye Khandro. Ithaca, NY: Snow Lion Publications, 2009.

Karma Chagmé. *Naked Awareness: Practical Instructions on the Union of Mahāmudrā and Dzogchen.* Commentary by Gyatrul Rinpoche. Translated by B. Alan Wallace. Ithaca, NY: Snow Lion Publications, 2000.

———. *A Spacious Path to Freedom: Practical Instructions on the Union of Mahāmudrā and Atiyoga.* Commentary by Gyatrul Rinpoche. Translated by B. Alan Wallace. Ithaca, NY: Snow Lion Publications, 2009.

Lama Chönam and Sangye Khandro, trans. *The Guhyagarbha Tantra: Secret Essence Definitive Nature Just As It Is, with Commentary by Longchenpa.* Ithaca, NY: Snow Lion Publications, 2011.

Longchen Rabjam. *The Precious Treasury of the Basic Space of Phenomena*. Translated under the direction of His Eminence Chagdud Tulku Rinpoche by Richard Barron (Chökyi Nyima). Junction City, CA: Padma Publishing, 2001.

Nāgārjuna. *The Root Stanzas of the Middle Way: The Mulamadhyamakakarika*. Translated from the Tibetan by the Padmakara Translation Group. Boulder, CO: Shambhala Publications, 2016.

Ñāṇamoli, Bhikkhu, and Bhikkhu Bodhi, trans. *The Middle Length Discourses of the Buddha*. Boston: Wisdom Publications, 1995.

Padmasambhava. *Natural Liberation: Padmasambhava's Teachings on the Six Bardos*. Commentary by Gyatrul Rinpoche. Translated by B. Alan Wallace. Boston: Wisdom Publications, 1998.

Pistono, Matteo. *Fearless in Tibet: The Life of the Mystic Tertön Sogyal*. Carlsbad, CA: Hay House, 2014.

Śāntideva. *A Guide to the Bodhisattva Way of Life*. Translated by Vesna A. Wallace and B. Alan Wallace. Ithaca, NY: Snow Lion Publications, 1997.

Sakya Paṇḍita Kün-ga Gyaltsen. *A Clear Differentiation of the Three Codes: Essential Distinctions among the Individual Liberation, Great Vehicle, and Tantric Systems*. Translated by Jared Rhoton. Albany: State University of New York Press, 2002.

Sonam, Ruth, trans. *Atisha's Lamp for the Path: An Oral Teaching by Geshe Sonam Rinchen*. Ithaca, NY: Snow Lion Publications, 1997.

Stanley, Matthew. *Huxley's Church and Maxwell's Demon: From Theistic Science to Naturalistic Science*. Chicago: University of Chicago Press, 2015.

Thupten Jinpa. *The Book of Kadam: The Core Texts*. Boston: Wisdom Publications, 2008.

———. *Wisdom of the Kadam Masters*. Boston: Wisdom Publications, 2013.

Tiso, Francis V. *Rainbow Body and Resurrection: Spiritual Attainment, the Dissolution of the Material Body, and the Case of Khenpo A Chö*. Berkeley, CA: North Atlantic Books, 2016.

Tsongkhapa Lozang Drakpa. *The Great Treatise on the Stages of the Path to Enlightenment.* 3 vols. Translated by the Lamrim Chenmo Translation Committee. Ithaca, NY: Snow Lion Publications, 2000–2004.

———. *A Lamp to Illuminate the Five Stages: Teachings on Guhyasamaja Tantra.* Translated by Gavin Kilty. Boston: Wisdom Publications, 2012.

———. *Ocean of Reasoning: A Great Commentary on Nāgārjuna's Mūlamadhyamakakārikā. Rtsa shes ṭik chen.* Translated by Geshe Ngawang Samten and Jay L. Garfield. New York: Oxford University Press, 2006.

Tucci, G., ed. *Minor Buddhist Texts,* vol. 2. Rome: Instituto Italiano per il Medio ed Estremo Oriente, 1958.

Varela, Francisco, and Jeremy Hayward, eds. *Gentle Bridges: Conversations with the Dalai Lama on the Sciences of Mind.* 2nd ed. Boston: Shambhala Publications, 1992.

Vasubandhu. *Abhidharmakośabhāṣyam.* 4 vols. English translation of Louis de La Vallée Poussin's French translation by Leo M. Pruden. Berkeley, CA: Asian Humanities Press, 1988.

Wallace, B. Alan. *Balancing the Mind: A Tibetan Buddhist Approach to Refining Attention.* Ithaca, NY: Snow Lion Publications, 2005.

———. *Minding Closely: The Four Applications of Mindfulness.* Ithaca, NY: Snow Lion Publications, 2011.

Willis, Janice D. *Enlightened Beings: Life Stories from the Ganden Oral Tradition.* Boston: Wisdom Publications, 1995.

# Index

## B



## C

**D**

**F**

**I**

identitylessness, 133, 134, 268, 274
ignorance, 170
  appearance and, 38, 142n14, 303
  connate, 57, 151
  of correct view, 284–85
  direct antidote for, 199
  of essential nature, 36
  mind and, 261
illumination, inward and outward, 173–74
illusory body, 78, 109, 153, 169
illusory vajra king, 102
impermanence, meditation on, xxx, 27–28
imputation, 256–58, 292–93, 300
"Inexpressible, Actual Confession," 52, 54
instructions, pointing-out, 22, 70, 119, 144, 164, 309
intellect, 69, 262, 290, 297
intellectuals, 237
intermediate period
  actual nature of reality, transitional phase of, 109–11, 169, 198–99
  becoming, transitional phase of, 109, 111
  liberation in, 81
  in lower inner tantra, 152
  sambhogakāya's self-appearance at, 21
  transforming, 236
introspection, 24, 65, 191
isolations, three, 153

**J**

Jamgön Kongtrul Lodrö Tayé, 15n34, 17
Jamyang Khyentsé Wangpo, xxii, 4, 16–17, 26n41, 100
Jamyang Mipham Namgyal, 273
Jamyang Zhepé Dorjé, 212, 214
Jewels, Three, 116, 286
Jigmé Phuntsok, Khenpo, xxii
Jikmé Könchok, 307–8
Jikmé Lingpa, 143n15, 199n13, 214, 219, 245
Jikmé Lingpa Khyentsé Özer, 220
Jina. *See* Buddha (Jina)
Jñānagarbha, 247, 266n48
Jñānapāda, 216
Jñānasūtra, 14
joy, xxiv, 255
  excellence of, 30
  futility of superficial, 29–30
  of pith instructions, 9, 239
  of rūpakāya, 157–58
  at threshold of first dhyāna, xxxv

**K**

Kadam lineage, 221, 242
Kagyü school, xxxvi–xxxvii, 216
Kālacakra (Śrī), 56
Kālacakra system, 79
*Kalama Sutta*, xxi
Kalu Rinpoché, xxx–xxxi
Kamalaśīla, 211, 274
karma, 56, 113, 129, 151–52, 161, 301–2. *See also* karmic energies
Karma Chagmé, xli–xlii
karmamudrā, 102
Karmaprasiddhi, 113
karmic energies
  absence of, 186
  binding, 309
  ceasing of, 194
  conceptual fabrication and, 148, 151
  extinction of, 93
  incinerating, 229
  increasing, causes of, 201
  methods for cutting, variations in, 179
  pacifying, 163
  during pointing out, 166
  power of, 167–68
  purification of, natural, 72
kāyas
  arising in phase of actual nature of reality, 111
  direct perception of, 9
  divine, 109
  five, 46
  four, 42
  in Kālacakra system, absence of, 79
  as primordially present within, 87–88
  ripening of, 308–9
  solitary, 93
  two, 172–73, 247, 281–83, 305
  vajra strands and, 92
  *See also* individual kāyas
kāyas, three, 12, 226
  in cultivating bodhicitta, 37–38

on dying and stability of practice while living, xlvii
homage to, 241
lineage of, 8, 15, 216–17
as personal deity, 162
on practice of Great Perfection, importance of, xxviii
on rainbow body, xlvii–xlviii
on releasing compulsive thoughts, 180–82
ultrasecret cycle of pith instructions and, xxvi–xxviii
Vajrakīlaya and, 231
on view and meditation, relationship between, xxiv–xxv
See also *Garland of Pith Instructions, A*
Padmovyūha, 112
palaces, 79, 173
*Paradigms of the Roots*, 230
Pāramitāyāna, 133–34, 135, 170–71, 196, 200–201
path
bringing death onto, 47
in Early and New Translation schools, common intent of, 281–83
nondual, 235
reality of, 55, 57, 60, 99
realization of one's own awareness as, 6
sets of five at time of, 10
taking impure mind as, xxxi
taking luminous visions/clear light as, 80, 81–82, 99, 149
taking phase of birth as, 109
two stages of, 281–83, 305
paths, five, xxxvi, 134, 195. *See also* individual path
Patrül Namkha Jikmé, 240n6
Pel Nyenmo Ri Namgyel monastery, 288n76
Pelgyi Lodröma, xxviii–xxix, 10, 119–20
Pema Tashi, xxxii–xxxiii
perception, arising of, 63
perfection, meaning of, 4–6
perfection of wisdom sūtras, 153, 222
perfection stage. *See* completion stage
perfections, six, xxx, 133, 134, 146
personal identity, autonomous, 129
phenomena
as creative expression, 69, 202
deceptive, 270
in Early and New Translation schools, common view of, 248–54
emptiness of, 130, 164–65, 197, 271
emptiness of, common views on, 248–54
as imputation, 256–57
indwelling and adventitious, differentiating between, 152
as mere appearances of mind, 175–76
mind and, xl–xli
nominal existence of, 303–4
as one taste, 75
perfection of, 5
subtle lack of identity in, 134
two realities and, 294
*phurba* (Skt. kīla), 226, 228
physical world and inhabitants, 61
appearance of, 275
causes and conditions of, 27
as displays of pristine awareness, recognizing, 201–2
as maṇḍalas, 163, 227
as manifest nature, 173
Pistono, Matteo, *Fearless in Tibet*, xix
pith instruction class, xxvi, 9, 217
placing knowable things into vase, 102–3
pointing-out instructions. *See* instructions, pointing-out
poisons, three, 151, 228
postmeditation
ascertainment of emptiness in, differences in, 213
of cutting through, 75
of direct crossing over, 85–86, 106
and meditative equipoise, merging, 185–86
recognizing appearance as pristine awareness in, 201–2
seven mind trainings in, 33
state of, 142
postures, 166, 185, 238
in direct crossing over, 85
in empowerment, symbolism of, 20
stabilizing, 96–97
of three kāyas, 22, 82, 86, 89
practitioners, 54–55
faults of, 117
of inferior faculties, 112–14

## T

## U



## V

# About the Translator

**B. Alan Wallace** is president of the Santa Barbara Institute for Consciousness Studies. He trained for many years as a monk in Buddhist monasteries in India and Switzerland. He has taught Buddhist theory and practice in Europe and America since 1976 and has served as interpreter for numerous Tibetan scholars and contemplatives, including H. H. the Dalai Lama.

After graduating *summa cum laude* from Amherst College, where he studied physics and the philosophy of science, he earned his MA and PhD in religious studies at Stanford University. He has edited, translated, authored, and contributed to more than forty books on Tibetan Buddhism, medicine, language, and culture, and the interface between science and religion.

After teaching for four years in the Department of Religious Studies at the University of California, Santa Barbara, he founded and currently serves as president of the Santa Barbara Institute for Consciousness Studies, which focuses on the interface between contemplative and scientific ways of exploring the mind and its potentials.

# Take Online Courses with B. Alan Wallace

# Also by B. Alan Wallace

**The Attention Revolution**
*Unlocking the Power of the Focused Mind*

"Indispensable for anyone wanting to understand the mind. A superb, clear set of exercises that will benefit everyone."—Paul Ekman, Professor Emeritus at University of California San Francisco, and author of *Telling Lies* and *Emotions Revealed*

**Stilling the Mind**
*Shamatha Teachings from Dudjom Lingpa's Vajra Essence*

"A much needed, very welcome book."—Jetsün Khandro Rinpoche

**Dudjom Lingpa's Visions of the Great Perfection**
Foreword by Sogyal Rinpoche

"These texts present the essential meaning of the Great Perfection with great clarity and precision."—Tsoknyi Rinpoche

**Tibetan Buddhism from the Ground Up**
*A Practical Approach for Modern Life*

"One of the most readable, accessible, and comprehensive introductions to Tibetan Buddhism."—*Mandala*

# About Wisdom Publications

Wisdom Publications is the leading publisher of classic and contemporary Buddhist books and practical works on mindfulness. To learn more about us or to explore our other books, please visit our website at wisdompubs.org or contact us at the address below.

Wisdom Publications
199 Elm Street
Somerville, MA 02144 USA

We are a 501(c)(3) organization, and donations in support of our mission are tax deductible.

Wisdom Publications is affliated with the Foundation for the Preservation of the Mahayana Tradition (FPMT).